PSYCHOLOGY, ART, AND ANTIFASCISM

PSYCHOLOGY, ART, AND ANTIFASCISM

ERNST KRIS, E. H. GOMBRICH, AND THE POLITICS OF CARICATURE

LOUIS ROSE

YALE UNIVERSITY PRESS
NEW HAVEN AND LONDON

For information about this and other Yale University Press publications, please contact:
U.S. Office: sales.press@yale.edu yalebooks.com
Europe Office: sales@yaleup.co.uk yalebooks.co.uk

Typeset in Adobe Caslon Pro by IDSUK (DataConnection) Ltd
Printed in Great Britain by Gomer Press Ltd, Llandysul, Ceredigion, Wales

Library of Congress Cataloging-in-Publication Data

Names: Rose, Louis, author.
Title: Psychology, art, and antifascism : Ernst Kris, E.H. Gombrich, and the politics of caricature / Louis Rose.
Description: New Haven : Yale University Press, 2016.
LCCN 2016015878 | ISBN 9780300221473 (hardback)
LCSH: Kris, Ernst, 1900-1957. | Gombrich, E. H. (Ernst Hans), 1909–2001. | Art historians—Austria—Biography. | Psychology and art. | BISAC: ART / Criticism & Theory. | BIOGRAPHY & AUTOBIOGRAPHY / Social Scientists & Psychologists. | PSYCHOLOGY / Movements / Psychoanalysis. | ART / Techniques / Cartooning.
Classification: LCC N7483.K75 R67 2016 | DDC 700.1/9—dc23
LC record available at https://lccn.loc.gov/2016015878

A catalogue record for this book is available from the British Library.

10 9 8 7 6 5 4 3 2 1

For Clelia and Asher

CONTENTS

ILLUSTRATIONS

Unless otherwise stated, all artwork featured is by Honoré Daumier.

ACKNOWLEDGMENTS

More than a few people assisted with this book. I am grateful to Edward Nersessian and Robert Penzer for their invitation to participate in the 2013 Helix Center conference at the New York Psychoanalytic Society and Institute on "Aby Warburg: Art, Neuroscience and Psychoanalysis" and to Steffen Krüger for his invitation to take part in the 2008 Berlin conference "In the Service of the Ego: Ernst Kris Today." Gary Cohen at the Center for Austrian Studies, University of Minnesota, Nellie Thompson at the New York Psychoanalytic Society and Institute, and Helen Fehervary in the Department of Germanic Languages and Literatures, Ohio State University, provided forums in which I could present my research. Otterbein University's School of Arts and Sciences, and its dean, Paul Eisenstein, provided continuing research support through the university's Ursula Holtermann and Humanities endowments.

I was fortunate to have the help of Margaret McAleer at the Library of Congress, Dr. Claudia Wedepohl at the Warburg Institute Archive, and Allen Reichert at Otterbein's Courtright Library. Carren Kaston provided invaluable research assistance. I want to thank Andy Spencer, past editor of *Communications from the International Brecht Society*, for his advice on issues of translation.

My thanks go to Judith Wechsler, Richard Woodfield, and the anonymous reviewers of Yale University Press for their very helpful recommendations on the manuscript. I am grateful to Robert Baldock, Melissa Bond, and Rachael Lonsdale at the London office of the press for their commitment to and support for this work.

This book began from a series of conversations with Anna Kris Wolff, Anton O. Kris, and Leonie Gombrich. I am very pleased here to be able to express my gratitude for their generosity, their time, and their perspectives. Eric Kandel, Arno Mayer, Debora Silverman, and Katharine Weber provided much appreciated encouragement as the book moved forward. Jim Amelang read more than one version of the manuscript as it progressed and I benefited greatly from his comments and suggestions.

Throughout, my wife Cindy patiently listened to, read, and responded to all and any of my thoughts on the book, from the first of them to the last.

It was my great good fortune to have known Carl Schorske as an advisor and friend, and the talks I had with him about the book remain with me. In these acknowledgments I would like to pay tribute to his work and memory.

. . . my library was dukedom large enough.

The Tempest, 1.2

CHAPTER 1

THE UNFINISHED PROJECT

The Manuscript

In 1936, two Viennese scholars, writing at the end of each day in the elder colleague's study, worked throughout the summer to complete a book manuscript before the younger of the two departed for London. The final crisis of the postwar Austrian republic gripped the capital and almost certainly the younger scholar would be unable to return to the city in the foreseeable future. The room where they now examined their manuscript became, like Prospero's cell, a lens through which to view both the pages of their book and the events of the outside world. Their intellectual labors provided them with an independent refuge and a source of solace. But as with Prospero's island, the shadow of politics intruded continuously at the edges.

The manuscript explored the subject of caricature—the art of comic distortion and willful exaggeration, of irreverence and, according to its most serious practitioners, absolute fidelity to truth. Inspired by recent advances in psychology and by contemporary innovations in art, the two scholars approached caricature not as a low form of creativity or a debased mode of communication but as a distinctive psychological and cultural phenomenon with its own functions and evolution. From the start of their project, they interpreted caricature as an ambitious psychological and artistic experiment, and their effort to grasp each aspect as fully as possible led them to employ theories and methods from both mental science and cultural history.

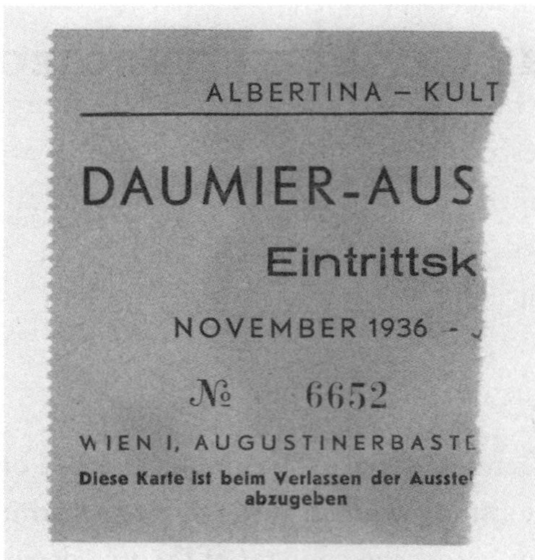

Ticket stub from Daumier's 1936 exhibition.

But caricature also included political dissent, and the two colleagues intensively explored that side of the experiment as well. In the same, decisive year of 1936—less than two years before the annexation of Austria to Hitler's Germany—they organized a Viennese exhibition of the work of Honoré Daumier. The art of the nineteenth-century French master of caricature embodied republican, anti-militarist, and internationalist impulses, which now in the 1930s opposed the forces of Austro-Fascism, Church conservatism, and pan-German nationalism that were abetting in the *Anschluss* with Nazi Germany. Bringing Daumier to Vienna, the two colleagues assembled the largest exhibition of the artist's works to appear outside of France since the First World War. The year following the exhibition, they completed their book manuscript. Here, in two hundred and fifty-four typescript pages, they traced the evolution of caricature from a Renaissance offshoot of portrait painting to a modern republican art form.

The elder scholar—whose private study served as both haven and workshop—was Ernst Kris, an art historian who had become a leading psychoanalyst within Sigmund Freud's circle in Vienna and a crucial pioneer of the new psychoanalytic ego psychology. As a university student, Kris had trained in the Vienna School of Art History, but soon after graduating he felt the influence of Aby Warburg's Library for the Cultural Sciences in Hamburg. Kris's gravitation toward the Warburg circle and their investigations into the psychology and history of image making coincided with his shift toward psychoanalysis, and the two tendencies produced mutually reaffirming, although not identical, intellectual directions.

Kris's colleague on both the caricature manuscript and the Daumier exhibition was E. H. Gombrich. Also trained as an art historian in the Vienna School, Gombrich acquired, like Kris, a strong interest in the new psychological sciences, especially the new cognitive psychology. Image studies held out for him the possibility of combining art historical researches with studies of mind and perception—and ultimately politics. Like Kris, he found support at the Warburg Library, which by the time he began his work there had been forced into exile from Hamburg and had re-established itself as the Warburg Institute in London.

The Daumier exhibition and caricature manuscript proved to be Kris and Gombrich's last collaboration in Vienna. The *Anschluss* forced both to emigrate to Britain, where they joined the anti-Hitler war effort as analysts of Nazi radio propaganda. Kris ultimately moved his family and his political activity to New York, whereas the younger Gombrich remained throughout the war in or near London. Although the two returned to the study of caricature after 1945, their book encountered new difficulties in the postwar world. They never published the prewar manuscript.

Yet, despite remaining unfinished—even because of it—Kris and Gombrich's caricature project represents a seminal twentieth-century effort at bridging scientific research and humanist scholarship. Nobel laureate Eric R. Kandel argues persuasively that Kris and Gombrich's psychological and art historical studies—which the caricature project helped initiate—marked out a path that ultimately led from Freudian depth psychology to neuroscientific models of brain functioning, perceptual processing, and artistic creativity.[1] Their study of caricature tested new psychological theories about mind and culture, articulated novel psychoanalytic conceptions of the ego and creativity, and helped to inspire Gombrich's own landmark theories on cognitive psychology and image making. It combined scientific questioning and humanist research not to produce a single, unified theory but to explore ways of integrating a broad range of concepts and methods. Their project thus offers insight into the kinds of collaboration, questioning, and support that such integrative efforts require in our own time—and will continue to require in the future.

The project also derives significance from another source. Kris and Gombrich's most extensive work on the caricature manuscript coincided with the emergence of the antifascist culture of the 1930s, and it derived impetus from that culture. But as a response to the European-wide crisis, it also became absorbed by that crisis. Yet, as historians and social theorists such as Herbert Marcuse and E. P. Thompson emphasized after the war, unrealized potentials offer vital—perhaps the most vital—subjects for historical inquiry. In the aspirations that moved them, in the obstacles that they confronted, and in the choices that they represented, such potentials possess ongoing relevance. The following chapters then do not set forth a dual biography of the two scholars, nor do they present an analysis of the corpus of their works across their careers. Rather, they trace the stages, possibilities, and outcomes of a joint project and shared inspiration from which we can still learn today.

A Model of Integration

According to his Viennese psychoanalytic colleague Robert Waelder, Kris was "at home in both history and psychoanalysis."[2] But while

Waelder saw this dual background as an exemplary model for professional training, Kris felt ill at ease with his divided career and treated his double education in art history and psychology as a highly problematic ideal. His persistent efforts to fuse his humanist training with his scientific pursuits never gave rise to a complete sense of personal fulfillment or intellectual satisfaction.[3]

Ambivalence, however, stimulated theory building. In his psychoanalytic studies of art and creativity, Kris developed the idea of *regression in the service of the ego*, which he introduced in 1934 in his first essay on caricature. There, and throughout his career, he argued that the creative liberation of unconscious primary processes strengthened rather than detracted from the functioning of the ego. Regressive mental processes did not necessarily lead to inward dissolution. Instead, through controlled regression or mental play the ego achieved an integration of psychological functions and impulses—what Kris described as a *restitution of the self*. Regression fostered a questioning of received notions from the past and restitution demanded new visions of the future. Both defined a psychological and historical condition of openness, ambiguity, and crisis, a process confirmed by Kris's own personal and political experiences.[4]

In the field of cultural history, Aby Warburg had devoted a lifetime of research to exploring the process of regression and restitution.[5] In pathbreaking studies of Renaissance artists and their Florentine patrons, he emphasized the ambivalence and instability—the Janus-like nature—of creativity and image making. Images served both as repositories of historical memory and as symbols of an idealized future, expressing simultaneously the violence of primal emotional needs and the promise of modern spiritual ideals. Renaissance painters and their patrons, according to Warburg, revived ancient symbols in a restless, always tentative search for psychological and cultural equilibrium. Warburg's concern with the "afterlife of antiquity"—the cultural appropriation of a buried and forgotten visual world—would resonate in Kris's work as he charted the processes of regression and restitution, of creative disintegration and reintegration, in both art and psychology. Maintaining contact with the Warburg Library after its escape from Hamburg for London, Kris relied on it to secure his friend and colleague Gombrich a way out of Vienna.

Initially as a research fellow and ultimately as director of the Warburg Institute, Gombrich carried out groundbreaking analyses in the psychology of perception and artistic representation. Kandel identifies the research that Gombrich undertook with Kris as a pivotal contribution to understanding the function of the brain as a "creativity machine" and to recognizing the psychological role of the beholder in completing the artist's creative work.[6] For Gombrich, artist and audience participated in the mutual construction of meaning. While he rejected Freud's theory of the unconscious in art—in fact, it eventually became an intellectual irritant to him—as well as Warburg's conception of historical memory, he did share Freud and Warburg's fascination with how artists and the public engaged in mental experimentation with images and how they transfigured visions from the past into workable models of the present. Throughout a long and tireless career, Gombrich continued to draw upon both experimental science and cultural history to interpret shifts in artistic perception and creativity and to analyze the psychological ambiguities and historical variations to be found in visual artefacts. He approached images as mental constructs, whose reception, modification, and alteration could be understood as both a cognitive and cultural process. His work with Kris on caricature became his first in-depth study of that dual process.

An impressive amount of material survives from the caricature project. Gombrich never discarded the prewar book manuscript, and as will be seen, he continued to revise it into the 1960s. The original German version and Gombrich's English translation, with later revisions, belong to the papers of the E. H. Gombrich Estate deposited at the Warburg Institute Archive. After emigrating to Britain, Gombrich also wrote, in English, a highly condensed version of the caricature manuscript, to which he added his own appendix; this abbreviated text can be found in the Ernst Kris Papers at the Library of Congress, while the appendix remains part of the Gombrich Estate. Finally, the Gombrich Estate contains a revised, thirty-five-page outline for the caricature book that Gombrich produced a few years after the war, when he and Kris planned to return to the manuscript.

Correspondence between Kris and Gombrich, preserved in the Kris Papers and the Gombrich Estate, dates from 1936, when Gombrich became a research assistant to Fritz Saxl, the Warburg Institute director in London.[7] Trained like Kris and Gombrich in the Vienna School, Saxl became Warburg's close collaborator after the First World War and, with Gertrud Bing, his designated successor and guardian of the library. Saxl sponsored the only public presentation by Kris and Gombrich on caricature—a lecture that Kris delivered at the Warburg Institute in 1937—and even considered publishing their book.

The *Anschluss* in 1938 forced Kris, his wife Marianne Kris, and their two young children, Anna and Anton, into exile in London, where he joined the BBC monitoring service as an analyst of German radio broadcasts. On his recommendation, the BBC offered a position to Gombrich, who joined the listening post in late 1939. A year later, Penguin Books published a highly abbreviated history of caricature that Gombrich had authored before the outbreak of the war. English reviews of the pamphlet-length publication—including a highly supportive piece by Herbert Read for *The Listener*—appeared in 1941, by which time Kris had emigrated to New York and taken a position on the Graduate Faculty at the New School for Social Research. There he received support from the Rockefeller Foundation's Project on Totalitarian Communication to undertake a detailed study of Nazi radio propaganda.

After the war, Kris offered courses at the New York Psychoanalytic Institute and directed research into early childhood development at the Yale Child Study Center, receiving an appointment in 1949 to the Yale University faculty.[8] In London, Gombrich returned to the Warburg Institute as a teaching and research fellow but without a permanent position until 1948. His academic prospects changed dramatically in

January 1950 with the appearance of his first monograph on art history, *The Story of Art*. The book earned nearly instantaneous success. Five months after its appearance, Oxford offered Gombrich the three-year Slade Professorship in Fine Arts.[9]

Despite the geographic and professional distance between them—soon after the war Kris became a naturalized American citizen and Gombrich a naturalized British subject—the two scholars attempted to revive the caricature book.[10] Yet, instead of reinvigorating the project, the early 1950s brought the story of the book to a close. In 1952, Kris published *Psychoanalytic Explorations into Art*, which collected essays from the previous two decades. Its topics ranged from metapsychology and clinical studies to literary criticism and aesthetic theory. Responding to intense postwar interest in both psychoanalysis and the increasingly popular field of applied psychology, the volume revealed an anti-reductionist temperament and interpretive range not easily matched by other psychoanalysts and psychologists. Yet, Kris regarded his essays—even those with prewar origins—as works in progress, as conscious experimentation with several lines of thought. Among them was the paper on caricature presented to the Warburg Institute, which Kris revised and included in the volume, and which now represented the final outcome of the caricature project.

After the collection appeared in print, Gombrich wrote to Kris that he regarded their Warburg Institute presentation as an important accomplishment. Stressing the significance of context for the interpretation of art, he stated: "It [context] is the problem which does justify a 'history' of art and I still think that in this respect our caricature paper is quite a model of 'integration'."[11] Like Kris, Gombrich saw in their caricature project a work of unrealized potential.

Daumier and the Choice of Caricature

In the ancient world, Plutarch—the Stoic moralist and Delphic priest—compared his aims as a biographer to those of a portraitist who searched both for character traits and for oracular signs within his subject's visage. The resulting biographies—like portraits—offered both the illusion of life and a symbol of the soul:

> When a portrait painter sets out to create a likeness, he relies above all upon the face and the expression of the eyes and pays less attention to the other parts of the body: in the same way it is my task to dwell upon those actions which illuminate the workings of the soul, and by this means to create a portrait of each man's life.[12]

In the Renaissance, portraitists reaffirmed the ancient conviction that a natural likeness of the body revealed hidden features of the soul. At the same time, according to Kris and Gombrich, they initiated the modern experiment with caricature. As the two scholars explained, caricaturists regarded supposedly natural likenesses as idealized or, at best, partial configurations. To communicate the soul's inward truth required that artists distort or reconfigure its external mask.

Seen as a process of de-idealization, caricature represented an innovation in portrait art, a radical psychological and artistic pursuit within the classical tradition, one that preserved an unobtrusive, even guilty, appeal to the humanist imagination. It persisted well beyond the Renaissance as the private creation of artists and a safe indulgence enjoyed by patrons—and perhaps especially by scholars. The composer Felix Mendelssohn drew caricatures of actors and fellow musicians: in 1845 he published in the notorious British satirical magazine *Punch* a group caricature of the chorus then appearing in Sophocles' *Antigone*.[13]

During the early nineteenth century, other caricaturists produced similarly entertaining and uncontroversial depictions of another sort of theater: the society of manners of the successful bourgeoisie. In such cases, their art remained a private amusement, an entertainment for an audience who could be let in on the joke without danger. Still other caricaturists, however, took far deeper and wider aim, targeting the injustices of the middle-class political and social system. Daumier and his colleagues regarded caricature not merely as a psychological and artistic instrument but as a civic action. In their hands, caricature became more than an alternative symbol for the soul: it documented social and political realities.[14]

Commentaries on caricature reflected its expansion. In Daumier's time, critics interpreted it as a response to everyday human folly and as an extension of the Romantic rebellion in art, as an examination of character and as a satire on society, as a creation of the salon and as a product of the street. Balzac referred to its technique as "abbreviatory signs," while Champfleury described its force as a "cry of the people."[15] Henry James perceived in Daumier the adroit manipulator of the bourgeois *imago*, whereas Baudelaire saw in him the heir to Bruegel and Goya, a figure who lowered the barriers between psychology, art, and politics.

Driven by the question of how an isolated activity of artists and a personal vice of the bourgeoisie became a public, political act of dissidents, Kris and Gombrich explored caricature as a dynamic, multilayered experiment that crossed creative techniques, historical time periods, and social strata. Scholars since have examined in detail caricature's separate origins in portraiture, satire, parody, humor, and political criticism, and analyzed its distinctive forms and functions in sketching, illustration, journalism, and photography.[16] In his own writings, in fact, Gombrich continued to write on subjects—such as cartooning—that reflected his early interest in caricature.[17] Yet, the work he and Kris did jointly remains unique in its approach to caricature as a continuous experiment—one with a long history and diverse uses but also, as Kris would write, with its own systematic or inner logic.

In Daumier, the experiment with caricature not only reached its most comprehensive incarnation but also, according to Kris and Gombrich, ran its course. By the time they brought the French artist's work to Vienna, they had concluded that caricature's constant and progressive innovation had come to an end. In their day, it had entered a state of disintegration, splintering into an esoteric play with symbolic forms on the one hand and an ominous, starkly propagandistic manipulation of thought and images on the other. The nationalist, anti-Semitic, and violent propaganda of the twentieth century did not represent to them the latest stage in the development of caricature but rather its collapse, a departure from its essential logic, a gross corruption, and a dangerous abuse that required its own study and response. Caricature, in its truest sense, was for them antipropaganda.

Scholarship and Exile

In exile, Kris and Gombrich shifted to the analysis of fascist propaganda, and waited for an opportunity after the war to revive their manuscript. In their commitment to both scholarship and war work—and in the difficulties they encountered in the pursuit of each—their situation recalls that of another refugee who shared ties to the Warburg Institute. In his memoir of émigré life in London from 1933 to 1936, Felix Gilbert—the great-grandson of Felix Mendelssohn—described his efforts as both a young Renaissance historian and a German refugee to salvage his career in a new country. His research into theories of the state, which combined his interests in cultural and political history, found no counterpart within the British academic universe: "I was surprised and somewhat shocked when I discovered that in England in the 1930s study of the Renaissance was left almost exclusively to art and literary historians."[18] Gilbert's focus on Niccolò Machiavelli and the rise of modern political theory received an indifferent and even cold response from British academics who still perceived Machiavelli as "an advocate of the devil."[19] Gilbert's political marginality as an antifascist compounded his intellectual alienation. He observed that the British political class—with the exception of Churchill's immediate circle and members of the Liberal party—remained smug or unconcerned toward Hitler.

Devoted to scholarship but without an institutional home, preoccupied by events in Germany but unable to influence them, frustrated by British myopia but with no access to opinion-making circles, Gilbert spent his days alone or among fellow exiles. At work he secluded himself in the Reading Room of the British Museum; in off hours he walked across the road to the bookshop of the German émigré Hans Preiss, where he conversed and debated with other anti-Hitler émigrés. The juxtaposition of museum and bookshop became a vivid reminder—and emblematic symbol—of the divided lives led by refugee scholars.

In 1937, in one of the first issues of the British *Journal of the Warburg Institute*, Gilbert published a commentary on Machiavelli and Florentine thought—his first article on Machiavelli in English, his first scholarly publication in exile, and a veiled self-examination.[20] In Florentine archives he had found an unpublished Renaissance dialogue composed *circa* 1533 by Luigi Guicciardini, the brother of the renowned historian Francesco Guicciardini.[21] Machiavelli, who had died several years before the date of the manuscript, appeared as a character in the dialogue, and his presence in the otherwise unexceptional work intrigued Gilbert. The only non-contemporary figure and the only participant who avoided a stock philosophic or religious stance, Machiavelli played the role of intellectual gadfly, the figure who set the dialogue in motion, in Gilbert's words, "the man who keeps the discussion alive by contradiction. Taken to task for his constant questions and objections, he declares quite openly that, for him, doubt is the beginning of all knowledge."[22] Unashamed, Machiavelli reminded his interlocutors of the power of necessity and especially the decisive role of materialism and selfishness in all human behavior: "Luigi Guicciardini, although he, like most of his contemporaries, saw mainly the paradoxical and contradictory features in Machiavelli's theories, nevertheless was aware of something more behind this mask of foolery."[23]

Guicciardini had aimed at producing a safe, acceptable philosophic and religious meditation. Yet, the presence of Machiavelli as Doubt betrayed a political thinker's nagging sense of disillusionment with human behavior.

Gilbert's analysis of the dialogue served as his own meditation on the unremitting conflict between scholarly withdrawal and the political impulse. Confronting that conflict in London, he produced a new historical image of Machiavelli—not the devil of British academic and moral imagination but a Mephistophelean spirit who led others first toward intellectual doubt and skepticism and from there into active political engagement. As in Guicciardini's dialogue, the movement from Doubt to political activity described not a self-confident, self-fulfilled journey but a conflicted, Faustian crisis. New knowledge of humanity brought with it an alienating, pessimistic appraisal of human action and motives. Machiavelli as Doubt reflected the fatalism that hounded all political commitment, the oppressive duality that fueled Gilbert's reinterpretation of Florentine thought.

In the mid-1930s both Gilbert and Kris had lost a strong intellectual foothold within traditional academia, but each had found a sympathetic hearing at the itinerant Warburg Institute. Through an analysis of Machiavelli and the Florentine origins of modern political science, the Berlin émigré tried to draw Renaissance scholars away from an exclusive focus on art toward engagement with contemporary political concerns. Through the study of caricature and the display of Daumier's artwork, the Viennese scholar sought to inject political concerns into the field of art history itself. But what plagued Machiavelli and Gilbert also vexed Kris—and Gombrich. As the two Viennese exiles moved from scholarly isolation toward political engagement, they, like Gilbert, confronted their deepening pessimism about the fate of Europe, a pessimism that the two Viennese never entirely shook off.

All three scholars found a way into the intelligence services. By the time that his commentary on Machiavelli appeared in print, Gilbert, who belonged only to the periphery of the Warburg Institute, had emigrated to the United States, where he took a temporary teaching position at Scripps College in 1936. During the war he served in the Central European Section of the Research and Analysis Branch of the Office of Strategic Services (OSS). There his functions included studying German propaganda, through which he worked at "finding out about the situation inside Germany, and about the 'mind of the German people.'"[24] Similar to Gilbert, Kris and Gombrich tracked Nazi radio broadcasts and tried to assess, in Kris's words, "the enemies' intentions."[25] In each case, the requirements of war work staved off emotional pessimism and political despair.[26]

Personal fatalism and political engagement expressed themselves differently in Kris and Gombrich. Kris, who had always sympathized with the ideal of a liberal Habsburg monarchy, eventually identified with and promoted Popular Front principles and strategies. He perceived the necessity of an antifascist alliance with the Left and took solace during the war from the rise of popular antifascist movements, although he questioned their ability to persist beyond the war. Gombrich, who did not identify strongly with the Popular Front, experienced a greater sense of disillusionment and felt a stronger temptation to withdrawal. Throughout the war, he continued to battle against a persistent fatalism, a struggle that gave personal urgency to his political reflections and wartime activities. After 1945, his pessimism about social progress only deepened. Gombrich's concentration on visual schemas and techniques of representation opened a new field of psychological inquiry into art, but it also reflected a persistent warding off of his brief yet determined engagement with politics.[27]

A Humanist Experiment

To stress the role of politics in Kris and Gombrich's study of caricature means also to acknowledge distinct limits. As scholars, they did not share Gilbert's focus on political thought. Within the world of central European psychoanalysis, Kris never belonged to that group of German-speaking analysts whom Russell Jacoby, in his study of the migration of European psychoanalysis to the United States, described as the political Freudians.[28] In the early 1930s, Kris saw no practical linkage between Freudian depth psychology and Marxist social philosophy and he rejected the program of those analysts who sought to bridge the two theories. Gombrich himself asserted flatly, "I have always been nonpolitical," explaining further that as a young liberal in his university days he associated the activity of politics with "mass processions."[29] As an art historian, he criticized efforts to join political and sociological, and especially Marxist, analysis to the interpretation of images. He finally adopted Karl Popper's antihistorical positivism and adamantly rejected Arnold Hauser's social history of art.

Unquestionably, the caricature project began as a collaborative effort in the psychology, not the politics, of art. That said, three crucial points should be noted. First, a project that began with the intent to bridge psychology and image studies ultimately called for methods of political and historical analysis. Second, both the Daumier exhibition and the book manuscript served as important steps toward direct political analysis and engagement during the war. Finally, Kris and Gombrich's manuscript did not take shape in a vacuum. Having persisted through decades of social upheaval, war, and exile, the caricature project came to an end under altered cultural and political conditions in the 1950s. The new Cold War atmosphere, as well as changes in the sciences, humanities, and visual arts, made it more difficult to pursue the model of integration. A new sense of pessimism supplanted in both scholars the political inspiration that had supplied a critical motive to the project and that had held it together despite differences over interpretation.

Like caricature itself, Kris and Gombrich's project never took on the shape of a finished masterpiece. It remained instead a suggestive, illuminating, and essential experiment in psychology, art, and politics. What follows is a history of that experiment.

CHAPTER 2

TOWARD A PSYCHOLOGY OF ART 1919–32

Kris and the Vocation of Art History

The caricature project derived from an undiminished friendship and continuous exchange of ideas that began in Vienna in the final years of Austria's First Republic and persisted through years of exile during and after the Second World War. As an émigré in England, Gombrich regularly sent to Kris in the United States detailed accounts of his work at the Warburg Institute and at the BBC monitoring service, including his analyses of German propaganda and his new theories on the psychology of art. He also shared with Kris his uncertainties about the postwar prospects for his family and career in Britain. Awaiting Kris's first visit to London after the war, he anticipated the restoration of their prewar Viennese contact: "I am tremendously looking forward to discuss[ing] the world and the future of the humanities with you."[1] For his part, Kris envisioned a revival of their original collaboration, stating,

> I have worked with many associates in these years, but I haven't found anyone with whom I got along so famously as I used to get alone [sic] with you. And getting along with me means always that I can learn from the other chap, and in these years I have often had the

> longing to sit down with you for a good many hours and to compare notes about the world and ourselves.[2]

Upon receiving Oxford's Slade Professorship, Gombrich expressed his sense of profound personal obligation: "Directly or indirectly of course I owe this like any other job I have ever had to your advice and encouragement."[3]

The friendship and collaboration between the two scholars reflected in part shared family and educational backgrounds. They belonged to the highly assimilated Jewish middle class of Vienna, both of their fathers practiced law, and members of each family pursued careers in the arts as scholars, teachers, or performers.

Still, a historical divide separated Kris and Gombrich—one far wider than the nine years difference in their ages. Born in 1900, Kris carried strong memories and influences from imperial Vienna. As a result, the collapse of the Habsburg monarchy during the First World War and the creation of the First Republic in 1918 registered more deeply, both personally and intellectually, with him than with Gombrich. When the republic entered its death throes in the 1930s, Kris foresaw the consequences more quickly and clearly than did his younger colleague.

Kris's father, Leo Kris, became a highly successful lawyer under the Habsburg regime and received the offer of a judgeship under the republic. The war years and the postwar inflation, however, had taken their toll. The offer of a judicial post was not enough to support his family and he turned it down.[4] In matters of religion, Leo Kris contemplated conversion and even spoke with Ernst about their converting to Catholicism together. He did not pursue the idea, but the father's religious leanings certainly encouraged the early interest in Roman Catholicism that Ernst shared with his older brother Paul. After his brother converted, Ernst, at the age of sixteen or seventeen, did so as well, only a year or two before centuries of Catholic rule came to an end in Austria. When in early 1919 he entered the University of Vienna, Kris recorded his religious affiliation as Roman Catholic.

His father had pointed the way and his brother had provided the model, but Kris's decision to convert also reflected his deep, personal fascination with the traditions of visual symbolism in the Church and can be seen as of a piece with his early commitment to art history. The Austrian republic had only just come into being and Vienna's Baroque tradition in art remained visible amidst the ruins of the monarchy. Kris's decision to convert remained a personal one: when the time came, he decided against baptizing his two children, a choice that acquired deep significance in the years immediately prior to the *Anschluss*.[5]

Kris's cousin, the art historian Betty Kurth, first instilled in him a serious interest in art. Thirteen years Kris's senior, Kurth defined her religious identity as *konfessionslos*—unaffiliated.[6] As an art historian, she concentrated on medieval German, French, and Flemish tapestry, but like Warburg, who had contributed to Baedeker's guide to Florence, she incorporated art history into an illustrated companion for sightseers. Writing a few years after the First World War, she composed a guidebook to Schönbrunn, the Habsburgs' former summer palace.

Labeled the Austrian Versailles, Schönbrunn survived as a historical relic, an impressive monument to the ambitions of the eighteenth-century empress Maria Theresa, who sought to solidify the Habsburg state as a central European Catholic empire by enforcing the Church's religious supremacy, expanding the territories under Habsburg authority, and imposing administrative reforms. Her summer palace—a closely controlled synthesis of architecture, decoration, and finely sculpted grounds—typified French classicism and imperial order. But "in the playful grace of the ornament, in the strong predominance of naturalistic flower motifs,"[7] it also, as Kurth pointed out, exhibited less orthodox features. Linked in memory to Theresian grandeur, Schönbrunn—and Kurth's description of it—pointed to impulses that led Kris into art history: a fascination with the treasures linking throne and altar; an interest in classically inspired forms that nonetheless rebelled against classical constraints; and a curiosity toward artistic techniques that reflected biological variations and physical excesses in nature. Politically, too, Kurth's interest in the Habsburg palace mirrored a trait that Kris exhibited throughout his life—what Gombrich described as his "soft spot for pageantry."[8]

Introspection and a New Realism

At the university, Max Dvořák became Kris's art historical mentor. The Czech scholar who held one of the university's two chairs in art history was, in Gombrich's phrase, Vienna's "champion of Mannerism and Expressionism."[9] During the war, while still a *Gymnasium* student, Kris attended Dvořák's lectures. A scholar of both ancient and contemporary culture, Dvořák called on art historians to reorient themselves toward the study of ideas, mentalities, and worldviews. His lectures and seminars—where he drew a small, dedicated group of followers—interpreted pictorial images as markers or symbols of intellectual and emotional concerns that were inaccessible through written documents.

Dvořák hoped the study of images would generate heightened cultural and spiritual awareness in his own day. His interpretation of Pieter Bruegel, the sixteenth-century Flemish artist whose paintings the Habsburgs had assembled into one of the most remarkable single collections in Europe, served as a crucial example. Bruegel's vivid depictions of peasants and commoners had dispensed with both classical balance and medieval severity. Instead, his faces and gestures depicted spontaneous emotions, daily pains, or temporary, joyful release. With Rabelais, Cervantes, Shakespeare, and the artist Jacques Callot, Bruegel brought about "the discovery and artistic expression of those vital truths which emerge when a careful observation is made of the psycho-physical characteristics of ordinary people."[10] His acute awareness and worldly vision produced, in Dvořák's phrase, a "new realism."[11]

By communicating the physical, sensual qualities of experience, Bruegel's realism embodied "the plenitude of life and in a way which makes all attempts to arrange and define seem utterly superfluous."[12] It reflected "the artist's insight which, in discovering the complex vitality of man's social life, is raised to a higher level of consciousness, a consciousness which, in turn, is passed on to the observer through the medium of art."[13] The counterpart to Montaigne's essays, Bruegel's satiric vision and stoic sensibility expressed a humble attitude toward nature and a belief in the inextricable union between the earthbound and the transcendent, between the grotesque and the ethereal. He rejected both classical heroizing and medieval spirituality: "eternal, changeless laws of nature stand above our desires and passions, indifferent to the lives of individuals; when we imagine that we are in control we are, in fact, being led by fate, as unknowingly as blind men, towards the abyss."[14] Such formed the basis of a religion of humanity that "was to become one of the most fundamental factors in seventeenth- and eighteenth-century European art and then in the nineteenth century, to gain a pre-eminence which it retained into the twentieth century where, almost at one stroke, it was replaced by a style that was its complete antithesis."[15] A modernist art that depicted metaphysical rather than material concerns, that renounced Bruegel's documentary and *politique* attitude, succeeded the new realism. And "the origin of this new style," Dvořák concluded, "is rooted in the work of the mannerist painters."[16]

For Dvořák, Mannerism contained the seeds of modern spiritual strivings and anxieties. Embodied in the enigmatic works of El Greco, Mannerist art depicted the same inner torment that Expressionists conveyed in the years leading to the First World War. Dvořák saw the war as the final crisis of modern materialism, and expected that its consequences would lead people to reject liberal egotism—which he identified with Austria's enemies and held responsible for the catastrophe—and revive the devotional search that anguished and inspired El Greco.[17] By its end, however, disillusion overcame him. According to Otto Benesch—one of his most loyal students—Dvořák ultimately adopted the Expressionists' aim to break with the past, teaching his pupils that "Expressionism exposed the absurdity of all earlier ideas of development and progress."[18]

Dvořák's disenchantment recalls the satirist Karl Kraus, who also advocated the Expressionist view of art as a moral astringent and instrument of spiritual chastening, and whose public readings Kris attended as a student in Vienna.[19] Unlike Kraus, however, Dvořák believed that Mannerist and modernist artists filled a therapeutic function. In their spiritual search, Baroque painters, according to Dvořák, had anticipated the twentieth-century emphasis on clinical introspection, the "effort to enrich man's life and understand its secret through psychological knowledge."[20] Mannerists thus possessed a kinship not only with Expressionist artists but also with scientists of the mind, and their creations foreshadowed the discoveries of scientific psychology and medical psychiatry.

From 1919 to 1921—the year of Dvořák's death—Kris enrolled in his lectures on the High Renaissance, Baroque art, and Albrecht Dürer, as well as in several of his art seminars.[21] There he would have heard Dvořák's explanation of the links between artistic experimentation and psychological analysis, as well as his ideas on the significance of art for documenting social reality. And when in 1936 Kris sought to characterize Daumier's artistic and political concerns in his exhibition catalog, he used the term Dvořák had applied to Bruegel and Callot: a "new realism."'

Entering the Museum

Kris admired the Dionysian Dvořák—the cultural historian of crisis, torment, and recovery—but for his professional training, he turned to the Olympian Julius von Schlosser. Under Schlosser's tutelage, Kris expanded his scientific vision and historical curiosity. Like Dvořák, Schlosser called for allying the study of art more closely to the discipline of history. Unlike Dvořák, he focused on tangible rather than intangible phenomena, adhering more closely to one of the founders of the Vienna School, Franz Wickhoff. Schlosser treated artworks not as records of psychological and emotional experiences that demanded symbolic or empathic interpretation but as material artefacts that required analysis of their distinctive features and components. His approach embodied the Vienna School's emphasis on academic expertise, archival experience, and museum work, as well as his predisposition as a collector and preservationist.

Claiming a multinational Austrian identity, Schlosser stressed his family links to artistic traditions from both northern and southern Europe. His mother was Italian and he referred to himself on occasion as Schlosser-Magnino.[22] A close friend of the eminent Italian philosopher-antiquarian Benedetto Croce, his *History of Portraiture in Wax* testified to Croce's influence. Schlosser followed Croce in asserting that objects of art were discrete, autonomous entities whose history "cannot be an organic phenomenon, cannot be the evolution of a 'species' as understood by modern-day natural science."[23] An artwork "by its very nature is an individual thing, containing its own framework of values, never, on pain of losing its unique identity, deriving them externally from 'history,' let alone from the realm of Platonic 'Ideas.'"[24] What was true of objects was also true of symbols. Schlosser's intense interest in typical images and iconic formulas—especially in medieval art—derived, for example, from a fascination with individual coins, the imprints stamped upon them, and the stories behind them.[25]

In 1901 Schlosser became curator of the collection of applied art and sculpture at Vienna's *Kunsthistorisches Museum*. There he carefully looked after the museum's gems, intaglios, gold and bronze works, artisanal creations, and small medieval and Renaissance statues almost as if they were his private possessions. His seminar students gained professional training and research experience by studying these distinctive objects. Beyond the curatorship, in his own scholarship, Schlosser produced an encyclopedic compendium and historical commentary on theories and conceptions of art from the Middle Ages through the Enlightenment—that is, the period before the modernist revolt shook the art world. After Dvořák's death in 1921, he succeeded to Dvořák's chair in the art historical institute, where he began to steer the Vienna School in a far more conservative intellectual direction.

Under Schlosser's guidance, Kris—whom Schlosser described as his *Urschüler*, his original or model pupil—chose for the subject of his doctoral thesis the work of Wenzel Jamnitzer, the German goldsmith whose highly detailed castings from nature crossed the boundaries between art and science. Many experts interpreted Jamnitzer's casts of plants, insects, and animals as purely technical accomplishments, but Kris found them intriguing for their combination of fantastic embellishment and precise observation. His choice fit within the decades-old tradition of the Vienna School—inspired originally by Wickhoff and Alois Riegl—to trace the history of art not only in the masterworks of well-known eras but also in the minor objects from less prominent periods, including figures and decorative objects produced for daily life.[26] Wickhoff and Riegl explored art from the period of Roman imperial decline; Kris chose the waning days of the Renaissance. The thesis earned him his doctorate in art history in 1922. The same year, he became a museum curator in his mentor's department of applied art and sculpture.[27]

Kris advanced rapidly in his profession, but, from the first, politics intervened in his career. During and after the First World War, his political inclinations remained steadfastly monarchist or *kaisertreu*. Such sympathies were widespread among much of Vienna's Jewish middle class, who perceived Emperor Francis Joseph as the guarantor of political stability and gradual liberalization.[28] The monarch seemed also the guarantor of the Austrian artistic patrimony that reached back to the late Renaissance. The *Kunsthistorisches Museum*—built in the nineteenth century as part of the *Ringstrasse* development—expressed Francis Joseph's intention to preserve and display that legacy in a grand public monument. As Carl E. Schorske described, constructing it, together with its companion museum of natural history, required that the imperial court reach a political compromise with Vienna's liberal municipal leadership.[29] Now presiding over a portion of that dynastic patrimony, Kris acted upon both his Habsburg loyalty and his Viennese civic responsibility. He reorganized the imperial holdings under his care and brought more of them to public view. Through the curatorship he not only indulged his early passion for art but also expressed his ongoing attachment to the liberal monarchist ideal.

But Kris's intellectual and political impulses derived from the last days of a fast disappearing political and cultural universe. He had embarked upon his university training and professional vocation after Francis Joseph's death, after Austria's overwhelming military defeat, and in the midst of the final disintegration of the Austro-Hungarian Empire. Remnants of the fragmented Habsburg world survived in the imperial family's art collections and in the imposing presence of the art historical museum, but that circumstance only emphasized the mutability and ethereal nature of Kris's situation. The vocation of art historian to which he had committed himself during the war belonged after 1918 less to a living present than to a decaying past. After the first years of his curatorship, Kris came to regard art history as a stillborn professional choice and an uncertain refuge.

Borderline Art

As curator, Kris immersed himself in researching and cataloging the museum's possessions in gold work, gems, medieval religious statues, and Renaissance craftsmanship—work that very soon won him an international reputation.[30] Furthermore, as the *Kunsthistorisches Museum* was transformed from an imperial institution of the old monarchy to a national institution of the new republic, he began to give the applied art collection its contemporary organization. Yet, neither the prestige of having followed Schlosser as curator at such a young age nor the opportunity to build and reorganize the collection at such a decisive point in the museum's history brought him personal satisfaction or professional fulfillment. By 1924, within two years after assuming his position, he shifted career directions dramatically.

Kris's growing disillusionment with the academic study of art and what seemed to him the stale atmosphere at the museum began to evidence itself in his disenchantment with even the Vienna School's new subjects and methodologies. He developed an increasingly intense interest in marginal artworks and pursued psychology as the most effective method for interpreting these borderline products. Like Schlosser, Kris explored such art as an overlooked cultural legacy; unlike his mentor, he hoped to find in it a key to the psychology of creativity.

An early inspiration to Kris's study of borderline art derived from the very sculpture and craftwork whose care he inherited from Schlosser. Those objects recalled the Austrian tradition of the *Kunst- und Wunderkammer*, collections of artistic and natural curiosities that ranged from the sublime to the grotesque and that possessed the aura of the magical, miraculous, or fearful, from rare gems and minerals to unique products of human design such as automatons. The seventeenth-century emperor and founder of the imperial art collection, Rudolf II, had lent early impetus to the mania for curiosities, which subsequently inspired a long line of Habsburg collectors. And Rudolf not only gathered mysterious and wondrous objects but also catalogued them. As Horst Bredekamp has explained, the tradition of the *Kunstkammer* led collectors in Austria and throughout Europe to devise scientific classifications for what astonished or mystified them.[31]

Schlosser developed an intensive interest in waxen images, technical marvels—including automatons —and similar uncanny products of art and nature. His book on the late Renaissance *Kunst- und Wunderkammer*, originally published in 1908 and reprinted in 1923, focused on a wide selection of such objects from the museum's collection. The pride and pleasure in possession felt by the original Habsburg collectors flourished anew in Schlosser's scholarly exposition. As the title page states, he wrote the book as a manual for the enthusiast as well as the professional collector, who could find in its pages a silver penholder and inkwell cast from shells and small animals in the manner of Jamnitzer; an animal's horn carved in the shape of a griffin that stood upon a tortoise and carried on its back a half-man, half-serpent; an ostrich-egg goblet; a whirring symphony of trumpeting figurines; and a mechanical, chiming bell tower. There appeared also a remarkable ebony cabinet carved in the design of an ancient temple and decorated with gold-encrusted satyrs and caryatids. Especially fragile objects provoked meditation on human transience and death, including a clock with a tiny ivory skeleton under glass and an ebony cabinet within which another small skeleton adopted a contemplative pose. Finally, Schlosser surveyed not only craftwork but also paintings, in particular Arcimboldo's depictions of autumn and fire, two of the well-known faces that the painter composed from images of fruits, grains, utensils, and weapons.[32]

As Christopher S. Wood has explained, Schlosser's antiquarian devotion reflected the reticence toward art historical speculation that he shared with Croce: "It was not indifference to art but the fastidious conviction that nothing pertinent could be said about art—that art could never be used as a document—that steered Schlosser away from the interpretation of the individual work of art and onto the unorthodox topics."[33] Deep conservative misgivings toward the intellectual value of art history had spurred Schlosser's willingness to seek out the unusual. Kris developed similar apprehensions—but he drew far different conclusions from them.

Outside the Vienna School Kris's questioning of art history received impetus from Emanuel Loewy, the historian and archeologist of antiquity who held professorships in both Vienna and Rome and who had strongly influenced Kris's thinking as a student. Like his contemporaries in ancient studies—such as Jane Ellen Harrison and her colleagues known as the Cambridge Ritualists—Loewy interpreted archeological and artestic artefacts as psychological residues of the ancient past. In 1900, in his widely read treatise on the imitation of nature in ancient art, he traced the way in which highly schematized and starkly linear images from archaic art evolved into the natural likenesses found in classical Greek creations. Archaic painting, drawing, and sculpture relied upon "memory-pictures," which kept before the mind's eye only the definitive or essential aspects of external objects.[34] They derived from a process of psychological abstraction or winnowing, and art that based itself on such memory pictures dispensed with natural contours, fluid backgrounds, and variable perspectives. Pre-classical artists reproduced these mental templates or prototypical images in their creations, leaving a storehouse of reminiscences and visions that classical artists later modified and adapted to nature.

The slaughter of the First World War compelled Loewy to rethink his notion of the links between art and mind. In contrast to his prewar ideas, he now interpreted archaic artwork as a technique of protective—or apotropaic—magic that aimed at defending against violent earthly and supernatural forces. Gombrich—who, like Kris, attended Loewy's postwar seminars—recalled the shift: "In his lectures and naturally in his exercises as well he frequently dealt with his theories of the rendering of nature in art, the migration of types, and later also theories of apotropaic symbolism."[35] Based on the belief in a magical identity between images and their objects, primitive artists created symbols that, like ritual performances, would, as Loewy wrote, "simulate the presence of certain objects or beings whose appearance is supposed to act as a deterrent."[36] Artists and craftworkers produced frightening depictions of animals—bulls, lions, snakes—and fantastic or lurid human faces to serve, among many such images, as defensive weapons against terrifying external powers. Classical mimesis—the artistic imitation of reality— thus derived not only from a lineage of archaic memory pictures but also from a separate stream of primitive anxieties, ritual practices, and grotesque imagery.

Psychoanalysis and Art History

In 1924, Kris met Loewy's close friend Sigmund Freud. An avid collector of ancient and Renaissance artefacts, Freud had asked Kris to evaluate his personal collection of cameos and intaglios. He contacted the young curator at the suggestion of Kris's fiancée, Marianne Rie. The daughter of the Jewish physician Oskar Rie—Freud's long-time friend and the pediatrician to Freud's children—Marianne Rie was at that time studying medicine at the University of Vienna. In 1925, the year after the first meeting between Kris and Freud, she received her medical degree, and immediately upon graduation began her psychoanalytic training in Berlin. During that same year, Kris began his analysis with Helene Deutsch in Vienna.

While working with Deutsch, Kris decided to pursue a career in psychoanalysis. Although she initially believed that his decision derived from an identification with her as his analyst, Deutsch eventually supported the choice.[37] Kris completed his training analysis with Deutsch in 1927, the year that Marianne Rie, having finished her own training, returned to Vienna. That year Kris and Rie married and both began to participate in the work of the Vienna Psychoanalytic Society, with Marianne Kris joining the recently founded seminar on child analysis.[38]

In January 1932, Freud asked Kris to become editor of *Imago: Journal for the Application of Psychoanalysis to the Cultural Sciences* (*Zeitschrift für die Anwendung der Psychoanalyse auf die Geisteswissenschaften*). He left Kris free to edit the journal alone or with Robert Waelder. Kris chose a co-editorship and informed Freud that he intended to move *Imago* away from traditional applied psychoanalysis. As he recalled in an interview with K. R. Eissler, he told Waelder: "[O]ne cannot edit *Imago* as a journal for applied psychoanalysis because there is no application of analysis, of psychoanalysis; there is psychoanalytic psychology and clinical psychoanalysis; there is no applied psychoanalysis in the old sense . . ."[39] Waelder agreed, and after the two became co-editors, they changed *Imago*'s subtitle to *Journal for Psychoanalytic Psychology, Its Allied Fields and Applications* (*Zeitschrift für Psychoanalytische Psychologie, ihre Grenzgebiete und Anwendungen*). Two years later Kris began to serve as a lecturer and training analyst in the Vienna Psychoanalytic Institute.[40]

From the start of his own psychoanalytic education, Kris turned his attention to the psychology of art, which, as he made clear with regard to *Imago*, he conceived not as psychobiography—the approach most common within the Viennese Freudian movement—but as an investigation into the creative process, and in particular whether that process enhanced or diminished the artist's and viewer's contact with the world around them. Thus, in 1926, he had published *Der Stil "rustique": Die Verwendung des Naturabgusses bei Wenzel Jamnitzer und Bernard Palissy,* an expansion of his dissertation on late Renaissance metalwork and sculpture to include Palissy's, as well as Jamnitzer's, castings from nature. Outwardly, the essay confronted the question of whether such artificially produced likenesses belonged to the mainstream of High Renaissance creativity. Inwardly, it dealt with the problem of whether art itself performed life-giving or life-denying functions. Natural castings conveyed rigidified, not revitalized, appearances, and Kris pointed out their links to medieval cults of the dead and the casting of death masks, a procedure revived by Quattrocento portrait sculptors in their efforts to achieve realism. Not only metallic casting but also the high art of portraiture derived original subject matter from figures emptied of life.[41]

Kris became increasingly interested in petrified or failed expression in art and life. He began to investigate the creations of persons suffering from severe mental illness, through which he explored the conflict between the vivid, living quality that sufferers perceived in their own artworks and the unlifelike, even lifeless, appearance that those same works conveyed to even sympathetic viewers. In 1932, he published his first paper on the subject: a study of the grimacing character heads created by Franz Xaver Messerschmidt, the famous eighteenth-century sculptor whom Kris diagnosed as suffering from psychosis. To their viewers the sculptures might appear as repetitive, frozen visages, but to Messerschmidt they functioned as magical devices or protective masks to repel the demons that in moments of illness he believed pursued him. But the grimacing masks that desperately defended against the world simultaneously expressed Messerschmidt's desire to engage directly with it and so they deserved to be seen as works of art. The meanings conveyed by the character heads did not supplant or cover each other; they combined within a single configuration. Messerschmidt's sculptures represented a recurrent, highly charged effort at social communication and "self-restitution."[42]

Kris's concern with the distance between art and life and the need for self-restitution reflected his deepening alienation from the art historical profession. He intended to relinquish his position at the museum but Freud convinced him to remain there.[43] The curatorship provided professional security. Furthermore, always searching out new disciplinary footholds for psychoanalysis, Freud knew that from such a position Kris could better contribute to the aim of Viennese psychoanalysis—expressed in the original masthead of *Imago*—to bridge the humanities and psychology. Perhaps Kris referred partly to his own life experience when in 1935 he wrote about the tendency of individuals in times of crisis to live what he called enacted biographies:

> In a world whose semi-darkness is again and again submerged in myths, the boundary between the individual and tradition grows hazy and identification with the ancestor decides the nature and direction of the individual's existence. Under normal conditions, in our society, this bond plays on the whole a subordinated role. And yet many of us live even today the life of a biographical type, the "destiny" of a particular class, rank, or profession.[44]

Kris remained an art historian but was never of one mind about his decision.

At the close of the nineteenth century, Henry James had described his own similar disenchantment with art and, like Kris, he had tried to heal himself by meditating on the work of Daumier. In his famous essay on Daumier as caricaturist, first published in 1890, James expressed his ambivalence toward visual art in general and toward the mysterious effect of Daumier's portraits in particular: "Art," James wrote, "is an embalmer, a magician, whom one cannot speak too fair."[45] Although most artists used their skills to conceal signs of morbidity in their subjects, Daumier displayed the contorted, deathly faces of his subjects among the French bourgeoisie, who for their part responded with macabre fascination. The bourgeois class could not resist art's capacity to preserve their images—their death masks—for posterity. That life-in-death, James explained, "puts method, and power, and the strange, real, mingled air of things into Daumier's black sketchiness."[46]

Through Daumier, future generations would recognize the bourgeois by his frozen grimace. At the same time, they would perceive in art a critical, documentary function that would offer it a new kind of life.

The Republican Interregnum

The museum gave Kris resources and contacts. Psychoanalysis provided conceptual orientation and a sense of intellectual community. Yet, doubt never abandoned him. The psychology of creativity offered no definitive resolution, merely an exploratory path. Furthermore, as he tested the possibilities of a psychoanalysis of art, the political ground again shifted beneath him. Soon, neither art history nor psychology promised personal or professional security.

By 1932, the Christian Social party had established a stronghold of antirepublicanism within the Austrian republic itself. Under the leadership of Karl Lueger, it had begun its political rise in the 1890s by opposing both traditional conservatism and the Socialist party. Lueger's appeals to Vienna's lower middle class and anti-Semites had won him repeated reelection as the city's mayor and established a new right-wing model of political success. Although the Christian Socials lost their hold on Vienna's local government after the First World War, they effectively used their antisocialist, conservative Catholic message to enlarge their base beyond the capital. The Socialist party and its supporters—the chief defenders of the new Austrian republic—now focused their activities on defending their municipal bastion of "Red Vienna."

During the 1920s, Monsignor Ignaz Seipel, Austrian chancellor from 1922 to 1924 and 1926 to 1929, consolidated the Christian Social grip on the new state. Seipel trained for the priesthood at the University of Vienna and taught moral theology at the university in Salzburg, where in previous centuries archbishops had ruled the diocese as princes and ecclesiastics, building the city into a political power in central Europe and a religious bastion for German Catholicism.[47] The palace-fortress atmosphere of Salzburg could not have been far from Seipel's mind when toward the end of the war he returned to the University of Vienna to teach theology and launch a career in national politics.

Seipel and the Christian Social leadership constructed a Catholic political front within the framework of the First Republic. While open to occasional compromise, they treated Vienna's Socialist civic and labor leaders as anathema and aimed at breaking the Socialist party and trade unions. At the same time, a feckless but nonetheless dangerous Austrian paramilitary organization—the *Heimwehr*—carried out its own assaults on the Left, trade unionists, and other republican supporters, thereby making its own claim to power, while strengthening the Christian Socials' political hand.

From the time of Lueger, anti-Semitism served the Christian Socials as a ready organizing and propagandistic tool. In the 1920s, they aimed an increasingly insistent anti-Semitic message not only at Vienna—where the postwar party continued to remain comparatively weak—but more importantly at provincial cities and rural districts. Radical anti-Semites within the Christian Social movement called repeatedly for legislation that would define Jews as a separate racial minority and drastically limit or exclude altogether their participation in government, law, medicine, journalism, and education, demanding that such measures also extend to Jewish converts to Catholicism. The Church leadership, which viewed the Christian Social party as their political arm, objected to the racial categorization of Jews and discrimination against converts as antithetical to winning adherents and rebuilding a Catholic state. At the same time, members of the episcopate—such as Salzburg's archbishop Sigismund Waitz—publicly declared that Jews represented an alien element within the Austrian population and therefore hindered the Church's religious and social mission.

Christian Social followers, their propagandists, and allied clergy called for the social segregation of Jews and the imposition of an official *numerus clausus*—a limit on the number of Jewish civil servants, academics, and students at or below the percentage of Jews within the population as a whole. Although Christian Social electoral platforms throughout the country promoted that agenda and party journals supported it, neither Seipel nor his Christian Social successors passed anti-Semitic legislation. Seipel personally approved of the *numerus clausus* proposals—early in his career he had supported placing a restriction on the number of Jewish students who could enroll at the universities—but as chancellor he resisted turning such demands into law. They risked arousing international opposition and they promoted a racial determinism that competed with the party's and the Church's Christianizing ideology.[48] Instead, under Seipel's governments and those that followed, Christian Social officials used administrative directives and party influence—rather than their law-making authority—to reduce the number of Jews employed in government ministries, the civil service, the universities, and the schools. They gradually but persistently remade the Austrian republic into a conservative Catholic state.

Seipel envisioned Austria as a strong link in a chain of similar antisocialist, Catholic states stretching across southern and Eastern Europe. His continental strategy overlapped and at times competed with that of Benito Mussolini, whose National Fascist party came to power in Italy the same year that Seipel first became chancellor of Austria. The Fascist leader sought to build an antisocialist alliance across the Mediterranean rim, with Italy as the political pivot. In 1928, his plan to negotiate an alliance between Italy, Austria, and Hungary against France and Czechoslovakia appealed to Seipel's Theresian vision, but the possibility of forging such a coalition dissipated in the face of Mussolini's call for Italian sovereignty over the South Tyrol. Seeking an eventual concordat with the Italian dictator, the papacy remained silent on the dispute, and in the following year, it agreed to the Lateran Accords. In the early 1930s, Christian Social governments allied more closely and openly with the Italian Fascist state. Following Seipel's chancellorship, Austrian leaders perceived Mussolini's Italy as a kindred regime, one that guarded European Catholic states against the dangers of socialism and the demands of pan-Germanists.[49]

In Austria, pan-German nationalists vehemently denounced Seipel's grand diplomatic design. The ultra-nationalist Greater German People's Party openly called for *Anschluss* with Germany. Far more crucially, however, the remnants of the supposedly apolitical Habsburg civil service rallied in growing numbers around the idea of a greater German state. From the time of Emperor Joseph II—Maria Theresa's eighteenth-century successor—the Habsburg monarchy had depended heavily on a secularized German bureaucracy to enforce imperial laws and policies and to contain or suppress the multinational forces that threatened to split the empire. Already inclined toward German nationalism before the First World War, Austrian civil servants after 1918 now saw their influence—and their jobs—disappearing under the new clerical state.[50] Discontented, insecure bureaucrats perceived a non-clerical Greater Germany—rather than a truncated Catholic Austria—as the state best suited to guarantee their employment and satisfy their political ambitions.

In response to pan-German nationalism, Seipel and his followers pursued a two-pronged strategy. To satisfy the nationalist Right and to win over former imperial servants, they appealed to bourgeois and bureaucratic animosity toward socialism and to Catholic hostility toward republicanism. At the same time, they avowed the ideological principle behind *Anschluss* by stressing Austria's cultural identification—rather than political unification—with Germany. In the 1930s, Christian Social leaders appealed to both Italy and Germany as partners in a mission to uphold Catholic conservatism and German nationalism in an independent central Europe state.

Reflecting its pre-1914 support for German unification, the Austrian Socialist party in the early 1920s advocated *Anschluss* with the new Weimar republic. But the emergence of a Catholic authoritarian government in Austria, the rise of Nazism in Germany, and the growth of an Austrian Nazi party dispelled the illusion of union based upon republican principles. By the 1930s, the Austrian Left still preserved its German nationalism but now focused on the struggle against the Christian Socials.

Under the new republic, the University of Vienna—including the art historical institute—became a recurrent political and physical battleground. The German student association—*Deutsche Studentenschaft*—declared Jews an alien racial presence at the university and called repeatedly for a *numerus clausus* on Jewish instructors and students. In early 1923, truncheon-wielding members prevented Jews from entering the university's lecture halls and laboratories. In November 1923—ten days after Hitler's failed coup attempt in Munich—Austrian Nazis charged into classrooms, removing and clubbing Jewish students while police stood by impassively. The Christian Social government—claiming that it had no power or jurisdiction to interfere with the university's traditional privilege to regulate its own affairs—refused to intervene against the attacks. Assaults on Jewish students, the storming of classrooms of Jewish professors, and violence against Jewish student organizations revived in the late 1920s. In 1927, the anniversary of the founding of the republic aroused particular fury: by then, *Heimwehr* members joined German nationalist youths in demonstrations and rampages.[51]

Nationalist students directed their rage also at non-students and non-academics. At the University of Innsbruck, Karl Kraus gave a reading from his antiwar drama, *The Last Days of Mankind.* A model of Kraus's documentary method, *The Last Days of Mankind* utilized statements, phrases, and claims—written or spoken—that Kraus culled from newspaper accounts, political speeches, and government reports. "Theatergoers in this world," he explained, "would not be able to endure it. For it is blood of their blood . . ."[52] The Kaiser's wartime statements and German generals' declamations, heard again in Kraus's drama, became self-caricature, and nationalist students in Innsbruck prevented a scheduled second reading.[53]

The historian Eric Hobsbawm, the son of a British father and Austrian mother, spent his youth in Vienna. He recalled that immediately after 1918 only devoted Habsburg loyalists rejected the idea of *Anschluss* outright.[54] That observation applied to Kris, whose political convictions originated in the pre-1914 image of an enlightened Habsburg monarchy safeguarding constitutional government throughout the Austro-Hungarian lands. Among Vienna's community of writers and artists, Kris encountered first hand the growing presence and pressure of the Austrian Right. He visited, for example, a circle that gathered at the studio of Trude Wähner, an aspiring artist who promoted Paul Klee's Expressionist work. Her father Theodor Wähner, however, not only sat on the Vienna city council as a Christian Social representative but also published the anti-Semitic *Deutsche Zeitung*.[55]

Given the official policy of the Church hierarchy, Kris's status as a convert to Catholicism temporarily provided him with professional and personal protection. His work abroad with international collectors, museum directors, and art patrons supplied a safety net beyond Austria if it became necessary. As his son Anton O. Kris recalled, Italian bishops readily gave Kris access to Church collections that they kept closed to the public.[56] When the Metropolitan Museum of Art required an expert to catalog its cameo collection, it brought Kris to New York in 1929 to undertake the job.[57] At the same time, Kris kept close track of deteriorating conditions in Austria and employed his contacts to find work abroad for his younger, Jewish colleagues.

A liberal royalist in post-imperial Vienna, Kris remained convinced of the irreversible disintegration of Austrian political life. At his first meeting with the university student Ernst Gombrich, he therefore made sure that the young researcher understood fully the uncertainties that attached to an art historical career in Vienna. In the years that followed, Kris became not only a professional mentor to Gombrich but also a political advisor.

CHAPTER 3

THE VIENNA–LONDON CONNECTION 1932–36

Gombrich and the Question of Art History

Like Leo Kris, Gombrich's father, Karl Gombrich, built a successful career in law. His mother, Leonie Gombrich, achieved equal success as a renowned pianist and music coach, whose friends included Adolf Busch and Rudolf Serkin. Both parents participated in the circle of culture critics and religious seekers who surrounded Gustav Mahler. Both converted from Judaism to Protestantism—the faith in which they baptized their children—adopting a tolerant and non-evangelical stance distinct from the religious mysticism that characterized others among Mahler's followers. Karl Gombrich joined a Masonic lodge, a place of social refuge for many assimilated Viennese Jews and an organization that still remained, at the behest of the Church hierarchy, illegal in Austria. Each Freemason committed himself to the Masonic vision of global citizenship.[1] His family's secularized Jewish background and liberal Protestant ethos thus combined to shape Gombrich's later sympathy with the skeptical and experimentalist traditions of English Dissent.

Like the Kris family, the Gombrichs suffered from the postwar economic decline that struck the Viennese middle class.[2] Leonie Gombrich's income as a teacher and her contacts as a musician became increasingly important to the household. Her pupils came from families throughout Europe, among them the daughters of Lady Violet Bonham Carter, the daughter of the last prewar Liberal prime minister of Britain, Herbert Asquith.

The link to the Asquiths embodied the Gombrichs' religious and political liberalism, but more importantly it would prove crucial to the family's escape from Austria. Educated in a Dissenting Protestant home in Yorkshire, Asquith attended Balliol College, Oxford, where he could have remained as a classical scholar. Instead, seeking an opening into politics, he pursued a career in law. Before the First World War, he fought for the disestablishment of the Welsh Church and confronted the combined forces of Church and peers in the struggle over eliminating the veto of the Lords in Parliament. He did not last as a wartime leader. His Liberal government split and finally collapsed under the pressure of political rebellion in Ireland and military stalemate along the Western Front. After 1918, the Liberal party went into irreversible decline; the scholar-lawyer had led Liberalism into the political wilderness. Still, after 1918, Violet Bonham Carter became active as a Liberal party organizer and candidate for Parliament—this despite her father's opposition to women's suffrage. Her ties to the Gombrichs remained strong enough for her to sponsor their emigration to Britain.[3]

Within the family Gombrich did encounter a spirit of political radicalism. His older sister Amadea—named for Wolfgang Amadeus Mozart—followed her mother's path into the world of music, becoming a respected concert violinist. But his younger sister Lisbeth joined Austria's Socialist party. Through discussions with her, he received an education in political argument.[4] But argument did not translate into conviction. Attached to a liberalism in decline, Gombrich, like Kris, regarded contemporary politics with mistrust. In accord with the Masonic tradition of his father and the Dissenting tradition with which he later identified in England, he deplored aristocratic privilege, on the one hand, and the politics of the street, on the other. He committed himself instead to scholarship.

The Gombrichs enrolled their son in the Theresianum, the prestigious classical preparatory academy that had once served as the educational bastion of the Viennese Catholic aristocracy and imperial officer corps.[5] After the war, the school had become a *Gymnasium* for the middle classes of the new Austrian republic. Yet, Gombrich felt himself "rather an outsider."[6] Certainly, his profile as a Protestant student from a Jewish and Freemason background ran counter to that of the traditional student at the once exclusive *Gymnasium*.

Devoting himself chiefly to the study of German literature and modern physics, Gombrich's interest in art history developed late. Vienna's Baroque artworks and architectural monuments did draw his attention as an urban explorer, but as the ubiquitous remains of Austria's past. It was Dvořák's inspired writings and the Expressionists' vivid artwork that led the young Gombrich to approach art not merely as a relic but as the living representation of an idea. He recalled:

> When I was about fifteen or sixteen, I read books on Greek art and on medieval art. As soon as Max Dvořák's book came out, with the title—not by him—*Kunstgeschichte als Geistesgeschichte* (*Art History as the History of the Spirit*), I was given it as a present and devoured it.[7]

The book had an immediate impact. Dvořák "convinced me that the art of the past offered an immediate and exciting access to the mind of bygone eras."[8] The intellectual curiosity that Dvořák generated gave him a professional direction: "With this idea in mind, that art was a marvelous key to the past—an idea which I learned from Dvořák—I decided I wanted to read the history of art at Vienna University."[9]

At the university, Gombrich chose Schlosser as an advisor. Under his influence he began to reject the idea that art conveyed a collective spiritual dilemma or shared consciousness. While researching his dissertation on the Mannerist artist Giulio Romano and his Palazzo del Tè in Mantua, Gombrich discarded much of Dvořák's approach, explaining years later that in studying the archival records of the citizens of sixteenth-century

Mantua he "found it hard to credit them all with that spiritual predicament Dvořák and others had found expressed in the style of Mannerism."[10] The Palazzo del Tè itself represented a conflicted product:

> At the time I maintained that Giulio Romano had two completely opposed aesthetic languages: one classical and relatively severe, the other extravagantly Mannerist . . . Much later, I realized that I had undoubtedly been influenced by Picasso; Picasso had worked in a Neoclassical style—in his designs for the Ballets Russes, and so on—and he had also carried distortion to an extreme.[11]

From the Palazzo del Tè to the workshops of caricaturists: despite Gombrich's rejection of Dvořák, Giulio Romano—and Picasso—helped prepare him to collaborate with Kris.

Loewy's classes on ancient archeology provided another source of inspiration. Years later, while with the BBC monitoring service, Gombrich transplanted Loewy's exegeses on magic to the English countryside. He informed Kris:

> The other day I "lectured" in a kind of studio, which one of our supervisors has opened for the benefit of bored colleagues and of the local population. I need scarcely tell you the subject I chose. It was, of course, "Art and Magic" and you can imagine that it was full of plagiarism of Loewy's and your work.[12]

Thus while Gombrich's work with Kris did not revive his early interest in Dvořák, it did encourage an interest in how to bridge cultural history and scientific psychology.

Confronting Doubt

Gombrich first met Kris during the academic year 1931/32, when in connection with a seminar assignment from Schlosser he came to the curator's office for permission to examine a medieval ivory pyx.[13] Almost instantly, Kris attempted to dissuade the student from pursuing a career in art history:

> But if your interest [in art] is intellectual, you must realize that you have chosen the wrong field. We really know too little about art to make any valid statements. The best our colleagues can do is to escape to some more advanced branch of study; they want to draw on psychology, but really psychology is not yet sufficiently developed to help the art historian. Take my advice, and change your subject.[14]

Kris's open alienation and his frank warning left a powerful impression on Gombrich—so strong that he worked the curator into a verse play that he wrote for end-of-term celebrations in summer 1932. The performance, with Kris in attendance, included a scene that "showed a young historian being tempted by Doubt, and Doubt was represented by Kris because he was so skeptical about art history by then."[15] In a letter written to Carl E. Schorske more than sixty years later, Gombrich—almost surely working from memory—reproduced his satirical tribute to Kris, titled simply "Doubt" ("Der Zweifel").[16]

In Gombrich's theatrical masque, Doubt attempted to open the eyes of a young novice standing before him in the museum. After sternly dismissing academicians and connoisseurs, he offered a blunt evaluation of job opportunities:

> Now tell me, to what end are you studying art history?
> What will you do with it, what do you have in mind? To expound expertly on Titians . . .?
> Are you that rich? No? And you are truly convinced
> Someone will employ you? Here? That is out of the question!
> Abroad?[17]

Doubt, unlike the professors of the Vienna School, rejected art historians as cultural or historical scientists. Archeologists, however, possessed a true scientific eye and with it a new power of vision: "You enjoy science? Then why do you not study Archeology? Those people can see!"[18]

Art history could not become a scientific discipline, but at most could turn to the new mental sciences for support:

> Are we a science? No, pay attention to me:
> We are not yet so far removed from the artwork to say that
> We can do absolutely nothing under our own power.
> At best one can flee to the sister science
> And attempt to draw psychology in with us.

Doubt's somber reflections on art history ended with a shudder of intellectual and personal despair:

> Here with us art will soon be no fun for you
> Neither art not science, my friend, can here be satisfied.[19]

Kris's challenge and his call to link art history to a true science of perception became a lasting impulse—as well as a lingering, Mephistophelean warning—within Gombrich's work.

Kris's disenchantment reflected the moment at which the meeting with Gombrich took place: he had begun—or would soon begin—to assume his duties as an editor of *Imago* and had to reconcile himself to sharing those desired responsibilities with his required obligations as a curator. Yet, as Kris indicated and Gombrich recorded, his comments did not simply, or even predominantly, derive from personal ambivalence or professional frustration. As Kris's alter ego, Doubt emphasized more than once that it was "here"—in Vienna—where the pure scholarly pursuit of art history—the "fun"—lacked fulfillment. As with Gilbert's Machiavelli, Kris's questioning of intellectual authority and academic convention accompanied recognition of political realities. Finding a job and institutional affiliation went, as he stressed, to the heart of the matter: Vienna's cultural institutions had become not only constricted but also menacing.

The Crisis of the Republic

In April 1930, the University of Vienna's Senate approved a proposal to categorize students according to their so-called nations: German, Jewish, mixed, and other, with Jewish converts to Catholicism classified as members of the Jewish nation. To be considered German, one's parents and grandparents had to have received baptism. A classification for "Austrian" did not exist. The Christian Social cabinet and the Ministry of Education voiced no opposition. Austria's high court, however, questioned the regulation's constitutionality and in June 1931 overturned the proposed measure. Nationalist and Nazi students reacted immediately. Armed Nazis laid siege to the Renaissance-style university building and attacked Jewish and socialist students. Campus police refused to respond and the university rector denied access to the city police. Only after three days of violence did the rioters leave the streets.[20]

As Nazi agitation extended into the university, Gombrich observed at close range how opposition to Nazi intimidation withered within the academy. At the art historical institute, his close friend—and Kris's first research assistant—Otto Kurz became the target of a savage anti-Semitic assault. Gombrich vividly remembered:

> The University enjoyed "extraterritorial" immunity from police interference, a fact which led to a reign of terror by Nazi thugs. Kurz was among the victims of their brutal violence when he was assailed at the University library and hit over the head with a steel truncheon.[21]

Kris soon secured employment for Kurz outside of Austria—a position at the Warburg Library in Hamburg. On one occasion Gombrich himself faced threats when a line of Nazis obstructed his entry into the art historical institute. Yet, almost as disturbing as the physical intimidation was the behavior of professors who remained silent when student organizations posted the virulent anti-Semitic invective from the pages of Julius Streicher's Nazi tabloid, *Der Stürmer*.[22] Neither academic administrators—"they employed 'marshals' who participated in the outrages of these student organizations"[23]—nor the mute professoriate organized a response. Instead, Christian Social chancellor Engelbert Dollfuss restored a temporary peace by providing greater policing against Nazi student agitation and prohibiting party leaflets and publications.[24]

Gombrich's experiences—particularly his disappointment at the university's response—led him to feel "a little clearer about my origins and about the situation."[25] Still, he fully intended to pursue a career in Vienna. "The professors could certainly have shown more backbone," he concluded, "but that the situation might become a danger to people's lives—that I never thought."[26]

In March 1933, Chancellor Dollfuss dissolved the Austrian parliament. After barely fifteen years of existence, the Austrian First Republic came to an end in all but name. To protect his new authority and contain pressure from Austrian Nazis, Dollfuss relied on a loose political alliance between the antisocialist middle class, Church authorities, rural townspeople, and homegrown *Heimwehr* paramilitaries. Through this conservative governing coalition—the *Vaterländische Front*—he aimed to stabilize the Christian Social regime in Austria and advance the cause of political Catholicism in central Europe. Dollfuss moreover aligned his government with Mussolini's. He admired the antisocialist, dictatorial cast of the regime, which had also been formally accepted by the Vatican in the Lateran Accords, and sought its protection against Hitler's mounting foreign demands. Ultimately, to gain broader international support—especially from the United States—and to solidify the new Catholic authoritarian state, Dollfuss outlawed the Nazi party in June 1933.

Temporarily more secure in his leadership and urged on by his patron Mussolini, in February 1934 the chancellor carried out his counter-revolution against the Socialist municipal government in Vienna. Fighting extended into Vienna's streets and housing projects, to Linz, and to isolated industrial centers beyond, but after several weeks, troops and police suppressed the last Socialist and worker opposition.[27] Dollfuss banned the Socialist party, abolished trade unions, and claimed sole governing power for the *Vaterländische Front*. As a self-described patriotic and Catholic organization, the Front imposed no racial laws. Dollfuss instead enforced an administrative *numerus clausus*: having ended Socialist power in Vienna, he removed Jews from the city's civil service and proscribed the employment of Jewish physicians in Vienna's hospitals and health services. In the meantime, Nazi party members and sympathizers—with the government's acquiescence—shifted their publications from party organs to private presses.[28] Announced at home and abroad as a defense of independent Austria, Dollfuss's counter-revolution installed an Austro-Fascist regime and initiated the first wave of emigration.

Shared Scholarship

In the summer of 1933—between the dissolution of Parliament and the suppression of the Socialist party—Gombrich graduated the University of Vienna with a doctorate in art history and began his search for an academic position. He soon realized the nature of the difficulties facing him. Finding a job, he recounted, "proved virtually impossible. There was a great deal of unemployment among intellectuals then, but my Jewish origins certainly also had something to do with it."[29]

Dvořák's follower Otto Benesch stepped in with an offer of support. As a specialist in northern Renaissance prints, Benesch served as curator at the renowned Albertina collection of graphic arts. He encouraged Gombrich to apply there for a position as a trainee:

> He was very nice, he thought a lot of me, and I was very pleased. It seemed like the first step. On his advice I therefore submitted an application and gave the necessary references. My application was turned down. That was not only a heavy blow, but also the first real proof that things could not go on like this. This happened still under Dollfuss.[30]

The expanding anti-Semitism that closed off his opportunity at the Albertina showed him that his parents' conversion counted for less and less within state institutions.

In 1934 Gombrich accepted an offer from Kris—who had recently begun a project on the psychology of caricature—to become his research assistant. As with his investigations into metal castings and sculpted character heads, Kris turned to caricature as a means of exploring the borderline regions of art history and psychological science. This new project contained richer, even more protean lines of inquiry. The caricaturist—the keen psychological observer and insensate scribbler—combined the mimetic receptivity of a classical painter with the aggressive experimentalism of a Mannerist or Expressionist artist. The fusion between life-affirming and life-negating motives, between generative and defensive patterns, and between magical and critical impulses nowhere came to the fore more clearly for Kris than in caricature.

Gombrich already knew that Kris functioned in several vocational capacities—as curator and consultant, as art historian and psychoanalyst—and pursued those various lines of research simultaneously. Experience had taught him that Kris spoke his mind openly with colleagues, questioned conventional professional assumptions, and struggled personally, like Gombrich, with the dilemma of how to bridge the studies of art and mind. An astute clinician and adventurous scholar, he also paid close heed to the world beyond his office.

Kris and Gombrich began their collaboration in an atmosphere of rapidly intensifying uncertainty and threat. Hitler's followers in Vienna assaulted their opponents on the Left and lashed out at their competitors on the Right. The crushing of the Socialists had not protected Dollfuss. In July 1934, during a failed putsch attempt, Austrian Nazis assassinated him in his office. The Austrian minister of justice, Kurt von Schuschnigg, succeeded the slain political leader as chancellor. A fervid Catholic, and as vehemently antisocialist as his predecessor, Schuschnigg continued to govern through the *Vaterländische Front* coalition. Attempting to maintain Dollfuss's previous balancing act, he sought the good will of France, Britain, and the United States, but like Dollfuss, he looked chiefly to Mussolini to protect Austria from Hitler's pressure. While he tried to keep his Catholic regime free of Nazi control, he opted at the same time to accommodate the demands of pan-German Austrians.

Schuschnigg's government staggered toward collapse. It refused to join with the Left in a genuinely pro-republican and anti-Nazi front. It fostered the steady spread of anti-Semitism, through which Schuschnigg hoped to strengthen his support among political Catholics, gain the approval of German nationalists, and consolidate his leadership over the Right. After Dollfuss's murder, Schuschnigg suppressed the vitriolic *Der Stürmer* but he continued to exclude Jews from government service and teaching positions, and in September 1934 he allowed his Education Ministry to issue regulations that would begin the religious segregation of classrooms.[31] For decades, Christian Social leaders had deployed anti-Semitism strategically; the stratagem now helped prepare the way for *Anschluss*.

The movement for unification with Germany drew growing support from the traditional Christian Social base. In April 1932, the Nazi party had already made significant inroads among voters outside Vienna, winning almost 17 percent in town and provincial elections.[32] As the political writer and sociologist Franz Borkenau explained at the time, after Hitler came to power, middle-class Catholics who previously supported the Austrian authoritarian government's cooperation with the Church hierarchy now called instead for alliance with Germany. Moved by antisocialism, German nationalism, anticlericalism, and anti-Semitism, increasing numbers advocated a pact with Nazism.[33]

Kris had already concluded that the Austrian government offered little or no hope against the spread of Nazism. He perceived that the *Kunsthistorisches Museum* provided at best a temporary refuge. Just as he had no hope that the Christian Social authorities or bourgeois elite would provide protection from above, he had no expectation that Hitlerism would be resisted from below: "He was convinced that the

Nazis would come to power."[34] Continuously evaluating the pace of the growing political danger, he assessed carefully the security of his academic, psychoanalytic, and Jewish colleagues. He remained highly conscious of the embattled position of young museum and university staff in particular and the dangerously tenuous position of Viennese Jews in general:

> It was particularly difficult for a person of Jewish descent. Kris was deeply aware of all the undercurrents of resistance he had to encounter within the Museum and in the University. Unlike many who were in the same situation he did not close his eyes to these dangers. On the contrary, he kept them wide open. He made a point of reading the *Völkische Beobachter* and he had no illusions. In Austria itself the scene had also darkened with the abolition of Parliament and the establishment of a dictatorship. It was when telling an anti-government joke at the office and being met with frozen stares that Kris began to reflect on the instability of the effect of the comic.[35]

In his colleagues' faces he saw the frozen grimaces that until then he had confronted only in works of art.

Like Freud, Kris followed especially closely the Catholic hierarchy's responses to the expansion of Nazi influence in Austria, monitoring as best he could the strength of its opposition to *Anschluss*. He had already experienced personally a shift within the Church. After the formation of the *Vaterländische Front*, pressure bore upon him to become public in his commitment to Catholicism and to place greater distance between himself and his Jewish background. One such occasion had been the birth of his son Anton in July 1934, the month of the Nazi putsch attempt. Acting on his own volition, a museum colleague visited the secretary of a cardinal to inquire into having this—Kris's second—child baptized. Through the secretary, the cardinal responded that he would be willing to remarry Ernst and Marianne Kris within the Church, baptize their son, and ignore the unbaptized state of their daughter

Anna. Kris had already confronted the political change within the museum; Jewish members of the Vienna Psychoanalytic Society had begun to seek safe haven abroad. Yet he refused the offer, a decision that would significantly compromise his standing with the Church.[36]

Thus at the moment they began their scholarly collaboration, Kris and Gombrich lived almost as outcasts within their own profession and their own city. Politically vigilant, Kris sought to convince his new assistant of the desperate nature of the situation, urging him: "You've got to leave, you have no prospects here, and things will get worse."[37] Soon London became the only city and the Warburg Library the only institution where either scholar could imagine a future.

Warburg, Freud, and the Psychology of Caricature

Writing shortly before the First World War, Aby Warburg stated in his famous essay on the Palazzo Schifanoia that art historians had to pursue research across disciplinary and national boundaries. Kris's career embodied Warburg's professional credo, but the affinity went much deeper. In both scholars an early passion for art history gave way to a more challenging, more expansive project: a psychology of the human being as imagemaker from antiquity to the present.

At the turn of the century, Warburg began to assemble a personal research library devoted to tracking the afterlife of antiquity in Renaissance and modern culture. The eldest son of the eminent Jewish banking family of Hamburg, he received his brothers' moral and financial support to live as an independent scholar. Before 1914, he began to open his holdings to others, and after the war, the library, with the support of the new University of Hamburg, expanded into a site for research and teaching. Warburg and his assistants Fritz Saxl and Gertrud Bing sponsored lectures and seminars, published journals and monographs, and supported a circle of researchers from the humanities and social sciences, including Erwin Panofsky and Ernst Cassirer. What had been a small, idiosyncratic library became during the 1920s a formal institution for the study of culture and psychology, and above its entrance was now inscribed: *Warburg Library for the Cultural Sciences*.[38] Following Warburg's death in 1929, Saxl became the library's director. Under his and Bing's guidance, it escaped Nazi Germany for London, where in 1933 the Warburg Library became the Warburg Institute.

Art history in Hamburg moved in fundamentally different directions than in Vienna. Like the Vienna School, Warburg demanded that art history acquire a firmer social scientific grounding. But to that end he immersed himself in the family papers, business files, and civic records of Florentine citizens, thereby initiating the systematic study of Renaissance patronage and the humanist institutional network. Again, like the Vienna School, he encouraged explorations at the boundaries of art. For Warburg, however, such efforts encompassed astrological tables, broadsheets, theatrical designs, and carnival pageantry. In travels to Italy and to the American southwest, he approached art as a branch of symbolic communication. Images functioned as visual signs and art history traced the creation, transformation, and psychological meanings of those signs over time, beginning with the ancient world.

Just as Loewy explored archaic memories, fears, and defenses within classical Greek art, so Warburg discovered their continuing presence within Renaissance painting. Seemingly modest gestures, which humanists found in ancient monuments and relics, and which painters incorporated into their creations, recalled violent Dionysian enthusiasms and mysterious Orphic ecstasies. Like Loewy, Warburg interpreted those disarming gestures as memory pictures—what the Hamburg scholar referred to as "pathos formulas." The use of such formulas not only gave renewed life to ancient images but also generated modern experimentation with visual thought and communication. Renaissance artists transformed fragments of pagan art and ritual into more highly spiritualized, Platonic symbols, and astrologists reworked mythic pictures of the universe into new, philosophic conceptions of the cosmos. Like Freud, however, Warburg believed that every artistic rebirth contained a *memento mori*, a regressive pull. The same premonition of death that

Freud recognized in Shakespeare's Cordelia, Warburg detected in Botticelli's Venus.[39]

Kris first made contact with the Warburg circle when in 1922—the year that he accepted his curator's position—he wrote to Warburg with a request for research information. Schlosser provided an indirect point of contact: according to Gombrich, Warburg had chosen Schlosser to serve as the executor of his will.[40] Saxl and Panofsky, as well as Kris and Loewy, contributed to Schlosser's academic festschrift.[41] Contact between Kris and the Warburg Library continued throughout the interwar period: Kris published in the Warburg journal; he contributed reviews to the Warburg Library's projected multi-volume bibliography of the classical tradition, of which two volumes were published; and he regularly met with Saxl during the latter's annual trips to Vienna.[42] Although Saxl, in Gombrich's words, "had no interest in the Psychology of Art,"[43] he did seek better understanding of psychoanalysis, at least so far as to strengthen the bridge between Hamburg and Vienna. In October 1932, he reported to Kris: "Just today I spoke at length and in breadth with our colleague Dr. [Edgar] Wind, because for the entire summer he studied Freud from his [Wind's] standpoint as a philosopher."[44]

Warburg reinforced for Kris the idea of image making as a vital psychological process with both life-denying and life-affirming potentials, a theme that Kris pursued in his first book, *Die Legende vom Künstler: Ein geschichtlicher Versuch* (The Legend of the Artist: A Historical Experiment), which he dedicated to the Warburg Institute.[45] Completed with Kurz's research assistance and published in 1934, *Die Legende vom Künstler* examined recurring formulas in the biographies of artists. Chief among those formulas was the artist as someone who gave life to inanimate objects, as had Daedalus, the fabled craftsman of self-moving automatons.[46] Just as Messerschmidt perceived in grotesque masks the power to guard against demonic forces, myth-making biographers and even scholarly experts saw in art a living presence. Such perceptions derived from the primal belief in image magic, a belief that, as Warburg had shown, lasted into the Renaissance. Kris cited Warburg's seminal study of Florentine portraiture, which established that sculptures continued to be perceived as effigies possessing magical power.[47] But unconscious attachment to image magic reverberated even among contemporary advocates of naturalism who argued that true art had to re-create lived experience. The psychology of ancient image making—the conviction in the identity between image and object and a belief in the power of effigies—still impelled people to seek from artwork the illusion of life.[48]

Kris's study of artist biographies confirmed his commitment to a new psychoanalytic psychology. Although he saw psychoanalysis as a necessary corrective to narrow biographical accounts, he never adhered strongly to the psychobiographical approach that gained great popularity among his colleagues first in Vienna and later in New York, and that risked promoting another species of illusion about the artist. His study of Messerschmidt instead had approached image making as a visual language, as a medium of thought and communication. For Kris, Panofsky's work epitomized that approach, in particular his 1924 book *Idea*, which explored the influence of Neo-Platonist philosophy on the birth of art theory in the Renaissance and Baroque periods.[49] As Panofsky described, art theory emerged not only as a theory of creativity but also as a theory of cognition, a philosophy of how human beings formed and communicated ideas about the self and the world.

Kris conceived of his book as a companion study to Panofsky's. Legends about the artist and myths about the vital, animating force within artworks accompanied the emergence of a genuine theory of art and mind. He hoped to publish his study as a Warburg Institute monograph. But Austrian politics compelled him to change plans. In a letter to Saxl in April 1934 requesting permission to dedicate *Die Legende vom Künstler* to the institute, Kris described the impact of immediate political circumstances:

> In good times, so it seems to me, the book could have become larger, more circumspect, and more technical. It would then have been

> destined for the Studies of the Warburg Library, and might have carried the modest title: The Typical Biography of the Artist or something similar. But what is useful in this book, which would like to be a first successor of Panofsky's Idea, is indeed connected with Warburg.[50]

Writing in the period of heavy, unnatural calm that fell between Dollfuss's February counter-revolution and the Nazis' July putsch attempt, Kris described the fetid atmosphere of Vienna. He looked to the Warburg Institute as a location to pursue his projects: "Perhaps I will still succeed in coming to London before summer. My longing is always for there. Here it is gloomy, narrow, and the possibility for work very limited."[51] Such was the environment in which, as he stated in the letter, "I am struggling with my large caricature work."[52]

In August 1934, at the international psychoanalytic congress at Lucerne, Kris presented his first and only psychoanalytic paper on caricature, which later that year he published in *Imago* under the title "Zur Psychologie der Karikatur" (On the Psychology of Caricature).[53] In caricature, art revealed itself to be not a life-negating illusion but a vital, continuous psychological experiment, requiring the engagement of the audience as much as that of the artist. In producing a likeness, the caricaturist "overcharged"[54] or exaggerated one or more of the subject's features. Messerschmidt's character heads had expressed the psychological method behind this distorted portrait: "In our thoughts, as it were, we cause our model's features to become twisted into a grimace."[55] The reconfiguration of the subject's countenance drew the beholder's attention away from the subject's visible persona and focused it instead on inward character: "the natural harmony of an appearance is destroyed, and this has the result in many cases of revealing a contrast in the personality between looks and character."[56] Similar to the mechanism of jokes as Freud had described it in *Jokes and Their Relation to the Unconscious*, the caricaturist rechanneled an inherently destructive impulse—"[t]he dissolution of unity in the interests of aggression"—into an inspired psychological insight, in this instance expressed not in words but in images.[57]

Kris traced the beginnings of caricature to the late Renaissance and early Baroque periods among artists who experimented with classical conventions. Such artists rejected portrait likenesses as idealized masks of the personality and turned instead to a de-idealizing art or "unmasking."[58] Again, as with jokes, their technique relied on the distortions and exaggerations, condensations and displacements that typified primary unconscious thought. In Kris's seminal formulation, caricature represented a "regression in the service of the ego,"[59] a functional, even intentional, retreat into primary unconscious processes. The ego withdrew its attention and activity from the world in order to allow the primary process to enter consciousness. This regression led not to inward disintegration or immobilization but to artistic innovation, psychological awareness, and a return to the world: "the ego enrolls the primary process in its service and makes use of it for its purposes."[60] Caricature thus reflected the ambiguous, hybrid nature of all creativity.[61]

Kris also traced mechanisms of caricature before the Renaissance into the distant past, in the regressive play with image magic. He asserted that whenever and wherever caricature became an artistic practice "we are invariably able to discover the use of effigy magic at some point in its development."[62] The effigy as a visual symbol, not as a lifelike illusion, elicited an acting out of aggression: "the action is performed in relation to an image which is regarded as identical with the person it represents."[63] Operating at a further remove from magical ritual, caricature manipulated not the effigy or bodily sign but the mask or portrait. Ancient and medieval effigies meant their targets to writhe and wince physically. Caricature left that result to the viewer's fantasy: "the pleasure gain in caricature is due to our imagination, as it were, forcing the features of the person caricatured to assume a grimace."[64]

Creator and spectator thus collaborated in the aggressive depiction of their targets, whose contorted reactions—real or imagined—remained part of a comic, experimental game and effort at criticism. In Messerschmidt's sculptures, grimaces had risked remaining frozen as ritualized defenses or deathly visages. But through caricature, artists and spectators reengaged with the world, breathing again, in the words of Henry James, "the strange, real, mingled air of things."

Saxl, Read, and the Art of Caricature

Kris's work on caricature received essential support from London, most importantly from Fritz Saxl. But it was caricature as an artistic experiment, not as a psychological paradigm, that held Saxl's interest. At the same time Kris presented his ideas to the psychoanalytic community, Saxl brought them to the notice of scholars at the Warburg Institute and art critics beyond it. His efforts reflected a commitment both to advance Kris's work—and perhaps ease his emigration—and to demonstrate the institute's value to the British art community.

In July 1934—less than a year after the Warburg Library transplanted itself to London—Saxl brought Kris's project to the attention of Herbert Read, who also saw in caricature a crucial artistic experiment. A poet, radical culture critic, and communitarian anarchist, Read assailed the tendencies in industrial society that isolated persons and undermined self-fulfillment. A veteran of the First World War, he became an uncompromising pacifist. A proponent of the Surrealists and of Carl G. Jung, he supported ventures in art and psychology that challenged the routinized or machine qualities of twentieth-century British life.

Saxl worked hard to convince Read, who had become editor of the *Burlington Magazine* the previous December, to have Kris review W. R. Juynboll's *The Comic Genre in Italian Painting During the Seventeenth and the Eighteenth Centuries: Contribution to the History of Caricature*. He prevailed and wrote to Kris:

> The Burlington Magazine would like to have a short critique of Juynboll, and I proposed to Herbert Read that I write to you about it. Read did not want to have the book reviewed at all. I could, however, imagine that it would be quite pleasant for you to say something already now on this topic in the Burlington Magazine and to

> have the book in return. R. [Read] requests that the review not contain more than 500 words.[65]

Toward the end of 1934, Saxl—with Kris's review in hand—directed Read to Kris's other writings:

> I immediately passed on the very nice review [of Juynboll] to Herbert Read. I also discussed with Read the review of the anecdotes book [Kris's book on artist biographies]. He is very interested in it. Hopefully he will also find a reasonable person as the reviewer.[66]

The *Burlington Magazine* never published a review of *Die Legende vom Künstler*, but when Penguin Books published Kris and Gombrich's wartime pamphlet on caricature, Read himself reviewed it for the BBC's *Listener*. By then he had become intrigued by Kris's psychoanalytic approach, which uncovered in caricature the aggressive passion and resolute individuality that for Read fueled innovation not only in art but also in politics.

In his Juynboll review, Kris showed that he had begun to consider caricature as not only an artistic but also a political experiment. As he emphasized, Juynboll—although neglecting Freud's psychology of jokes and the comic—identified key artistic foundations of caricature in late Renaissance and Baroque Italy: the upsurge of interest in Leonardo's drawings, the realist approach taken by the Carracci school in Bologna and its particular interest in street life, and the Roman tradition of portraiture. But just as importantly, Juynboll recognized how the stage types of Florentine *commedia dell'arte* resurfaced in the work of Jacques Callot, who transmitted them to caricaturists and who, like Read, became a critic of modern war:

> Through Jacques Callot, whose style was formed during his stay in Florence, this source of Italian caricature became of decisive importance. The types which Callot had created were copied for two

> hundred years by engravers and craftsmen of all European countries, so that we can hardly compare any other artist's influence with his on the evolution of this branch of art.[67]

Although Daumier—Callot's modern successor—did not receive mention in the review, the exhibition of his work in Vienna would soon enter the planning stage.

While composing the *Imago* essay and the Juynboll review, Kris sought to secure positions for both Kurz and Gombrich at the Warburg Institute. For more than two years, Kris had urged Gombrich to leave Vienna. The events of 1934—the antisocialist crackdown and Dollfuss's murder—led to even more urgent pleas. In October, Kris waited no longer. He provided Saxl with information about Julius von Schlosser that he thought would impress upon him the precariousness of Kurz and Gombrich's situations. Kris had already explained to Saxl how Schlosser had begun to distance himself from the Warburg Institute after the Nazis had come to power: in a letter in December 1933, he had characterized as "grotesque" Schlosser's refusal to include any reference to the Warburg circle in a soon to be published overview of the Vienna School.[68] Now, in October 1934, Kris wrote:

> I hear nothing from Kurz, I am as apprehensive on his behalf as I am for my other friend and collaborator on caricature, Gombrich, who here despite protection and despite advantageous paperwork—only his race still remains Jewish—has no chance. No wonder, when one hears that a man like Schlosser in a private letter to a friend (with Jewish wife) expresses himself to the effect that his blood draws him to Hitler! That is confidential![69]

Thus Schlosser—the Austrian son of an Italian mother, the advisor who looked upon Kris as his model pupil, the art historian who preached the autonomous quality of imaginative creations, the seminar leader who counseled against interpretive speculation, the sober and cosmopolitan collector—at the moment of political decision aligned himself with Nazi enthusiasts.[70]

Kris knew the significance in Vienna of private utterances such as Schlosser's. Surrounded by museum objects that he inherited from his mentor and that cast increasingly oppressive intellectual shadows, his alienation from art history had now reached its extreme. The gloom receded only at those moments when he contemplated pursuing a research program in London on the psychology of art and creativity.

The program Kris had in mind combined the perspectives of Freud and Warburg, and would permanently attach Kurz and Gombrich to the institute. Writing to Saxl in December 1934, he spelled out his plan: "You know," he began, "how my work, divided between art history and psychoanalysis, converges toward a place of connection."[71] The "preoccupation with caricature"[72] reflected this ambition to build a bridge between the two fields in general and between the circles of Warburg and Freud in particular:

> The more detailed work, which I am now preparing with my other young collaborator, E. Gombrich, should be a treatise of a mixed character, as far as possible an aesthetic rather than a history of caricature and attempting somewhat in the Hegelian sense to sketch the system in the outline of the history.[73]

The caricature book, together with the studies of Messerschmidt and artist biographies, set out a consistent intellectual vision: "All three works constitute for me introductions to the more central problems, which in decades to come should help to sketch some principles of a 'psychology of visual art.' The idea of such a work I carry with me."[74] A psychology of visual art would begin with psychological anthropology, in particular the question: "What is image magic, what are its historical, its psychological foundations?" It would then move toward a study of "the art of the untrained"—primitive drawings as well as cross-cultural creations by children—all intended to answer: "Where is the commonality between visual representations that are primitive in the ontogenetic sense?"[75] The Warburg circle provided crucial direction: "It is easy to see, and I do not have to describe for you just now, where both follow from A. Warburg's life work and what they could mean art historically."[76] The third object of study derived from Freud: the representation of dreams and dreaming in the visual arts.

Kris knew that he could not realize this program in Vienna. As long as he remained bound to that city, his plan amounted to little more than a creative fantasy:

> I seek themes, as you know, without committing myself in advance to the more particular problem, which can emerge only in the course of the work. In this case, too, I can do nothing else than stick to this imaginative habit.[77]

A month later, in January 1935, he wrote to Saxl that the hours he spent reorganizing the museum's applied art collection left little time for realizing his psychology of art: "I am at present in the middle of the work of conversion in the museum and my remaining workday, gradually growing to 16 hours, is now dedicated in part to caricature and in part to psychoanalysis."[78] Kris resigned himself to remaining in Vienna but he intensified his efforts to find positions for Kurz and Gombrich. Relying on his contacts with the psychiatrist Bettina Warburg and her cousin Edward Warburg in New York, he attempted to secure a stipend for Kurz at the Warburg Institute.[79] He assured Saxl that an assistantship for Kurz would not commit the institute itself to Freudian research: "The relation [of Kurz] to the Library could also be as loose as you want, so that you and your circle will not through my engagement with psychoanalysis be burdened by it."[80]

In January 1935, he wrote to Edward Warburg about his personal plan to bridge the schools of Freud and Warburg, explaining that Kurz, who had held assistantships at the Warburg Library in Hamburg and at the institute in London, would act as Kris's assistant. Kurz could not return to Vienna: "In his homeland of Austria, as a Jew he has no prospects whatsoever; a position abroad is his only possibility."[81]

Kris summarized his plan to investigate the role of image magic in art, explaining that such a study required the help of Kurz, whose "comprehensive"[82] intellect ranged across specializations:

> It is also no accident but rather a proof of my assertion, according to which the life's work of your uncle points the way toward psychoanalysis, that Dr. Kurz, who is employed at the Warburg Library, represents an immediate connection between this [Aby Warburg's] direction and my labors devoted to the application of psychoanalysis.[83]

In March 1935, Edward Warburg informed Kris: "I think your plan for the use of the Warburg Institute for scholarship from a Freudian standpoint naturally a most interesting one."[84] He provided Kurz with a stipend for another year in London —an essential stopgap for the young scholar, who would remain at the institute throughout his career.

Although the idea of leaving Vienna for London appealed greatly to Kris, for the time being he felt protected in a way that his younger associates did not:

> I actually would have every reason to think of my own future more than I do, but I suffer extraordinarily from the disturbing feeling of being able to do nothing for my younger colleagues although I know that I am so closely indebted to them and they have such pressing need.[85]

In April, he stated, "I set the [Warburg] Library as a workplace above all others."[86] Looking forward to a planned meeting with Saxl in London, he emphasized that he intended to initiate collaboration between the Freudian movement and the Warburg circle—most immediately through the caricature project. At the same time, with the help of Ernest Jones—Freud's close associate and the leading Freudian in

Britain—he hoped to draw the international psychoanalytic movement closer to the institute:

> I believe also that I can bring along the disposition, that is, an exact and very detailed disposition of the book about caricature, on which I work in my few spare hours together with Ernst Gombrich . . . For the summer I plan to take up again Warburg's writings in order to try to frame the question concretely as to what depth psychology could accomplish toward the extension of this line of research. In the meantime, with some not completely uninfluential London friends who are at present in Vienna, I made propaganda for the Library. One of them, Dr. Ernest Jones, the president of our international association and the director of the London psychoanalytic institute, is very interested, I believe, in making personal contact with you above all.[87]

Kris continued to seek a position for Gombrich. He had already suggested to Saxl that when a place was finally arranged for Kurz, a position should also be worked out for Gombrich, although "the circle of themes of the works that would absorb him would presumably be defined somewhat differently."[88] In January 1935, Gombrich had begun to correspond directly with Gertrud Bing.[89] Later that year, Kris suggested that Saxl bring him to the institute to assist with Saxl's plan to publish Warburg's papers. Finally, in September 1935, during one of his last visits to Vienna before the *Anschluss*, Saxl arranged with Gombrich a two-year fellowship. Bing looked forward to his arrival:

> I have not for a long time had such a feeling of relief and absolutely correct judgment as when Saxl said that you would be ready to collaborate on the Warburg-Nachlass . . . I do not want, however, to encroach on your work with Dr. Kriss [sic] and would only ask you to tell me when you want to come.[90]

In January 1936, Gombrich arrived in England to work with Saxl on editing and annotating Warburg's copious manuscripts and cryptic, fragmentary notes, as well as composing a biographical study to accompany the papers.[91]

That summer Kris traveled briefly to London. Bing wrote about the visit to Gombrich, who had returned to Vienna to work on the caricature book: "I was very glad to speak with Dr. Kris here. I did not know him or rather only very superficially and now for my part I have the feeling that the London–Vienna connection has been very much strengthened."[92] Kris derived crucial intellectual and personal sustenance from the London connection, as he expressed to Saxl: "[T]he lonelier one stands in art history—I mean here in Vienna—the more convincing appears that direction which today attaches only to Panovsky [sic] and you."[93]

He always remained sharply aware of *here*. He repeated the word—*here*—in his meetings with Gombrich and in his correspondence with Saxl. And each trip abroad intensified his consciousness of isolation and made him more insistent. *Here* referred not only to his city and the museum but also to the unavoidable sensation that they produced in him. But not yet ready to leave for London, Kris created a temporarily protected, alternative refuge in Vienna where he could exhibit the work of Honoré Daumier.

From spring 1935 to autumn 1936—the period coinciding with the inception and rise of the Popular Front movement in France—Kris organized the Daumier exhibition. Through Daumier, he and Gombrich—who assisted with the exhibition—moved beyond the psychology and theory of caricature to engage directly with its history. In the world of European galleries, the exhibition became unique: in continental Europe, Daumier's art appeared in no other place outside France during the 1930s. By displaying Daumier's work in Vienna at that moment—*here* in 1936—Kris and Gombrich attached their scholarly researches to the antifascist cause. The space for examining Daumier's artwork would allow the public to view a culture of republicanism and internationalism that was disappearing in Austria but that still survived beyond its borders.

CHAPTER 4

DAUMIER IN VIENNA 1936

The Discreet Charm of the Austrian Bourgeoisie

Kris first brought caricature to a Viennese museum-going public in autumn 1933. Sponsored by the *Kunsthistorisches Museum*, the exhibition displayed caricature sculptures by the little known French artist Jean-Pierre Dantan.[1] From an Austrian *palais*—perhaps with its own *Kunstkammer* stocked with such objects—an anonymous private donor lent Dantan's statues to Kris.[2] Dating from 1831 to 1839, the caricatures belonged to the first decade of Louis-Philippe's bourgeois constitutional monarchy, which had come to power after the popular revolt of July 1830 and was overthrown by the French Second Republic in 1848. Amidst crossing political and cultural currents, Dantan steered an uncontroversial course. As Kris wrote in his introduction to the exhibition catalog, Dantan "primarily chose as his subject leading stage artists, musicians, and writers, the representatives of the intellectual culture of the bourgeois monarchy—the world between two revolutions."[3] Surrounded by former Habsburg possessions, Dantan's sculptures recalled the twilight of the liberal royalism that had defined Kris's early political convictions.

But if the demise of Francis Joseph's monarchy during the First World War recalled the collapse of Louis-Philippe's rule in 1848,

Dollfuss's dissolution of the Austrian parliament in 1933 evoked Louis Napoleon's disbanding of the French Chamber of Deputies in 1851. Backed by a coalition of antirevolutionary bourgeoisie, French Church leaders, rural conservatives, police officials, and paramilitary gangs, Louis Napoleon dismantled the government of the French Second Republic and replaced it with his Second Empire. In Austria, Schuschnigg governed through a similar political alignment inherited from Dollfuss. He saw his Bonapartist coalition as the embodiment of both the Theresian and Josephan traditions, through which he would unite supporters of authoritarian Catholic government and bourgeois German rule, limit the hostility of Austrian Nazis to clerical government, and negotiate a compromise with Hitler.

What was formally known in Austria as *Kulturpolitik* reflected the confused, dual character of Schuschnigg's policies. Scholars and novelists who identified with official, antirepublican cultural politics claimed fidelity to both a Catholic homeland—the Austrian *Heimat*—and a German heritage.[4] In the performing arts, a parallel movement promoted a non-bifurcated Austrian identity at once devoutly Catholic and ethnically German, a movement that thrived at the Salzburg Festival where productions of classical German theater reinforced German national traditions and performances of Christian morality plays evoked European Catholic legacies.[5] Salzburg, which had for centuries preserved doctrinal orthodoxy and followed its prince-archbishops, now in its yearly theatrical pageant joined the ages-old longing for a universal Church with the contemporary passion for a single German state.

At the art historical institute in Vienna, *Kulturpolitik* and German racial ideology made significant inroads, as evidenced by the work of the young scholar Hans Sedlmayr and his university colleagues. Saxl had met Sedlmayr, a former student of Schlosser, in 1932 and tried to draw his attention to Edgar Wind's work on Warburg's aesthetic philosophy, as he wrote Kris at the time: "I asked Wind to forward to you his essay on Warburg and aesthetics, about which I spoke with you and Sedlmayr."[6] That year Sedlmayr joined the Nazi party. Although ceasing party membership in 1933, the up-and-coming scholar continued to advocate openly what Schlosser supported only quietly: *Anschluss* with Germany.[7]

In 1934, Sedlmayr published his *Habilitationsschrift* on Pieter Bruegel's *macchia*, a lengthy and detailed essay on Bruegel's compositional techniques and their relation to Mannerist and modernist tendencies. Although acknowledging a debt to Dvořák's lectures, Sedlmayr showed disdain for Mannerism and moral repugnance toward modernism. Appearing in the same year as Kris's paper on caricature, Sedlmayr's essay examined artistic phenomena familiar to Kris: the Mannerist distortion of bodies, the impenetrability of facial expression, the manufacturing of masks, and the depiction of demonic fear. In Sedlmayr's view, such phenomena gave Bruegel's creations an aura of estrangement. Relations between individuals lacked organic qualities, gesture and expression appeared disjointed, inner reality hid from and remained closed to the viewer. Such features in Bruegel and in Mannerism—and by extension in their modernist counterparts—corresponded to the inchoate behavior of the masses and the pathologies of the mentally ill. The subjects of Bruegel's paintings, Sedlmayr concluded, lingered at the fringes of humanity as sources of distress and dissociation.[8]

Neither Dvořák nor Kris had seen a threat to art in Bruegel's concentration on depth psychology and mass behavior. In his study of Messerschmidt, Kris described the use of masks or masklike visages as the ego's attempt at self-restitution and the artist's effort to communicate with the outside world. The petrified, alien quality of Messerschmidt's character heads represented a defense against private, demonic terrors, not an effort to represent for the public an unstable, deranged universe. Far from inducing immobilizing anxiety or disorientation, Bruegel inspired social and political recognition—"a new realism." As Dvořák had explained:

> If, and of this there can be no doubt, artistic form is the result of social involvement, then, and this is particularly evident in the

> work of great artists, the way in which it is developed represents a genuine contribution on the part of the artist to his contemporaries' understanding of the age in which they live.[9]

The estranged stare that Sedlmayr perceived in Bruegel's figures emanated from Sedlmayr not Bruegel.

Elsewhere Sedlmayr's views did not meet with disfavor. In 1936, he was elevated to Schlosser's chair at the art historical institute. The promotion established him as the leading representative of the New Vienna School both in and outside of Austria.

In June 1936, in collaboration with Leo Planiscig, the curator of bronze work at the *Kunsthistorisches Museum*, Kris resumed his exhibitions of borderline art, beginning with a display of small sculptures and craftwork from the early Italian Renaissance. The exhibition catalog announced:

> After a long pause, that was filled with the labors devoted to the reclassification and rearrangement of the collection for sculpture and applied art, it has now become possible to take up again an old program: to organize, within the scope of our collections and corresponding to their character, temporary displays of existing art objects in private or public possession that are difficult to access and so supplement the museum's stock from time to time in another direction.[10]

Before the end of the year, with the Austrian republic entering its death throes, Kris brought from France Honoré Daumier's equally "difficult to access" works.

Looking Toward France

In France, Vincent van Gogh and Paul Cézanne had openly acknowledged their artistic debts to the caricaturists in general and to Daumier in particular. A collector of Daumier lithographs, van Gogh asserted that in Daumier's work "the proportions will sometimes be almost arbitrary, the anatomy and structure often anything but correct in the eyes of the academicians. But it will live."[11] Cézanne himself "liked to talk about the caricaturists, Gavarni, Forain, and most of all Daumier. He loved their exuberant movement, bulging musculature, the impetuosity of their hand, and the bravura of their pencil lines."[12] For van Gogh and Cézanne, Daumier belonged to the ranks of those avid experimenters and rejuvenators who removed the dead hand of the academy from French art.[13] That same experimental drive also forged a weapon against Bonapartism.

Early in his career Daumier contributed illustrations to Honoré de Balzac's *La Comédie humaine*, attaching visual images to the novelist's finely grained psychological portraits and scathing social criticisms.[14] Inspired by a personal, mystical faith, Balzac believed in the transmission of influence between body and spirit, a near heretical pantheism that contained proto-Freudian insights. The spirit—in the form of a resolute will, a powerful idea, or even divine inspiration—acted through the pathways and synapses of the nervous system to arouse and guide external behavior. Simultaneously, physical nature—whether as bodily inheritance, material surroundings, or social environment—shaped the inner being with a deep, determining force.

Yet, however close he may have come to biological determinism, sociological predestination, or outright religious heresy, Balzac as a young man remained loyal to the ideal of a Catholic monarchy shepherding and instructing its flock. The prolific French writer opposed radical republicanism and reacted with horror at the revolutionary politics of the barricade. At the same time, however, the venalities of the aristocracy and the artificial pieties and soul-destroying ambitions of the French bourgeoisie infuriated him. Modern society, reducing all human relations to status and business transactions, emptied both the spirit and the flesh of their intrinsic worth. Building upon outraged moral sensibility and detailed social analysis, Balzac's human comedy became a recurrent scourge and ruthless documentary of a world where "life has no longer anything sacred or real."[15]

Balzac sympathized with those in Paris and the provinces who had been cruelly used, whose hardships multiplied, and whose everyday lives succumbed to forces beyond their control. In the decade before the 1848 uprisings, he supported the idea of a Catholic republic to replace the bourgeois monarchy of Louis-Philippe. Catholic teaching would give legitimacy and direction to republican government and republicanism would restore the Church to its rightful mission. In such a republic, the physically destitute and spiritually abandoned would continually challenge the Church's indifference and the bourgeoisie's inveterate bad conscience.

Balzac's literary landscape inserted the pattern of Dante's divine comedy into a non-transcendent, earthly framework. Victims and perpetrators alike wandered through infernal social realities to arrive at stark, pitiless illumination—flashes of oppressive clarity that provided insufficient recompense to victims and only meager punishment to perpetrators. Balzac documented social ills not to encourage revolution but to demonstrate the absence of spiritual consolation and the impossibility of atonement. Foreseeing the day when writers, journalists, and publishers would be hired agents in the new business of mass communication, he declared his deepest inward fear: "wrong will be done without anybody being guilty."[16]

There were those in interwar Austria who received Balzac's prescient, disenchanted vision with desperate sympathy. In the final years before his suicide in 1942, the exiled Viennese writer Stefan Zweig wrote a biography of Balzac. In *The World of Yesterday*, his testament to the lost universe of the Habsburg monarchy, he recalled:

> For years I had been accumulating material preparatory to a large two-volume study of Balzac and his work but had never had the courage to start on so comprehensive a labor that was calculated to occupy a long period. But it was just my gloom that produced the courage.[17]

Balzac—who overcame repeated literary setbacks with "uncurbed spirit and stubborn determination, as after every disappointing crisis throughout his life"—provided one of Zweig's final, brief inspirations.[18]

Equally despondent, Kris also turned toward Balzac's moral example and literary imagination. Like Balzac, he and Zweig remained attached in memory to the ideal of a protective Catholic monarchy. Also like Balzac, both he and Zweig dwelled among a decorous but cruel and self-protective middle class. And like him, they lived under an unconstitutional and unprincipled bourgeois regime that, despite claims to the contrary, sacrificed both its independence and its faith—in Austria's case, on the altar of *Anschluss* and a pan-German Reich. Ultimately, Kris—like Balzac—adopted republican ideals as the necessary political embodiment of his earlier convictions. Daumier provided visual images for those ideals.

During Louis-Philippe's monarchy, Daumier and fellow caricaturists began to test the limits of governmental censorship and bourgeois tolerance. The first turning point came in the 1830s with the publication of "Les Poires"—Charles Philipon's and Daumier's famous portraits of Louis-Philippe, in which the head of the politically hybrid king slowly transformed into a visually hybrid pear.[19] (Figs. 1 and 2) But Daumier's vision, like Balzac's, extended to the margins of society, to the innocent souls betrayed by a crass and rapacious society. His illustrations of Balzac's stories, in Ségolène Le Men's words, "made palpable the erosion of the individual life force that Balzac . . . sought to demonstrate throughout the entire *Comédie humaine*."[20] Thus, unlike caricaturists such as Dantan who depicted on-stage performers, Daumier, when he turned to the theater, focused on the despairing, off-stage world of *saltimbanques* and other itinerant entertainers whose struggles to survive remained beyond public view. Self-display, self-aggrandizement, and emotional manipulation belonged to the new skills of the politician, and Daumier—like Karl Marx—recognized that the farcical aspect of such behavior—finally crystallized in Louis Napoleon—represented a new type of political threat.

After Louis Napoleon's overthrow of the Second Republic, Daumier became an unseen observer of his agents and an unofficial portraitist of his victims. His stark vision targeted government warmongering and documented the spread of political violence. It was with the rise of Louis Napoleon that Daumier created his most widely recognized figure: the pathetic yet disturbing Bonapartist agent Ratapoil, who united the appearance of the out-of-luck performer with that of the disingenuous politico, and who began to appear in Daumier's work during the Second Republic's final disintegration. Ratapoil, according to T. J. Clark, epitomized the arch-manipulator who himself became the puppet of his political handlers.[21] To Daumier, Ratapoil also resembled a sadly corrupted Quixote, badly treated but incapable of resisting Bonapartist propaganda.

An increasingly fatalistic mood clung to Daumier's drawings. As Clark suggests, the pessimism that pervaded Daumier's early work never left him completely and even led him into long periods of silent withdrawal. The sense of desolation that enveloped the *saltimbanques* captured their portraitist as well. Unlike Marx, Daumier possessed the heart not of an unwavering revolutionist and hard-bitten theorist but of a restive experimentalist and skeptic who struggled against his own fatalism. When he turned his energy to political causes, he mobilized a combative pessimism rather than an unshaken spirit.[22]

Before and during the Daumier exhibition, Kris maintained steady contact with associates in France, including at Pontigny. There the Cistercian abbey provided the site for an annual conference that brought French scholars and writers into contact with European counterparts. The conference—a series of ten-day symposia held every summer—often featured new psychological research. Jane Ellen Harrison—the Cambridge classicist who combined the ideas of Freud, Jung, and James Frazer in her studies of ancient religion—made at least one visit to Pontigny. Regular participants included André Gide and Roger Martin du Gard, both of whom recognized a vital identity between literature and psychology as records of ego development and products of self-examination. In the 1920s, Pontigny devoted a meeting to "telling one's own story—autobiography in fiction and fiction in autobiography" and in 1930 it posed the question: "Are there three psychologies—infant, primitive, abnormal—or are the three the same?" Such topics converged directly with Kris's research, and after Charles de Tolnay—one of Dvořák's Viennese followers—introduced him to the conference, Kris attended several times in the 1930s.[23]

Kris felt an immediate intellectual affinity with modern Pontigny. Through the conferences, he developed a lasting friendship with Martin du Gard, not only a renowned novelist but also a supporter of French socialism. According to Albert Camus, Martin du Gard felt highly protective of his literary detachment and deeply uncertain about political activity. With Gide and fellow members of the *Nouvelle revue française*, he belonged to the circle of writers who prior to the First World War began by "entering literature (the history of the *Nouvelle revue française* group is clear proof of this) rather as one enters the religious life."[24] Martin du Gard, however, recognized "the collapse of bourgeois Christianity"[25] and shifted his concern toward history and politics. Thus, the characters in his massive novels fight against personal, professional, and intellectual confinement, and ultimately "leave their private universe to rejoin the world of men."[26]

Kris knew their choices. In Martin du Gard's *Jean Barois*, a young Catholic renounced his conservative faith to join the Dreyfusards in defending the republic and advancing a new rationalist ethic. Like Kris, the title figure not only suffered in youth from a chronic heart ailment, the effects of which returned in adulthood, but also moved gradually toward political engagement. Introspective questioning of doctrinal belief produced a temporary acceptance of religion as a "symbolist compromise"[27] but finally ended with a commitment to new scientific teachings that brought him "outside the pen, in the clear light of day" and ultimately led him to support Alfred Dreyfus.[28] Kris would have recognized the influence of Balzac and Daumier on the novel's depiction of Zola's trial. Present among the observers, Barois saw the courtroom's combination of theatrical display and political menace:

> The courtroom is filled with a seething, chattering, gesticulating crowd, amongst which one notices a sprinkling of uniforms, gold epaulettes, smartly dressed women. People are eagerly pointing out to each other well-known figures—staff officers, popular journalists, leading lights of the stage and political world. A black phalanx of gowned lawyers separates the spectators from the still-empty Bench, over which hangs Bonnat's melodramatic "Christ" . . . A clock strikes three and the crowd heaves, as if rocked by a ground-swell, while a flood of new-comers seeps into the smallest crannies of the all-but-solid mass. Students in berets, lawyers in their gowns, clamber over the high barrier separating the public from the Bench and Bar and perch themselves on window-sills and ledges.[29]

The chief judge, "a burly, moon-faced man whose shaven lips are like a narrow horizontal line drawn between the bushy side-whiskers, scowls darkly."[30] Despite his combativeness, fatality weighed upon Barois. No intellectual or ethical ideal countered the force of his self-doubt. Instead, he questioned the value of his profession as editor and scholar. Witness to the rise of a Catholic authoritarian movement from the vortex of the Dreyfus affair, he finally lost faith in political progress.

In *On Aging*, Jean Améry, the Viennese-born wartime resister who survived Auschwitz, recalled that *Jean Barois* became a defining book for young men of his generation and educational background.[31] Thus, even in the final years of his life, he wrote in his book *On Suicide* that he wanted to believe in the greater authenticity of the Barois who was "a declared atheist,"[32] not the Barois who called from his deathbed for a priest. Like Améry, Camus recognized Barois'—and his creator's—inner struggle. Martin du Gard represented the modern stoic whose socialism arose not from determined hope or commitment but rather from "the refusal to despair."[33]

Pontigny's organizers confronted that struggle in the theme of the 1937 conference: "The Social Vocation of Art in Epochs of Mental Confusion and of Despair." Kris had his response: he described for the participants the oppression of Jews in Austria, where a republic had for all practical purposes met its fate several years earlier.[34]

Daumier and Austrian Politics

Bringing Daumier to the crumbling Austrian state required Kris to take advantage of Schuschnigg's remaining willingness to placate Britain and France and demonstrate independence from Germany. As Gombrich recalled, Kris

> was determined to stay as long as Freud stayed in Vienna. But he knew very well that time was running out and used his diplomatic skill to make contacts abroad. Thus he arranged a Daumier Exhibition in Vienna to help us with our researches, but also to have the pleasure of displaying subversive cartoons and to collaborate with French colleagues.[35]

The sheer organizational ambition of the exhibition demanded those professional and diplomatic talents that Kris had honed through his years as a museum curator, as a friend to churchmen, and as an advisor to private collectors.

In the Dantan exhibition, Kris had relied almost exclusively on holdings in Vienna and the *Kunsthistorisches Museum*. Now he called upon not only private Viennese sources but also contacts in France and associates in the émigré community. He drew extensively upon collections in Paris and Rotterdam to secure the widest possible selection.[36] In early summer 1936, Saxl granted Gombrich a leave from the Warburg Institute to return to Vienna so he could work not only on the final draft of the caricature book but also on the exhibition.[37] Otto Benesch, the art historian and Albertina curator who had once offered support to Gombrich, now helped Kris obtain sponsorship and gallery space at the Albertina.[38] In Vienna, this kind of support for international cultural events would become increasingly scarce. Thus, in March 1937, the

Viennese *Konzerthaus* demanded that two Jewish musicians from the United States alter their names for a performance program.[39]

In August 1936, Kris had warned Saxl—who still planned on making his annual trip to Vienna—about the unstable conditions in Austria. The letter began with a brief, unusually direct political comment that Kris wrote in English, the only time that he used English in letters to Saxl from Austria:

> This only to tell you that you can come to Austria, as quietly as last year. You wont [sic] find any German. I was told that after the Nazi riots in Vienna (July 29th) the present government is resolved to make no further steps in the pro-German direction. Of course—the strength of the government seems to be considerably diminished. But this concerns the future and does not concern the present situation.[40]

The Nazi riots and the Austrian government's pro-German direction referred to the events surrounding the July 1936 agreement between Hitler and Schuschnigg.

On 11 July, after completing negotiations with Hitler's loyal emissary Franz von Papen, Schuschnigg had signed the Austro-German Agreement, in which Hitler formally recognized Austria's international sovereignty and its autonomy in domestic affairs, while Schuschnigg agreed to pursue foreign policies in line with Austria's identity as a German state. That much of the agreement became public, and led the writer G. E. R. Gedye—one of the most astute English-speaking journalists in Austria—to state that Schuschnigg had just signed Austria's "death-warrant."[41] The consequences of the agreement's secret clauses, however, might also have suggested to Kris that he protect his communications to Saxl.

Under the heading of a "Gentlemen's Agreement," appended privately to the treaty, Germany and Austria pledged to prevent criticisms of each other's countries appearing in print, in film, on radio, or on stage. As a result, a new wave of Nazi propaganda began to flow to and from Austria: Hermann Goering's *Essener Nationalzeitung* crossed the border and Austrian newspapers friendly to the Nazis in Graz and Linz—the *Grazer Tagespost* and the *Linzer Tagespost*—circulated in Germany. At the same time, the Austrian government suppressed émigré and anti-Nazi literature. Schuschnigg—who steadfastly refused pardons for incarcerated leftists—agreed to grant amnesty to Austrian Nazis imprisoned, or merely indicted, for any but the most serious crimes. Perhaps of greatest political consequence, he promised to offer cabinet positions to the so-called "National Opposition in Austria," a coalition of Catholic conservatives and German nationalists who lobbied persistently in support of Hitler. The Austrian chancellor soon conferred ministerial posts on future wartime collaborators, including the interior minister, Dr. Arthur von Seyss-Inquart, who envisioned the Catholic Austrian state becoming a full and equal ally of Hitler's Reich. He briefly replaced Schuschnigg as chancellor after the *Anschluss*, and became Reich commissioner for Holland; the Nuremberg tribunal convicted him of crimes against humanity.[42]

The Austro-German treaty and the Gentlemen's Agreement led immediately to Nazi street riots. On 29 July—the day that the Berlin Olympic torch passed through Vienna—Austrian Nazis and the still banned Austrian stormtroopers demonstrated in Vienna's *Heldenplatz* in front of the imperial Hofburg. Under the eye of police, Nazis and their sympathizers greeted the torch with chants of *Sieg Heil*, *Deutschland über Alles*, and the Horst Wessel song—the Nazi Party's anthem, illegal in Austria. They drowned out the Austrian national anthem and for several hours easily blocked half-hearted police efforts to disperse them. Schuschnigg responded by revoking amnesty for Austrian Nazis—a near meaningless gesture, as most had already gained release. At the same time, using the excuse of a renewed threat to public order, he kept socialists and other leftists in their prison cells. On the day following the Nazi torch rally, Schuschnigg organized a *Vaterländische Front* counter-demonstration; without the participation of the Left opposition, it sparked little enthusiasm.[43]

These events might also help to explain a brief, incomplete change of attitude among Viennese psychoanalysts toward the Left. In 1934, both the International Psychoanalytical Association and the Communist party had expelled Wilhelm Reich from membership: neither psychoanalysts nor Communists accepted Reich's linkage of sexual and political revolution. Later that year, Robert Waelder published in *Imago* a critique of Reich's theories as unscientific and politically driven. The psychoanalyst and Marxist theorist Otto Fenichel drafted a rejoinder, which in 1935 and early 1936 produced a series of negotiations with Waelder and finally Kris.[44] Neither Kris nor Waelder supported a sociological revision of Freud—Kris criticized that direction when it appeared in Erik Erikson—but they arrived at a compromise to have Fenichel publish his own overview of psychoanalytic theory in *Imago*. Unlike Reich, Fenichel remained an orthodox Freudian psychologist: he advocated Freud's instinct theory while also emphasizing the psychological impact of social structures and institutions. Further, by 1935, the Popular Front between Socialists, Communists, and republicans was gradually taking shape. Echoing the recent Communist call for an alliance with socialists and labor reformers, Fenichel described his negotiations with Kris and Waelder as an effort to produce a "united front."[45]

In the weeks following the Austro-German treaty, Kris began to serve as one of the first Austrian contacts for London's Academic Assistance Council. The AAC—later renamed the Society for the Protection of Science and Learning—identified scholars and educators who needed to escape the Continent, assisted with their emigration, and sought employment for them in Britain. Kris sent names and résumés of Austrian scholars to Saxl and Bing, who relayed the information to the council. On 14 September 1936, soon after Saxl's visit to Vienna, Kris mailed to him by registered parcel a copy of the University of Vienna's personnel directory; in it Kris marked the names of "the ones living under the cloud of suspicion."[46] Kris stressed that the situation in Austria already resembled that of Germany. Thanks to the rule of the Christian Social government and the rise of Nazism, there remained few working Jewish scholars: "You will be convinced of how extraordinarily small is the number of those who come into consideration for the A.A.C."[47]

In Vienna, some whom the Nazis labeled "half-Jews" ("*jüdisch Versippte*")[48]—men whose wives were Jewish—kept their jobs, but only a small number of those, if any, remained in the humanities and social sciences. Among the recent generation of scholars, Catholic authoritarianism had done its work:

> Naturally the list is very deficient, although I do not believe that many eluded us. But it is deficient for the reason that there are half-Jews of whom one does not know; people with grandmothers or wives. That does not hold for the Philosophy Faculty and not for the last ten years, during which that too [intermarriage] was already causa exclusionis.[49]

Kris offered to gather names of scholars and researchers employed outside the university, but those figures would merely confirm the picture that emerged from within official academia. He enumerated:

> 1) I could try to obtain from the Ministry of Social Welfare a list of the Jewish doctors still employed in hospitals outside of the university system whose habilitation recently was refused or not attempted as being senseless. The number also cannot be large. Estimated under 10.
> 2) I could try to sort the entire class of scientific employees in public services. For the sphere of the scientific institutions in Vienna I have done that, so far as it concerns the cultural scientific institutions. The result is that in all libraries, archives, and museums—including a one-eighth Jewess, including the chair of the Association of German-Catholic Academic Women, further including two roughly 55-year-old and pension-qualified supervisory librarians in the university library of whom one is likewise only a one-quarter Jew, further

> including my person, a young man in the Albertina (one-quarter Jew) and Dr. Schwarz (Austrian Gallery)—the number 7 can be accepted as the maximum number. This number, however, is incomplete because the possibility exists that outside of Vienna one Jew might be found; further, it would take into account the non-cultural scientific institutions, but it still would not result in doubling the proposed number.[50]

Kris concluded that for the AAC to protect academics and scientists outside the university, the council would need exact numbers of the intermarried:

> 3) What is really absent are people with Jewish wives. That can hardly be determined.[51]

Kris relied on well-placed contacts, among whom he counted an associate at the museum who for his own reasons kept track of the backgrounds of other scholars: "Dr. Hans von Dehmel, the director of our Egyptian department, four-fifths Nazi with strong racial standpoint."[52] The National Socialist Egyptologist exhibited no personal hostility toward Kris, but the museum had ceased to be a secure workplace. Thanking Saxl for his recent visit, Kris described his personal isolation: "The evening with you was enjoyable, almost too enjoyable, for here there is otherwise hardly anyone with whom I can speak freely."[53]

On 22 October 1936—only days before the opening of the Daumier exhibition—Kris sent to Saxl a report for the AAC that further described the situation confronting Jewish scholars in Vienna, most particularly the younger generation. In it Kris pressed the council to focus especially on the fate of colleagues who had embarked on careers at the moment Nazism came to power, among whom he included Karl Popper:

> The real conditions in Austria appear somewhat differently than the way they are used to being viewed abroad or even at home. The

> anti-Semitism predominant since the Eighties has become so much stronger in the last twelve years or so in Austria that one can speak of a systematic exclusion of the Jews from all academic and scientific positions. This exclusion was never a complete one, but in the time period to which I refer, it is a growing one. It first laid hold of the teaching profession in the high schools, then the scientific institutes, and finally, since about 1926/27 in increasing measure also the hospitals and clinics. Since the year 1933, the barring of the Jews has been a total one, so that the question what would happen if National Socialism came to power in Austria must be replaced with the question: What should happen since it is not only the case that a dominant tendency debars a rising generation of Jews and those of Jewish descent from research but also that no opportunity for development is given to an indeed small number of young Jewish scholars who have already been admitted to training?[54]

Concerned that word of his ties to the AAC might find its way back to Austria, Kris had been adamant that Saxl and Bing keep his work anonymous—including to AAC members, who at this time also were helping arrange for the Warburg Institute to remain in London beyond 1936. When forwarding the first report, however, Bing had allowed his identity to become known within the council. Kris repeated his demand for anonymity, emphasizing that the Church hierarchy's once friendly attitude toward him had begun to turn cool and even hostile:

> I believe I am not mistaken that in the course of time severe difficulties await me and that certain Catholic ecclesiastical authorities are preparing to act against me. The reason lies on the one hand in analysis and on the other in my family circumstances (children not baptized). In any case, one of the most prominent representatives of the Viennese clergy refused to appear at the same time with me in a neutral lecture program. I know very little still about this affair, will report to you in more detail when I know more, and ask that for the

time being you treat this communication as strictly confidential (namely from all Austrians).[55]

Dispirited by Schuschnigg's policies, marginalized by the New Vienna School's nationalist *Kulturpolitik*, and disowned by Church leaders, Kris worked on the Daumier exhibition. His attempt to turn Austrian eyes from Berlin toward Paris would be his last significant project in Vienna.

A Republican Art Exhibition

In Austria, Schuschnigg's government continued its political and diplomatic maneuvering. Against this background Kris secured for Daumier's artwork a last trip outside France before the war.[56] With two hundred and sixty-nine drawings, watercolors, sculptures, and lithographs, the extensive survey held in the Albertina in November–December 1936 was nearly twice the size of the Daumier exhibit organized in Berlin a decade earlier.[57]

To accompany the exhibition, Otto Benesch contributed an essay on Daumier to the *Österreichische Rundschau*. Appearing in February 1937, it reinforced the vision of the artist as psychological portraitist, artistic experimenter, and political tribune. Daumier's early paintings revealed the artist's interest in the monumental and heroic, but his later drawings, lithographs, and sculptures—and most importantly caricatures—reflected his concern with the quotidian, revelatory details of daily experience and his deepening attachment to the life he saw immediately around him. The combined figure of Quixote–Ratapoil expressed both sides: Daumier instilled in Quixote the "vital intensity"[58] of a classical poetic character, while he gave to Ratapoil a documentary realism, creating "a concrete figure, of which one could believe that it had actually lived."[59] Daumier's mastery of light, his use of color, and his preoccupation with antiquity recalled late Renaissance and Baroque artists—Tintoretto and the Venetians, Rubens, and most tellingly Rembrandt. His heroic impulse ultimately derived from a deep sympathy for the common citizen: in his last images, the social mass itself became the monumental figure of his art. But the individual subjects within the collective remained distinctive personalities and all too human.

By the end of the 1920s, left-wing critics had begun to deplore the fact that, in France, only Daumier the painter, not Daumier the caricaturist, received recognition.[60] Kris's exhibition restored the balance. The Albertina presented Daumier's full depth and range, from the contemplative and psychological to the moral and political. The works on view combined self-examination, artistic invention, and social criticism, demonstrating to Viennese spectators Daumier's well-known credo, "One must be of one's time."

In the exhibition's first rooms, drawings and lithographs displayed middle-class existence as a revel of acquisition. Bourgeois sociability suppressed the qualities of inwardness and meditation; more dangerously, it provided a cover for possessiveness, complacency, and heartlessness. Art offered a source of light and a spirit of genuine communion. In Daumier's tribute to the artist Auguste Raffet, the prints illuminate a trio of intent collectors (cat. no. 24, Plate 3), while in his image of a single beholder examining a copperplate, the light from the beloved engraving inspires purely private contemplation (cat. no. 59, Plate 4).[61] As in his images of collectors browsing tranquilly through an art shop rack or losing themselves in thought, this solitary figure embodied the vision of a humanity still capable of inward communion.

Bourgeois self-conceit, absence of conviction, and pitilessness denied that vision. In the law chambers, legislative halls, and courts of justice, Daumier witnessed and recorded self-dramatizing defense lawyers, sedentary deputies (cat. no. 99, Plate 5), and splenetic judges (cat. no. 29, Plate 6). Daumier's depiction of the bourgeoisie, Kris wrote in the exhibition catalog, reflected the disfigurements that they caused in others: "To the Parisian bourgeois he holds up a mirror in which the life of the little man appears in grotesque distortion."[62]

Under conditions of extreme poverty, even introspection became unnaturally distorted, as revealed in the unsparing vision of *The Soup* (cat. no. 37, Plate 7). At the table, inwardness turns visceral. Each exhausted figure—father, mother, and infant—withdraws into the state of desperate concentration demanded by survival. An intense, enforced introversion pervades the dismal scene, producing between the mother and the child at her breast a tragic, mutual obliviousness.

In sharp contrast to the somber, self-engrossed world of *The Soup*, Daumier's Ratapoil conveyed calculated, unnerving gregariousness. Thus his relentless attention to the goddess of the Republic can only arouse suspicion (cat. no. 108, Plate 8). Still, his exaggerated, histrionic bow betrays something more than the insincerity of his republican sentiments: it exposes his instinctive deference, of which Ratapoil himself is unaware and which his Bonapartist managers manipulate to their advantage. Ratapoil insists on his nobility of character, yet proves always willing to sell himself to the highest bidder. Aggressive in pursuit of his political targets and submissive toward authority, he recalls the Balzacian agent, the *claqueur*, both "ferocious and fawning."[63] Without reliable social standing or self-direction, Ratapoil's highest aim is to become indispensable. His freedom and power to act depend on being another's agent: indispensability, as Balzac lamented, redefined the meaning and limits of liberty.[64]

Daumier's famous sculpture of Ratapoil, brought to the Albertina, explored in detail the fractured personality of the political agent (cat. no. 84, Plate 9). Completed a year before Louis Napoleon's coup d'état, the small statue communicates its subject's unstable, fragmented identity.[65] Comparing the figure to distant precursors, including creations by El Greco, Clark explains that the "only parallels are with Mannerism at its most extreme and expressive."[66] He describes the grim and evocative nature of the small statue:

> In *Ratapoil* the broken surface, marked with the comb at every point, seems to eat into the solid of the figure, making it tenuous and fragile. That is why the sculpture conjures up skeletons and the dance of death: the wrinkled trousers and the great billow of the

> creased tail-coat are mimicked, on a smaller scale, by the folds and openings of every surface, so that there seems to be no flesh inside the clothes.[67]

In the twisted and rumpled bronze figure, Daumier produced a psycho-political case study. The theatricality and sense of self-importance that emerge from one angle cannot hide the caustic anger visible from another or the vacant stare that appears from yet another. Ratapoil's outward persona as the agent of someone else's designs cannot protect against disintegration from within. Whatever aspirations he claims for himself, they fail him. His excess of sociability signals a wasted personality and empty superfluity, marking him as the first modern agent of propaganda and foreshadowing Jacques Ellul's characterization: "In the very act of pretending to speak as man to man, the propagandist is reaching the summit of his mendacity and falsifications, even when he is not conscious of it."[68]

According to Kris, Daumier later transferred the disheveled and disjointed features of Ratapoil to the figure of Quixote—but a Quixote who senses approaching death, seeks rest in this world, and whose visionary struggles exist only in his memory. Quixote–Ratapoil represented the mass exhaustion of republican ideals, the wearing away of hope by a corrosive, Bonapartist society, and the feeling of political weariness and personal alienation in those who, like Daumier, lived through the bourgeois monarchy and Second Republic and who, after becoming disenchanted by both politicians and the people, devoted themselves to remembrance. As Kris stated:

> When he shows us the lawyers who swarm around clients in the Palace of Justice, shows us the multitude in the theater, in the railway train where the individual is swallowed up by the masses and the masses react as a totality, when he—critically disillusioned—casts an eye over the Second Republic and parliamentary government or with unrelenting severity scourges the menacing danger of

> Bonapartism and its representatives, that is more than satire or broadsheet. "Ratapoil," whom he brought to life in a fine statuette and in numerous lithographs, Ratapoil, who advocates for the golden days of a second empire, is more than a swaggering agent of Napoleon III. He is at the same time a dreamer from the line to which belonged a great favorite of Honoré Daumier; Ratapoil is a descendant of Don Quixote. Satire becomes character portrait.[69]

From the distorted, shattered lines of Ratapoil emerged the faded, disappearing outline of Quixote.

And of Daumier. Henry James looked on Ratapoil as Daumier's alter ego—and James's own double. Thus his essay on Daumier conjured an image of himself loitering in a print shop. There he discovers Daumier's lithographs and ponders their effect: he is, in other words, the bourgeois art connoisseur examining prints in a Daumier drawing, a character within a Daumier creation. James becomes uneasy about his admiration for Daumier's antibourgeois images—especially their leaning toward the ugly and grotesque—and wonders how they can strike such a sympathetic chord in him and in others. He regrets having placed himself within Daumier's shops and streets and suddenly fears that his decision reveals a sense of morbidity. Like Ratapoil, Daumier exploits that fear and subtly "bribes"[70] his targets with thoughts of restored grandeur. Just like Ratapoil, who "in a whisper"[71] twists the mind of his mark, so the figure of art "whispers even to the great"[72] that only art guarantees their survival in the eyes of posterity. Ultimately, James must assimilate Daumier to his own self-image. Baudelaire had stated, "Caricatures are often the most faithful mirror of life," to which James responds that Daumier was in fact the essential bourgeois artist, but one "to whom a big cracked mirror has been given."[73]

In Daumier's drawings the bourgeoisie paraded in their death masks, their crisis well advanced. But in their last gesticulations they clutched desperately at phantasms of Bonapartist glory and control, inevitably dragging the exhausted masses into a lethal arms race and disastrous militarist adventures. In the Albertina, one could see the giddy firearms inventor whose dreamscape was a wasteland (cat. no. 113, Plate 10), the figure of Peace accepting a crown ringed with bayonets (cat. no. 122, Plate 11), and the images of Bonapartism's last gamble: the Franco-Prussian War of 1870, which ended in political self-destruction, foreign occupation, and the starvation of besieged Paris. In Daumier's drawing from that year, "The Empire is Peace," smoke descends upon the ruins of an empty town, and the unburied bodies reveal the absolute tranquility that Louis Napoleon had promised the French people after he seized imperial power (cat. no. 126, Plate 12). But the title–"L'empire, c'est la paix"—did more than recall the emperor's declaration from the year following his coup d'état. It revived Victor Hugo's memorial to the victims of the first imperialist slaughter: the civilians shot down in the streets of Paris by Louis Napoleon's soldiers in the coup's immediate aftermath. In *Les Châtiments*, Hugo condemned Bonapartism in the name of the innocent: "Dormez dans vos cercueils! taisez-vous dans vos tombes! / L'empire c'est la paix. [Sleep in the coffin! be calm in the tomb! / Empires, we know, bring peace.]"[74]

In the room adjacent to Daumier's drawings of modern war, the exhibition placed his depictions of classical heroes and foot soldiers. Selected from the artist's early collection, *Ancient History*, these parodies of Homeric myths foreshadowed Daumier's broadsides against militarism. "Menelaus the Conqueror" (cat. no. 131, Plate 13) exposed the falseness of the heroic code. It did so neither in the self-righteous pose of the sybaritic king, nor in the disdain for him shown by his wife Helen, but instead in the contempt both figures display toward the corpse of the nameless soldier, face buried in the sand, lying at their feet. Even before the Franco-Prussian War, Daumier had extracted the lesson of Troy: heroism meant self-glorification, sacrifice imposed anonymity. For Kris, Daumier's vision conveyed a shattering impact, both morally and emotionally:

> The travesties of ancient scenes that show the poor bourgeois, the commonplace man playing the part of the hero of antiquity, in which the comic contrast reaches the point of being frightening or often

> moving, are as alive as the political sheets of the later period. These are the sheets in which, out of a deep longing for peace, is depicted the armaments fever of a sick Europe on the eve of the war of 1870. These are the sheets in which the sorrow and pain brought by the war of 1870 are portrayed with stirring pathos; across more than two generations they have lost none of their power to affect us and many of them might be more powerful today than at the time.[75]

In a similar spirit, the "Page of History," also on display at the Albertina, depicted the Bonapartist eagle lying punished and powerless beneath the weight of Victor Hugo's *Les Châtiments* (cat. no. 124, Plate 14).

Daumier reached far beyond Dantan's stage world, expressing what Benesch described as a concrete vision of society or what Kris—reviving Dvořák's description of Bruegel—called in the exhibition catalog a "new realism."[76] Daumier's realism encompassed both mind and society:

> In his works, what stands before us are not the types that the English caricaturists and their French imitators circulated in the eighteenth and early nineteenth century, but rather human beings who are deeply familiar to us, human beings who live, breathe, and suffer, human beings in their physical and psychological reality. Caricature unmasks; it seeks the essence, it makes us laugh, but with Daumier it teaches us to know human beings. They are the human beings whom we find as heroes in the epic written by Daumier's friend, Balzac.[77]

Like Balzac's *La Comédie humaine*, Daumier's visions became a documentary record, bearing witness to the endurance demanded by daily survival.

The Disasters of War

In London, Saxl understood clearly the political significance of displaying Daumier's artwork in the Albertina and the personal meaning that the exhibition held for Kris. Immediately after the First World War, with the support of Austria's Socialist government, he had organized in Vienna an antiwar exhibit that featured Goya's etchings, *The Disasters of War*.[78] He now circulated Kris's exhibition catalog at the Warburg Institute and in January 1937 conveyed to Kris his own and the staff's praise: "The Daumier exhibition must have been splendid. Everyone in this library enjoyed the catalog with delight and admiration, and were also very glad that the foreword [to the catalog] does full justice to you and your work."[79]

Support such as that shown by Benesch in Vienna and by Saxl in London would have helped relieve Kris's sense of isolation, but the most crucial sign of fellowship came from France. The months when Kris prepared and displayed the Daumier exhibition coincided with the first triumphs and final crisis of the French Popular Front. In May 1936, led by the Jewish socialist Léon Blum, the Popular Front had formed an antifascist government in Paris, where it struggled to survive against internal dissension and unrelenting middle-class, Church, and nationalist opposition, until it fell in June 1937. For his efforts in organizing the largest Daumier exhibition between the wars, and the only European exhibition outside France during the 1930s, a presidential decree signed on 12 August 1937 bestowed on Kris membership in the *Légion d'Honneur*. The Grand Chancellery of the *Légion d'Honneur* certified it on 22 September. Receiving membership so soon after the collapse of Blum's ministry indicates that it was his government that made the nomination, a sign of recognition that, Gombrich recalled, Kris "valued as a safeguard."[80]

By the time of the Daumier exhibition, Kris no longer expected the Viennese art historical profession or the Austrian Church to offer any reliable protections. In bringing the French artist's work to his own city, he now identified himself intellectually and politically with a broad Popular Front movement. The French *Légion d'Honneur*—and the presence of a European audience that the honor confirmed—both justified the exhibition and encouraged Kris to continue the caricature project.

Gombrich, who had assisted with the exhibition, would not present his work again to an Austrian audience for decades. His career and new family became firmly rooted elsewhere. During his return to the Continent in 1936, he married Ilse Heller, who came from a Jewish family in Prague and had been a piano student of Leonie Gombrich in Vienna. Their wedding took place in Czechoslovakia. In 1937, their son Richard was born in England.[81] Much later, when Gombrich described his ties to his original and adopted homes, he discarded national identifications, characterizing himself simply as "a Central European working in England."[82]

In summer 1937, the Spanish Popular Front government displayed in the Spanish pavilion at the Paris Exhibition Pablo Picasso's *Guernica*. Depicting the recent German bombing of a defenseless Basque town, it presented a riveting vision of anguish that defied all previous traditions of mural painting. Both Saxl and Kris immediately regarded Picasso's creation as the highest artistic achievement of the twentieth century. In a lecture presented immediately after the war, Saxl recalled: "It made a deep impression on hundreds of thousands of visitors, and I think it will go down in history as one of the few great and prophetic works of art created between the wars."[83]

During the war, in a talk delivered at the Dayton Art Institute, Kris placed *Guernica* within a lineage of centuries of antiwar art, a lineage that included caricature. Both types of art exposed ugly material realities and unmasked false ideals:

> In the beginning of the 17th century engravings of the Frenchman Jacques Callot depicted neither the glory nor the excitement, but the horrors of war. And since that time, three spheres of war imagery have coexisted: The imagery of victory which commemorates; the imagery of the reporter which describes, [sic] and the imagery of the anti-war movements. The three types correspond to three social areas: The first, the imagery of victory, is that of the official painters: they usually paint large canvasses, murals and battle prospects; the

> second is the area of popular imagery, of the artisans, the picture reporters of the past; the third is that of a few enlightened leaders of mankind, of artists like Callot, Goya, or Daumier, who kept the torch of higher convictions and human ideals alive.[84]

In the contemporary world, Picasso's antifascist and antimilitarist mural sustained this line of prophets:

> I do not pretend to know where in this complex world, in which the polarity of individualism and conformity splits our lives, the artist's place should be. But let me quote at least one instance, well known to all, illustrating the potential function of the individual creator where art and war are concerned. I refer to Pablo Picasso's *Guernica*. If the great artist turns to war as his subject, he—accidentally—may become propagandist as well. His choice, it appears, will be to join the small group of those who have endeavored to show the horrors not of this war or that but of war as an institution.[85]

Picasso had brought Daumier's experiment into the twentieth century.[86]

CHAPTER 5

THE CARICATURE BOOK 1936–38

Completing the Manuscript in Vienna

In the months that led up to the Daumier exhibition, in the undisturbed quarters of Kris's study, the two scholars continued their work on the book manuscript. Gombrich recalled the routine that they had adopted from the start of their collaboration:

> I well remember visiting him in the Museum in those days when he was physically so tired from standing on his feet all day that he was close to collapsing, but he not only carried on, but would rush home in a taxi to receive the evening's patients. After a rapid supper I would then come at about nine o'clock and we often sat together till midnight talking about caricature and about many other things as well. When it came to writing we really wrote together, he sitting on one side of the desk and I on the other. Usually it was he who held the pen but we would jointly formulate every sentence before he wrote it down.[1]

They intended the caricature book, in crucial part, for the Warburg circle in London, so that before Gombrich returned to England in

February 1937, they packaged a still unfinished draft and sent it off to Saxl.[2] In March, Saxl wrote to Kris offering to assist with the book's publication:

> I hope that you do not believe that I did not immediately read the caricature. I find it extraordinarily well-done in the arrangement. About the execution we must still speak. I believe that the book, as it is, would already find its readership in England—where I can help with that, I would very much like to help.[3]

In fall 1937, as *Anschluss* approached, Kris wrote to Saxl that he planned to complete the book's final chapter, covering the psychology of caricature, in November.[4]

Gombrich translated the full German manuscript, *Die Karikatur*, into an English version, *Caricature*, for publication in exile. He kept the London manuscript to the same length as the Viennese: two hundred and fifty-four typescript pages of text and citations. On a separate sheet inserted in the Vienna version, he placed the rough draft of a German foreword with a partial, typed English translation of it, including handwritten revisions.[5]

Both the German and English versions of the foreword leave no doubt that the book aimed to bridge Kris's Freudian researches and the Warburg circle's art historical approach. Describing psychoanalytic theory as critical to bringing art history in line with science, Kris accepted the sole burden for applying Freud's concepts:

> When we speak of psychology, we mean a certain psychological school. One of us (Kris) is also a psychoanalyst and pupil of Freud; he carries the responsibility for the fact that the thoughts developed here conform closely to the Psychoanalytic approach. This should be specially stressed, because the nature of psychoanalysis has suffered from many misunderstandings. We base ourselves [superscript-lean

> upon] its findings, because it is the first, and to date the only scientific doctrine of the central psychic processes in man. We [take-crossed out] the approach of psychoanalysis, but use its terminology with reticence: we have attempted [to] formulate in the simplest possible fashion all psychological insights which we turn to account. The (type of) problems, then, posed in this work took this point of departure from psychoanalytic studies [here Kris's first paper on caricature is footnoted]; which indicated the usefulness of extending the range of our work into this field.[6]

Behind the disclaimer remained the question: would Saxl associate the Warburg Institute with the book?

Aby Warburg interpreted symbolic images as vessels of memory that invited scientific investigation and he believed that Jung's theory of the collective unconscious confirmed his view. Like Jung, he regarded image making as a spiritualizing process and rejected Freud's theory of sexual sublimation as irrelevant to artistic creativity. As for Saxl, he explored the mnemonic and emotive power of images, but did not look for reinforcement from mental science or, as Gombrich later noted, seek a psychology of art. Kris and Gombrich kept Saxl's ambivalence clearly in mind:

> From our preoccupation with the historical material we have gained insights, which we neither expected nor sought. For these insights, as presented here, we are both responsible in equal degree. We worked on them together for several years, whereby Gombrich attended on his own to the collection of material in many areas. Although finally not living in the same place, thanks to the help of the Warburg Inst. we were able nevertheless to work over [superscript-revise] and set down this work together. We owe [feel-crossed out] a longstanding debt to [this Instit-crossed out]ute's orientation in research and [the] scientific proficiency of this [Inst-crossed out] [sphere of work (brackets in original)].[7]

There followed a crucial parenthetical comment: "(We would not however make it responsible for the basic attitude of this study of whose problematic nature we are perfectly conscious[.])"[8] Following this remark Gombrich added in German: "Except if Saxl strikes this sentence."[9] The foreword concluded with acknowledgments that emphasized first "the guidance of the Warburg Institute and namely the personal participation of F. Saxl." They included, from Vienna, Otto Benesch, Leo Planiscig, and the cultural historian Hans Tietze, and from the Warburg Institute, Gertrud Bing and Rudolf Wittkower.[10] Neither the German nor English manuscript of the book included a dedication, but Kris planned to dedicate it—as he had done his study of artist biographies—to the Warburg Institute.[11]

What now follows in this chapter will retain the book manuscript's original order of presentation and adhere to its division into five chapters. Although Gombrich after the war became dissatisfied with this organization, it strongly reflects how his and Kris's attitudes toward psychology, art, and politics developed during the crisis of the interwar republic and how their project evolved in response to that crisis. As threats to republicanism intensified, Kris and Gombrich broadened their conception of caricature. The study of an experiment in psychology and art expanded to consider how that experiment evolved into political protest. Ultimately, Kris and Gombrich came to see that the success of the psychological and artistic experiment depended strongly on its political fate.

The Classical Mask

The book's first chapter, "Caricatura," reviewed early theories of caricature. Defined as "portraits which show the features of the subject in comic distortion, without losing the resemblance,"[12] caricatures raised fundamental questions about the ancient conception of art. Thus theorists made various attempts at reconciling caricature's embrace of distorted and unstable appearances with the classical tradition's search for ideal forms and universal laws of proportion. Perhaps the most prominent theory held that caricature art represented a different type of idealization, one that located perfection not in beauty but in deformity—the *bella deformità*. Other arguments suggested that it provided a unique form of escape for working artists, or a useful recreation for divinely inspired geniuses, or, more technically, a generative *modelletto* or sketch. One Neo-Platonic theory asserted that caricature sought to depict the essential quality—or Idea—of a person: "caricature is more like because it gives more than mere physical information about the subject: it grasps his essence."[13]

For Kris and Gombrich, Renaissance-era caricature made a crucial discovery: the ignoble in human beings hid *not behind* the mask of nobility but *within* it. As they wrote:

> [O]ne could even say (cum grano salis) that caricature, at least that of the 17th century, is a special order of the ideal portrait, an ideal portrait with inverted signs, in which it is not the noble [and] elevated in man which shines forth, but the low and ugly which stands unmasked.[14]

Like Karl Kraus, they asserted that caricaturists revealed new truths not by removing the mask but by reconfiguring it.

The great eighteenth-century satirist and empiricist William Hogarth explained the creation of such reconfigurations psychologically: a series of rapid mental associations produced a quick, unexpected connection between a familiar likeness and an unfamiliar distortion. Modern psychological theories, Kris and Gombrich pointed out, described the same cognitive shortcut as the "surprising realization of a similarity in the apparently dissimilar."[15] Caricature art thus appeared untrained, accidental, playful, and even childlike. And by producing pleasure and discomfort simultaneously, it became after Hogarth's era a volatile art form: "In the 19th century all comic or aggressive art, particularly that reducing reality to a few lines, will come to be called caricature."[16]

Kris and Gombrich traced caricature's beginnings to a confidential, even secretive, activity within the neo-classicist artistic circle of Annibale Carracci in late Renaissance Bologna. The Bolognese engaged in isolated games with portraiture, surreptitiously drawing and privately distributing humorous or iconoclastic portraits for their own entertainment. Away from the view of patrons and public, they banished classical lines and proportions from their drawings, choosing instead to distort or exaggerate features of the face and body into comic configurations. The studio became an invigorating laboratory, closed off from the world of patronage and commissions.

Carracci and his circle eventually took their activity into the streets. The results survived in what became known as the "Munich notebook," a compilation of sketches believed to be drawn by members of the Carracci circle or its later followers. In this notebook or sketchbook faces came to life from various angles and at various tempos: "distortions set in experimentally," the caricaturists acting with "experimental swiftness."[17] These instantaneous products of the closed atelier or open-air street recalled well-known comic types from popular theater:

> Thin and fat, dwarfs and giants point to a world familiar to contemporaries from the Comedia dell'Arte [sic]; the actors in a scenario which starts its triumphal march through European 17th and 18th century graphic art in the work of Jacques Callot.[18]

But although caricature derived inspiration from the comic stage performer, it acquired no social function or public audience. Indeed, it seems a strong peculiarity of caricature that at each phase of its evolution, it had first to pass through the filter of stage life before entering the public domain.

Not long after the Carracci initiated their experiment, Bernini steered it in a new direction, focusing not on the body but on the face alone and the perceived unity of facial expression. Rather than singling out and exaggerating distinctive physical traits, Bernini "compresses the multiplicity of form into a schematic shape."[19] Reminiscent of Loewy's early theory of archaic art, Kris and Gombrich emphasized that Bernini reproduced only those facial features and expressive gestures that comprised a viable memory picture. And anticipating Gombrich's theory of the transmission of conceptual schemas, they explained that Bernini produced those pictures by modifying pre-existing mental constructs:

> Bernini starts with the whole, not with the parts; he conveys the image which we fix in our mind when we try to recall someone in our memory, that is with the unified expression of the face—and it is this expression which he distorts and heightens.[20]

Bernini represented an isolated phenomenon. For centuries caricature art remained socially ostracized, a mere private amusement. Caricaturists themselves let their spontaneous, unforgiving imaginings run riot, but in so doing acquired no reputation as artists.

Public recognition finally came when Roman patrons and connoisseurs took an interest. In Rome, Pier Leone Ghezzi developed a routinized, step-by-step memory technique for producing caricature portraits. Working from the mental image that he formed of the subject, Ghezzi introduced distortions into it only as he first sketched the image on paper. The finished portrait, however, toned down or removed the most severe deformations, safely muting the sketch's offensive or confrontational aspect.

Roman elites now avidly sought caricatured likenesses of themselves and of their social circle. Caricature became a teachable technique and its images served as badges of status. Yet, it remained sequestered—an exotic curiosity or hothouse growth, like other objects invented or nurtured for the enjoyment and edification of aristocratic households. As Kris and Gombrich explained:

> Nothing could better characterise the cultivated sceptical atmosphere of the early 18th century than the fact that it allows caricature,

> if only in adulterated form, to become a category of art in itself. The theory of the bella deformita[sic][,] of the unmasking function of a caricatured portrait, attracts a social stratum and a period which welcomed criticism of man in epigram, epic and satire. But this criticism was at once limited to a narrow, private circle; Ghezzi caricatures the friends and acquaintances of his patrons. Caricature acted as criticism, as unmasking—but criticism and unmasking are a game played by art-lovers. Caricature has become a branch of art, but a branch for connoisseurs. It has left the world of the artist's workshop, but it has not wandered very far: it has found its new abode in the libraries and reception rooms of the nobles, the protectors of the arts, men of learning. It has never quite left this social milieu and is still today very much alive in the entourage of artist and art-lover. But that was not to be its most effective domain.[21]

Eventually, to draw caricatures—and to be caricatured—came to signify more than membership in the cognoscenti. Reconfiguring the mask ceased to languish as an esoteric game.

The Switch

As discussed in the manuscript's second chapter, "Comic Art and the Pre-conditions of Caricature," caricaturists flourished outside the elite world of aristocrat and patron because they maintained ancient but still thriving contacts with popular, borderline regions of art. In particular, caricature preserved faded but protean images of the grotesque—the surviving remnants of archaic anxiety and pagan excess. But the incorporation of grotesque imagery reflected also the inherent "switch character"[22] (*Kippcharakter*) of vision. The human countenance formed a composite image, a mask containing alternative configurations and alternative truths. Relying on the switch nature of perception, caricaturists therefore directed viewers' attention to possibilities already residing within the mask. Distortion and exaggeration functioned not only as mechanisms of horror or humor but also as techniques of subtle reconfiguration bringing new truths—psychological, social, and political—into view.[23]

Loewy had taught that the ancients incorporated visions of demonic creatures into ritual magic in the belief that the sight of their grotesque, grimacing faces would deter evil. According to Warburg, Renaissance imagemakers endeavored to detach those symbols from their archaic, violent memories. As Kris and Gombrich now described, the use of grimacing or grotesque visages remained a highly fluid, ambivalent activity:

> The sinister expression of the threateningly distorted face is the direct predecessor of comic mimicry. The grimace, the distorted human face which is the autoplastic equivalent to the mask, plays even today this dual role in the human consciousness, which is revealed as it were in many a folk-custom. There is only a hair's breadth dividing the grinning grimace from the laugh.[24]

Kris himself knew all too well how thin was this distinction: at the *Kunsthistorisches Museum* he had expected laughs in response to his joke directed against the *Vaterländische Front*, but instead met with frozen silence.

That same, unsettling switch between the humorous and demonic surfaced in Sedlmayr's essay on Bruegel's *macchia*. Kris and Gombrich now argued that with Bruegel the switch image "may have lost some of its terror because of its closer proximity to the didactic and illustrative."[25] It functioned as a visual pun. Sedlmayr, they knew, took the opposite view: Bruegel's calculated ambiguity "such as also appears in the caps of the 'Children's Games' which in conjunction make up a grimace, has an effect which Sedlmair [sic] has described as 'alienation' (Entfremdung)."[26] Bruegel's paintings indeed evoked a distancing effect: "Medical psychology shows that an impression of the uncanny is always accompanied by a feeling of depersonalization. A milder feeling of this sort gradually slips into the comic."[27] Comic art, however, "utilises feelings of alienation in the smallest quantities."[28] Sedlmayr's interpretation rested on views other than medical psychology: "Discussion of Sedlmair's [sic] provocative arguments would start from this basis, which give only partial access, of course, to his attitude."[29] Behind Sedlmayr's theory of estrangement loomed the grim countenance of Austro-Fascism.

The switch nature of caricature pointed not only to its hybrid background in pagan antiquity but also to its multivalent quality in seventeenth-century Bologna. Like Bruegel, Annibale Carracci applied non-classical techniques to his own *mestieri*, or figures from the street:

> If one considers the scenes in context and amongst works of art contemporary with them, one is amazed at the freedom with which it has been possible to view the various and typical forms of life. We have here some relationship with art north of the Alps in the spirit of Bruegel: the far-ranging eye for life, falling on the low-class as on the anti-decorous in the sense of antiquity, has an affinity with the Fleming's basic attitude.[30]

Unlike Bruegel, Carracci did not produce a new vision of the masses or create a new type of portraiture; that accomplishment fell to the great Mannerist Caravaggio. Instead, he pursued the experiment of caricature within—not against—the classical tradition. His images served as commentaries on classicizing portraits rather than as borrowings from everyday popular art. Yet, the *mestieri* and caricatures brought Carracci—even if against his will—to a documentary perspective, one that benefited from a close observation of the world and a well-developed sense of irony toward his own classicizing art:

> They [the *mestieri* and the caricatures] are connected through a common relationship to everyday life. If in the "mestieri" we have parodic application of the formal means of the "reformed" grand

> manner, then in caricature we have an analogous parody of the new theory of portraiture.[31]

Kris and Gombrich's discussion of Carracci's street drawings recalled Dvořák's lectures: "The 16th century, as in Bruegel, went so far as to take typical figures such as peasants directly from the life, identifying them as members of a class; this gradual advance leaves one step to works like the mestieri."[32] Like Bruegel's paintings, Carracci's sketches and caricatures provided a visual record of the variety within everyday social existence.

Carracci's faces also conjured imaginative, playful visions. His reconfigurations became comedic formulas: "The external appearance of the individual is generalised, transformed into a type. This world of types is comic even without comparison with the individual, even without a thought to the model caricatured."[33]

Not surprisingly, after his death, Carracci's figures came back to life not as images in visual art but as characters on the popular stage. And the agent of their revival was Callot, the master of switching between on-stage and off-stage visions:

> The types which make their appearance in the Munich sketch-book are constantly resurrected in the comic art of the following century as variations on the theme of man. They pass from hand to hand and become basic to the repertory of comic pictorial types. The fame acquired through their dissemination is associated with the name of Jacques Callot, who arrived in Italy shortly after the death of Annibale Carracci and must have known caricatures by the Carracci and their circle such as were preserved in albums.[34]

Callot himself never drew caricature portraits. Instead, he fused actors' masks onto the visages of real human beings and in doing so offered both a critique of society and a documentary vision of humanity. Enlivened and sharpened by the influence of Carracci, Callot went beyond sketchbook reflections and self-irony: "For the grotesque types of dwarf and Capitano, of figures from the Commedia dell'Arte and the street, provide a critical theory of man as in the work of Bruegel."[35] In the galleries of the Albertina, Kris and Gombrich had displayed Daumier's work as the culmination of an anti-idealizing, documentary art. In the caricature manuscript, they traced its historical lineage in Bruegel, Carracci, and Callot.

Highly attuned to the switch character of images, caricaturists challenged the very stability of human vision. They thrived on the inherently fluid nature of seeing—on the visual and cognitive shortcuts that Hogarth described as the essence of caricature—and they exploited the mind's capacity to alternate between opposite constructs of a single feature, gesture, or expression. Just as Arcimboldo manipulated the fluidity of perception—its power to switch between alternatives—to produce his famous heads of the seasons, so Carracci drew faces out of animal features.

Here Kris and Gombrich directed the reader to Schlosser's work on the chambers of wonders. Arcimboldo had painted his images "out of fruit and animals, so that one can see them in two ways: as still-life, or as part of a face."[36] Carracci's animal-like caricatures and Arcimboldo's fantasized faces each relied on the viewer's ability to respond to "the artist's invitation to various modes of seeing and of interpreting shapes."[37] In the objects that Schlosser had guarded and cherished, Kris and Gombrich now recognized the vital and disconcerting switch character of appearances.

Hogarth's satiric analysis of human nature took the switch technique to its furthest limits. In his drawings, play with form—not ritual magic—produced the switch between the grotesque and the comic: "Line and dot are according to Hogarth the ideal caricature of the singer; line and dot, seen as a man, are at the same time a grotesque image."[38]

But Hogarth did not pursue the political implications of his insight. Daumier, however, did.

The Pear

Kris and Gombrich's third chapter, "The Satiric Image," opened with Daumier's world and its defining image: "La Poire." Even in our day, it is not difficult to call to mind Philipon and Daumier's depiction of the head of Louis-Philippe metamorphosing slowly into the pear: *la poire* in the caricature, fool or fathead in Parisian vernacular. The transformation of Louis-Philippe's head into a pear challenged his competence as a leader; more importantly, it condemned his betrayal of the revolution that brought him to power. It exposed not an ineffective monarch but an illegitimate ruler who overthrew the July Revolution, turned against the people of Paris, and transformed into "the hated symbol of reaction."[39] The image marked a decisive moment in both the history of caricature and the politics of culture: "The visual game of the Carraccis which transforms a face into an object has not changed in principle. The joke for the few, however, has become an appeal to the masses, a private aesthetic has become a social phenomenon."[40]

Daumier developed the pear into a vision of French politics—past, present, and future. A reminder of the republican revolution betrayed, his and Philipon's image became a call to action. The monarch and his officials viewed it as "a prelude to depriving him of actual power."[41] And so, after a long period of private experimentation with artistic form and content, caricature in the century of Daumier generated a civic language and popular symbolism that inspired public responses.

Whereas the nineteenth-century pear evoked anger at the abandonment of the republic, in the twentieth century, such defamatory images—as the work of a "mob"[42]—became more dangerous, especially in the hands of nationalists and anti-Semites. Bringing strongly to mind Heinrich Heine's prediction that those who burned books would end by burning people, Kris and Gombrich recalled that attacking effigies now provided training in the use of lethal violence: "Target practice with the enemy image has become all too familiar to us from the wars of our own time. Contempt and hatred here serve as pretexts for the primitive character of the action."[43] Defamatory images facilitated a hellish descent from symbolic to actual violence.

This volatility of visual images had been Warburg's chief intellectual concern and consuming private fear, and in art history he had searched continuously for signs of progress away from defamatory magic toward reliance on symbolic communication. His seminal essay on Protestant broadsheets during the Reformation claimed to find spiritualizing signs even in the fevered propaganda and counter-propaganda generated by religious warfare: illustrators who used grotesque and demonic imagery to depict their religious adversaries wielded a visual vocabulary, not magical incantations. Despite, or perhaps because of, their own fears, Kris and Gombrich supported Warburg's thesis. Acts such as overturning statues or carrying mock coffins revealed "a fluid tr[a]nsition here from true magical identification of man and image, to symbolic action."[44] Pictures of the devil or images that identified an enemy with the devil evolved from depictions of Satan incarnate to visual allegories and finally to comic personifications: "This supersession of the literal by the metaphorical is of a typical nature, for it characterises that development from sensory representation to logical signs, to which A. Warburg devoted his research."[45]

Caricature thus could overcome defamation to become an instrument of social dialogue and political criticism.

The Moderns

The fourth and longest chapter, "Caricature in the Modern Sense," detailed the rise and decline of caricature after it left the studios and salons and entered the public arena. Kris and Gombrich identified three tendencies of caricature in the modern sense: social commentary, psychological analysis, and technical experimentation. As social critic, psychological researcher, and technical innovator, Daumier integrated the three tendencies, and in doing so, created modern political art. No caricaturist had repeated his accomplishment since.

Caricature art as social criticism emerged with the growth of print media during the Enlightenment, as Kris and Gombrich emphasized: "Caricature finds its social role in the broadsheet."[46] The audience for caricature came from the widening political universe in which openness meant literally being open to view: "the public to which it appeals, before which the victim is to be mocked, must already be familiar with the appearance of the victim."[47] Civic spectacle and public confrontation created the necessary environments for caricature, which "presupposes a conception of public and publicity, a stage on which the individual moves, a forum where he can be judged."[48] Modern politics as performance stage and as popular forum generated two types of caricature, each with its defining practitioner. Politics as a communal theater inspired Hogarth, and as a collective tribunal, Daumier.

While connoisseurs in Italy exchanged caricatures within private networks, artists in Britain began to produce drawings for popular consumption. The closed world of Roman salons gave way to the open life of London streets, where British political and social critics transformed caricature into a public discourse:

> Caricature found in England such fertile ground where it might flourish. Only here was there at the time of Ghezzi, after the "Glorious Revolution", that atmosphere of publicity which can only be created by democratic institutions; here the broadsheet becomes "cartoon" in the modern sense, and the defamatory image caricature.[49]

Like Jonathan Swift and the literary satirists who followed him, caricaturists came fully into their own amidst the parliamentary deal making, backroom skirmishing, and popular agitation that characterized political life from the age of Walpole to that of George III and Pitt the Younger. The new caricaturists possessed far greater willingness to depict the street than did their Renaissance forebears:

> The flood of satirical prints which sweeps in when the first phase of the reign of George III cedes to a more democratic period of active political participation in political affairs, carries unheard-of potency in pictorial satire as a whole. The display-windows of the booksellers and publishers Holland and Fores, who also hired out portfolios of the evening, are an expression of the new social role of this satire, in which portrait caricature is predominant and to which it gives its name. For these prints, which caused congestion of pedestrian traffic around the windows where they were displayed, which became universal "conversation-pieces" at social gatherings, and which were sometimes banned while their authors were imprisoned—are now called "caricatures" themselves.[50]

Caricature brought together visual satire and popular protest. What Hogarth grudgingly accepted as a limited experiment now threatened to break its artistic and social bounds. As Kris and Gombrich explained, "That fusion, which the old Hogarth feared would be detrimental to art as a whole, is now complete."[51]

The caricaturist James Gillray shared Swift and Hogarth's anxieties toward the new democratic masses and popular movements. Gillray directed his most scathing caricatures not at political institutions but at political personalities—Pitt being his chief object—and at national enemies, above all Napoleon. Although he used art chiefly to expose his target's corrupt character, he also at times employed it to "unmask his politics."[52] Gillray and other English caricaturists displayed their portraits in shop windows and in widely distributed pictorial broadsheets. But having helped transform the broadsheet into a critical mass medium, they refused to ally their artwork with any popular political movement.

In Paris, under the bourgeois monarchy, Daumier took the step that Hogarth and Gillray rejected. Although not yet ready to associate themselves or their art with a revolutionary party or radical street movement, Philipon and the illustrators of *La Caricature* and *Le Charivari*—

including the young Daumier—used caricature to critique the sham constitutional government. In the case of Daumier "the pictorial joke is addressed to an educated public with a preference for indirect representation through symbols which regular readers of the journal learn to understand. The pear is such a symbol, standing for the fathead Louis-Philippe."[53] Daumier pushed the use of classical language even further to make a political point:

> Daumier's impressive adaptation of Raphael's Cartoon, where Paul preaching in Athens becomes Demosthenes appealing "Atheniens [sic], prenez-garde à Philippe", is not intended as a mockery of Raphael, but as a meaningful re-use of a famous figure. The pathos of classical sculpture is not to be degraded, but exploited.[54]

Daumier's experimentation with classical themes, according to Kris and Gombrich, injected the popular broadsheet with "figurative energy."[55]

Political criticism in turn inspired artistic innovation. Daumier and his associates found their chief model not in British satire but in Goya's documentary scenes and fantastic visions: "It is in the work of Francisco Goya that the broadsheet found, for what is probably the first time, and surely in the most magnificent form, true pictorial dignity."[56]

In *The Disasters of War*, Goya employed a private visual symbolism to depict the sufferings of the Spanish masses under Napoleonic occupation. Building on Goya's legacy, Daumier developed in caricature a "lingua universal,"[57] which combined naturalist depictions with magical imagery and which moved beyond classicism to integrate the documentary and the symbolic. Artistic experimentation and political engagement reinforced each other. Further, as French censors became more active, symbolic inventiveness became more crucial to transmitting political messages. Philipon published the famous series of pears as a public defense against the charge of lese-majesty.

But censorship and the increasing use of symbolic language also encouraged a counter-impulse toward non-political play with visual imagery. The union of documentary substance and symbolic form that Goya had initiated and that Daumier had strengthened began to disintegrate. Grandville, who used caricature to construct ever more fantastic visual designs, attracted the notice of Baudelaire, who perceived in his artwork a fascinating dream world. Kris and Gombrich cited Baudelaire's commentary in which the poet explained how Grandville—unintentionally—caricatured his own art:

> Before his death he applied himself stubbornly to the noting of his successive dreams and nightmares in a plastic form, with all the precision of a ste[n]ographer writing down an orator's speech. Grandville the artist really wanted his pencil to explain the law of the association of ideas! Grandville is indeed very comic, but he is often so without knowing it.[58]

Grandville's broadsheet drawings reflected not worldly engagement but extreme introversion, as Kris and Gombrich wrote,

> for in Grandville's designs the game with form serves illustration no longer, it has abandoned all pretence to propaganda. It is even questionable how fantasies of this sort may still be brought within the realm of comic art. It is a psychic event which is represented, an inner sequence of images.[59]

The art that reproduced dreamscapes surfaced again in the next century, not as caricature but as Surrealist imagery: "Only with 20th century surrealism could such experiments become once more the object of artistic interest, and at the same time finally removed from the realm of the comic."[60]

The Surrealists' use of caricature epitomized its fate after 1900. What Daumier elevated to a medium of universal expression became a language not of urban politics but of dream psychology.

Political art as practiced by Callot, Goya, and Daumier, which forged caricature as its chief weapon and the broadsheet as its mass medium, declined rapidly in the twentieth century. As psychological art replaced it, the experiment with caricature turned inward. And as Kris and Gombrich considered this new psychological direction, they turned to Hogarth as the model of innovation—Hogarth, who had abhorred the use of caricature as a political tool and had been the first to mold visual parody into a psychological technique.

In psychological art, as in political art, caricaturists exploited the switch nature of images. The Carracci circle, followed by Bernini, had dispensed with stable physical likenesses and explored instead the intrinsic fluidity of facial appearances and expressions. Like other late Renaissance artists, the Bolognese became attached artistically and scientifically to physiognomics—"the theory of clues to character in the human face"[61]—and they searched the human visage for indicators of "concrete psychic states or particular mental attitudes."[62]

Yet, the more closely caricaturists observed the human countenance, the more instability they discovered there. Bernini became the first caricaturist to focus on the "mobile human countenance."[63] He and the artists who eventually followed his lead emphasized not physiognomy but pathognomy, the approach that originated with Leonardo da Vinci and called for scrutiny not of physical or anatomical traits but of the "play of features."[64] Their observations centered on "forms of expression."[65] While Leonardo's studies of human emotional expression extended beyond facial features to encompass gesture, action, and behavior, in the age of the Carracci the face began to serve artists as the crucial indicator. Thus the Bolognese and Bernini accepted "the primacy of facial mimicry in the representation of emotions,"[66] and artists by the eighteenth century began to use the play of facial expressions as a tool of psychological analysis.

Hogarth's revolutionary achievement was to create a lingua franca for psychological art. His accomplishment went far beyond a heightened mastery of facial reactions: "It is only in Hogarth that this type of human description takes on universal significance; finding its richest form in those prints in which the artist represents people singing[,] laughing or listening to a lecture."[67] For Hogarth the secret of portraiture lay in capturing outbursts of human spontaneity: "For spontaneous expression distorts man and unmasks him in the distortion."[68] Psychology became the great equalizer: "He shows us [how] man en masse lets himself go, how the similarity of reaction has a levelling effect: man is robbed of his rank and composure, he is just one man laughing amongst many."[69]

A throng, helpless with laughter, appeared on the subscription tickets for *A Rake's Progress*, the "curtain-raiser to a sequence of pictures which he wanted to be viewed as tableaux from the stage."[70] In that series of prints, elite society became the stage performers and the crowd their audience—necessary observers of the social drama, but transfixed, confined, and immobilized by it. For Hogarth, the crowd as an object of psychological study demonstrated the liberating effects of inward release and the rich diversity of emotional responses. Its social function, however, had to be limited to that of an astute and receptive audience.

Among the satirists who succeeded Hogarth, Thomas Rowlandson also located in crowds the extremes of human emotion from hilarity to sorrow. Yet, Rowlandson emphasized above all else the presence of untamed avarice and wild fear. As Kris and Gombrich stated, "he too unmasks mass-man, but his unmasking serves to reveal not only the absurdity but also the innate ugliness of the human being."[71] Rather than replicate Leonardo's "experiments of the scientific artist,"[72] Rowlandson implemented "Swift's vision of the Yahoos."[73] For him, the grimace represented not the exception in human emotion but the psychological norm: "The art of Rowlandson might be summarised in the notion that the noble expression of the human face is artificial, a fake. It is only genuine where the elemental breaks through in the form of the ugly."[74] Rowlandson's caricatures depicted the crowd not as the audience of a grand spectacle but as the arena of the grotesque.

Psychological art found a necessary corrective in the work of Daumier, whose crowds expressed more than spontaneous catharsis or repulsive excess. His masses exhibited a shared pathos: "In Daumier too, all people in extreme situations are similar, yet not only similarly comic, but also similarly pathetic—similarly great."[75]

Like Benesch, both Kris and Gombrich stressed Daumier's perception of the crowd as heroic. Far surpassing Rowlandson as both a collective psychologist and group portraitist, Daumier recognized that the so-called mob embodied a common fate: "The Daumier crowd poseeses [sic] a p[a]thos to itself . . . In this he transcends Rowlandson."[76] Crowds revealed not merely the comic or grotesque extremes of emotional behavior but, more importantly, the core of psychological suffering: "He is the contemporary of the great naturalists in literature, of Balzac, Flaubert and Zola, for whom not only comedy, but also tragedy knows no more social boundaries. Daumier alone can claim this position."[77]

But his images conveyed not only empathy for the supposedly disreputable masses but also insight into what passed for reputable behavior in the bourgeoisie. Carefully worked out angles of illumination revealed the switch nature of the bourgeois countenance, as astute contemporaries recognized:

> The greatness od [of] Daumier and his role as a critic of the contemporary social scene has nowhere been better described than by the Journal (for March 13 1865) of the Goncourt brothers: "I saw the other day, apssing [sic] by Rue Lafitte, some magnificent Daumier watercolours representing panathenaeas of the judiciary, lawyers' meetings, and judges' processions against pale backgrounds, illuminated by the sinister glare of an examining magistrate's study, by the grey light of a corridor in the Law courts. They are treated with fantastically spectral washes of Chinese ink. The heads are hideous, with a frightening ribaldry and gleefulness. These black men have some of the ugliness of repulsive antique masks, in the record-office. The smiling solicitors have a corybantian air, there is something of

> the faun in these macabre lawyers." The switch-character of the satire has surely never been seized with greater precision.[78]

As in the later art of photography, manipulation of light could be enough to reconfigure the elements and reveal the truths that resided within the bourgeois mask of respectability.

Just as Daumier mastered light, so Hogarth mastered staging. And in his universal theater, he relied on character masks for his psychological portraits. Reproducing the switch between stage and stalls, spectator and actor, his drawings transformed middle-class theater-goers into figures on stage, where their behavior became the object of public scrutiny and the stuff of comedy: "The 18th century brings these actors into the auditorium itself."[79] Hogarth rejected what he saw as the forced, artificial instruments of caricature in favor of the ironic, unguarded potentials of theater. He constructed his scenes and positioned his performers with the eye not of a caricaturist but a moralist: "comic unmasking of the men about him is not the essential purpose of his art, for the didactic is foremost."[80]

Hogarth's genius consisted in revealing his subjects' personalities even as they kept their masks in place and performed their accustomed roles. As Kris and Gombrich explained:

> Hogarth accordingly creates the portrait of his figures the way an actor makes his mask: he represents them in their "character"—and it is no coincidence that this word bears in English the dual sense of "role" and "personal psychology".[81]

Hogarth contended that the childlike distortions and irrational exaggerations of caricature detracted from art's moral purpose and psychological effectiveness: "He therefore condemns *caricatura* which makes jokes instead of interpretations of character."[82] Hogarth made his point in the subscription tickets to *Marriage à la mode* on which "various Hogarthian heads are confronted with caricatures from Ghezzi and

Carracci, but also with heads from Raphael's Cartoons as examples of Character."[83] Whereas Daumier's experiments culminated in the political broadsheet, Hogarth's ended in the clinical case study and moral tale.

Beyond serving as a medium of political protest and instrument of psychological investigation, caricature in the modern sense for Kris and Gombrich eventually came to represent a technique of visual perception. In the nineteenth century, the citizen of Geneva Rodolphe Töpffer moved caricature in this third direction—away from physical distortions and toward elemental formulas. Töpffer borrowed a reductionist style from graphic arts and simplified it as far as possible to a few strokes, lines, and points: "The outline drawing, the 'trait graphique', represents the essence of things by suppressing all subsidiary matter."[84] The viewer's imagination built upon a schematic design to construct a fuller image: "'trait graphique' allows one to guess at what it omits; while in a fully-fledged picture every gap in representation is disturbing, in the schematic drawing the observer assists the draughtsman; he completes the drawing."[85]

Töpffer's caricatures not only recalled the efforts of Bernini but also anticipated the findings of Gestalt psychology: "Every line which we see before us can be taken as a sign in the context of an expressive system."[86] The Swiss artist in fact transformed his artistic program into a laboratory test. He drew a series of facial expressions—"schematic masks of human faces"[87]—which he varied slightly from face to face and which he presented to diverse observers, gauging the effect of his variations on the viewer's perceptions. Through such tests, as Kris and Gombrich described, "he tries in general to explain the emergence of various expressions in the picture by pointing to the conditions under which we interpret expression, and showing us just how few signs determine the character of an expression."[88] Although they sought to identify certain irreducible components of perception, Töpffer's experiments instead demonstrated the inherently variable, unstable quality of human expression and communication.

The nineteenth-century German caricaturist Wilhelm Busch deliberately exploited that instability. In his portraits of Napoleon, Busch pictured the French emperor's downfall through the metamorphosis of his face from momentous triumph at Austerlitz to final defeat at Waterloo, "revealing one by one the formative elements of the head, or the constituent elements of his expression."[89] The intrinsic malleability of the human face exposed, even foretold, Napoleon's reversal of fortune: "The comic effect here relies on the ease of changeability, on the lability of expression."[90] Busch took advantage of this lability both to present a cautionary tale and to readjust his audience's perception:

> We find thereby a perfect, dual realisation of the potential latent from the beginnings of caricature: first, the victim's face has become a true formula. For the Carracci and Bernini, this reduction to formula was a device for unmasking; it has now become a teachable essence in the literal sense. Second, and more important, we now reach a climax of the "process" of caricature as already described. By this we meant that caricature gives direction for seeing, initiates a visual re-interpretation ("Umsehen"). Here we are invited to pass from visual reinterpretation to visual re-creation.[91]

Caricature derived not only from the visual depiction produced on the illustrator's page but also from the mental picture constructed by the audience. Only the observer's psychological working through of the image conferred on the portrait its momentary stability.

Here caricature drawing converged with the modernist conception of art as technical construct. Rather than offer falsely unified products, it instead presented the visual components from which the beholder could piece together authentic images. It promoted the technique of "turning the picture into a mental exercise"[92] and ultimately gave that method universality in cartoon illustrations and graphic stories. In keeping with Freud's "theory of wit, when the essential remains unspoken,"[93] cartoons relied on schematized pictures that left as much as possible to the imagination. Audiences enjoyed filling in the missing elements of the scene or story. Thus, after the political journal and the psychological portrait, the "dissemination of the simplified cartoon-style is the third reason for the expansion of the concept of 'caricature'."[94] But unlike Daumier, the twentieth-century caricaturist no longer attempted to integrate political critique and psychological analysis with technical invention.

Kris and Gombrich worked and wrote in what they described as "a historic phase in the development of European art, the great stylistic crisis of Expressionism."[95] That crisis overwhelmed caricature art, just as modernist artistic currents swept away the original Renaissance experiment. Expressionists approached all reality as a mask of inward truth:

> If art is not an imitation of the real world, but purely an expression of its inner processes, it becomes meaningless to differentiate between summary and detailed representation. The work of the more extreme Expressionists blurs for us once again (and now deliberately) the boundary between the comic and the serious. Before the poems of the Dadaists or the drawings of a Paul Klee or Max Ernst, the question of the boundary of intentional, i.e. comic distortion becomes again meaningless. This is not intended in a critical sense, but as a statement of a historical situation. The introverted imagery of Expressionism is fed from other sources, draws closer to man's unconscious mind. Without wishing to interpret this phenomenon any further, let us summarise our thesis: many features of comic art are exploited by Expressionism, to the extent that a bra[n]ch of art becomes a movement of art.[96]

The methods of caricature merged with Expressionist techniques. Only the reduction and reconfiguration of reality could convey essential truths.

Outside the world of art, advertising posters now replaced broadsheets as the illustrators of daily life. Marketeers exploited the schematic formulas of caricature to attract an audience's attention:

> In much advertising imagery, simplification is pushed to the limit. For all the precursors discovered by the histories of advertising, the poster-designer of today is faced with a new task. The artist is often obliged to simplify, inviting the question "what is represented here? (What product are they trying to sell?)" This question may not remain with us for more than a fraction of a second, for the success of the advertisement depends on the immediate solubility of the problem. Simplification here serves as an eye-catcher, contributing a momentarily unsolved image which requires completion. The poster has be[c]ome [a] picture-puzzle.[97]

Once modern caricaturists had transformed image making into a mental exercise, advertisers remade the exercise into a business strategy, grafting it onto the narrow and tendentious aims of salesmanship. And as illustration sacrificed its documentary and critical content, the political mission of caricature, as epitomized by Daumier, lost its vitality and direction.[98]

Thus the twentieth century brought not the triumph but rather the disappearance of caricature both as an independent visual form and as a call to radical action. But the end came differently in art and politics. In art, the experiment underwent an apotheosis. Expressionists adopted caricature's stylistic innovations and incorporated them into a more extensive and more profound artistic rebellion. In politics, modern marketing and political engineering co-opted caricature's techniques, leading the civic experiment into the netherworlds of advertising and propaganda.

The Fate of Political Art

The experiment that had reached its apogee with Daumier had by the early twentieth century run its course: caricature ceased to exist as an independent political and artistic phenomenon. In the fifth and final chapter, "The Theory of Caricature," Kris and Gombrich considered whether caricature, having lost its creative and critical function in art and politics, could still claim psychological significance.

From Carracci's notebook to Daumier's sculptures and lithographs, caricaturists had de-idealized not only the outward persona but also the ego that hid within it. The exaggeration of facial or bodily features, by creating a disproportion between parts, "enacts a dissolution of the totality of the person, the difference in physical dimension standing for its destruction."[99] Thus, on the eve of the Second World War, the British caricaturist David Low depicted Hitler as only forelock and moustache:

> Nothing is exaggerated, but the isolation of a characteristic which is made to stand for the whole person, means an unmasking in the most vivid sense: this man is nothing but nose, he is nothing but monocle and forelock. These externals make up the whole man, therein lies his power, it is as easy as that to imitate or replace the powerful.[100]

By reconfiguring the ego's mask, the caricaturist reconfigured its identity, a psychological procedure that began when Carracci remade human visages with animal-like features and Bernini reinvented human faces from a single expression:

> When we next see the victim in life, the memory of the caricature makes us laugh, for we find ourselves changing him back again in the spirit of the caricature. The caricaturist has achieved his uttermost goal, he has appropriated his victim's real-life appearance; the man drags the caricature after him, he is bewitched.[101]

Just as Callot transformed a living personality into a stage figure, the modern caricaturist remolded the subject's face into an altered persona. The audience welded that new visage into an iron mask.

The complicity between artist and audience reanimated the visceral emotional power of image magic. Here Kris and Gombrich followed both Freud and Warburg in giving fundamental psychological significance to visual signs: "The image has greater archetypal value than the word . . . Magical beliefs cling longest to the image, and image-magic is still alive in the thinking of sophisticated man."[102]

The mutability of the human countenance allowed caricaturists to reassemble—even disassemble—a supposedly coherent persona:

> The practice of magic in the portrait as performed by caricature exploits the great mobility of physiognomic impression. The line which turns laughing into weeping can twist the portrait round. This lability of expression (familiar to students of the psychology of perception) appears in caricature as evidence for the artist's power of control. With a single stroke, the transformation is effected, the similarity created or destroyed.[103]

The game that had begun in late Renaissance Bologna initiated an unpredictable, variegated experiment with inherently ambiguous, unstable images.

In its urge to control volatile powers, art replicated and ultimately spiritualized magical practice: such had been Warburg's interpretation of Renaissance culture. For Kris and Gombrich, portrait caricature reconfirmed his account. The invention of caricature marked the final decline of pagan magic and the opening of a new period of artistic innovation. As subjects and viewers lost their fear of image magic, they began to take pleasure in caricature. Kris and Gombrich interpreted the change as the conclusion of a three-stage, psycho-historical process. At the stage of primitive image magic, "the hostile action is performed on the person through the image."[104] Subsequently, effigies or defamatory images became substitutes for the persons depicted, and aggression became redirected toward images alone. With the Renaissance, image-makers finally channeled the aggressive drive into play with form, into the manipulation of symbols, and into the reconfiguration of masks. Caricature therefore represented "a step in detachment from the magical associations of art."[105] But such detachment remained tinged with ambivalence, as the lure and fear of image magic persisted as unconscious elements of art.

The decline of magic alone, however, did not account for the emergence of caricature in the late Renaissance: the rise of Mannerism proved essential. The Cinquecento origins of caricature brought to mind Dvořák's lectures on Mannerist art, and when they described those origins, Kris and Gombrich revived his art history as the history of ideas. To give visual representation to the internal, invisible world of the self, Mannerists developed new rules of artistic creation, free from the constraints of external likeness:

> Something has changed in the figurative arts, not only in style or in form, but in its whole purpose. This becomes evident if one compares a Cinquecento sketchbook, which may contain visions, compositions, private visions of scribblings, with skecthbooks [sic] of earlier times. If the medieval pattern-book represents the repertory of tradition, and the Quattrocento sketchbook a utilitarian repertory of pictorial reality, one may, roughly, speak of the Mannerist sketchbook as a repertory of the possible. The work of art is more detached from reality, not because it is less true to reality, but because it opposes reality with a world of its own. This general and essential feature of Mannerism, which has constantly been stressed in all the recent books on the subject since it was first emphasised by Dvorak [sic], takes on a particular significance with the precursors of caricature. The deliberate ambiguity of form which makes a visual game of seeing, which consciously exercises the beholder's power of perception, demonstrates this new level of freedom: a given picture is no longer a sign of reality, no longer imitation or prescribed ornament, but a playing with form in itself. This does not invoke external models, or iconographical substance, but the human imagination, the dream itself. This new world of themes is called "Sogni", "Traumwerk", "Songes Drolatiques". The appearance of a tenet of

> Chinese art-theory in Quattrocento Europe, with Leonardo and others recommending the artist to exercise the imagination on chance configurations, is the preparatory stage to this inner freedom vis-à-vis the object. Peeling walls, clouds and stains are visually transfigured by the artist. They are occasions for the projection of inner visions. Caricature may be seen as the last step along this path. It is now the most concrete form, the external appearance of an individual which can occasion the artist to substitute for it the inner image evoked in him by this man. Just as he can heroise his subject in the idealised portrait, he can render him in comic distortion for purposes of aggressive criticism.[106]

Dvořák's interpretation of Mannerism affirmed Kris and Gombrich's account of the evolution of caricature. In the age of the Carracci—the time of Shakespeare's Prospero—caricaturists channeled the aggressive and power-seeking impulses of image magic into artistic independence and invention. Thereafter, in the age of Hogarth, they turned to a psychological analysis of the mutability and volatility in human expression and perception. Finally, in the era of Daumier, they developed the full potential of caricature as a political tool. From Carracci to Hogarth to Daumier, from art to psychology to politics: points that defined the logic and history of modern caricature also marked Kris and Gombrich's personal and intellectual paths.

After the First World War, the sharp split in caricature became increasingly visible, producing on the one hand a remote depoliticized art and on the other a dangerous demagogic weapon. As an experiment with artistic technique, it merged with the reductionist, introspective tendency in modernist art:

> On the level of abstraction provided by Bernini, caricature might be termed timeless; the less "disegno" it contains, the mote [more] it approaches Hogarth's formula of "dot and line", "the purer" it is, the nearer it comes to what may be considered the "ideal type" of caricature.

> This ideal type is no longer an historically determined work of art, but the graphic crystallisation of a psychic process.[107]

But as a political instrument, caricature thrived in the arenas of crowds and propagandists, where defamatory images served the aims of emotional and ideological manipulation. In such forums the necessary condition for art had ceased to exist: "This condition palses [passes] when a social group acts en masse and regresses toward primitive modes of behavior; we know only too well how this happens in our own times."[108] Yet, the nature of caricature itself—as a plea for creative complicity with the audience and as a vision of control over its target—lent itself to demagogy:

> Every game with words is a game with conventional signs, while the game with forms is a game with the thing itself. That is why the relationship with the legacies of magic is inherent in all caricature, particularly in the participation it invites of the beholder. By completing the act of seeing we experience for ourselves the caricaturist's achievement. [W]e win with him, with his transformation, power over his victim.[109]

Whereas modernist artists used caricature to explore universal components of vision, contemporary propagandists wielded it to perform image magic: "The propaganda value of caricature is thus particularly marked, for it stands nearer to action than all forms of verbal comedy."[110] Caricature in the twentieth century had broken into two opposing identities: an ethereal mental pursuit and a profane demagogic activity.

In the 1936 exhibition catalog, Kris had written that Daumier's comic art had compelled viewers to see themselves and their own social world as they actually existed. In the book manuscript, he and Gombrich now described the need for a new Callot or Daumier, for artists who used caricature to combat false idealizations. But the manuscript's final pages expressed little confidence that contemporary caricaturists would recover Callot and Daumier's comic purpose, artistic legitimacy, and critical spirit. In the closing paragraph of *Caricature*, they wrote: "No justification of caricature as art has ever quite succeeded. Like all forms of the comic, it stands at the edge of art."[111]

Masters of magical techniques, most caricaturists never fully justified their reductionist or destructive aims. Only those committed to a transformative vision intuited the full creative potential of caricature. In his pure allegiance to classical form and his absolute commitment to documentary content, Daumier had created the republican hybrid: political artwork that was true art. He readjusted his audiences' perceptions by helping them to see their accepted views of society as distortions. Caricature held up a corrective, not cracked, mirror to reality. To recover its purpose as political art, it had to revert to what it had been in Renaissance Bologna and Daumier's Paris: a classical experiment of the street.

The caricature manuscript offered, in Gombrich's phrase, a model of integration, one that approached image making and creative experimentation as evolving processes moved by intersecting and conflicting currents from art, psychology, and politics. Grounded in the Freudian principle of the overdetermination of meaning—now including cultural and political layers together with the psychological—it provided not only a language that bridged psychoanalytic and cognitive psychologies but also an awareness of the problems and methods that linked the humanities, the mental sciences, and the social sciences.

As depth psychology and art theory, *Caricature* identified the conflicting impulses of aggression and restitution that drove artistic experimentation from one period to the next. As ego psychology and art history, it traced artistic innovation as a ceaseless search for stable frameworks of cognition and vision. As a cultural history covering diverse media and images, it located the sources and aims of experimental activity not only in the studio and salon but also on the stage and in the city. Finally, it took into account how, especially at moments of crisis, societal conditions and political realities influenced artistic, technical, and cultural innovation. The rebellion within classicism started as a game with portraiture but became an experiment with politics. It merged symbolic, documentary, and critical imagery, giving rise to a civic art and a universal language capable of responding to the disintegrative effects of crisis. Yet by 1900, mutually reinforcing tendencies of self-isolation and public demagogy undermined it.

Kris and Gombrich's conclusion that caricature culminated with Daumier and only began to recover its potential with Low reflected their judgment that it had all but lost its direction in Germany and Austria after 1900. German Expressionists embraced caricature but only to incorporate it within their psychological art, while nationalist, anti-Semitic movements transformed it according to their own demonologies. The book manuscript did not track these post-1900 developments in any detail. Rather, Kris and Gombrich would do so a few years later, when they worked as political analysts for the Allied war effort.

The manuscript's most dynamic, intriguing, and innovative themes—that the truth of personality hid within and not behind the mask, that visual and mental images possessed a switch character, and that gesture, expression, and perception were fluid, volatile phenomena—represented in crucial part immediate responses to the corrosive, deteriorating conditions in Vienna. At the museum and university, Kris and Gombrich recognized the switch character in the faces of colleagues and professors. And they could see in the labile countenances of Austro-Fascist politicians and their supporters the grinning, grotesque masks known since ancient times.

Looking back on his training as a chemist in the late 1930s, Primo Levi recalled in *The Periodic Table* the moment when he realized the vital importance of chemical impurities. Pure zinc, he discovered, did not react with sulfuric acid; only impurity elicited the reaction that created zinc sulfate. Levi drew the political and moral conclusion, presented as a dialogue with himself:

> In order for the wheel to turn, for life to be lived, impurities are needed, and the impurities of impurities in the soil, too, as is known,

> if it is to be fertile. Dissension, diversity, the grain of salt and mustard are needed: Fascism does not want them, forbids them, and that's why you're not a Fascist; it wants everybody to be the same, and you are not. But immaculate virtue does not exist either, or if it exists it is detestable.[112]

More than a century before Levi wrote those words, Daumier exalted the *bella deformità*, the *grano salis*, as the universal language of republicanism. His and Levi's insight marked the authentic culmination of the Bolognese experiment.

The story of caricature that Kris and Gombrich wrote from 1934 to 1937 moved from a study in the psychology of art to a study of republican political culture. The story's conclusion came when caricature, serving as a tool of marketeers and propagandists, became a source of advertising formulas and demagogic typologies. Ceasing to document social and political realities, it failed to preserve or integrate its life-giving impurities. And when it lost its vital links to republicanism, it ceased functioning as an ever evolving artistic innovation. The symbiosis broke down and it became a deadened and deadening form. As a record of that story, however, the caricature manuscript itself remained an experimental grain of salt, a *bella deformità*, within a Vienna that now tried to dissolve all irritants within a new national body.

CHAPTER 6

FROM VIENNA TO LONDON AND NEW YORK 1938–41

Leaving the Museum

In May 1937, Kris traveled to England to present a paper on caricature at the Warburg Institute, the first public presentation of his joint work with Gombrich. A year later, he would return to England as an exile from Vienna, hoping to make London his permanent residence, the Warburg reading room his workshop, and British psychoanalytic circles his new professional community.

When Kris arrived at the Warburg Institute in 1937, no prospect existed for publishing the caricature book on the European Continent. Saxl had expressed a desire to promote it and in his presentation Kris emphasized points that met the interests of Saxl and his fellow listeners. Warburg's study of Botticelli and Freud's analysis of Shakespeare's *King Lear* had interpreted Renaissance artworks as hybrid products—compounds of magical thinking, symbolic imagery, and humanist criticism—and Kris adopted a similar perspective. Focusing on the relation between the emergence of caricature and the decline of magic, the paper sketched the development of caricature from the Carracci and Bernini to Hogarth and the eighteenth-century English satirists. Yet, in the following year, it appeared under Kris and Gombrich's names not in the Warburg journal but rather in the pages of the *British Journal of Medical Psychology*, which provided an outlet in Britain for Freudian ideas. Kris might have had several reasons for placing the article here: his concern that Saxl not feel pressured into accepting a psychoanalytic contribution, Saxl's own hesitation, or Kris's simultaneous efforts, as seen in earlier letters to Saxl, to create a bridge between the Freudian community and the Warburg circle in London.

Psychoanalysts within the British Psychological Society had spearheaded the creation of the *British Journal of Medical Psychology* in 1920. At the time of Kris's Warburg presentation, John Rickman served as its editor, while Ernest Jones acted as an editorial advisor. A Quaker, Rickman joined the Friends' War Victims Relief Unit in Russia after completing his medical training in 1916. A friend and colleague of William H. R. Rivers, the eminent Cambridge neurologist and anthropologist who applied Freud's theories to the treatment of war neuroses, Rickman acquired a broad psychiatric training before gravitating toward psychoanalysis and undertaking sessions with both Freud in Vienna and Jones in London. Freud urged Jones to find a role for Rickman in England and by the 1930s he had become a leading figure in the British psychoanalytic community.[1]

Publishing in Rickman's journal allowed Kris to associate the caricature project more directly with Freud. As a result, the article's preface sounded a far different note than the foreword to the book manuscript:

> With the turn of the century came a new means of grasping the ways in which the mind plays with elements of sensory experience and out of them shapes new patterns. Freud's *Interpretation of Dreams* (1913) marks a turning point in the history of aesthetics just as it does in psychiatry.[2]

Psychoanalysis offered a scientific perspective that possessed the unity and integrity of an artwork:

> In passing it might be noted as one of the aesthetic pleasures of psychoanalytic research that a study such as this which starts out as a survey of pictures of a bygone time may throw some light on the problems of the clinician to-day—there are no boundaries in science, and in none, perhaps, do we meet with so many cross-illuminations as in psychology—the science of the integration of sensation, perception, and desire.[3]

The article further explained that the study of caricature relied on Panofsky's insight into the role of ideas in art history. Caricaturists sought the Platonic Ideas—the true realities—hidden within external appearances. Portraitists accomplished that aim by *re-forming* their vision of the world; caricaturists achieved the same goal by *de-forming* it:

> By the seventeenth century the portrait painter's task was to reveal character, the essence of the man in an heroic sense. The caricaturist has a corresponding aim. He does not seek the perfect *form* but the perfect *deformity*, thus penetrating through the mere outward appearance to the inner being in all its littleness and ugliness.[4]

The Neo-Platonic mission altered neither the aggressive nature of caricature nor its fundamental reductionism: "The deeper sense of such an action is obvious: by singling out and reproducing an outstanding part of a personality, we destroy its unity, its individuality."[5]

In this more strongly Freudian essay, Bernini's line drawings and the work of Hogarth, who stressed the necessity of primitive simplification and absence of design, became the chief touchstones for interpreting caricature. "Even now," the article stated, "caricature has its strongest effect in reduction, in formulae"[6]—and they cited David Low's caricatures of politicians as the clearest evidence. In an earlier century, Mannerism had encouraged such imaginative abstraction, and under its influence art became conceived as a mental sketch projected onto the external world:

> The work of art is—for the first time in European history—considered as a *projection* of an inner image. It is not its proximity to reality that proves its value but its nearness to the artist's psychic life. Thus for the first time the sketch was held in high esteem as the most direct document of inspiration. Here is the beginning of the development which culminates in the attempts of expressionism and surrealism to make art a mirror of the artist's conscious or unconscious.[7]

The practice of image magic receded and "play with forms"[8] replaced it. Ambiguous hybrids of human and non-human features culminated in Philipon and Daumier's nineteenth-century pear—"a catchword, a symbol in the battle of the French people for their freedom"[9]—and in Low's contemporary political animals.

Although caricature recalled image magic in its power to reconfigure the viewer's "memory-picture,"[10] Freudian psychology showed that, as with jokes, the caricature already existed within the picture. The primary process, wrote Kris and Gombrich, "cannot produce a joke which is not hidden in the language. Neither can the caricaturist follow his arbitrary will alone. He is bound to follow the rule of his language, which is form."[11]

The aggressive and reductionist techniques of caricature built upon a learned, experimental process:

> This innermost primitiveness in style as well as in mechanism, in tendency as well as in form, is the secret of the caricature's appeal. Here, too, the pretext of humour has first conceded what nowadays seems to have conquered a vast field of modern art. But it has since, perhaps, become clear how artificial is this primitiveness and with what difficulty it was acquired.[12]

Caricature could be interpreted both as a liberating psychological transformation—a regression in the service of the ego—and as an acquired mental construct. Kris and Gombrich made reference to French republicanism in the article, but they left full discussion of political art to the book manuscript, stating only:

> This paper is based on a lecture given by Dr Kris at the Warburg Institute on 25 May 1937. A book on the same subject by the lecturer and Dr Gombrich is in course of preparation. Many questions which are only touched on here will be dealt with fully in the book.[13]

In September and October 1937, the *Kunsthistorisches Museum* presented Kris's last exhibition in Vienna, titled simply *Forged Artworks*. As he described in the catalog, forgery thrived in periods when the public, out of hostility to its own artists, exalted artists of the past. Relying on that exaltation, forgers exploited the "passion for collecting."[14] In the late Roman world, copyists plied their trade among patrons who, scorning imperial art, sought objects from the Greek past. The modern bourgeoisie—committed to eclectic, historical revivals—created an avid market for forgeries: "in art, it was the fate of the consciously retrospective nineteenth century to be presented with forgeries of all those periods which it pretended to reanimate."[15] The bourgeois desire to live vicariously through art became symptomatic of an age that sustained itself through falsity.

How then could art specialists and the public recognize and appreciate authenticity? "The forms of forgery are always new," Kris warned, "and always new must be the means of their unmasking."[16] What could the museum curator bring to the task? Investigating and exhibiting the extent and power of artifice remained possible but led inexorably—like all art history—to disillusionment: "Every piece [of forgery] attempts to cover a treacherous nakedness [*eine verräterische Blösse*], and the society of other 'unmasked objects' is thereby no succor, but creates only an even more sobering atmosphere."[17] A treacherous nakedness. The term brought to mind Austrian politicians and jurists who claimed that they defended the republic by bringing the *Vaterländische Front* to power, churchmen who asserted that they protected the soul of man by siding with authoritarian movements, and scholars who claimed that they advanced the study of art by exposing its supposedly degenerate tendencies.[18] Surrounded by unmasked figures from his workplace and city, Kris's exhibition of forged art conveyed his farewell message to the museum and to his Viennese public.

The End of the Republic

In 1938, the *Anschluss* with Germany destroyed the remaining republican façade in Austria. In the final, crucial hours, the European powers failed to provide necessary support from the outside, but by that time Austria's Christian Social party, as well as large segments of the population, had deserted the republic from within. Politicians and citizens now poured forth to welcome Hitler. Crowds in Vienna's *Heldenplatz* and intellectuals in places such as the art historical institute joined together in proclaiming the end of the republican era. When Hitler entered Vienna in March, Theodor Cardinal Innitzer allowed Viennese churches to sound their bells and display the swastika. He supported the circulation of a pastoral letter calling on Austrians to approve the *Anschluss* in the April plebiscite and appended to it his own epistle, signed with "Heil Hitler." Like Seyss-Inquart, the new Austrian chancellor, Innitzer regarded attachment to a Greater Germany as the long hoped-for opportunity to secure a Catholic Austrian state in central Europe and to rid Austria of the socialist threat. During the *Anschluss*, he extended protection to Jews who had converted to Catholicism but refused assistance to the unconverted and offered no word of protest against Nazi violence directed against them.[19] At the university, Sedlmayr announced his support for *Anschluss* in a scholarly festschrift and concluded the declaration with his own "Heil Hitler."[20]

In the Gombrich family, the *Anschluss* aroused concern for the fate of Lisbeth Gombrich. Karl and Leonie Gombrich recognized that their younger daughter, as an active socialist, faced immediate danger. A

Swiss piano student of Leonie Gombrich—and a former competitor for the hand of Ilse Heller—promised to accompany Lisbeth across the border into Switzerland. The day after the *Anschluss*, she left Austria. Her parents, however, persisted in the conviction that they and their older daughter Amadea could survive in Vienna. Their determination to remain did not alter until the Gestapo called Leonie Gombrich in for questioning, during which it became clear to her that the state police had intercepted and read her private letters. After returning home, she decided that the family must leave Austria.[21]

On the day of the *Anschluss*, Kris resigned his position with the museum's sculpture and applied art collection. Museum authorities pressed him to change his mind and stay on as curator, and later, when he was brought before the police, he was given to understand that political authorities would not interfere with the museum's offer. Kris refused it.[22] In May, two months following the *Anschluss*, he, his wife, and their two children departed Vienna. He had the British consul's office notify Saxl of their imminent arrival in London. On May 6, 1938, the consulate telegrammed the Warburg Institute, "Your friends arriving Monday 16.20 Victoria Station" and requested that the institute "Advise Dr. Ernest Jones."[23] Following Freud's recommendation, Kris had remained in his curator's job until political circumstances forced him to leave.

Seeking a Public in London

Unlike many émigré scholars, Kris and Gombrich could tap a potential public in London—but an audience still, perhaps, unaware of its own existence. From 10 March to 6 April 1939—the weeks during which Hitler occupied Czechoslovakia—the Anglo-French Art and Travel Society and its sister organization, the *Comité de l'Association Art et Tourisme*, sponsored an "Exhibition of a Century of French Caricature 1750–1850 with some English Caricatures of the Napoleonic Period" at the New Burlington Galleries. The previous year, the same association had exhibited in Paris a selection of English caricatures.

The return display of French caricature in London emphasized the ties that now bound the two countries. With two hundred and forty-two French caricatures, the size of the show approached that of Kris's Daumier exhibition. The curator of the print collection at the *Bibliothèque Nationale*, P. A. Lemoisne—who had provided Kris with prints for the Viennese exhibition—wrote an introduction for the catalog. Highlighting caricature's non-revolutionary impulses and downplaying its republican instincts, Lemoisne emphasized the influence of Hogarth, Rowlandson, and the English satirists on French caricature—especially "the caricature of manners."[24] The London exhibition displayed the work of Philipon, Daumier, and their colleagues at *La Caricature* and *Le Charivari*, but Lemoisne derided their politics, describing their caricatures as "drawings of obvious artistic value and of biting satirical power, but of such violence that Louis-Philippe, in spite of his liberalism, was compelled to restrain a liberty which too often degenerated into licence."[25] Daumier's artistic ability received high but qualified praise: his drawing "amplifies reality and transforms it—sometimes at the expense of his models."[26]

The cut-off date of the exhibition—1850—allowed the display of several caricatures of mid-century mores but prevented the viewing of Daumier's images of the destruction of the French republic and the spread of European militarism. Fittingly, the exhibition's French galleries concluded with a room of Dantan's sculpted, pre-revolutionary caricatures of English lords and politicians. At the moment of its appearance, the Art and Travel Society's exhibition reflected the self-contained, self-protective world of the European bourgeoisie, who even when confronted by post-Munich realities shuddered not at the specter of fascism but at the thought of republican excess—the same bourgeois world that Jean Renoir targeted in his own scathing caricature of manners, *La Règle du jeu*, which also appeared in spring 1939. The London exhibition shunned the spirit of the Popular Front that infused Kris's Daumier exhibition.

For Kris and Gombrich, the Warburg circle represented the genuine audience for their caricature project. Perhaps they believed that Kris's presentation at the institute in 1937 confirmed Saxl's intent to publish their book, but when Saxl finally faced the decision, he delayed. Gombrich recalled: "He gave it to someone else to read, who was against psychoanalysis."[27]

Another opportunity appeared. Penguin Books invited Gombrich to write a volume for its King Penguin series. Working from the unpublished manuscript, Gombrich composed a highly abbreviated history of caricature and included Kris's name with his own on the title page; as he recalled, "although I wrote it alone, the book really had two authors."[28] Also titled *Caricature*, it proved to be their only book publication on the topic.

The publisher of Penguin Books, Allen Lane, began to commission King Penguins a year before the war and chose Elizabeth Senior from the British Museum as the first series editor. Modeled on a collection printed by Insel Verlag in Germany, King Penguins were hardbound, pamphlet-sized art books that included color illustrations and cost only a shilling. Appearing originally in November 1939, King Penguins quickly became a popular wartime series. Print-runs averaged 20,000 copies.[29]

Kris and Gombrich's slim volume—twenty-seven pages of text, with sixteen color plates and nineteen black-and-white illustrations—appeared in 1940. It traced the background of caricature to Greek vase paintings and travesties of mythic heroes, all of which exposed the "contrast between crude reality and lofty idealism."[30] Mimicry—as seen in grotesques and effigies—combined comedy, derision, and aggression: "To copy a person, to mimic his behavior, means to annihilate his individuality."[31] Caricature art could emerge in the age of the Carracci and Bernini because fear of mimicry had begun to lose its hold over the mind:

> We think that portrait caricature was not practiced earlier because of the dire power it was felt to possess; out of unconscious fear of its effect. Before caricature as an art could be born, mankind had to become mentally free enough to accept this distortion of an image as an artistic achievement and not as a dangerous practice.[32]

Hogarth distanced caricature even further from physical mimicry by linking his masks of personality to roles within society: "the figures in his pictures are actors who are meant to express in their outward appearance the parts they have to play."[33]

Gillray and Rowlandson took the next step by aiming their art specifically at those who enacted roles on the political stage. What began with ancient travesties culminated with Daumier, who created an art that "far transcends any such division as that of the ridiculous to the sublime."[34]

The contemporary style of caricature and comic illustration—the style that characterized Edward Lear and Max Beerbohm, as well as Töpffer and Busch—sought to "simplify the world and reduce its representation to an easy game."[35] Through the old magic or the new style, caricature continued to attract a public, to whom it offered a playful and controlled release of aggression. The King Penguin book ended with a psychoanalytic conclusion: Freud had shown that jokes released unconscious impulses through word games; caricature offered the same release through play with images.

The book received four brief reviews. Three of them—by Clive Bell in the *New Statesman and Nation*, John Piper in *The Spectator*, and an anonymous reviewer in the *Times Literary Supplement*—focused on the book chiefly as an example of what to expect from the King Penguin series. Bell, the theorist of significant form in art, and Piper, the painter of architectural ruins and local landscapes, reviewed the book as a companion to Ernst Kitzinger and Elizabeth Senior's *Portraits of Christ*, which King Penguin issued at the same time as *Caricature*. Both Bell and Piper praised Penguin's effort to provide the broad reading public with an affordable source of color prints and both deplored the quality of the reproductions. Their reactions to Kris and Gombrich's book, however, reflected separate cultural concerns.

Tapping new audiences remained the heart of the King Penguin mission and Bell urged Allen Lane, Elizabeth Senior, and the King Penguin authors to rally the public against the twin evil of the private film industry and government-sponsored mass culture. The hopeless, rearguard nature of his cause seems to have made it all the more appealing to Bell:

> If the Penguin publishers really intend to issue a series of short, readable, illustrated monographs at a shilling each, edited and written by scholars and people of taste, it is just possible they will arouse such interest in visual art that when that government comes into power which is to decree the conversion of all picture galleries and museums to movie-houses there will be quite a brisk opposition.[36]

Bell searched artworks for their defining form and he examined Kris and Gombrich's book, as well as Kitzinger and Senior's, for what they had to say about artistic technique. Depictions of Christ interested Bell far more than caricature drawings, but he did find in the caricature book "bright ideas and ingenious theories,"[37] if also some questionable art historical judgments, such as the claim that Hogarth worked from the tradition of Dutch genre painting.

John Piper evaluated the King Penguin books in light of early wartime efforts to bring art to the masses. Public institutions and private sponsors organized popular concerts, lectures, theater performances, and radio talks that both reminded the general population of the common danger and promised an oasis of normalcy. They ranged widely, from projects for historical preservation to the antifascist film documentaries of Humphrey Jennings. Piper, who before the war had already turned away from non-representational art to history and nature paintings, now depicted wartime landscapes. His paintings of the Blitz and the ruins left by German raids focused attention on the immediate threat, while his nostalgic visions of the countryside and its ancient relics satisfied a longing for quietude.[38] Supported by the War Artists' Advisory Committee (WAAC) and the Council for the Encouragement of Music and the Arts (CEMA), Piper—unlike Bell—regarded wartime mass communication as essential both to preserving the national heritage and regenerating the visual arts. A neo-Romantic concerned with how monuments from the past communicated their spirit to the present, Piper believed that both King Penguin books would strike a meaningful chord with readers: "These two books look more modest than they are, for if they are successful and if the series grows there is a chance that fine art will be disseminated by them much as the wireless disseminates fine music."[39] Yet, he regretted that the caricature volume relied too heavily on what he considered to be popular psychology. Reaching the masses was better left to the artist than to the psychoanalyst.

Like Piper, the anonymous reviewer in the *Times Literary Supplement* found the use of psychology intriguing but suspect: "The suggestion that portrait caricature was delayed by fear of its magical effect upon the victim is so ingenious that one hopes it to be true."[40] This last statement represented the furthest extent to which Bell, Piper, and the *TLS* reviewer concerned themselves with Kris and Gombrich's psychological theory.

No longer needing Saxl's urging to show his support for the caricature project, Herbert Read—the fourth reviewer—gave the King Penguin book its most thorough and serious reading. In his *Art and Society*, first published in 1937, Read had drawn attention to the identity between caricature and Expressionism. Like Kris, Read interpreted caricature as a rechanneling of aggression that required the hard-won complicity of the audience. The caricaturist and Expressionist, in his view, confronted modern spectators with unprecedented challenges:

> Expressionism lives up to its name; that is to say, it expresses the emotions of the artist at any cost—the cost being usually an exaggeration or distortion of natural appearances which borders on the grotesque. Caricature is a department of expressionism, and one which most people find no difficulty in appreciating. But when caricature is carried to the pitch and organization of a composition in oils, or a piece of sculpture, then people begin to revolt. The artist is

> no longer "appealing" to them—he is not flattering their vanities nor satisfying their super-egoistic idealism in any way.[41]

In Britain, Read became an active and outspoken advocate of the German and Austrian Expressionists, not only advancing the work of individual artists but also promoting one of the most important interwar exhibitions of Expressionist art in the English-speaking world. Held in July 1938 at the New Burlington Galleries, the London Expressionist Exhibition offered a response to the infamous 1937 Degenerate Art Exhibition in Munich, which Nazi officials had organized to demonstrate the supposed decadence of modernist art.[42] The New Burlington exhibition, which contained a significant number of Expressionist paintings, included Oskar Kokoschka's *Portrait of a Degenerate Artist.* Read had promoted Kokoschka's work in particular and eventually wrote the preface for a 1947 English-language biography. In Kokoschka he perceived what Dvořák had seen in the Expressionists after the First World War: "there is no other artist of the present time," Read stated, "so near to El Greco as Kokoschka."[43] Kokoschka's was the art of exposed, lacerated nerves, of "the mute suffering of the individual, of the person crucified on the codes of false social values."[44] It recalled not only the images of El Greco but also Goya's disasters of war. In October 1938, Read helped to bring Picasso's *Guernica* to London.[45]

Kokoschka's spirit did not strike Read as utterly foreign to British art. The Austrian's landscapes recalled Turner, who abandoned classical restraint for "a return to nature, to nature in the sense of the English landscape, a return which involved an honest attempt to render the sensations experienced in the observation of nature."[46] Turner's images of nature—a proto-Expressionist venture "to make the work of art a symbol of the artist's inner or subjective feelings"[47]—exerted a near hypnotic effect on later painters, including Piper: "Even the landscapes of John Piper, though they may be controlled by a conscious desire to make a topographical record of the scene or building, are generally inspissated with a romantic melancholy which is essentially expressionistic."[48] For

Read, the vital force in art came from subterranean, psychological drives. Piper and others tried to diminish or deny the influence of those drives; Turner, Kokoschka, the Expressionists, and the caricaturists confronted and released them.

Read's review of *Caricature* appeared in the BBC's weekly, *The Listener*. Founded in 1929, *The Listener* reached 52,000 readers during the 1930s—a total greater than the readerships of the *New Statesman and Nation* and *The Spectator* combined—but the number dropped to just below 50,000 on the eve of the war.[49] Read's review, which also covered Kitzinger and Senior's volume on portraits of Christ, praised Allen Lane for bringing color illustrations to a wide public. But he dismissed as mere grumbling any objection to the quality of the color. Lane had successfully adapted scholarly commentary to a popular format, an achievement that set him apart from other publishers: "each volume is not merely the kind of entertainment we expect to pick up on a bookstall, but also a work which every student will want to add to his library."[50]

Read demonstrated his familiarity with Kris's psychoanalytic writing and his own interest in caricature as an art form. What Piper dismissed as popular psychologizing, Read recognized as the book's critical core. He drew attention to Carracci's claim that the classical artist and caricaturist remained allied to each other in seeking and exposing the subject's true personality. Read stressed that psychological revelation and controlled aggression linked caricature to Expressionism:

> [T]he caricaturist must reveal the essential ridiculousness of his subject, contrasting the pretentiousness of his ideas or actions with the absurdity of his personal appearance. The art of caricature is therefore essentially a destructive art, and it is this fact which gives it its psychological significance—a significance which has been studied by Dr. Kris from a psycho-analytical point of view.[51]

A zealous supporter of modernism, Read argued that the caricaturist reduced art to its most fundamental elements, calling upon "a deep knowledge of the sources of expression such as will enable him to build up a life-like face out of a few strokes."[52] Analysis of caricature thus required not only a psychology of instincts, such as Kris brought from Vienna, but also a psychology of perception, as Gombrich later pursued in London.

Read's diverse interests as poet, art critic, and anarchist thinker inspired a sympathetic review. His devotion to artistic experimentation and political iconoclasm led him to recognize clearly the crucial principles of caricature as Kris and Gombrich saw them: unmasking, controlled aggression, and social documentation.

The BBC and the Journey to New York

The King Penguin *Caricature* appeared in the first year of the war, at a time when the power of spoken language, not of visual imagery, still remained the decisive tool of wartime communication. As Asa Briggs pointed out, whatever the sway of poster art or motion pictures, the Second World War on the political and cultural fronts remained predominantly a war of words.

At the beginning of the struggle, the new British Ministry of Information as well as the BBC moved to create offices to transmit British radio messages to the Continent and to monitor Nazi broadcasts in Germany and the occupied territories. At the BBC, Richard Marriott and Oliver Whitley assembled a listening and translating cohort that drew chiefly from émigré scholars but also included young British academics in search of professional employment. Less than a month after the start of war, the group began its routine. Monitors submitted relevant portions of broadcasts to BBC staff who then distributed them to the Ministry of Information, the Foreign Office, and the service branches. The monitoring corps kept lengthy daily digests, as well as highly condensed summaries, of all information that they recorded from German radio, materials that provided the chief sources for Kris and Gombrich's wartime research.[53]

After Britain went to war in September 1939, Kris immediately joined the BBC monitoring service as a researcher and analyst of Nazi propaganda. The position grew out of his vocation as an art historian and museum curator, as well as his work with the London Press Exchange, where he had served briefly as a consultant on advertising and propaganda. Jessica Mitford, employed as a polltaker by an advertising firm in London on the eve of the war, recalled the dreary and often unedifying nature of advertising and opinion research:

> Market research was considered slightly above selling or office work; the pay was higher and it was the kind of employment that might "lead to something better." It attracted a mixed assortment; my co-workers, all women roughly between twenty-five and forty-five, were ex-chorus girls, wives of businessmen, friends of copy writers, aspirant newspaper reporters. We traveled by train in teams of six or eight, herded by the supervisors, to manufacturing towns in the Midlands or the north of England . . . The work itself was based on a very new idea recently imported from America. We were told that its originator was Dr. George Gallup, a person with the unusual but descriptive title of Pollster. The objective was to compile information for the use of the advertising agency about public reaction to various products, and to this end we were provided with elaborate forms to be filled out in the course of door-to-door interviews. The questions, of course, varied widely according to the product. Interviewing for a breakfast food or household cleanser was fairly plain sailing, while the form dealing with deodorant was likely to contain the question: "How often do you find it necessary to wash under the armpits?"—with the attendant risk that the market researcher might face swift ejection by the housewife thus approached. The supervisor cautioned us that the Dr. Gallup method included a built-in safeguard against cheating on the part of interviewers, and inferred that somehow *he* would know if we should be so dishonest as to fill in the questionnaires over a nice cup of tea in the nearest Lyons.[54]

Although mass advertising had appeared suspect to Kris, the new business of public opinion research opened an avenue to participation in the war effort. In a curriculum vitae that he submitted to the AAC on 4 June 1939, he wrote the following about his employment skills:

> I think that I have a vast experience in any kind of practical work as connented [sic] with exhibitions. Propaganda by pictures is of special interest to me and I have devoted many years of research to it. I have in the last months been consulted by the London Press Exchange, in connection with questions on Propaganda. I am collaborating with the scientific staff of this firm in developing psychological principles of advertisement, a research carried out mainly on practical lines.[55]

At the BBC, Kris quickly advanced to the post of senior research officer and began training a sizeable staff of broadcast monitors.[56]

On the morning of 10 May 1940, German armies crossed into Belgium, Luxembourg, and the Netherlands, moving toward France. British government tribunals had already begun to identify and classify enemy aliens, dividing them according to those who posed an imminent risk and had to be interned immediately, those who bore watching, and—the greatest number—those who seemed to present little or no cause for concern.[57] Now on 10 May the British War Cabinet issued its first order for general internment of German and Austrian émigrés, calling for the incarceration of all male enemy aliens residing in coastal areas threatened with invasion. That same day Winston Churchill succeeded Neville Chamberlain as prime minister and six days later, in one of his first acts as head of the War Cabinet, Churchill expanded the internment directive to cover the entire country.[58] Although the Home Secretary Sir John Anderson opposed the policy as a xenophobic reaction, which could revive the domestic hysteria of the First World War, the military chiefs of staff pressed for internment and Churchill backed their demand.[59]

In June, the War Cabinet concluded that internment had not proceeded intensively or rapidly enough and called for a concerted roundup of the majority of enemy aliens, with little regard for age or political loyalties. Police officials no longer had to determine a refugee's attitude toward the Allied war effort.[60] By August 1940, authorities had interned 22,000 German and Austrian émigrés.[61]

The BBC could offer no assurance to Kris that his family would escape internment or that he would preserve his position with the monitoring service. Officially, BBC supervisors offered him temporary protection by transferring him to Canada to assist with creating a Canadian listening post. Unofficially, they held out the possibility of bringing him back to England. Uncertain of his future, Kris also considered an offer from the New School for Social Research in New York. In a letter of 10 July 1940 he explained the alternatives to his British contact with the AAC, Esther Simpson:

> It is possible that I shall be leaving this country on a semi-official mission towards the end of next week or a little later. The work I am supposed to do will take me to Canada and possibly to the United States, where I have been offered a Chair at the New York [sic] School of Social Research ... I wish I could explain the situation more fully to you, but this is impossible for obvious reasons. I hope, however, to be able to do so on my return—in a few months' time if things go well.[62]

In August, writing to Simpson from the offices of the Canadian Broadcasting Corporation, he expressed deep personal and political frustration. The Battle of Britain had begun and he had no opportunity for direct engagement. He merely waited for a visa to the United States: "I need not tell how I feel in these days: as an exile from Britain. My heart is with all of you and my only wish is to know that the attack fails. I wish I were there in the midst of it."[63]

He continued to receive broadcast digests, special studies, and weekly summaries from colleagues in the monitoring service and he sent back his own propaganda analyses, especially on the state of opinion in the

United States. His reports included advice on where to aim antifascist propaganda in the United States and on how the British and Americans could begin cooperation in listener research.

Kris's communications from Canada reflected his view that the United States needed to have a coalition along the lines of a Popular Front to ensure that Roosevelt won reelection, that the country continued with rearmament, and that the United States entered the war against Hitler. In September, writing from Montreal, he analyzed American public opinion. On the Right he found "unconditional isolationists of the old school, which are up to a point, but not totally, amalgamated with the fifth columnists."[64] Of far greater concern was the

> Wall Street section of isolationism; this section does, at present, not interfere with rearmament. Their whole interest seems to be concentrated in getting Roosevelt out of office. Their intention—"Appeasement" and "business with New Europe"[—]is not yet outspoken . . . On the whole, these people seem to assume that some kind of peace between a weakened [British] Empire and Hitler might be a good thing."[65]

Kris worried deeply about the large numbers who remained defeatist toward Hitler out of "the belief in his invincibility" and "the disillusionment in democratic resistance (France!)."[66] Support for the war came from rearmament advocates, but perhaps more importantly from the Left—"the unconditioned anti-fascist and those for whom Britain was not an empty word."[67] In another report Kris advised that British overseas broadcasts stressed to listeners that the war meant not only a military struggle against Germany but also a political fight to bring social change. He was well aware of the sensitivities that such a Popular Front approach aroused in both Britain and America, but he remained convinced of its necessity:

> People here are not aware of the fact that Britain is experiencing a social evolution which may lead her very far, that Mr. Chamberlain

> is without influence, and that the British people are not just "tough" but conscious of the new spirit. I know it is a ticklish problem. How far is it true and how far will people on this side appreciate it. I feel however that it ought to be emphasized over and over again. It will help in convincing the people in Canada and in America that this is a serious war. And I suggest that prominent Labour leaders should be asked to broadcast more frequently in "Britain Speaks". They should mention the subject of the "future" as frequently and as tactfully as possible. My reasons for making this suggestion is that no other slogan of nazi propaganda has had more success than that of "British plutocracy". It ought to be exterminated. "It" means here the slogan.[68]

After Roosevelt's reelection, writing from the United States to monitoring chief John Salt, he criticized BBC officials who

> are obviously well connected but the USA they know is not that of the people, [w]ho have, [sic] just now entered upon social revolution on a minor scale. Make no mistake about it, this election was one in terms of social problems. Only the people are prepared to fight this war. The wallstreet people are still if not appeasers, at least without any real conception of the issues at stake.[69]

A month later he expressed support for the appointment of Lord Halifax—one of the advocates of appeasement—as ambassador to Washington but hoped that "somebody with appeal to the labor, comes with him. The Wall Street racket is overwhelmingly powerful. They are just everywhere."[70]

In December 1940 Kris joined the Graduate Faculty of the New School. There, with the German émigré sociologist Hans Speier, he quickly designed a project to collect and analyze German radio propaganda. Speier had been teaching at the New School since 1933. He was one of the earliest members of the University in Exile, which the school's director Alvin Johnson had assembled to rescue scholars threatened by Hitler. The Rockefeller Foundation had provided support for the program as part of its effort to promote American social sciences in Europe and advance non-Marxist scholarship in the United States.[71] In 1934 the foundation had also paid for half the salaries of Fritz Saxl and Edgar Wind in London, playing its part in keeping the Warburg Institute in England.[72] As Speier recalled, Kris suggested they seek foundation support for their project analyzing Nazi propaganda. He assured Speier that the BBC would provide access to monitoring reports and digests.[73] Speier recognized the unique potential of access to BBC material: "There was at that time no better opportunity in the United States for closely examining the Nazi mentality while trying out new methods of content analysis."[74] And Kris intended the plan extend beyond a single project, as he had written to Salt: "I hope to get a research Institute going, which would study totalitarian propaganda . . . The intention of the work, which would be stricklty [sic] academic, is to supply material for commentators, agitators, jou[r]nalists, which could use the Institut[e]'s publication."[75]

Marshall, Lynd, and Content Analysis

At the Rockefeller Foundation, the associate director for the Humanities, John Marshall, provided crucial support for Kris and Speier's proposal. Trained in medieval literature, Marshall implemented the Humanities Division's new policy to shift support away from, in the words of the foundation's appraisal and planning committee, "a cloistered kind of research" to projects that could reach a mass audience. Toward that end, he began to organize projects and grants on how to use mass media—including radio, photography, and film—to bring the humanities before a wider public. Marshall built a network of thinkers and activists who evaluated not only the contemporary social functions of mass communication but also its political impact.[76] More clearly than many at the foundation, he recognized that radio, cinema, newsreels, and popular art created unprecedented opportunities for scholars to serve as mass educators and opinionmakers. Marshall intended his projects to help define long-term principles of cooperation between traditional academics, government agencies, cultural organizations, and expanding media empires.

In the near term, as war approached, Marshall sought to direct foundation support toward antifascist activities in general and to émigré intellectuals in particular.[77] In contrast to other foundation administrators, he steered grants toward Jewish scholars, socialist theorists, and left-wing artists, for example, funding the young Viennese émigré and Jewish social democrat Paul Lazarsfeld in the investigation of radio and mass communication and the composer Hanns Eisler in the study of film music.[78] By contrast, Tracy Kittredge, a Rockefeller official who served in Paris, nervously reported in 1933, "Many of the leaders in this field are Jews or social democrats, or worse."[79] Similarly, Marshall's Rockefeller projects differed from those of his counterparts at the Ford Foundation in that his efforts did not aim at forming an anti-Communist intellectual network. In September 1940, as Kris prepared to come to New York, Marshall urged the foundation to promote more extensive research into German and Italian media. His plans envisioned not only the analysis of totalitarian communication but also the organization of an antifascist response.[80]

Kris's plan to study German radio broadcasts and to create a corps of propaganda analysts in North America coincided closely with Marshall's aim to prepare American scholars for intelligence gathering and counter-propaganda. In the curriculum vitae that Kris provided Marshall, he sketched in rapid outline a self-portrait from the prewar years. It included the political essentials: "I was born in Vienna, Austria of Jewish extraction, and I lived there until to [sic] Hitler's invasion of Austria."[81] With equally concise strokes he commented on the split in his scholarly endeavors and his effort to resolve it through research into image making: "Though my fields of work—the history o[f] art and psychology—seem little connected I have never experienced the diversity of subjects, the common problem being that of man's reaction to the appeal of symbolic stimuli."[82] After interviewing Kris in December 1940, Marshall described for foundation officials the personal necessity behind his journeys to Canada and the United States: "When it seemed likely that all enemy aliens would be interned, he was sent to Canada on a temporary mission, on the completion of which he entered this country on a quota visa."[83] Marshall reported on the strongest message conveyed by Kris: "[H]e cannot associate with anyone who is not interested in seeing Germany defeated. Interestingly enough as later appeared, this referred to the Institute of Propaganda Analysis, whose work seems to Kris neutral to the point of defeatism."[84] Kris informed Marshall that he admired the work of Harold Lasswell, Marshall's academic *éminence grise* and a pioneer in the new field of political psychology. In his first psychoanalytic essay on propaganda, Kris would apply Lasswell's definition of propaganda as the "management of collective attitudes by the manipulation of significant symbols."[85] Having studied briefly in Berlin with one of Freud's early Viennese followers, Theodor Reik, Lasswell interpreted politics in part as an arena of unconscious projections. He drew, however, far more strongly on the ideas and practices of George Gallup and the new pollsters, with which he sought to transform political psychology into a quantitative science.[86] Kris, Marshall reported, indicated that in this regard "he feels Laswell [sic] bound by his techniques."[87] Interpretation of mass communication, Kris told Marshall, must penetrate "even to the instructions that underlie it, and definite instructions can safely be taken for granted in the totalitarian countries."[88] As Kris later wrote, propaganda had to be approached on two levels: as "the images he [the propagandist] has created in the minds of his audience"[89] and as the conscious "configuration"[90] propagandists produced as an instrument of state.

In March 1941, with Marshall's strong recommendation, the officers of the Rockefeller Foundation approved Kris and Speier's proposal. They supported the project as a contribution to communication studies and not as an arm of the British war effort:

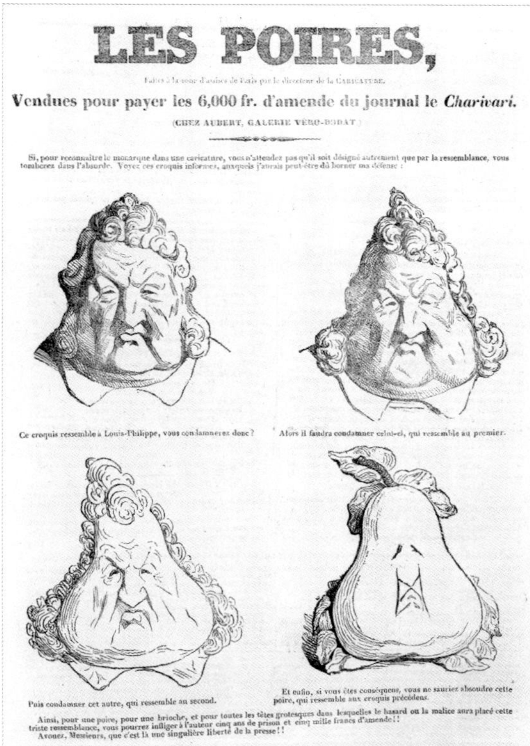

1. After Charles Philipon, "Les Poires." Philipon originally depicted the king's transformation into a pear as a satiric, unsuccessful legal response to charges of sedition. At a court appearance on 14 November 1831, he submitted into evidence a sketch of the four figures to show the extremes to which the government would have to go if it intended to suppress all possible likenesses of the king. After the trial, references to and depictions of the pear resurfaced in Paris, not only in Daumier's rendering in Philipon's *Le Charivari* but also in newspapers, on stage, in graffiti, and even on storefronts.

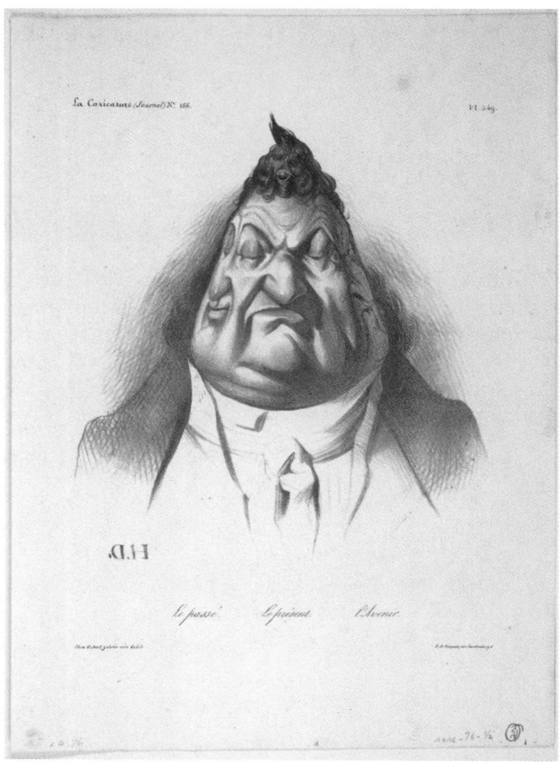

2. "Le passé. Le présent. L'avenir." Here Daumier combines within a single configuration the features of the self-satisfied bourgeois and the oppressive monarch. The bourgeois past contains the authoritarian future.

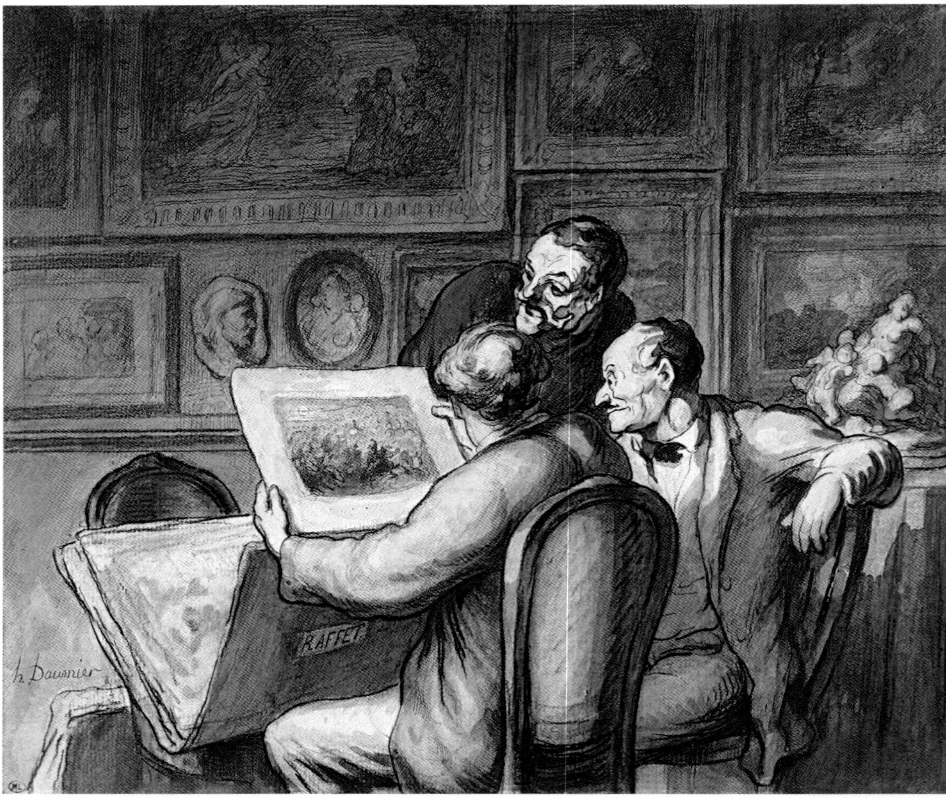

3. "Trois amateurs devant 'La revue nocturne' de Raffet." Daumier admired the work of Auguste Raffet, whose well-known lithograph of Napoleon I reviewing his troops at night draws the three men's attention here. Daumier's reminder of Raffet's somber, ethereal print perhaps meant also to provoke a comparison between the first and second Napoleons, of whom Marx famously wrote in the opening of *The Eighteenth Brumaire of Louis Napoleon* that all great historical events happen twice, the first time as tragedy and the second time as farce.

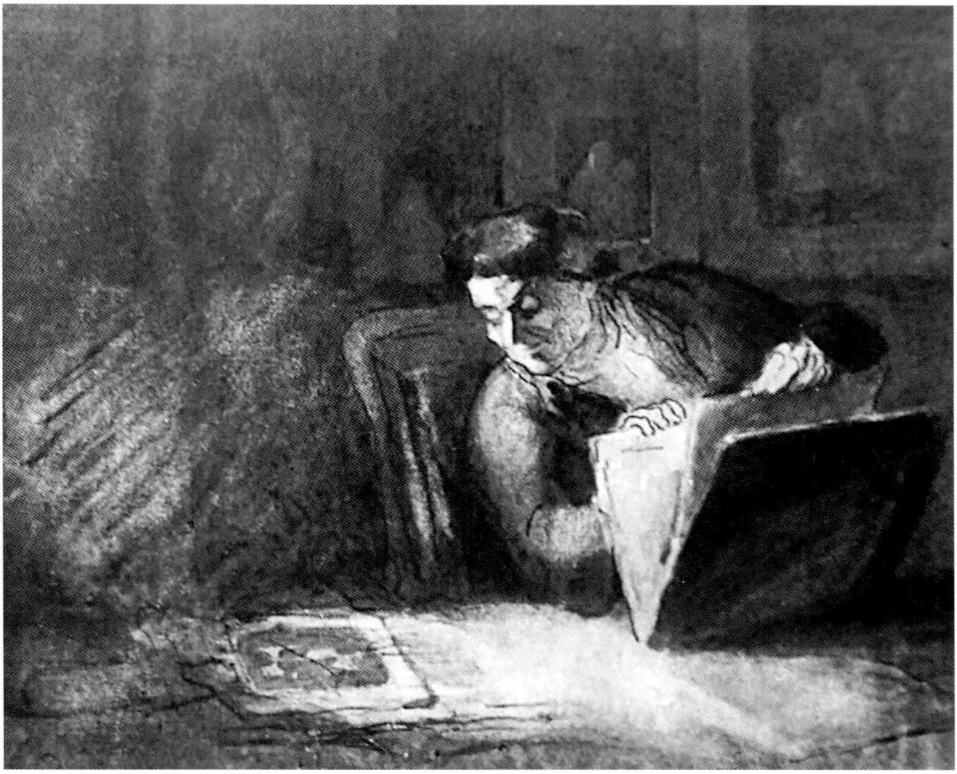

4. “L’amateur d’estampes.” The exhibition in Vienna was likely the first time this print appeared in an exhibition devoted to Daumier’s work.

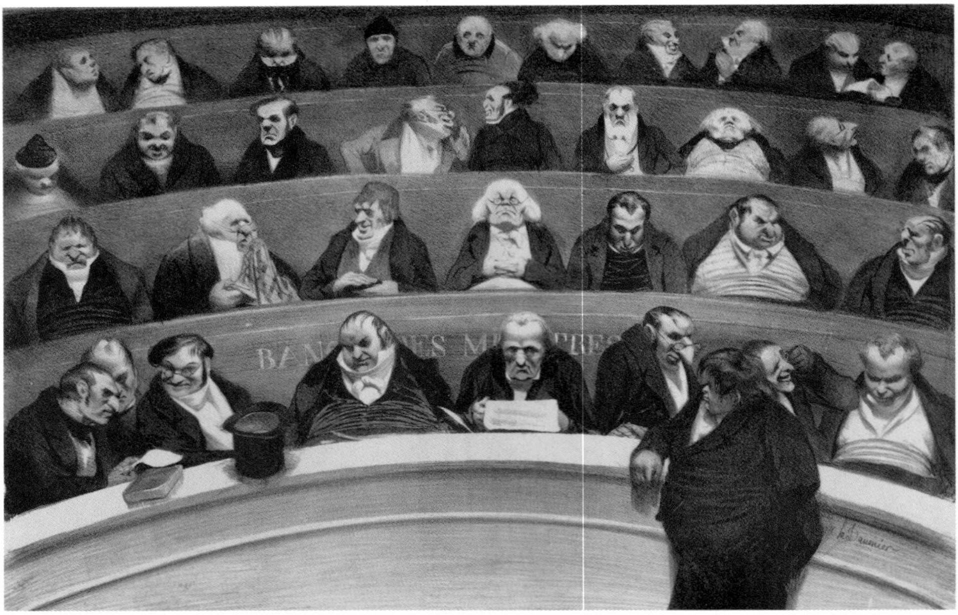

5. "Le ventre legislatif." The image included the subtitle: "Aspect des bancs ministériels de la chambre improstituée de 1834." (View of the ministerial benches in the improstituted house of 1834.) Daumier's depiction of the legislative benches, with the deputies assembled in rows, provided a group portrait of the bourgeois representatives of the people. Two months later, the people of Paris built barricades against their government.

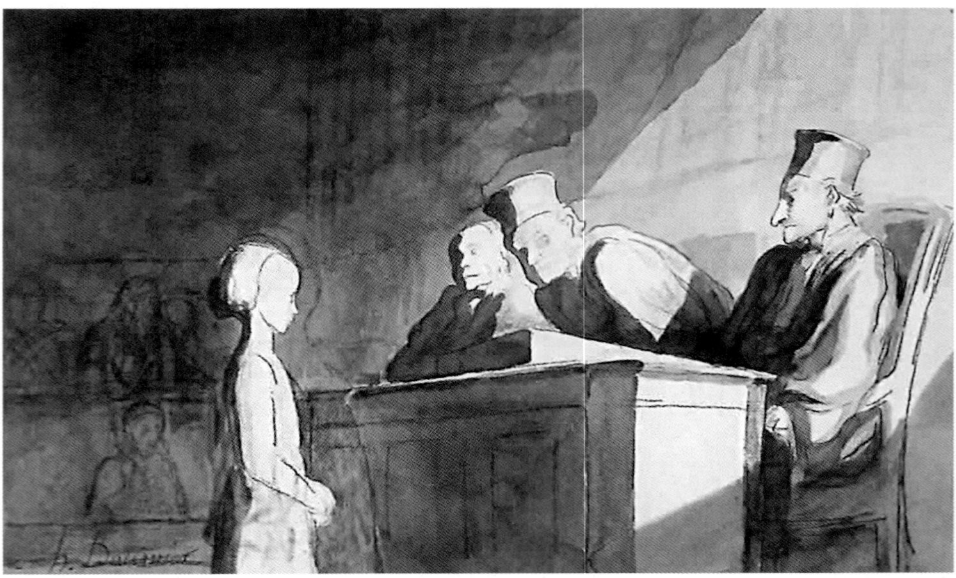

6. "La déposition d'une mineure." The session in which the judges question the girl's testimony is closed, intensifying the remoteness and harshness of the process. At one time, this picture belonged to Edgar Degas.

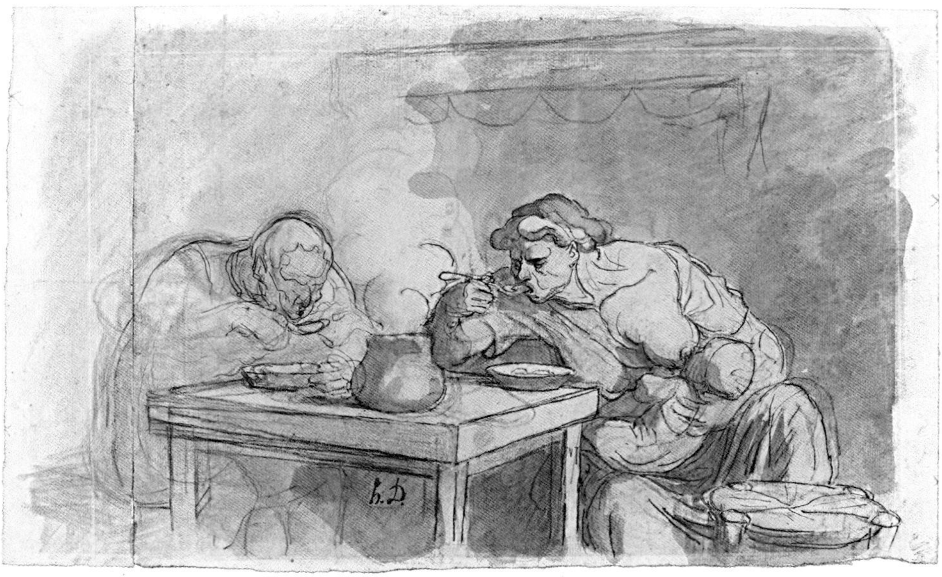

7. "La Soupe." Daumier might have intended this drawing to serve as an initial study for a larger painting of the family.

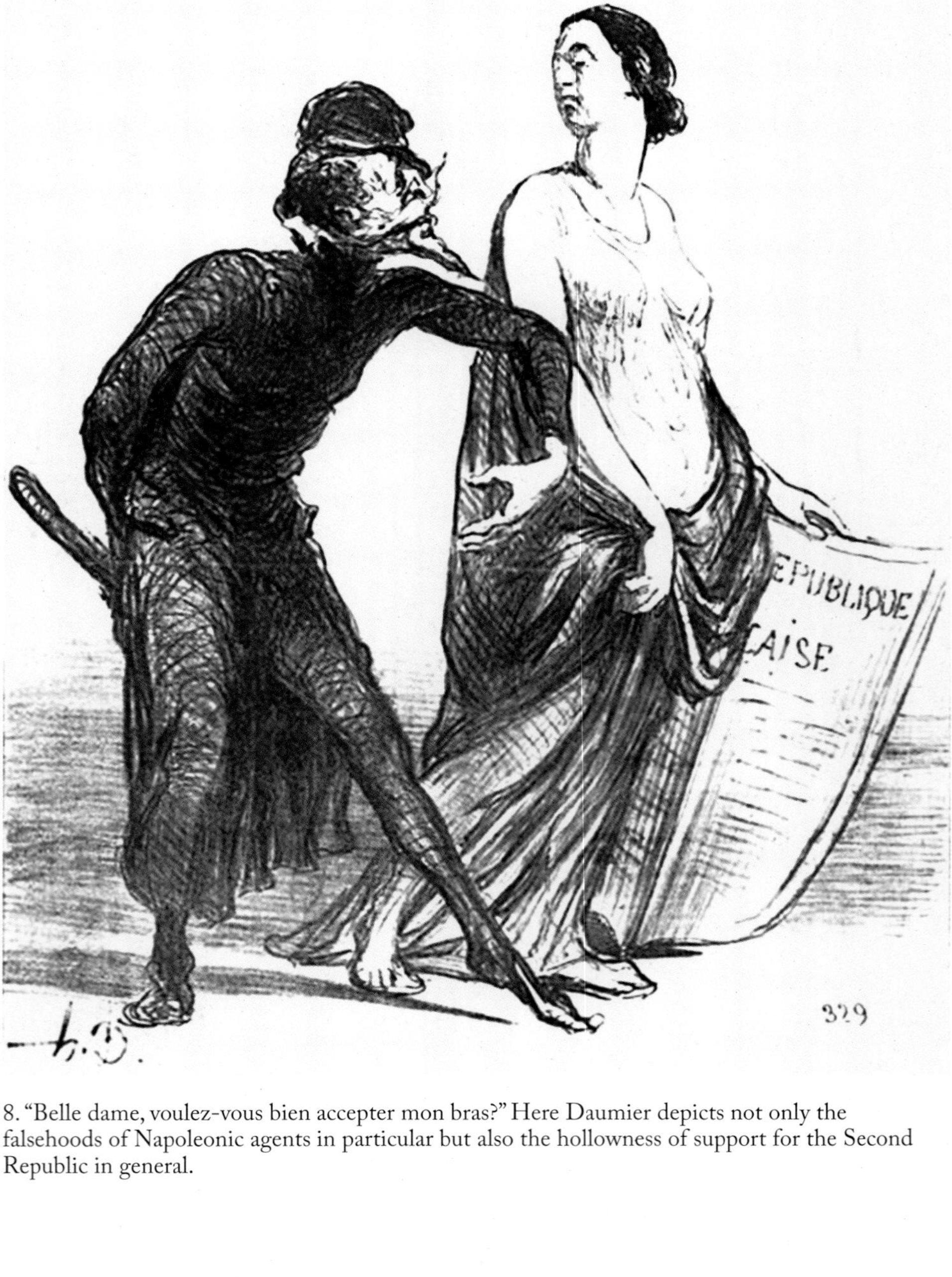

8. "Belle dame, voulez-vous bien accepter mon bras?" Here Daumier depicts not only the falsehoods of Napoleonic agents in particular but also the hollowness of support for the Second Republic in general.

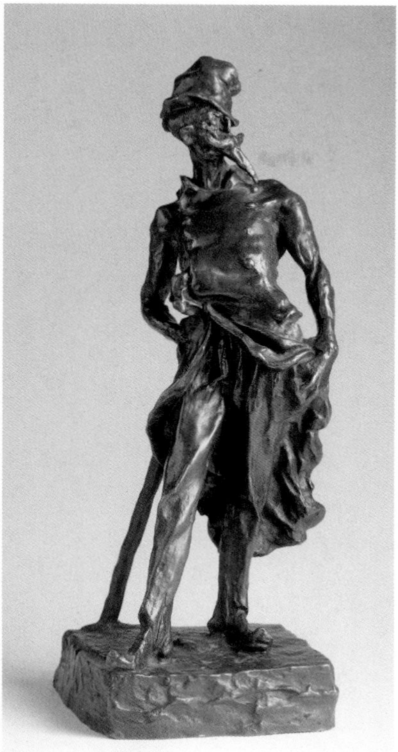

9. “Ratapoil.” In spring 1851, Daumier created a clay model of the figure of Ratapoil, who already had begun to appear in Daumier’s lithographs. Soon after, it was cast in plaster. In 1891, under the Third Republic and at the instigation of Armand Dayot, Inspecteur des Beaux-Arts, a bronze casting was made, although it was not initially displayed in public.

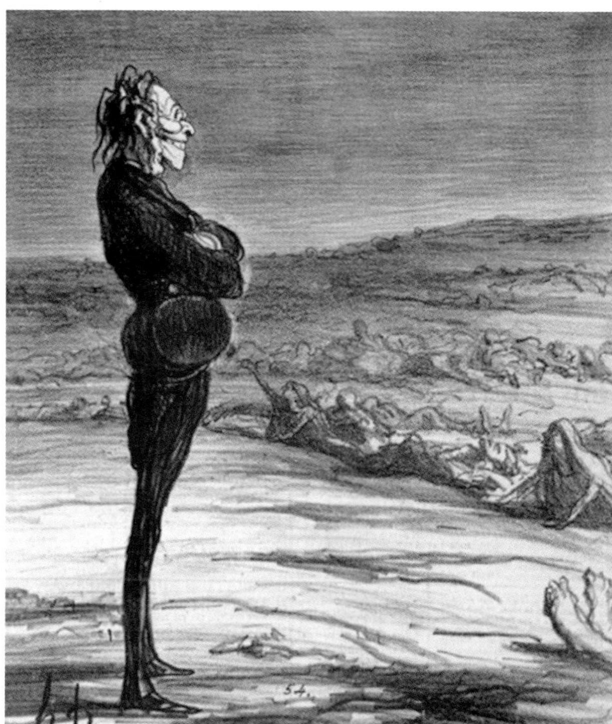

10. “La rêve de l’inventeur du fusil à aiguilles le jour de la Toussaint.” On All Saints’ Day, the inventor of the machine gun visits, in his fantasy, a graveyard of his making. Louis Napoleon had intended to keep the manufacture of the French *mitrailleuse* in 1866 a military secret, but word of its production began to leak out. This lithograph was included in the antiwar collection *Daumier und der Krieg* (*Daumier and War*), published in Leipzig, Germany, in 1926.

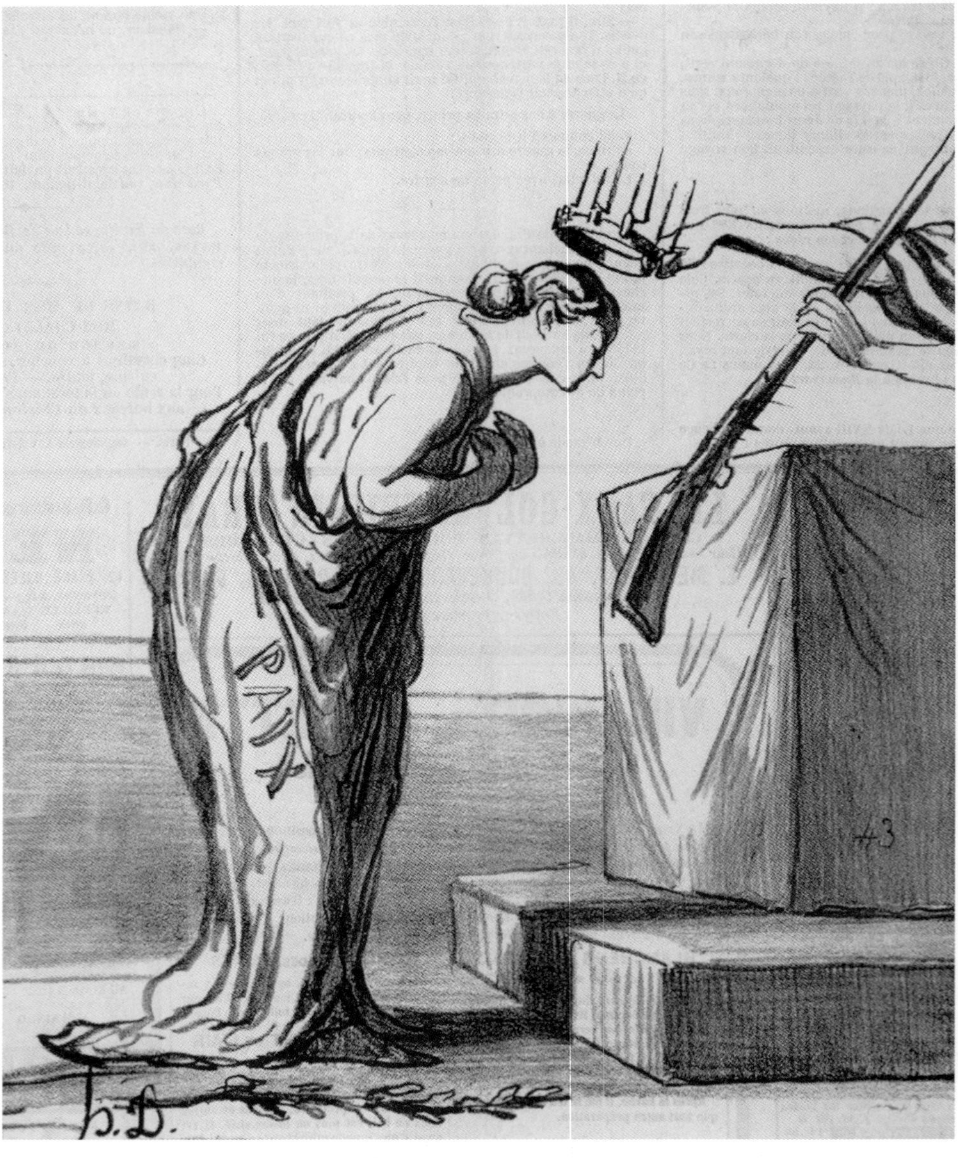

11. "Une lauréate en 1868." Frequent European treaty negotiations had followed continuous military actions—the 1864 French occupation of Mexico to install Emperor Maximilian, the Prussian occupation of Schleswig-Holstein in the same year, and the Prussian defeat of Austria in 1866—and they preceded the build-up to the Franco-Prussian War of 1870. This lithograph was also included in the *Daumier und der Krieg* collection in Leipzig, 1926.

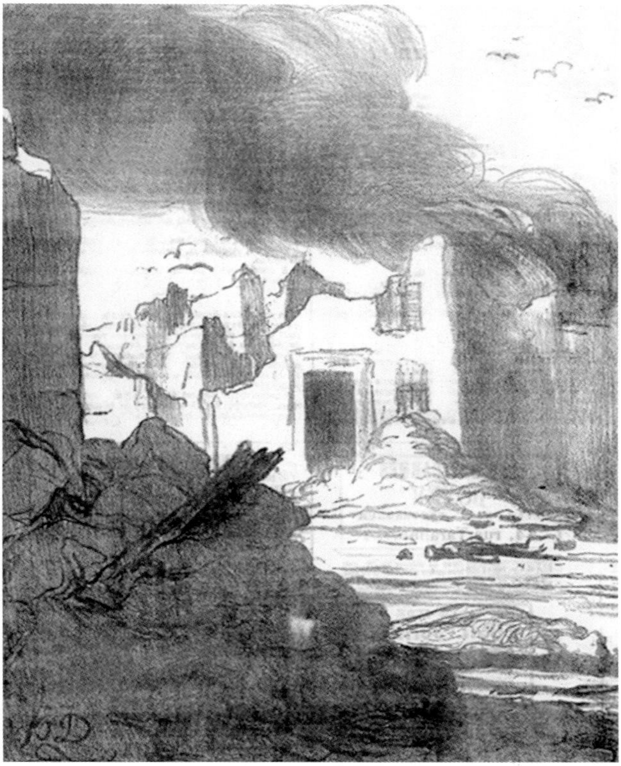

12. "L'empire c'est la paix." Prior to the November 1852 plebiscite that confirmed his imperial title as Napoleon III, Louis Napoleon declared that he would bring peace to the nation. The Franco-Prussian War, whose consequences Daumier depicts here, brought an end both to the emperor's military campaigns and to his Second Empire. This is another lithograph from *Daumier und der Krieg*.

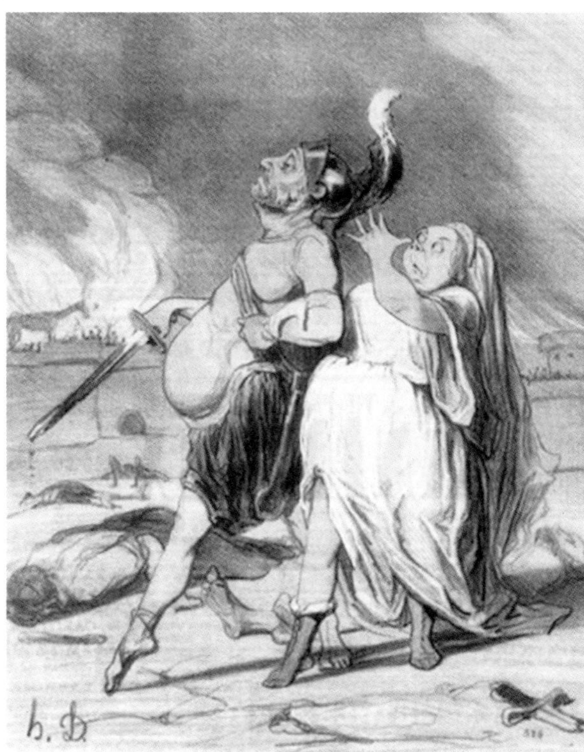

13. "Ménélaus vainqueur." This image of Menelaus the conqueror originally appeared as the first plate of the *Histoire ancienne*, Daumier's series of drawings from 1841 to 1843 that explored the classical tradition in art and education. The series sharply criticized the conventional, deceptive idealization of antiquity.

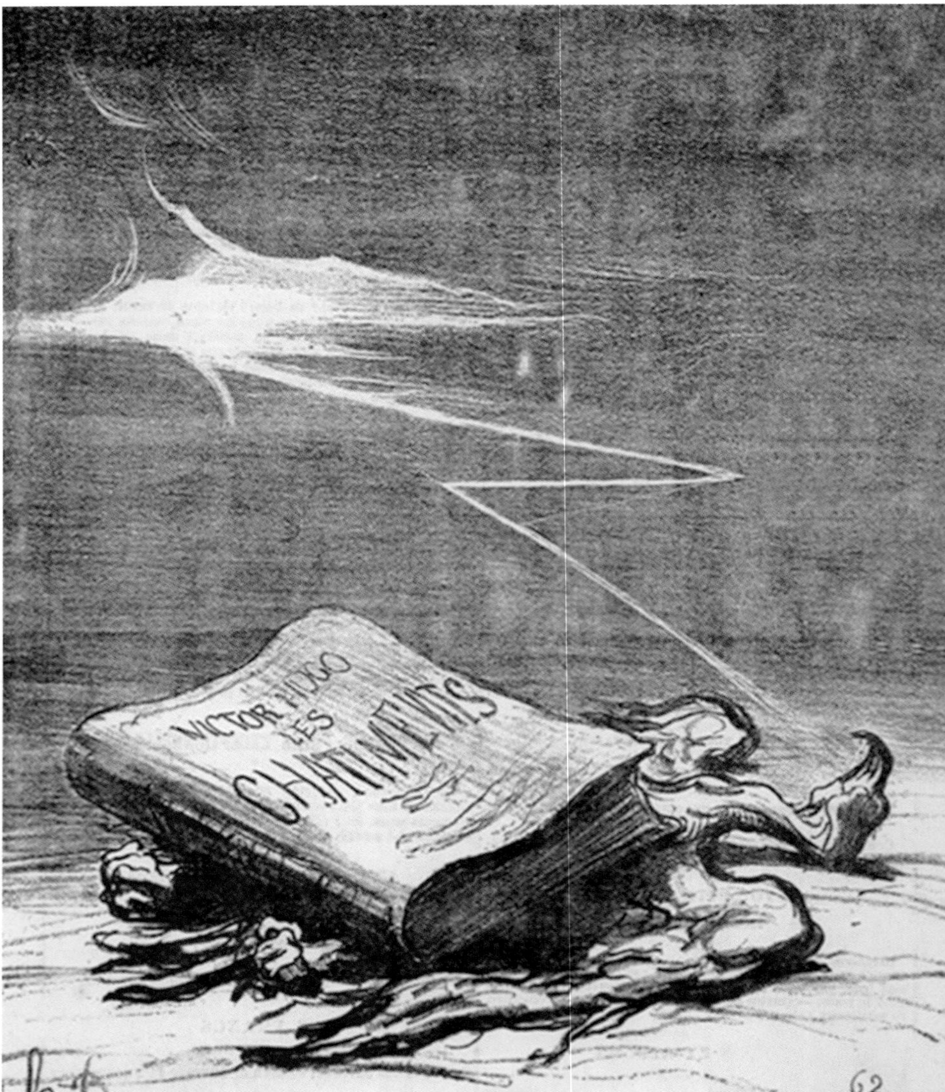

14. "Page d'histoire." Hugo's anti-Napoleonic *Les Châtiments* had been prohibited in France since its publication in Brussels in 1853. In October 1870, it finally appeared in France, confirming the collapse of the Second Empire and recalling the republican past.

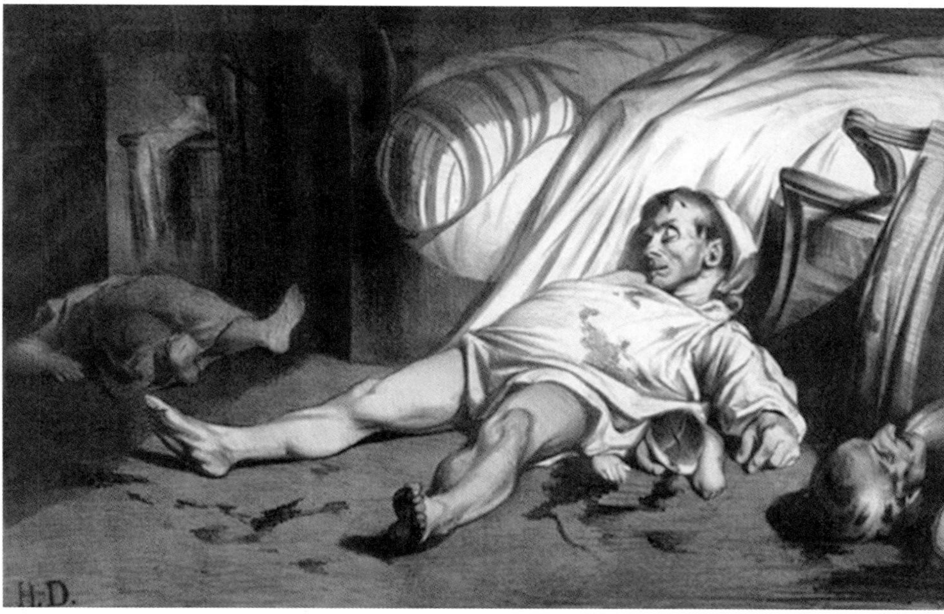

15. "Rue Transnonain, le 15 avril 1834." On 13 April 1834, following an earlier uprising in Lyons, republicans in Paris rose up in revolt against Louis-Philippe. On the following days, troops seized control of the streets with brutal force. Daumier's image depicts the slaughter of a worker's family in their dwelling on the rue Transnonain, where innocent residents had come under severe fire.

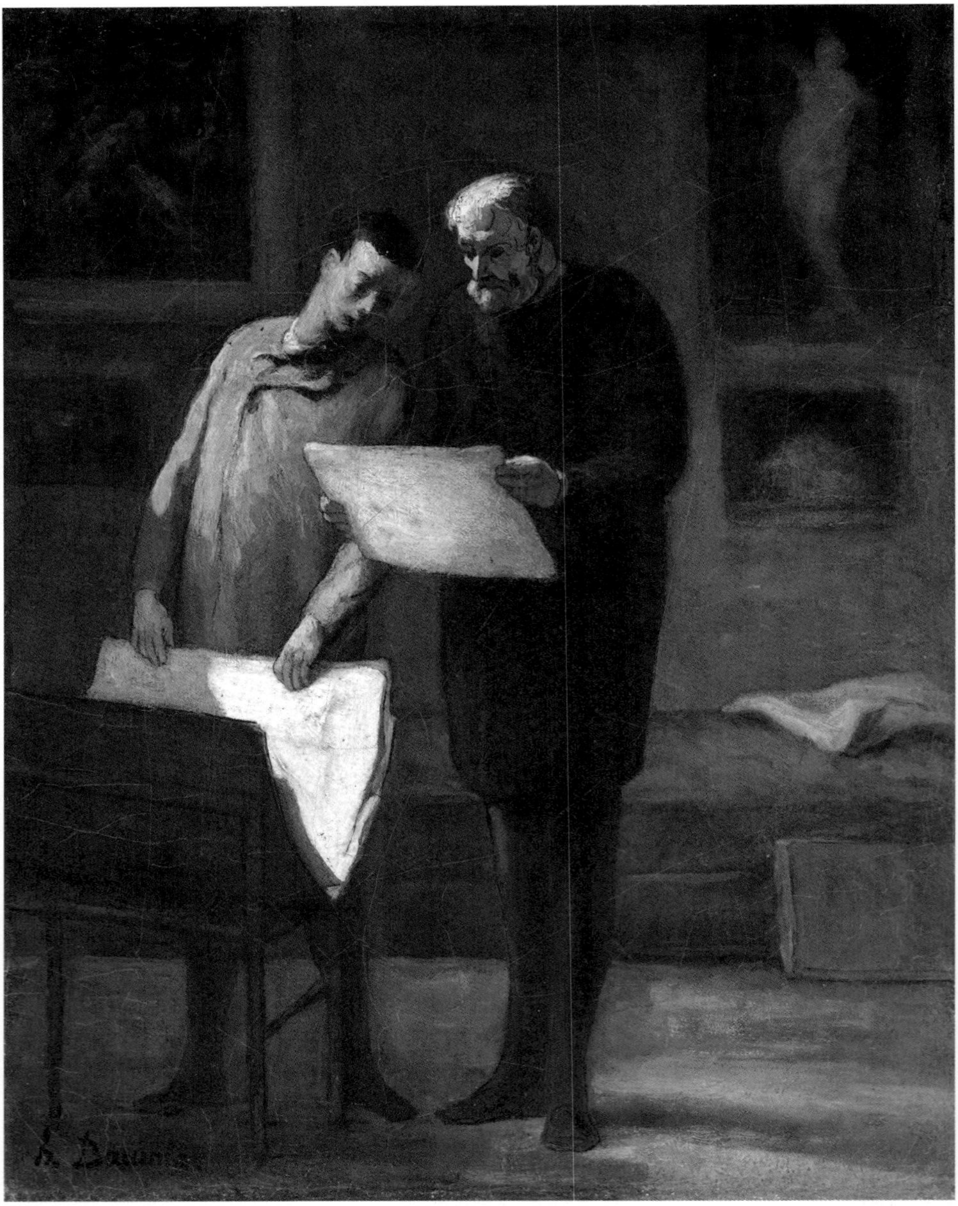

16. "Conseils à un jeune artiste." This painting originally belonged to the nineteenth-century master Corot, Daumier's friend, colleague, and fellow rebel within the classical tradition.

> Dr. Kris's earlier analysis of these materials [British monitoring digests] was necessarily hurried and largely directed toward meeting governmental needs. He will now assemble the evidence these materials afford on the trends and purposes of totalitarian communication, both within Germany and in programs which the Germans have directed toward other countries.[91]

Kris informed Salt that Marshall, however, was "extremely anxious to know as much as possible about the process of [monitoring] work. The idea of my cooperation with the Rockefeller Foundation is, of course, a double one. While research is one aim, another is to get ready for action by securing influence and training people."[92]

Kris, Speier, and their research team at the New School began work in April 1941.[93] Like Kris, Speier questioned the American over-reliance on opinion polling, standardized interviews, and marketing surveys. After receiving his doctorate in sociology from the University of Heidelberg, he had written poetry, stories, and part of a novel, and worked closely with the economist Emil Lederer, a colleague and follower of Max Weber who later became the first dean of Johnson's University in Exile. A socialist youth who opposed the Marxist sociology of class conflict and class consciousness, Speier interpreted the German bourgeoisie's contempt toward workers and its rejection of an antifascist alliance in Weberian terms—as the result of a middle-class preoccupation with traditional prestige.[94]

Speier shared both the Left's opposition to Bonapartism and liberalism's fear of mass politics. He admired the 1864 critique of Louis Napoleon, *Dialogue in Hell between Machiavelli and Montesquieu*, written by Maurice Joly, who had "stood between the political fronts, perceiving the hazards of popular sovereignty as well as abuse of power by social engineers."[95] Joly's Machiavelli combined the views of a "modern caesar"[96] who ruled through the "unscrupulous use of force and cunning"[97] and the insights of a modern politician who saw the instability of revolutionary movements and "corruptibility of the masses."[98]

In 1942, Speier moved to Washington to direct the German section of the FCC's Foreign Broadcast Intelligence Service—an agency similar to the British monitoring service—and in 1944 he joined the Overseas Branch of the Office of War Information (OWI) where he organized American broadcasts into Germany. In 1948, he became director of the RAND Corporation's Social Science Division. Years later the scholar who had denounced Bonapartist caesarism and censorship continued to the last to condemn Daniel Ellsberg's publication of the Pentagon Papers as "an act of sensational insubordination."[99]

While he remained firmly attached to his contacts within the psychoanalytic movement and the Warburg Institute, Kris found new colleagues and exemplars within Marshall's network of American social scientists and émigré scholars. Important among them was the Columbia University sociologist, and consultant to Marshall, Robert S. Lynd. Like Marshall, Lynd urged the Rockefeller Foundation to pursue an explicitly antifascist agenda by countering neutralist sentiments and profascist sympathies within the mass media and wider populace.[100] In 1939, Lynd incorporated Marshall's radio research project into the new Bureau of Applied Social Research at Columbia. There he organized the series *Radio Research*, in which Kris would publish an early analysis of German propaganda.[101]

As he later wrote to Gombrich, Kris came to regard Lynd as an intellectual model. In 1929, Lynd had published with his wife Helen Merrell Lynd the groundbreaking *Middletown: A Study in Modern American Culture*, a seminal work of cultural anthropology and a profound social psychological case study. Researched in 1924–25 and published on the eve of the Depression, *Middletown*—in actuality Muncie, Indiana—examined an American community undergoing rapid, disorienting change and suffering from the dysfunctional gap between early twentieth-century cultural institutions and the new social reality forcing itself upon them.[102] The book combined the social scientist's accumulation of quantitative data on collective behavior with the humanist's exploration of the content of the individual's choices and responsibilities. Culture functioned as a crucial analytic and dynamic concept that encompassed the mass communication of institutional values and pressures, the spectrum of personal responses to them, and the numerous points of friction among private aspirations, institutional demands, and communal needs. In the scientific rigor of their analysis and the literary consciousness of their presentation, the Lynds offered a new methodology and shared direction to psychology, the humanities, and the social sciences.

Through Marshall and the Totalitarian Communication Project, Kris briefly collaborated with the émigré critic and film scholar Siegfried Kracauer. As a reporter for the *Frankfurter Zeitung*, Kracauer—who had studied Kant with his friend and colleague Theodor Adorno—incorporated the Frankfurt School's critical Marxism and Freudianism into his film writings.[103] While still a working journalist, he began to accumulate and organize the material that after the war he built into his pathbreaking work on film psychology, *From Caligari to Hitler: A Psychological History of the German Film.*

Kracauer left Germany in 1933, lived in France until the German occupation, and settled in New York with the help of Marshall and Iris Barry, the curator of the Museum of Modern Art's Film Library, recently created thanks to a Rockefeller grant.[104] In New York, Kracauer approached both Marshall and Barry about utilizing MoMA's library to undertake a study of Nazi film. Marshall stipulated that Kracauer coordinate his proposal with Kris and Speier, who both agreed to serve with Barry as his references.[105] In her May 1941 letter supporting Kracauer's request for support, Barry characterized the significance of his work: "A coordination of the two studies in radio communication and in film communication would thus be effected, which seems desirable in the interest of an integrated content-analysis of totalitarian communication in wartime."[106]

Marshall not only approved funds for Kracauer's research into Nazi film propaganda but also provided him with a crucial recommendation to the Guggenheim Foundation when it considered whether to support the completion of *From Caligari to Hitler*. Seeking to pre-empt political objections at the Guggenheim, Marshall stressed Kracauer's journalistic approach to film and his experience of American social—not socialist—research:

> [H]e brought to this country an unusual acquaintance with German films, but more unusual still is the context of his view of them. As Kracauer has said, he regards himself, and quite properly, primarily as a "social reporter." If he were less modest he would probably claim status as a socialist, but he is both modest and just in holding himself to the function of "social rapportage" . . . His painstaking ability in research was amply evidenced in the work which underlay his report on the German propaganda film. In that work he adopted the best objective techniques of analysis, particularly those developed by Dr Ernst Kris and Dr Hans Speier at the New School for Social Research in their analyses of German radio propaganda.[107]

In his wartime study of Nazi film, Kracauer analyzed German propaganda to show how it corrupted and exploited republican art forms that the German middle class had abandoned, a theme that he explored in detail in *From Caligari to Hitler*. In contrast to Herbert Read, he viewed the radical pacifist and antibourgeois current within Expressionism as a sign of withdrawal into an alternative inner world, an irresistible "retreat into a shell."[108] In a prewar essay comparing interwar German film to Russian cinema, he similarly asserted: "What is more essential is that Eisenstein and Pudovkin—in contrast to a mere caricaturist such as George Grosz—are informed about human affairs."[109] Manipulating an art form already robbed of its substance, wartime German propagandists employed the outward appearances of a realist vision to transmit a "pseudo-reality,"[110] turning nineteenth-century documentary art against itself. The emptiness of the images reflected Nazism's lethal void, "its own nihilism."[111]

Kris also came to admire one of Kracauer's other supporters—Meyer Schapiro, the young art historian and lecturer at the New School, who, like Kracauer, applied both Marxist and Freudian understandings to cultural history.[112] In 1936, in one of the first substantial critiques of the New Vienna School, Schapiro had warned that although Sedlmayr and his colleagues invoked Riegl's notion of *Kunstwollen*—the inherent direction or moving principle within an artwork—in practice their interpretations either relied on conventional antiquarianism or emphasized vague national traditions and racialist mentalities. The followers of the New Vienna School, Shapiro explained, "tend to isolate forms from the historical conditions of their development, to propel them by mythical, racial-psychological constants, or to give them an independent, self-evolving career."[113]

Marxist analysis provided a corrective: "[A] materialistic view of art history is not necessarily a theory of materials but of the concrete historical determination of forms as against a purely immanent, automatic, logical, or animistic determination."[114] Treating the artwork as a self-contained artefact led to historical mystification. Schapiro could have written much the same about Sedlmayr's teacher, Schlosser.

Marshall and Lynd had thus organized a circle of American and émigré scholars who approached the study of images and propaganda as a combined scientific, humanist, and activist endeavor—in Barry's phrase, as integrated content analysis. Yet Kris continued to feel deeply ill at ease both with politics in the United States and with his own immediate situation. He reached a particularly low point in early 1941, writing to Salt:

> Since I believe that any progress in Britain will have to lead to a further strengthening of the left wing movement, any such progress will reflect upon the internal situation in the United States and public opinion will not be at peace, as I see it, and no unity of action will here be achieved for a long time.[115]

The atmosphere of the Warburg reading room and a psychoanalytic office felt far more natural than did the New School with its quasi-governmental status as a think-tank. Although a Foreign Broadcast Monitoring Service existed by the time he began his research at the New School, and propaganda analysis and counter-propaganda moved forward at the FCC, OWI, and Library of Congress, Kris, unlike Speier, avoided joining government departments.[116] Nor did he accept the Rockefeller Foundation's mission of creating a new academic discipline of mass communication studies. Kris had preferred educating and agitating; he saw his chief work in New York as countering neutralist attitudes and convincing young scholars to join the war effort. Throughout the years of his Rockefeller research, he looked forward to returning to London, resuming his activity with the BBC, and renewing contacts with the Warburg circle.[117] He wrote to Salt from New York as he had written to Saxl from Vienna: "The feeling of complete isolation remains strong and unchanged."[118]

As he moved forward with the Totalitarian Communication Project, Kris continued to hope that colleagues in Britain would act on his behalf. By the end of 1942, he decided against applying for an extension of Marshall's grant beyond the following spring, indicating to Bing that he wanted to remain a propaganda analyst, but with the BBC monitoring service rather than the Rockefeller Foundation:

> My Rockefeller Project expires in March and I shall not apply for a prolongation. I do not know where my future will be enacted. But since the British authorities here did not, last summer, wish to dispense with my services when I requested them to send me back to England, I do not know whether attempts to that end which I will repeat have a chance of succeeding. I am acting as a "brain-truster" and I am now fed up with the ridiculesness [sic] of this situation.[119]

As before his forced exile, Kris continued to view his personal and professional destinies as in some sense enacting themselves, beyond his will.[120]

Kris, Speier, and their research team completed the Rockefeller project in 1943 and published the results the following year as *German*

Radio Propaganda: Report on Home Broadcasts During the War. Although it focused on radio broadcasting, the psychology and history of images remained relevant. Wireless broadcasts, according to Kris, generated mental projections as visceral in their impact as visual symbols:

> The German propagandist talks about the world to his audience in terms of images. These projections are not only simplified to the utmost, but are also of remarkable coherence. In the ideal instance no inconsistent traits appear in them. The words that are to build up the image are vivid, composed like a poster, seductive, easy to remember, and meant to be "taken for real," but deprived of the complexities of reality.[121]

Such images reinforced ideological manipulation, intensified political terror, justified militarism and expansion, and—when Hitler's war failed to go as predicted—rationalized mounting German failures. But Kris held to the belief that countervailing anxieties—fears of military defeat and economic uncertainties—would ultimately counteract the workings of Nazi propaganda and prepare the ground for effective antifascist messages.

Psychology and Propaganda

From the early war years on, in published and unpublished analyses of fascist propaganda and public opinion, Kris stressed the symbiosis between propaganda and terror.[122] Fascism as a movement did not arise from crowd psychology, he argued, but instead aimed to create one. It used propaganda as a conscious instrument toward that end. He discussed these views in his inaugural lecture to the New School faculty, which he delivered in December 1940 and which was reported on in the *New York Times*.

Hitler's propaganda, like all hypnotic strategies, targeted the instincts, but the "extremes only, apathy, panic or frenzy." Although Hitler and

Nazi propagandists manipulated such instincts, and in particular the "desire to be dominated," their propaganda appealed to a psychology that it sought first to manufacture politically and ideologically. Politically, "Hitler must transform men by this [totalitarian] force in order to make them into what his conception says they are." Furthermore, "there must be an ideology behind it, something to inspire the imagination, and whatever you say, you must repeat it." As a combined instinctive, ideological, and political phenomenon, propaganda functioned without regard for contradictions. In fact, as a conscious political tool aimed at different audiences, propaganda demanded self-contradiction. Nazi propaganda to the United States sought to re-enforce already existing American isolationism and anti-British attitudes, but to Canada and Latin America, it warned instead of Yankee empire building and warmongering, tendencies promoted especially by "Jewish New York." Political strategies, in the end, proved of greater concern than instinctual or hypnotic tendencies: as a result of repeated Nazi propagandizing, "distrust extends to all news, first to all news from belligerents, and then to all news in general. One of the ultimate aims of Nazi propaganda is to create doubt, confusion, and thus, apathy."[123] Kris's chief concern remained not a supposed mass or crowd psychology but the ideological conditions for resistance and the emotional obstacles to it, especially a pervasive indifference or neutralism that he feared was taking hold in both occupied and unoccupied countries.

In published and unpublished papers, Kris concluded that theorists—in particular the psychologist Gustave Le Bon—who characterized the human being as subject to an instinctive crowd mentality did not depict psychological reality but instead described a strategic, instrumental policy. Propagandists targeted the ego before the instincts. They mobilized existing anxieties or aroused new ones to produce hallucinatory, suggestible conditions in their audiences. Their thought-experiments conjured images of control over a feared object or enemy so as to generate identification with political leaders and their symbols. In an unpublished draft, "The Place of the Audience in German Propaganda," Kris summarized this psychological and political process, by which paramilitaries and propagandists consciously functioned together as the instruments of Bonapartist intimidation and coercion:

> German propaganda aims at paralyzing the critical judgment of the audience, at canalizing its emotions and at finally terrorizing it into panic . . . In "Mein Kampf" Hitler has dealt with propaganda and organization as two most important weapons; he has in wartime entrusted the military machinery with the function which in civil war the Stormtroopers and after access to power the Gestapo exercised; in all three cases the real power was planfully exaggerated in order to supplement fear by anxiety. These devices of German propaganda are clearly correlated to a certain conception about the nature of man; he is considered only as a member of a crowd. It is the conception of Gustave Le Bon. If we keep that in mind one aspect of the relation of National Socialist organization and propaganda becomes clear: the organization is supposed to drive man into the mass, to bring him into that state in which he will be a playball of propaganda. Propaganda in a preliminary phase intends to attract him, in order to "deal with" him in the end. The relation between Le Bon's doctrine and National Socialist practice goes however further. Le Bon has stressed the necessity of illusions for mass formation. Psychological research has since enlarged upon that aspect and Freud has shown that we can distinguish masses according to their allegiance to concrete persons as leaders or to leading ideologies, which may to some extent, alternate in their function.[124]

In his published essay "Some Problems of War Propaganda: A Note on Propaganda New and Old," Kris explained the background and reception of the psychological theories of Le Bon, a nineteenth-century, old-guard conservative who in the twentieth century applauded the fascist new guard. Le Bon, Kris wrote,

> was one of those French reactionaries who had seen revolutions in plenty. He was terrified by the specter of socialism. His life—a peculiar sequence of endeavors on the fringe between journalism and science—was intrinsically devoted to warding off this peril . . . In Eastern Europe, this pupil of Gobineau learned to hate the Jews. In his own country he opposed the forty-eight hour week, the abolition of child labor, the expansion of education to lower-income groups . . . The success of Le Bon's writings, especially his Psychology of the Crowd, was largely dependent on a public of specific occupation: translations, except into English and German, were sponsored by Grand Dukes, Ministers of Justice, and General Staffs . . . When Mussolini came to power he professed the influence of Le Bon's doctrine. Le Bon, almost ninety years of age, became the admirer of the "new order" in Italy.[125]

Here Kris emphasized again the close functional connection between organized propaganda and organized violence. "Propaganda," he wrote, "becomes a supplement of violence, and violence a prerequisite of propaganda."[126] Fascist propaganda thus possessed a dual emotional and instrumental nature, provoking both psychological anxiety and political violence. Measuring the psychological impact on audiences was difficult if not impossible in the midst of war, but an integrated analysis of the content could at least give insight into the political purposes and strategies behind it.

CHAPTER 7

WAR WORK
1941–45

Scholarship and War

Several months after the Allied landings in Europe, John Marshall undertook a fact-finding mission to Britain to explore the role that the Rockefeller Foundation could play in postwar reconstruction. At Kris's urging, he arranged to meet with Gombrich. Kris pressed upon Gombrich the importance of Marshall as a professional contact and awaited Gombrich's account of their meeting. In November 1944, Marshall and Gombrich spoke in London. During their conversation, Marshall posed a question regarding the caricature project and Gombrich's work as a monitor of German radio propaganda: "He asked me," Gombrich reported to Kris, "whether it had ever struck me how natural was the transition from Caricature to Propaganda, I said it had."[1] Gombrich described Marshall as "a serious person, alive and progressive and likely to do a lot of good."[2]

Twenty-five years later, Gombrich recounted the path that led him and Kris from interpreting caricature to analyzing propaganda. He wrote:

> [T]he evil art of hate propaganda is not so far removed in technique from the mechanism of real art ... Unconscious projection merges

> into conscious distortion. Sometimes the stereotype will automatically modify the motif he [the artist] wishes to portray, another time the transformation becomes more conscious in the interest of an artistic aim, as happens in caricature and cartooning.[3]

By personifying and demonizing imagined types the propagandist created the equivalent of modern myths: "Just as the primitive myth studied by anthropologists tends to personalize the forces of the natural universe into beneficent or malign beings, so the Nazi propagandist transformed the political universe into a conflict of persons and personifications."[4] From caricature to propaganda, experimental visions had transformed into self-animating constructs, Daedalus' demonic, ill-begotten creations.

Since the Warburg Institute had been established in London, Fritz Saxl had provided a place of refuge for émigré scholars—Gombrich secured a space in the institute's reading room for Elias Canetti[5]—and from 1939 on he worked strenuously at demonstrating the relevance of the institute for the war effort. He photographed buildings threatened by bombing, organized photographic exhibits for CEMA, and sponsored public slide lectures, including a series on the links between British and Mediterranean art that he later published as a book.[6] In his own research and lectures, Saxl explored the influence of politics on art, as in the design of the Vatican Appartamento Borgia under Pope Alexander VI or Velázquez's paintings for the court of Spain.[7] He carried on such efforts, perhaps with all the more intensity, despite the fact that the University of London, on instruction from the government, had closed the Warburg Institute's facilities in September 1939. Bing explained the situation to Gombrich, who had moved his wife and two-year-old son to safety outside of London: "We shall probably only have a much reduced war budget at our disposal, and carry on for the time being with a skeleton staff at the old address."[8] With the help of Rudolf Wittkower, a mainstay of the institute faculty, Saxl continued to publish the English-language *Journal of the Warburg Institute*.[9]

Throughout 1939, Gombrich expressed his restlessness to participate in some direct way in the antifascist cause. In April, a month after Hitler's invasion of Czechoslovakia, he wrote to Esther Simpson that "one feels that reading the papers and [of] 16th century humanists is really not enough these days."[10] Immediately after the start of war, he repeated his dissatisfaction to Bing, who counseled patience: "I feel quite sure that you will find something to do in the way of public service before the war is over."[11] News in September that the institute was losing its space at the university deepened Gombrich's sense of marginality. The reading room that had been his refuge and workplace was now shutting down:

> That the Warburg institute should actually be packed away again belongs to the many things which one might know today without being quite able to realise them. On the other hand[,] the atmosphere of the reading room belonged so intimately to peace and everything it implies that it might have been difficult mentally to adjust it to "war-conditions." I find it difficult in any case. If one accepts it as inevitable—as surely one must if one wants to survive—all the efforts of the last years seem so utterly futile. I do not mean my private efforts—though I won't pretend that I would not have wished them to bear some kind of fruit—but the whole history of the last 21 years with all its illusions and incompetence which doom the last war and all the years we have lived through to something next to meaningless. Well—I should not bore you with this kind of useless sentimentalities, it seems that one has to pass from reflection to some kind of action and I wish we were given the opportunity to do that step as soon as possible.[12]

The opportunity he awaited was official approval from the Home Office to serve in the National Emergency as a non-British resident. He had submitted the paperwork but had yet to receive a response.

The Home Office's delay represented only one aspect of the situation that troubled Gombrich. Speaking before Parliament in September and October 1939, the prime minister and chief architect of appeasement

Neville Chamberlain described Britain's decision to go to war as a response not to European fascism but to German aggression, even implying that he would accept Hitler keeping power in Germany if he ended the occupation of Eastern Europe.[13] A government that mistrusted German-speaking refugees still showed willingness to reach an understanding with the Third Reich. Gombrich feared the spread of xenophobia toward émigrés and a return to the policy of accommodating Hitler:

> I do not want to pose as a hero but I am afraid [that] for the sake of our future position in this country one has to take every opportunity to serve – Not that it helped the German Jews very much that they had done it but there does not seem to be an alternative –. You know me well enough to know that I am rather pessimistic again and find the outlook for the future in general rather gloomy, for the Jews in particular worse and perhaps for what we used to call civilisation worst. Did you notice by the way how far the slogan "no talk with Hitler" has receded already? But much as they may wish it they can't go back now.[14]

Gombrich had not yet succeeded in convincing himself.

Waiting for word about his future, Gombrich considered reviving projects from his past. In October 1939, he wrote Bing that he had essays in mind for the Warburg journal, including one on caricature and another on Warburg:

> I promised Dr. Wittkower an article cut out from the corpse of our caricature-book, on Physiognomics in art but this means a good deal of reproductions to be of any value (comparisons etc.) Would you care to consider to take my article on Warburg's philosophical ideas instead, that means of course if you think it worth printing and approve of its content?[15]

The essay on Warburg would explore the philosophy of historical recollection behind the *Mnemosyne*, Warburg's vast, uncompleted visual atlas identifying links between images across time and cultures. Gombrich did not write on the *Mnemosyne*, but in late 1939 or early 1940, he did, it seems, prepare for Wittkower a work on caricature: an undated draft of one hundred and twenty-nine pages typed in English, with revisions in Gombrich's hand. It cited the article published in the *British Journal of Medical Psychology* but not the King Penguin book. After discussing the psychology of caricature, the paper devoted a separate section to the work of French political caricaturists under the bourgeois monarchy and then traced the history of caricature from the Carracci to the British satirists. A commentary on "Caricature and Physiognomics"—with Leonardo as its starting point—served as an appendix.[16]

In this unpublished work, one sees Gombrich's concern over the persistence of appeasement within conservative political circles. The essay discusses David Low's famous creation from the 1930s, Colonel Blimp—the supporter of appeasement, defender of Empire, and model of deference. The farcical Blimp revealed the tragic dangers of a time-worn ideology and outmoded sense of honor. Here Gombrich depicted Low as carrying on the French tradition of Callot. Like Callot's comic, fantastic stage figures, Blimp represented a disturbingly real social type. Low himself explained his art in *Political Parade with Colonel Blimp*, which Gombrich quoted:

> I regret that contrary to the custom now established among authors, I am unable to declare, that "the characters of this book are entirely ficticious [sic]"[.] As one convinced sceptic of human greatness to another, I agree that Hitler, Mussolini, Roosevelt, Baldwin and MacDonald have no real existence; but I am perfectly sure that Colonel Blimp exists, obstinately and ubiquitously[.][17]

In December 1939, Gombrich contributed to *The Listener* an article on art and propaganda. There he cited the example of two fifteenth-century English students in Prague who, prohibited from preaching their Hussite, antipapal ideas, painted on the walls of their lodging images that opposed a humble Jesus to a power-mad pope. The story of English students in Prague might have brought to the minds of British readers not only the first city occupied by Hitler after the Munich agreement but also the political risks taken by émigrés. Gombrich reproduced Daumier's searing image of the family of Parisian workers murdered in their home by agents of the bourgeois monarchy:

> To make things "plain appear" simply and silently has sometimes been the most powerful effect of great propaganda artists. Among Daumier's 4,000 lithographs there is perhaps none more stirring than the one that portrays with grim objective realism the interior of a proletarian home at Rue Transnonain after the ruthless quelling of revolt under Louis Philippe. But pictorial art can do more. It can give visual reality to the wishes and desires of the masses. It can show the menacing opponent as humiliated and defeated, pilloried, hanging on the gallows or tortured in hell.[18] (Plate 15)

With Daumier political protest generated a new form of art and communication, as Gombrich stated: "generally speaking opposition has more chance of finding genuine and even artistic expression than official adulation."[19] He contrasted the artistic bankruptcy of Nazi images:

> What hopeless results had not Diderot's exhortations to his friend the painter J. B. Greuze, that he should depict the alluring qualities of bourgeois life and glorify the charm of happy family with as many children as possible! It gives a kind of foretaste of the results of a similar effort, magnified through totalitarian efficiency, in the official art—and there is no other—of the Third Reich.[20]

No stronger antifascist message could have been conveyed to British readers. Nazi propaganda celebrated *Kinder, Küche, Kirche*, while Daumier documented the murder that occurred at the behest of guardians of middle-class domestic bliss.

Saxl and Bing kept the Warburg Institute running with a highly restricted budget and virtually no assistance. In October 1939, with the institute's needs and the authorities' treatment of refugees in mind, Bing strenuously advised Gombrich against seeking government employment: "Saxl with whom I talked about it this morning is under the impression that you will all feel compelled to join up as time goes on, but I would advise you not to do anything rash."[21] Yet, as Kris had predicted, art history now seemed personally inconsequential and socially irrelevant. In December, Gombrich made his decision and accepted a position with the BBC as translator and analyst of German radio broadcasts.[22] Kris provided the necessary recommendation.

From Reading Room to Listening Post

At the BBC monitoring service, Gombrich met those who had believed even before September 1939 that Britain had to commit itself to an antifascist war. Richard Marriott, who with Oliver Whitley organized the original monitoring group, recalled:

> I think we were all praying for the war to begin, which is not as ghoulish as it sounds, because we had probably none of us been in agreement with appeasement at any stage, and by that time it had become clear to practically everyone that war was inevitable.[23]

In February 1940, only weeks after he began his work at the listening post in Evesham, Gombrich wrote to Bing that he had finally found a political outlet:

> I really have no intention of giving up my line and becoming a professional monitor for [a] life time. I only feel that it is a kind of mental safeguard to put that in the foreground which after all pushes itself into the foreground sooner or later. I admit that i [sic] sometimes felt the tension and inconsistency rather hard when all the

> posters shouted "Barcelona bombed" or "Hitler asks Jews to quit" and I went to the Museum to order Philostrat or Gyraldus. I admit that Gyraldus is more "real" than Hitler but only after Hitler is disposed of.[24]

War work and, at this moment, reading outside the monitoring center about ancient Judaism lessened his feeling of detachment and helped him manage his sense of fatalism:

> It may seem odd but after having listened to the Nazi-news for eight hours I feel much more free to read, say, Wool[l]ey's book on Abraham, or to work on the Atlas, then [sic] I did when all that was only looming at the background. "Activation"—if ever such a word does exist—is certainly the best way of fighting anxiety. And to hear the most pessimistic version first—over the German wireless—is strangely enough the most efficient antidote against my inborne [sic] pessimism which I have yet discovered. One does no longer fear that this country may lose if one hears the German shouting that all the time. I do not mean that I have developed into a radiant and beaming optimist, I am pretty sure that we will have to face hard times, and may be [sic] very soon, but this hysteria over there does not sound very confident.[25]

Gombrich continued his researches into Jewish historical memory and the psychological transmission of memory fragments. He read Freud's *Moses and Monotheism*, and offered an opinion on its psycho-historical theory to Bing:

> The points of contact between the Moses and some of Warburg[']s mnemic thoughts are however so surprising that I must urge you to read the book in spite of the obvious Widerstaende [resistances] whcih [sic] you are sure to feel. Dont [sic] give up before reading the last chapters because it is there that Freud reveals that [sic] he really believes, that strong experiences of the past like the killing of the

> primaeval father survive as memory traces in the unconscious of the nation and can be evoked through a new experience or return after a long "latency period" with all their power. I could not say that he has convinced me but the similarity with some of the basic conceptions of the Mnemosyne is really surprising.[26]

After several weeks such reading and reflections seemed to belong to a distant, unfamiliar world. In May 1940, Gombrich contrasted the nervous intensity at the Evesham listening post to the quiet atmosphere at the British Museum reading room where so many exiled scholars had once found a haven:

> I need hardly tell you that the world looks pretty ghastly now. Not even I find it exhilarating to listen to these [sic] news although I must confess that I find the tension and rush during our working hours (they are working-hours) more in harmony with my state of mind than I would probably find the Reading Room of the B.M.[27]

The hastily assembled monitoring center had displaced the bookshop and museum.

Despite their connections to the Bonham Carters and the BBC, the Gombrich family still felt the antirefugee backlash in 1940. Gombrich's parents and his sister Amadea lived in Stratford and, through former students and contacts, his mother began to give piano lessons in Oxford.[28] An accomplished violinist, Amadea Gombrich performed in Stratford and was allowed later in the year to take her university exams at Edinburgh.[29] Gombrich's own activities remained restricted, as he described to Bing in June 1940: "I do not think that I am allowed to enter the Bournemouth area at all, all male 'enemy' aliens between 16–60 have been interned there."[30]

Days later, the general internment order went into force. On 7 July, Gombrich wrote that his father Karl Gombrich had been incarcerated in a camp outside Liverpool:

> I am afraid life must be rather gloomy in your circles now with all the xenophobia which is rife—have there been other victims? My father has been interned a week ago and we have not even got his address yet! All this is rather sad, but probably inevitable from the point of view of mass psychology. I see in todays [sic] paper that even recruiting of refugees has been stopped and I wonder what all these people are going to do. Our position here seems as yet—knock wood—comparatively safe but of course nobody can know what is going to happen when the so called "real thing" starts.[31]

Gombrich knew that Otto Kurz had been caught up in the anti-alien reaction, and wrote dejectedly to Wittkower at the end of July that: "I fully appreciate my undeserved luck to have escaped internement [sic] by virtue of my occupation. My father has been interned and so have practically all non British people I know."[32]

At the end of the summer, Karl Gombrich was released, which Gombrich reported to Kris in October:

> My father, by the way, has returned to Stratford about a fortnight ago, he looked quite well and is alright. Strangely enough he seemed to have minded the actual hardships of the first weeks much less than the drab and dreary routine camp life under the somewhat improved conditions later on. Particularly the last period of waiting for the release which he expected every day seems to have had a very depressing effect on him and also the small and comparatively trifling indignities which are inevitably connected with these things. But I think that my mother suffered more than did he.[33]

During Karl Gombrich's internment, the phony war ended and the "real thing" began: from July to September bombing raids on Britain increased heavily in number and intensity. From 7 September to 2 November, German planes attacked London every night. Gombrich's sister Lisbeth, having made her way from Switzerland, held a temporary job in London and carried on through the Blitz:

> She had one very narrow escape in a basement shelter but as a rule she says that she sleeps alright and that the behavior of the Londoners is really admirable. Personally she is most concerned about health conditions in winter with most of the windows smashed, people crowding in cold shelters and the danger of any 'flu epidemic taking very serious forms most obvious. Unfortunately her bosses have now preferred to leave and to close down their shop so that she had (more or less) lost her job. They still talk about transferring it elsewhere, but she does not believe that they are serious about it.[34]

After the Blitz, Lady Violet Bonham Carter secured Lisbeth an employment interview at Bedford College, University of London, the first women's college in Britain. In 1942, she moved to Oxford with her parents, and worked there in the same office as her father.[35] Gombrich's family survived the Battle of Britain. German bombs, however, killed Hans Meier, the Warburg Institute's librarian in 1941. A year later Gombrich learned that a German bombing raid had also taken the life of Elizabeth Senior, the editor who had published the King Penguin caricature book.[36]

By the summer of 1941, Saxl, Bing, and Rudolf and Margot Wittkower had relocated the Warburg staff safely to Denham where they now stored the only remaining catalog of the library's holdings, reassembled collections of books and photographs, and supported research and preservation activities as best they could for the duration of the war.[37] Gombrich kept in contact with the Denham circle, which included the Wittkowers, Otto Kurz, and the medievalist Hugo Buchthal. He agreed to Saxl's requests for art historical talks and articles and contributed to the lecture series on Britain and the Mediterranean with a presentation on "Heroic Landscape in England." Saxl attempted to dissuade him from further work on caricature, writing in August 1941:

> I don't think you should again take up the subject of Caricatura. Not because we wouldn't like to have it but I think it would be more amusing for you to deal with the "heroic landscape", as you first suggested. An imperfect lecture on the "heroic landscape" seems to me preferable to an almost perfect lecture on Caricature.[38]

The topic of landscape art would better assist Saxl's plan to connect the institute to the wartime historical preservation campaign.[39]

Yet, Saxl perhaps underestimated the relevance of Gombrich's interest in caricature, a relevance that Allen Lane and the King Penguin editors still appreciated. In 1943, the King Penguin series reprinted an abridged version of *The Microcosm of London*, a collection of color plates originally published during the Napoleonic Wars in 1808 after the victory at Trafalgar but before the end had come into view.

In the *Microcosm*, one hundred prints depicted sites of London's political, economic, and cultural life: the House of Commons, law courts, and royal palaces; the Guildhall, board rooms, and Stock Exchange; churches, schools, and hospitals; the Royal Academy, Christie's auction room, and the comic stage at Sadler's Wells. Every location conveyed the message that the home front had not succumbed to fear and isolation but instead successfully maintained normalcy and continuity. A. C. Pugin—the architectural illustrator, preservationist, and father of the architect and medieval revivalist A. W. Pugin—drew the buildings and meeting places, coloring them by hand. But the caricaturist Thomas Rowlandson drew the people who lounged about, crowded within, and streamed through the streets and interiors.

The introduction to the King Penguin prints reminded readers that the original *Microcosm* had been the brainchild of the émigré publisher and bookseller Rudolph Ackermann—"German by birth, cosmopolitan by nature."[40] Ackermann's *Microcosm* embodied the spirit of Londoners who "lived their lives against a background of world war, of sweeping armies and mass fanaticism."[41] From Napoleon to Hitler, questions and fears remained the same: "'Can he invade us?' 'Will he attack Spain?'

'Can the Russians hold him?' 'What is America thinking?'"[42] Pugin's colors and backgrounds transported readers into an old, nearly mythic London; Rowlandson's "sharp observation"[43] of people returned them to the present.

Caricature art accorded far better than landscapes with Gombrich's state of mind. Having contributed to *The Listener* articles on artists, propaganda, and the art of war, he wrote to Saxl that he envisioned writing another for the same periodical on "'war artists' in the sense of officially appointed chroniclers of war."[44] In Saxl's view, Gombrich had lost his commitment to the projects Saxl believed were crucial to the institute's wartime survival and long-term future; from Gombrich's perspective, Saxl refused to accept his decision to join the listening post and had—without saying so outright—withdrawn any vestige of support for the caricature book. Their mutual sense of disappointment persisted beyond the war, becoming a source of tension in what remained a still vital professional collaboration.

While Gombrich's decision to join the BBC stemmed from several motives—including his desire to provide security for his wife, his son, and his émigré parents—his determination to follow Kris into the monitoring service signified a political choice. In his letters to Kris, Gombrich grappled with the changing realities of wartime politics. Writing frequently and at length, he tested his ideas and sought Kris's responses to them. The correspondence reflected the thoughts of a concerned scholar, attentive to ideological debates within the anti-Hitler coalition and well attuned to the layered meanings of political language.

The life that Gombrich had pursued in the reading rooms of London yielded completely to the listening post at Evesham. Yet, the monitoring service produced its own disappointments. As he wrote later, he knew that as a toiler at the bottom grades he would gain only a "frog-eye view"[45] of the war. Still, he grew frustrated with rapid analyses, inexact translations, and lax reporting, the results of bureaucratic pressures and political myopia in the BBC. In August 1941, he accepted promotion to monitoring supervisor in part to introduce some reform in procedure.[46] But early in 1942 he wrote to Kris about his ongoing disenchantment with "the germ of journalism in our place which I try in vain to combat."[47] He continued:

> You cannot imagine how few people there are left with the sort of scholarly approach you and your work stood for . . . My own job as a "supervisor" still does not give me an awful amount of satisfaction. I am not ambitious, as you know, at least not for "authority," and I preferred being an actual ear witness of events and racking my brain over translations of such beauties as "Freiheit ist Bindung" to a[n]swering umpty telephone calls about little matters and passing on requests for special carbon copies. Still, it is not always quite as bad as that, and perhaps I can do a little for the preservation of the standard.[48]

For Gombrich, the heads of his department—Marriott and Whitley—embodied that standard. They protested when the BBC ignored the work needs and professional opinions of the large émigré staff at Evesham, and in January 1942 they left the listening post to enlist in the armed forces.[49] Gombrich reported the news to Kris:

> Both Marriot[t] and Whitley resigned and have already joined up. For me personally the whole affair was extremely sad and worse than that for I had come to have a very high regard for both of them, for their absolute integrity of motive and their almost fanatical devotion to duty. I daresay they were no diplomats in the way they handled their conflict with the powers that be but it is not easy not to feel bitter about it all.[50]

Oliver Whitley provided a political as well as professional model for Gombrich. His father J. H. Whitley, a Yorkshire Liberal and religious Nonconformist, had been both Speaker in the Commons and chairman of the BBC governors. Not only did the elder Whitley's background mirror Asquith's Yorkshire and Nonconformist upbringing but his continued devotion to Asquith's party after its steep decline in 1918 paralleled the interwar activism of Violet Bonham Carter. Gombrich traced the younger Whitley's self-discipline, his lack of deference toward BBC superiors, and his independent political commitment to his family's Dissenting and Liberal roots, writing to Kris: "Whitley in particular (who, as a son of the speaker in the House of Commons) is a real embodiment of fairness and non-conformist ethical standards."[51]

Gombrich's pessimism returned at Evesham, where he directly confronted the limits of Asquith's Liberalism in wartime. He had already experienced the revival of xenophobia in Britain; now he encountered an anti-intellectual, antiforeigner, status-conscious mentality—Low's Blimpism—at the monitoring service. Most importantly, new alliances had reshaped wartime politics, at home and abroad. In 1940, Churchill—a rebel against his Tory family and once a Liberal ally of Asquith before the First World War—had returned to power as Conservative party leader and given the crucial post of wartime Foreign Secretary to Anthony Eden, the representative of post-Munich conservatism. But only a year later, with the invasion of Russia and the entry of the Soviet Union into the war, the possibility of victory over Hitler now meant joining forces with Stalin and Communism. Committed to principles from the age of Asquith, hesitant to embrace Popular Front politics, and isolated as an Austrian émigré, Gombrich immersed himself in propaganda analysis. But he sought also to define for himself, for Kris, and for his colleagues his position in the antifascist movement.

Theories of Propaganda

From the German invasion in June 1941 until the turning of the tide against German armies in Russia in February 1943, the antifascist cause experienced its worst military setbacks and most severe tests of endurance. For many observers—Gombrich among them—the shock of Hitler's attack on the Soviet Union reinforced their fatalism about the war. In a letter to Bing, Gombrich confessed his profound apprehension and complained of his dull political sense. His conception of Soviet prospects turned bleak:

> Incidentally, I proved once more completely ignorant of politics—I never believed a word of the rumours concerning an impending attack on Russia . . . It is surprisingly like Napoleon—but Napoleon did reach Moscow, after all, and only committed the blunder of starting his campaign so late in the year. One really wonders whether the Russians have much chance.[52]

The Soviet entry into the war sent political and ideological reverberations throughout Britain and the United States. During the next two years, antifascism confronted renewed anti-Bolshevist and xenophobic tirades from individuals and groups fearful that the alliance with Russia against Nazism would pull the war effort and domestic policy toward the Left. The war in the Soviet Union and reactions to it on the home fronts now provided new background to Kris's propaganda research in New York and Gombrich's political analyses in London.

Before June 1941 the British government not only had conducted the sole military defense against Hitler but also controlled political and ideological warfare, which it had divided among various ministries and departments: the Foreign Office under Eden; the Office for Economic Warfare under the Labour minister Hugh Dalton; the military service branches; the Ministry of Information; and the BBC. Churchill gave little direction to messages broadcast to the Continent but deferred to the Foreign Office and military service chiefs, eventually removing Dalton—one of a small number of Labour leaders who supported rearmament in the 1930s—from propaganda work. Official ideological strategy mirrored Conservative foreign policy concerns and Anthony Eden's diplomacy.

Before the war, Eden had served as minister to the League of Nations where he advocated principles of collective security but also offered a territorial settlement to Mussolini in advance of the invasion of Ethiopia. He became Stanley Baldwin's Foreign Secretary during the Ethiopian occupation and remained in that post when Neville Chamberlain became prime minister. Agreeing with Chamberlain that Britain should enlist Mussolini's aid in protecting Austrian independence, Eden advised that Britain officially accept Italy's occupation of Ethiopia if Mussolini would withdraw his soldiers from Spain. His strategy aimed not at defending the Spanish Republic but at negotiating a favorable settlement with Germany and exerting greater pressure on Italy. In February 1938, a month before the *Anschluss*, he resigned from the cabinet, distancing himself from Chamberlain but not actively opposing appeasement.[53]

As Churchill's Foreign Secretary, Eden sought to maneuver collaborationists away from Germany to the side of Britain, and following the Battle of Britain, his Foreign Office remained intent on preserving friendly contacts with Catholic authoritarian governments in Vichy France and Franco's Spain. Eden insisted that Britain's war against Hitler aimed at the defeat of German aggression and expansionism rather than the overthrow of fascist collaborators and sympathizers. The British fought the war, he and Conservatives argued, not to transform governments and reshape societies but to suppress a threat to peace in Europe and to Britain overseas.

Critics on the Left—from Labour and trade union leaders to independents such as J. B. Priestley and George Orwell—called for popular antifascist mobilization and demanded a statement of war aims that included plans for political and social reform. Some served as members of Dalton's Economic Warfare division, which maintained liaisons with partisans and resistance groups. Others brought their message before the public as BBC broadcasters.[54] By 1943, a Radical Action group had formed within the Liberal party to press the government for a new social agenda and to recruit candidates for parliamentary elections.

British Labour representatives and trade union leaders demanded that the government develop proposals to protect health, disability, and retirement; to expand the educational system; and, most crucially, to end chronic unemployment and housing shortages. Such programs would require nationalizing major industries and creating a comprehensive system of health care. Early in the war, trade unionists had suspended workplace rules and contracts in the name of the war effort; after the Battle of Britain, they sought to regain their shop floor rights.

In military strategy, the differences between Conservatives and their critics arose over the need for a Second Front to relieve pressure on the Red Army and Russian civilians in the east. In October 1941, as German armies neared Leningrad and Moscow, demands in Britain for a Second Front grew more insistent. Approval of the War Cabinet's military plans declined sharply. The head of the Ministry of Supply, Lord Beaverbrook, pushed for the shipment of a far greater number of tanks to the Soviet Union and sounded the call for a Second Front in the newspapers of his press empire. In 1942, after Stalin ordered a halt to the Red Army's retreat at Stalingrad, pressure on the government to create a Second Front became unrelenting. From July to September, Stalingrad remained continuously in the dailies' headlines and Conservatives became increasingly concerned that the movement for a Second Front in Europe would strengthen the Left at home.[55]

In the trade unions, Communist shop stewards campaigned for a Second Front and pressed for the revival of a workers' Popular Front in opposition to the national coalition of party leaders and independents in the War Cabinet. Yet, many union members—now that the country had survived the Battle of Britain—wanted changes not in the War Cabinet's military tactics but rather in its economic planning. At the Labour party conference in 1943, trade unionists soundly rejected the Communist party's request for a renewed Popular Front from below, but the question of how to connect the military struggle against Hitler to a political movement for reform remained a pressing issue for the Labour party leadership and on the shop floor.[56]

From his liberal royalist background, Kris saw in communism the nucleus of a totalitarian state. Furthermore, he believed that Stalinist propaganda in the years of the Hitler–Stalin Pact had helped fuel anti-British sentiments in the United States.[57] But Kris also recognized the danger posed by ideological anti-Bolshevism. After the German invasion of Russia, he and his research team in New York painstakingly charted the revival of anti-Bolshevik propaganda on German radio.[58] Following the Hitler–Stalin Pact, Nazi propaganda against the Soviet Union had been comparatively quiescent. In November 1941, however, German broadcasts both at home and in the occupied countries proclaimed the construction of a *Festung Europa*—a Nazi fortress of Europe—within which European civilization would find security against Bolshevism. From then on, German radio propagandists repeatedly conjured the image of an anti-Bolshevik citadel to be built and defended by national fascists and political collaborators throughout the occupied Continent. Kris and his colleagues detailed the symbols that Nazi broadcasters presented continuously to their listeners:

> But the fortress was more than just a military fortress. It was a munitions factory, a brotherhood, a living testimonial to Nazi justice, a new ideology, a concatenation of all the victories. It provided the newest of the new orders.[59]

When the German invasion of the Soviet Union stalled, Nazi propagandists stressed even more adamantly the threat from communism and the need for an anti-Bolshevik political fusion of Europe.

Months before the invasion of Russia, Gombrich began to prepare his own treatise on the messages and mechanisms of German propaganda. Monitoring the German wireless for long hours both day and night, he developed a numbing familiarity with Nazi claims. As early as February 1941, in a memorandum for the monitoring service, he began to outline a theory of propaganda on paper.[60]

To explain Nazi propaganda Gombrich first applied an analytic framework within which to interpret the nature of fascist regimes. Although the writings of the medieval cleric and historian Giraldus Cambrensis—Gerald of Wales—had seemed less inspiring after he moved to the listening post, he continued to read them and found there a version of the dual state theory of fascism. In March 1941, Gombrich wrote to Saxl that the cleric had anticipated the competitive alliance between state and party that existed in contemporary fascist regimes:

> I am now reading "The Autobiography of Giraldus Cambrensis" (De rebus a se gestis) XIIth cent. which I found in the Evesham public library in a modern translation. I find it amazingly interesting. It gives a very vivid picture of the conditions in Wales and probably everywhere with the constant tussels [sic] and conflicts between various dioceses and between State and Church[;] that dualism was really something like the dualism of "party" and "state" in authoritarian states nowadays.[61]

Gombrich added to the duality of the party and civil service a third institutional partner: the Church.[62] In July 1941, he wrote to Kris that he had progressed far enough in his thinking that he was "sometimes toying with the idea of writing something very general on propaganda."[63] Eventually, he approached colleagues at the listening post to join in a compendium of essays on Nazi propaganda.

Just as Kris sent Gombrich drafts of his book chapters and copies of his articles, so Gombrich kept Kris apprised of the ideas that he intended to incorporate in his treatise on propaganda. Before the invasion of Russia, he focused on formal techniques of Nazi communication, distinguishing between various types of propaganda. A smooth brand was "carried out at dinner tables by semi-official business envoys"; radio propaganda, however, was "as subtle as a steamroller."[64] *Mein Kampf* had given instructions in propaganda methods and German radio adhered to the techniques absolutely. Hans Fritzsche, who served under Reich press chief Otto Dietrich, applied them most adroitly. As a radio broadcaster and eventually the chief of Nazi radio propaganda, Fritzsche avoided overt ideological indoctrination. Rather, his speeches persistently spread the myth of Germany as the victim not the aggressor in the current war, a conflict which was "always represented as horrible and as a ter[r]ible necessity 'forced upon us' rather than as a climax of life."[65]

But Fritzsche's image of Germans compelled to wage war against their will represented more than a strategic effort at legitimizing expansionism and arousing retaliation: it revealed the obsessively formulaic and projective nature of Nazi propaganda. Gombrich gave particular attention to propaganda as a mental construct and mode of political perception, emphasizing that the propagandist aimed above all at preserving a schema. Thus, after the German invasion of the Soviet Union, Nazi propagandists devoted continuous and increasing energy to solidifying the mythic construct of German history and destiny. A month after the invasion, Gombrich explained to Kris the theory that now guided him:

> The main "point" of my story would be that it is a misconception to think of "propaganda" as of a means to put "something" across—say the idea, that America is an invincible industrial ally or so. It is first and foremost a way of se[e]ing things, an interpretation of events, not of some events but of <u>all</u> events, past, present and <u>future</u>. Everything must fit in and the "moral" of ever[y]thing must always be "I told you so" . . . [T]he myth to which everything is reduced is, of course, born out of the most simple and primitive mechanism of that kind: projection. That is to say, the "stop thieve[s]" technique which [one] can always enjoy with so much pleasure in German propaganda—(the <u>others</u> strive for world domination, regard Europe as "a mere reservoir of slave labour", play the socialists to dupe the masses, and have stolen the V sign from the Germans who invented it)—has very deep roots in the whole technique.[66]

Although agreeing with Kris that propagandists sought both to manipulate emotional states and promote instrumentalist goals, Gombrich stressed the nature of Nazi imagery as a projective construct. Only by approaching propaganda as the imposition of modes of seeing and interpretation could one fully explain its hegemonic reach and purpose.

The Dilemma of Antifascism

Propaganda analysis led Gombrich, as it did Kris, to examine the political and ideological difficulties confronting the antifascist war effort. In early January 1942, Kris wrote to Gombrich that his research team had nearly completed its first Rockefeller Foundation report on German radio broadcasts. In the letter, Kris detailed his ongoing concern about the obstacles that stood in the way of building a strong antifascist movement in the United States and forming a political alliance with Britain. Anti-Bolshevik hostility toward Russia and anti-British sentiment among Catholics posed the most difficult barriers:

> As to the future of the war: I feel that it may take much longer than any of us are inclined to believe and I am anxious to detect any chink in the Allied armour; the one I mind most is the antagonism against Russia, prevailing in this country and supplemented by the catholic [sic] prejudice against England; catholics [sic] here are largely Irish or Italian.[67]

Antifascism in the United States had still to become a strong unifying force. Kris conveyed his most dismal assessment of global prospects at any time during or after the war: "I take the view that the world war has just begun and that many more wars are going to start before they all can be composed by victory."[68]

In reply, Gombrich pointed out that the antifascist cause suffered inevitably from having to reject in principle any schematic construct, any comprehensive formula. All propaganda—past and present—meant the propagation of a faith and the manufacture of a myth to justify that faith:

> As long as it is not, as it was originally[,] a "propaganda fides" it is no propaganda at all. That is to say it is more and more my conviction that its function is to interpret events (all events) in one given sense, to fit them into a pre-existing pattern rather than to advertise them.[69]

Regarding the search for a unified antifascist movement, Gombrich cautioned Kris against accepting the framework of the Marxist Left:

> Marxism with its primitive interpretation of history and politics has an easy game, Nazism with its far more primitive myth of a world in which the radiant [illegible] Siegfrieds are fought by a Jewish conspiracy has an even easier task.[70]

Gombrich despaired at the Allies' disappointing and half-hearted efforts at political warfare and he shared Kris's frustration with those who impeded the creation of a broad antifascist message: "But that does not mean that we can dispense with any interpretation . . . But as one can't concoct a 'fides' (at least we can't) the whole thing makes me rather sick."[71]

Gombrich acknowledged that the unhealthy miasma of Allied propaganda derived not from the ideas of the Left but from the attempt to construct an instant ideology of Christian democracy. Not only Eden but also Franklin Roosevelt wanted to placate the Vichy government and draw it over to the Allies:

> Roosevelt has most of it, but the background [of] this christian democratic creed is historically and sociologically so far removed from the past of continental nations (where progress and enlightenment was championed by the Voltaires) that I doubt whether it can have much appeal there.[72]

A Christian democratic creed, which emphasized that the danger represented by Nazism was the spread of pagan belief, would not stir French citizens "who suffer from the betrayal of their Catholic Pétains."[73] Such propaganda would do nothing to undermine the reactionary nationalism that helped give rise to Nazism in Germany: "the trouble there seems to me that since the days of the French Revolution the national enemy happened to coincide with the champion of progressive, liberal ideas."[74]

Gombrich had lived under a Christian Social regime and understood its nature. He opposed the rehabilitation of Catholic collaborationist regimes in the guise of postwar Christian democracies. Instead, antifascist propaganda had to focus on building a secular, reformist European identity. But unlike Kris and despite his criticism of Christian democratic ideology, he recoiled from advocating Popular Front politics as the means of realizing this Voltairean vision.[75]

At the listening post, the idea of the externalization and modification of conceptual schemas in both art and politics took ever stronger hold of Gombrich. In March 1942, he wrote to Kris that he had been preparing the promised lecture on English heroic landscape. Intended for the Courtauld Institute, it interpreted eighteenth-century landscape painting through "the whole process of 'projection' which is going on."[76] He summarized his argument:

> At the first stage (roughly) there is an "ideal landscape" (illustrative of the literary genres of pastoral and epics) and, somehwere [sic] below the threshold of "art"[,] topographical painting. Then travellers etc. "project" Claudes into English landscape and admire the "prospects" never forgetting to compare them with Claude etc. Gardeners "improve" sceneries to conform to Claudian standards (there are plenty of documents for this), and painters start selecting beauty spots to paint Claudes from Nature (slightly adjusting the composition to make nature conform to the rules of the game)[.] Only then landscape painting in our sense becomes "possible" (in the

> Woefflin sense) . . . Well, there it goes, the whole thing should end in Turner on the one side who starts from this convention but transcends it by expanding it and Constable who breaks it with the help of the Dutch convention.[77]

Gombrich had turned Saxl's request for a talk on landscape art into a lecture on experimentation with mental and cultural constructs:

> [T]he evolution as outlined is really very typical of evolutions as such because you know that this is an old hobby of mine that "nature" can only be grasped (in art) in terms of some pre-conceived pattern which is streched [sic] and adapted to conform to new demands but not easily exchanged for a new one.[78]

The Courtauld presentation contained the theoretical kernel and the visual image—Constable's depiction of the English countryside—that inspired Gombrich's postwar analysis of the manipulation and transformation of artistic schemas. Saxl had been right: English heroic landscape would provide Gombrich with a vital stimulus. At the same time, Gombrich responded by integrating it with, not isolating it from, his political analyses of conceptual constructs in image making. Paradoxically, in Gombrich's view, art might possess greater power to combat propagandistic formulas than did the strategies of politicians, information officers, or monitors—a conclusion that reflected less his confidence in the artist than his growing pessimism toward politics.[79]

An Integrated Front

A new resurgence of xenophobia in Britain coincided with the invasion of Russia and intensified the difficulty of sustaining a coherent antifascist message. One highly public form of antiforeign attitudes went by the name "Vansittartism," a term that referred to Conservative diplomatist Lord Vansittart and his series of published radio talks,

"Black Record." His talks drew the attention of large numbers of listeners and readers, including Kris and Gombrich. A revived chauvinism now attached itself to the debates over the social aims of the war.

Throughout the 1930s, Lord Vansittart served as permanent undersecretary to the Foreign Office. After Mussolini's invasion of Ethiopia in 1935, he helped to construct the Hoare–Laval proposal for a partition of the occupied country. If implemented, the proposal would have satisfied Mussolini's territorial demands while allowing him to avoid oil sanctions by the League of Nations. In September 1938, Vansittart supported conceding the Sudetenland to Hitler but insisted on a statement promising British action in case of any further German annexations of Czech territory. Vansittart's stance led Chamberlain to demote him to the status of chief diplomatic advisor. In May 1940, with the defeat of France looming and the British Expeditionary Force falling back to the sea, Vansittart—still with contacts in foreign embassies and the intelligence services—helped to arrange a meeting between the Italian ambassador to London and the Foreign Secretary, Lord Halifax. Vansittart hoped the government would use Mussolini to seek favorable peace terms for France, and, if necessary, to organize a conference with Hitler. After the meeting, Halifax thought the idea worth exploring further; Churchill, supported by Labour's Clement Attlee, rejected it.[80]

In November and December 1940, Vansittart delivered seven BBC radio lectures on the war. The *Sunday Times* immediately printed portions in its New Year's edition. Published as *Black Record: Germans Past and Present*, the talks went through fourteen printings by December 1941. According to various estimates, copies reached tens of thousands to one million people—not including radio listeners.[81]

Vansittart's lectures sounded a single theme: Nazism represented the most recent and most extreme incarnation of the ancient Germanic danger to Latin civilization and European Christendom. From the Roman Empire to the present, Vansittart explained, the German people—"*Germans* in the plural"[82]—had posed a recurrent threat to a peaceful Europe. For confirmation he referred to the *Germania* and

Annals of the Roman historian Tacitus, who gave a detailed account of the society and customs of early Germanic tribes and whom Vansittart had read as a student. The main point for Vansittart was that Tacitus, who "admired them in some ways, but found them disquieting neighbors,"[83] recognized in the Germanic population and their leaders a hatred of peace. As a self-conceived, modern-day Tacitus, he now stressed, "there is nothing new in Hitler."[84] Nor was there anything new in the contemporary response of the German people to Hitler and his expansionist mission: "there have been potential reformers in Germany," Vansittart explained, "but they have always been a weak minority, and have never been able to impede the iniquitous habits and courses of the majority."[85]

According to Vansittart, only the Church and the British Empire could impede German ambitions. The German churches, he acknowledged, had offered almost no opposition to the spread of Nazism. But in an early formulation of Christian democratic ideology, he asserted that Latin Christendom—which he associated with both Austria and France—represented an essential barrier to Hitler's "anti-Christian"[86] regime. Both Bismarck and Hitler had perceived Austria, which in Vansittart's vision was Hitler's first victim, as the initial obstacle to subduing Latin civilization, a mission that they both completed with the conquest of France.[87] It now remained for British soldiers and citizens to undertake not only an imperial duty but also a Christian obligation to defeat Nazism.[88]

The term "fascism" never appeared in Vansittart's talks, which interpreted the war as a patriotic and Christian fight against German expansionism. Emphasizing the weakness of internal opposition to Germany's leaders, he discounted German social democracy as an agent of reform. Not surprisingly, conservative editorialists applauded Vansittart. Conservative Foreign Office officials, however, remained mixed in their reactions: they supported Vansittart's stress on the German nation, not fascism, as the enemy and welcomed his support for the Churchill wing of the Tory party, but they saw no reason to bring a loose cannon back into decision-making circles. Among Labour members of government, the figure in the strongest position to answer Vansittart—Hugh Dalton, the early opponent of appeasement—had also promoted xenophobic counter-propaganda.[89]

Excluded from the Foreign Office, Vansittart zealously exploited his access to the radio microphone and his position in the House of Lords. Yet, despite their xenophobia, his talks brought attention to two questions that would become decisive after the war: how to identify the nature of the German people's complicity in Hitler's crimes and how to confront the denial of responsibility for those crimes. As Vansittart emphasized, Goering's bomber pilots destroyed Guernica but the "Old-School Neurath"[90] oversaw the violence against the Czechs. Concluding his lectures, Vansittart demanded: "Above all, never be duped by the type of German who says that he disapproves of atrocities, but was obliged to commit them out of loyalty to the Fatherland."[91] Responsibility reached not only to "camp-followers"[92] but also to those who averted their gaze: "All these will join unctuously in long litanies of denial."[93] Those indictments and predictions carried weight beyond Vansittart's historical views and political motives.

Black Record brought swift and strong responses from the émigré community and from the Left. Like a long line of polemicists before him, Vansittart had brought Tacitus into the political arena, and the German refugee Heinrich Fraenkel immediately questioned his claim to be educating a British audience in the same way that the ancient writer had educated the Romans.[94] In a pamphlet published by the Fabian Society, Fraenkel responded that unlike Vansittart, Tacitus never exploited xenophobia in his readers. A great deal was at stake to Fraenkel and writers on the Left: not only how émigré opponents of Hitler were being treated in Britain but also how the government and public viewed the rise of fascism in Europe and how they intended to prevent a fascist resurgence after the war. As Fraenkel wrote, Vansittart ignored how Germany's aristocratic, military, and industrial elites raised Hitler to the chancellorship, and he intentionally overlooked how British and French policies from 1936 to 1939 abandoned republican Spain to dictatorship and indulged Hitler's territorial claims. Perhaps of most concern to Fraenkel, Vansittart refused to acknowledge the German opposition. According to Fraenkel, of the many who supported Hitler, the largest number did so not from active conviction but from feelings of passivity, indifference, or selfishness. Not only had a unified German resistance slowly come into being among exiled Social Democrats, but a growing segment of the German masses were ready also to engage in resistance once the prospect of victory came closer:

> Next to the vanguard of heroes and martyrs comes a group of those who hate Nazism no less but are not prepared to risk their lives in active oppositional work, at least not so long as they cannot see an immediate chance of success. That group does run into millions; it contains the bulk of the politically-minded workers and peasants, and a good many intellectuals from all strata of the population.[95]

Vansittartism, which refused to take that possibility into account, foreshadowed a Draconian peace that would hinder the process of postwar recovery and reform.

More than one reply to Vansittart appeared on the British Left, including contrasting responses from Victor Gollancz and George Orwell. In early 1942, as editor of the Left Book Club, Gollancz published a rejoinder that reasserted the antifascist principles he had spelled out before the war, including that the anti-Hitler struggle must adopt no imperialist claims and contain "no trace of the wrong sort of war feeling."[96] Like Fraenkel, Gollancz stressed Vansittart's ill effect not only on wartime behavior but also on how Britain would make the peace and undertake reconstruction.

By contrast, Orwell regarded Vansittartism not as the ideology of a single, well-placed government figure but as the reflection of an existing, increasingly widespread political assumption. In one of his first London Letters to the *Partisan Review* in New York, written in April 1941,

Orwell explained that Vansittart's ideas fit with the recent upsurge of nationalism:

> Propaganda enters into our lives more than it did a year ago, but not so grossly as it might. The flag-waving and Hun-hating is absolutely nothing to what it was in 1914–18, but it is growing. I think the majority opinion would now be that we are fighting the German people and not merely the Nazis. Vansittart's hate-Germany pamphlet, *Black Record*, sold like hot-cakes.[97]

As Kris had observed about the United States, anti-Hitler feeling did not represent an antifascist mentality; rather it expressed a patriotic, wartime reaction. As Orwell continued, "nor is 'anti-Fascism', of the kind that was fashionable during the Popular Front period, a strong force yet. The English people have never caught up with that."[98]

In a London Letter published in January 1942, Orwell returned to the topic of Vansittartism. Nationalist feeling had produced xenophobic outbreaks. Governing circles—fearful of egalitarian tendencies within the resistance movements—welcomed those outbursts:

> Vansittart's thesis is that the Germans are *all* wicked, and not merely the Nazis. I don't need to tell you how gleefully the Blimps have seized upon this as a way of escaping from the notion that we are fighting against Fascism. But of late the "only good German is a dead one" line has taken the rather sinister form of a fresh drive against the refugees.[99]

Not only British elites but antirepublican émigrés also sought to convert the war against Hitler into a struggle against socialism and the reformist agenda:

> The Austrian monarchists have fallen foul of the German left-wingers, whom they accuse of being pan-Germans in disguise, and

> this delights the Blimps, who are always trying to manoeuvre their two enemies, Germany and socialism, into the same place. The point has now been reached where anyone who describes himself as "anti-Fascist" is suspected of being pro-German.[100]

Orwell rejected Fraenkel's view that there existed a latent anti-Nazi resistance within Germany, but he did not renounce the radical aims of the antifascist struggle: "The pinks cannot admit that the German masses are behind Hitler any more than the Blimps can admit that their class must be levered out of control if we are to win the war."[101]

For his part, Vansittart supported the émigré organization "Fight for Freedom," which had been founded by the German exile Walter Loeb. This nebulous group feared that British workers might veer too far toward the Left, especially if they believed that a socialist uprising in Germany would defeat Hitler. It published its own polemical literature, including a broadside against Gollancz, and lobbied trade unionists to reject socialism and communism.[102]

Gombrich reacted strongly to Vansittart's radio address. Having seen the excerpts that appeared in the press on New Year's 1941, he wrote to Kris the following day: "By the way, what is your opinion on Sir Robert Vansittard's [sic] talks to overseas? I read them in the Sunday Times yesterday and I found them rather deplorable from all points of view."[103]

Vansittart made a travesty of the historical record. His argument from Tacitus was "bad history because it should be wellknown [sic] by now that Tacitus is not a source but an adaptation of 'topoi' to the Germani whom he, incidentally[,] represents as the virtuous natives."[104] But the significant issue was political, not academic. Vansittart's tirades closely resembled fascist broadcasts:

> But most of all it is bad propaganda because it is so entirely irrelevant and why waste the time and the air with past sins when the present ones are crying to heavens and why spoil a noble cause with so ignoble arguments. After all if one would stop to take them

> seriously for a moment they would boil down to a theory of racial determinism, that is to say just what we are fighting against.[105]

In the months that followed, Gombrich—like Orwell—concluded that the "anti-Hun" mentality reflected more than momentary fear and zealotry: it received impetus from the political classes who used it as an ideological diversion. In a January 1942 letter to Kris, Gombrich described the combination of reactionary nationalism and political calculation that sustained Vansittartism and that threatened to revive fascist sympathies within British political life:

> I can't help feeling however that apart from being a most natural and comprehensible reaction to events the "Hun propaganda" here is fostered by quarters who want to blur the issues of this war. This seems to me more dangerous than it may look at present but we can't help it anyhow. There are other signs here of a possible fascist mentality after the war but there is nothing we can do about it.[106]

To the end of the war Gombrich remained mistrustful of the propaganda that emanated from governing circles and wary of the chauvinism that circulated within and beyond them. For him, European fascism, not German Nazism alone, was the enemy and in that struggle British anti-Hun propaganda proved as misbegotten as Christian democracy.[107]

In March 1942, Gombrich wrote to Kris that the most serious discussions of the war occurred within the working class. The Labour movement—in contrast to the behavior of Conservatives—did not blur the issues. What concerned Gombrich was that the debate over the Second Front would lead Labour to discard its political moderation and succumb to appeals from the Communist party. After 1945, Gombrich would condemn what he called the "glib and irresponsible talk of civil war"[108] coming from the émigré Austrian socialist press after the Dollfuss coup; he interpreted the demands for an immediate Second Front as equally self-destructive. Yet, while he opposed the popular agitation for a Second Front—especially the arguments from the Communist party—he just as strongly rejected Red Scare tactics:

> On the other hand I fear that where there is less complacency and more thought, that is to say with the workers, there is precious little understanding of the situation as it is. This constant call for "action" and for "taking risks" and, naturally for the "second front now," is naturally (and openly) fostered by the Communists, but I wonder whether it is not rather ill considered and dangerous. Strangely enough words have lost all meaning becuase [sic] if people talk of taking risks they never seem to think what the risks are and what we can afford to stake. I have sometimes the impression, which may very well be wrong, that some of this activist shouting is fostered, through some devious channels, by Axis propaganda, mostly because of the restiveness and sense of frustration which it creates but perhaps for even more sinister reasons. I could well imagine, though I can't, of course, prove it, that some Communist or pseudo communist elements who have been Nazi dupes before Hitler's attack on Russia, are still, without knowing it, the dupes of some Nazi-fostered whisper propaganda. Don't think that I am bitten by the anti-Bolshy scare, for I am not in the least . . .[109]

Gombrich remained profoundly hesitant toward the call for an immediate Second Front. But faced with a revival of nationalist hysteria and fearing the reemergence of fascist political sympathies, he continued to argue against Christian democratic, anti-Bolshevist strategies.

In November 1942, Kris completed an essay in which he detailed his own concerns about the reemergence of xenophobic propaganda. To sustain the German war effort, especially at a time of German military setbacks in Russia, Goebbels had repeatedly stressed the threat of retaliation from Germany's enemies, claiming that the Allies would make no distinction between Nazis and Germans in taking their vengeance. Kris argued that material such as "Lord Vansittart's pamphlet"[110] indirectly assisted such propaganda. His last contacts with Germans in 1938 and recent reports that some Germans had shown signs of sympathy toward Jews after the imposition of the Yellow Star led Kris—like Fraenkel and other émigrés—to conclude that perhaps "still the urge to oppose exists in Germany."[111] Opposition, however, did not mean a commitment to resistance. Rather, now that the military tide was beginning to turn, those who had denied knowledge of brutalities, evaded responsibility, or applauded early military successes simply disavowed the regime. German military failures suddenly led such persons to rediscover their souls:

> The preconscious belief in the ultimate divine protection of the successful will, when disappointed, give rise to a different reaction; and the voice of conscience, so long in check, will gain in strength. "After all, my original feeling that this is evil was right; what looked like inspired leadership is crime after all."[112]

Those who showed gestures of support toward Jews included "many who were in search of alibis,"[113] as well as "those whose wavering conscience was awakened, since the approach of failure had broken the spell."[114] According to Kris, propaganda analysis would yield more information about the actual extent of opposition within Germany, especially the relative significance of long-term resistance as opposed to immediate defections.

In August 1943, several months after Russian victories in the east and Allied victories in North Africa, Gombrich commented on the revival of chauvinism, both within the general population and the intelligentsia. In a letter to Kris, he lamented that British universities had no professors like Robert S. Lynd. On Saxl's recommendation, Gombrich had read Lynd's *Knowledge for What? The Place of Social Science in American Culture.* Ten years after *Middletown* and on the eve of the Second World War, *Knowledge for What?* described the same dysfunctional state in the social sciences that Lynd had discovered in Middletown. Calling on scholars to incorporate the sciences of psychology and sociology into their thinking, he warned that academics risked marginalizing themselves as a profession if they refused to confront pressing societal problems.[115] Gombrich now agreed: "Recently I read some of the essays in Robert Lynd's 'Knowledge for What'? (Saxl drew my attention to them) and I found them very stimulating and very 'American'—are'nt [sic] they?"[116]

Gombrich informed Kris that recent xenophobic attitudes could very well last beyond the war:

> There is a definite danger of a pseudo fascist reaction here with talk of the kind one hears already "the foreigners and Jews stayed behind and took all the cushy jobs etc." and though my job is anything but cushy it is difficult for outsiders to see it in this light. In this respect too you are better off as an immigrant in the USA then [sic] we here who are only here on toleration. As you know naturalisation does'nt [sic] make any difference here.[117]

Service with the monitoring center had not counteracted Gombrich's sense of social isolation. Yet, despite harboring a similar feeling of dislocation and pessimism, Kris still found in popular reform movements and in the ideas of the Left the possibility of a new direction. He agreed with those in Britain and the United States who urged wartime policymakers to prepare blueprints for postwar reforms. If the antifascist struggle did not bring about change, Britain and the United States risked a relapse into political ideologies and economic conditions that produced the Depression and Nazism. In September 1943, Kris responded to Gombrich's concerns about close-minded scholars and resurgent xenophobes in Britain:

> As far as the general situation goes the concern of common people about the future is the one hopeful sign I can see. Peace plan[n]ers have as yet not been able to integrate their work and policy makers

> have failed or avoided to publicize their plans. The concern of the common people however remain the motiv[e] power which will help to overcome inertia and may well guarantee that easy go lucky back to normalcy speakers won[']t find followers. Their kind is naturally more rampant in this country than in England. Here normalcy means "free" enterprise, anti new deal policy, and in the long run the old mess.[118]

Like Gombrich, Kris perceived the danger of a fascist revival in peacetime and thus intellectuals like Gombrich would have important roles to perform after the war:

> I like to think of the day when people like yourself will be busy debunking the mythology they carefully recorded. Our anti Nazi propaganda must start when the war is won, or we may well see the third world war emerge from the second as the second emerged from the first.[119]

Kris sought more information about Vansittartism. He feared that it would split Labour and become an influential postwar doctrine:

> May I in this connection solicit a comment of yours on Vansittartism. What do you, what do progressives in Britain think about V. [Vansittart] and the fight for freedom Loeb who has swayed the labour party and was rebuked by the T.U.C. the other day? I am asking you since after a careful study of British views, (pamphlets, speeches, articles) I am unable to guess how the majority of people are likely to react to Vansittartism in say a year from now.[120]

Thus in the months after completing his essay on defections from Nazism, Kris had again become more sullen. He could not agree with those in the émigré community or on the British Left—represented by Richard Crossman, assistant editor at the *New Statesman and Nation*—

who claimed that an incipient German resistance was looking for the correct moment to rise up. Like Orwell, he believed that Vansittart—however misguided strategically and politically—sounded an important warning. After the war, German citizens would refuse to confront the full extent of their participation in Hitlerism. Almost all would find reasons to convince themselves that they had been good Germans:

> You may suspect that I myself hold profound views on the question. In fact I don't. I do however feel that V. is more nearly right than those of the Crossmanites who expect German social democrats to wait for their liberators. There are those who wait and there are those who will say that they have been waiting. To my mind the latter will be so numerous that nobody will be able to distinguish between truth and pretense; not even those who pretend, i.e. the Germans themselves.[121]

Kris stressed to Gombrich the value and relevance of the work of Left intellectuals such as Robert S. Lynd, whose ideas in fact did not represent the thought of a generic American social scientist:

> Robert Lynd, whom you seem to consider as typical American, is undoubtedly one of the leading if not the leading American sociologist; he is a true leftist, to the left of ordinary Marxists, and is undoubtedly a brilliant man. You may have met him or [will] meet him in England since he is supposed to act there as a[n] OWI speaker, as Margaret Mead is doing. She is one of my close friends and again typical only of herself. There are not many of his or her kind around.[122]

And among such scholars and writers Kris's letter included not only Harold Lasswell but also Meyer Schapiro.

Kris's political advice had limited effect on Gombrich. To counter wartime xenophobia and "Blimpism"—whether among Vansittart's supporters or in the BBC bureaucracy—Gombrich turned not to contemporary critics on the Left but to an older, conservative tradition. Responding in November 1943 to Kris's request for information about Vansittart, he began:

> Now to your question about "Vansittartism". I am afraid I know very little about it. My own views on this subject in general were anticipated by a certain David Hume in his essay "On national character." (Generally I am inclined to think that human intelligence progressed till it reached its peak in England round about 1730–1760 with people like Swift or Hume or young Burke and that it declined afterwards till it reached the nadir in the brains of my present superiors, but this is a digression).[123]

Gombrich likely recalled the opening sentence of Hume's essay "Of National Characters":

> The vulgar are apt to carry all *national characters* to extremes; and, having once established it as a principle that any people are knavish, or cowardly, or ignorant, they will admit of no exception, but comprehend every individual under the same censure.[124]

In Gombrich's view, however, Vansittartism had not yet sunk permanently entrenched roots in society:

> The other people I know are hardly very characteristic examples. My Evesham landlord, for instance, is an utterly egocentric brutal retired market gardener and horsedealer who does'nt [sic] really care but who is all for the view that the only good hun is a dead hun. But generally this problem plays only a minute part in his mental universe for his only real interest is horse-prizes and profit making. He is not an exceptionally bad or unkind man but this is [h]is world—we have had three years of "fieldwork" studying it.[125]

At the listening post, however, other analysts shared Gollancz and Crossman's opinion that Vansittartism represented a more widespread phenomenon: "People whom I meet in the course of my work here naturally incline towards the opposite view—for they are more often than not of a leftish New Statesman hue."[126]

Gombrich rejected both the wartime ideas of the Conservative ruling circle and the criticisms leveled against it by the British Left. But he now distanced himself even from the position of Labour moderates. Instead, as at the start of the war, he turned toward the past—toward an older British philosophy that reflected his own persistent sense of alienation.

Combative Pessimism

Gombrich's analysis of fascism and fascist propaganda derived chiefly not from his experience of monitoring German broadcasts, nor from his feeling of displacement within British political culture, but from his vivid memory of the Austrian debacle. The experience of Austro-Fascism, especially the political and moral collapse of both the Austrian Church and Austrian liberalism, remained strongly in his mind.

In April 1943, writing from the listening post's new home in Reading, Gombrich responded vigorously to Kris's draft of a chapter for *German Radio Propaganda*, which stated: "Before each of the great holidays, the radio broadcast comments on its meaning in Teutonic mythology."[127] Gombrich warned that the statement was misleading:

> The notion that Nazidom is "pagan" is only true if one implies with it the denial of what is called the values of Christian Civilisation. It becomes ludicrous if one hints that they are worshipping Wotan. They don't. They worship nothing at all.[128]

Rather, the Catholic hierarchy's political collaboration with Nazism—to the point of adopting its signs and symbols—exemplified pagan behavior far more closely:

> On the other hand it was Innitzer, still Archbishop of Vienna, who added with his own hand "Heil Hitler" to the Church's pronouncement on the invasion of Austria and for a Prince of the Church to do that is, I think, "Paganism". I really don't think, for all [the] respect I have for the Faulhaber's and von Galens, that the Church is fundamentally anti Nazi. There is a Kulturkampf going on, that's all, none is on in Italy or Spain and they might just as well come to terms in Germany.[129]

In Austria, the *Kulturkampf*—the cultural war between Nazi party officials who wanted to install a new Germanic religion and Austrian clericals who advocated collaboration as spelled out in the Concordat between Hitler and the Church hierarchy—had stretched from the year of the *Anschluss* to the invasion of the Soviet Union. In 1938, Innitzer expected to reach his own accord with Hitler that would allow the Church to keep control of its schools, property, and pastoral work; the fact that the majority in Seyss-Inquart's cabinet belonged to the Catholic National Opposition gave him confidence in his negotiating position. Although the Church offered compromise, the Austrian Nazi party, with the support of Seyss-Inquart in Vienna and Hitler in Berlin, imposed state control over education, closed parochial schools and seminaries, and confiscated Church property. Yet, led by Innitzer, the Catholic hierarchy continued to affirm its political loyalty to the Reich and seek accommodation with the regime. Religious worship as well as spiritual instruction remained under its supervision. Ultimately, after the invasion of the Soviet Union, Hitler ended confiscations so as to unite pan-Germans and Austrian clericals in the anti-Bolshevik crusade.[130] As in Spain and Italy, the *Kulturkampf* in Austria subsided when the two sides joined against a socialist enemy.

Against this background, Gombrich remained skeptical toward the Church as a source of antifascist opposition. As he wrote to Kris:

> Naturally the Church, as an organised body outside the State and the Party[,] is a potential center of resistence [sic] but the whole

> sphere of problems would require a very very dispassionate and thorough analysis far removed from any facile labels and slogans.[131]

For Gombrich, it was essential that no one construe from Kris's reference to Teutonic mythology that there existed any hope of the Church hierarchy resisting Nazism. It had already shown itself all too willing to compromise.

If the *Anschluss* exposed the collaborationism of Austrian clericals who served the Church, neither did it permit illusions concerning the behavior of anticlericals who served the state. Gombrich did not forget the Josephan civil servants who had defected to pan-Germanism after the First World War. Joseph II's enlightened German administrators, who in the eighteenth century had enforced limited religious toleration toward the monarchy's Jews, revealed in the twentieth century their fervid German nationalism. Then, after 1933, they readily pledged fealty to Hitler's Third Reich rather than support a restored Austrian Catholic state, as Gombrich recalled to Kris: "Nor need I tell <u>you</u> that anti clericalism drove many liberals in Austria into the Nazi camp, people who essentially embodied the "'Josephinische Tradition' of liberalism."[132]

Like the Church hierarchy, the secularized civil service had made its peace with Nazi politics and ideology. The moral collapse of clerical and anticlerical authorities alike—the almost complete absence of either religious or liberal resistance—reflected the crisis from which fascism emerged:

> My view, in a nutshell, is that the rise of Nazidom has much to do with the decline of religion in Germany and the crisis of European civilisation caused by this momentous fact but it is vital not to take cause for effect. Nor did Nazidom put Paganism in the place of Christianity but simple Nihilism, Opportunism and Cynisism [sic], disguised as a worship of force and of the Survival of the Fittest.[133]

Both devout clericals and statist liberals refused to offer protection against fascism. Instead, they submitted to it and advanced it, sacrificing both faith and reason. Gombrich's reflections on Austria recalled Balzac's furious judgment against sacrilegious churchmen and unprincipled bourgeoisie in a society that discarded what was both sacred and real.

For Gombrich, at that moment of history, the aim of propaganda analysis was therefore to combat intellectual nihilism. In August 1943, he responded irately to an essay on Goebbels's conception of propaganda written by Hans Herma, a member of Kris's research team:

> Though there are passages in it which I would heartily endorse, I do not only think that the whole paper is rather inadequate but, in parts it is definitely wrong. You can imagine that owing to my particular occupation the note 2 "as a result of the peculiar use of language by totalitarian authors their meaning is not always clearly ascertainable" drove me into harness . . . Forgive this outburst but I am sure you will realise that I had plenty of opportunity to ponder general problems of translation and meaning and that "I stand no nonsense" in this respect.[134]

Meanings remained accessible through their contexts, a spectrum that ranged from the scientific and philosophic to the ideological and political to the institutional and social. Summoning inspiration from the young Burke, Gombrich concluded:

> Apart from this "spectrum" there is, in the Nazi use of language, a definite attempt to increase the evocative character of certain words as emotional stimulus and, consequently a blurred logical meaning, this, incidentally[,] is nothing new but was described with supreme insight by Edmund Burke in one of the last chapters of the "Sublime and Beautiful". But even so it seems ridiculous to say that these words have no "meaning"[,] they have a very strong emotive meaning

which is quite easily ascertainable. (Through the study of contexts, like all meanings.) Basta.[135]

Toward the end of his *Philosophical Enquiry into the Origin of Our Ideas of the Sublime and the Beautiful*, Burke had examined the impact of language by virtue of sound, imagery, or the "*affection* of the soul produced by one or by both of the foregoing."[136] Emphasizing that words exerted strong emotional effect even without producing clear images, Burke lamented that he found it "very hard to persuade several that their passions are affected by words whence they have no ideas."[137] Here as elsewhere Gombrich's intellectual model derived from the early Enlightenment, from the time when the young Irishman and émigré liberal Burke experienced a profound sense of social alienation and before political disenchantment and fear of revolution took hold of him.

By November 1943, Gombrich had produced "my mammoth study of totalitarian propaganda."[138] Several colleagues contributed to the volume and Gombrich hoped that the monitoring service would publish it. But in April 1944 he wrote to Kris that his effort would never see print, the chief problem being that "all the contributions together came to some 100 000 words which is madness."[139] Yet, the fragments of his propaganda study that surfaced in letters to Kris reveal not madness but an engaged and divided spirit, one plagued by an increasing pessimism and a deepening mistrust of popular politics.

Gombrich's mood recalled the mindset of his Tory exemplars: Swift, Hume, and the young Burke, all critics from the age of Hogarth and Rowlandson, the first golden age of caricature. Disgruntled and caustic writers, hard-bitten satirists, and disenchanted caricaturists, they built their polemics not only on psychological analysis and moral iconoclasm but also on an inveterate social pessimism and deep aversion to mass political action—the ideologies for which the aging Burke became the famous spokesman. Throughout the war, Gombrich became increasingly drawn toward that worldview, toward the fatalism of an alienated, exiled liberal who identified neither with a Conservative political class in power nor with a popular alliance on the Left. When the monitoring service rejected his manuscript, he thus saw nowhere else to turn with it.

Although he persisted in a sweeping rejection of Marxism, Gombrich continued to remain immune to wartime anti-Bolshevism and anti-Labour ideology. Moreover, despite his later criticism of the socialist press, his letters to Kris contained no signs of dissatisfaction or hostility toward the political behavior of Austrian Socialists, and he would later characterize the Austrian Christian Social regime as "the semi-fascist government of Dollfuss."[140] For Gombrich, political xenophobia and intellectual nihilism posed the great threats of his time—and those threats, he believed, would persist beyond the war. Nazism had combined nationalist counter-revolution with nihilist ideology, a phenomenon to which Allied propagandists gave little or no account. If they had, then they would have appealed to the European Enlightenment tradition rather than to the Christian democratic creed—the phoenix that rose after the war from the midst of the discredited Church hierarchy and self-serving civil bureaucracies. Gombrich had respected the wartime spirit of the Labour moderate, but he could not shed the political pessimism of the disaffected Tory. He remained an ambivalent, isolated liberal, pulled in opposing directions and unable to accept the wider identity that Kris derived from Popular Front culture.

Fatalism had also accompanied Kris's odyssey, in his case from liberal royalism to antifascist republicanism. He had seen the collapse of his monarchical ideal, lived through the disintegration of the Austrian republic, and witnessed the succession of defeats suffered by the Popular Front. Yet, in Vienna and in New York he continued to support a broad antifascist front and held onto the idea that military victories would undermine support for Hitler in Europe. Thus too, in his 1943 article on "Some Problems of War Propaganda: A Note on Propaganda New and Old," he contrasted the propaganda system of totalitarianism to that of the democracies. Totalitarian propagandists acted on Le Bon's theories of mass suggestion and the hypnotic susceptibilities of the crowd to transform their audiences into a psychologically fused organism—or rather to convince them to perceive themselves as such. By contrast, antifascist propagandists approached their listeners as an integrated body of individuals or groups who still retained their distinct identities. Authentically democratic appeals tolerated new information and critical viewpoints, and provided the foundation for a new postwar propaganda generated not by government leaders but by opinionmakers—writers, editors, broadcasters, and scholars—utilizing mass media for instructive purposes. Kris's vision of postwar social communication incorporated the full range of his political ideas and values: a sense of royalist guardianship, commitment to the civic task of the intellectual as Marshall, for example, had defined it, and ongoing support for Popular Front republicanism.[141]

Reacting to Kris's analysis in "Some Problems of War Propaganda," Gombrich stated that in his own manuscript on totalitarian propaganda he too had "tried to uncover the symptoms of this distrust of propaganda in totalitarian countries and the way its managers are trying by a number of makeshift arrangements to counter this distrust and to adopt some of the externals at least of democratic or 'new' propaganda."[142] He came, however, to a far different conclusion:

> For in this one respect I find your paper a little too optimistic. I see no reason why the insights of the "new" approach should not also be used for very sinister ends—that is to say no intrinsic reason.[143]

Briefly revising his argument in April 1944, Gombrich wrote to Kris that he had drafted an essay explaining that the Nazi effort at imitating Allied propaganda techniques would ultimately fail at winning over the German people—but only because defeat now loomed close at hand.[144] But in January 1945, he returned to his previous desolate judgment. Unconvinced that even military defeat would uproot fascist influence from Germany, he wrote:

> [T]ime has shown that the view expressed in your +++book [*German Radio Propaganda*] that Nazi propaganda thrives on victories and

> cannot cope with defeats is wrong. I don't blame you for that, I also thought so and tried to prove it at some length. Or is it our propaganda that keeps them going?[145]

The schematic mental constructs of fascism that had preceded the war would outlast it.

In 1945, however, Gombrich's somber appraisal of events generated a new impulse for political work. Although unshaken in his original decision to join the BBC, he remained acutely aware of the disruptions, strains, and loss that exile imposed on wartime scholarship. In January, he reflected on his choice to leave the Warburg Institute:

> I do not think I could have "survived" the war in the manner Kurz[,] Buchthal or Saxl are doing it though I know that a good many people are genuinely grateful to the Warburg Institute for keeping "the torch burning" while nearly everything closed down and stopped.[146]

Gombrich's decision to leave the institute had reflected his impulse for immediate wartime activity. Now his concern that Nazism would reemerge in Germany, that the Allies would fail to inculcate an antifascist mentality on the Continent, and that neo-fascist, anti-alien attitudes would reappear in Britain almost physically demanded in him further engagement:

> What I should probably like best of all after the war, would be taking part in some positive reconstruction work, educational or antiquarian or in the field of intellectual cooperation. I have the feeling that things are bound to be in a fearful mess and that one will feel little more inclined than one is now to remain altogether aloof from what is happening. Though I think that theoretically the persuit [sic] of pure knowledge is probably the best service one can undertake in the circumstances it may need stronger nerves than mine to stick that out.[147]

After Germany's surrender, Gombrich remained with the monitoring service where he joined the work of German and Austrian denazification. In September, he briefly explained to Kris that he was participating in "the vast field of 're-education' into which I have already been drawn through various confidential activities of lecturing and translating and which also threatens to get hold of me."[148] In 1946, after having returned full-time to the Warburg Institute, he continued to devote himself to the denazification effort:

> The only outside activity I allow myself at present is a once-monthly lecture tour to Austrian Prisoners of War connected with the general re-education schemes about which you may have read in the papers. I am not very suitable for this job but they want me and I did not think I could refuse it. It is strenuous and not un-exciting. Since most of the audience usually consists of rather dumb and poor peasant lads I always feel that despite my desperate efforts to be popular we still talk a different language. Can you imagine me in a huge Nissen hut all by my little self discussing politics with, say, 300 men? I can't, in fact I often have the feeling of playing a role in whi[c]h I am rather miscast, but the others do not seem to feel it to the same extent.[149]

In fact, Gombrich—who had worked with Kris on the Daumier exhibition, left the Warburg Institute for the listening post, and compiled his own study of totalitarian propaganda—had been preparing himself for the role of a political educator for several years.

During the war, Kris and Gombrich had acted from a disenchanted mindset that nonetheless abhorred intellectual nihilism and loathed political defeatism—a combative pessimism. That divided spirit had characterized Swift, Hogarth, and the young Burke—Enlightenment critics who condemned humanity's self-elevation and self-admiration and who seconded Swift's lament from his *Meditation upon a Broom-Stick*: "Partial Judges that we are of our own Excellencies, and other

Mens Defaults!"[150] As psychologists and moralists, they had exposed the human being as a self-idealizing creature who sought from society only a role to play, a mask to wear, and a small stage on which to perform. Human reason, as they conceived it, was a limited, surgical instrument of self-criticism or, at best, a defense against illusory pride. Their discontents led them into deep personal disillusionment and finally political reaction. Their image of humanity conformed to Swift's broomstick, the literary parallel to Hogarth's vision of man as a line and a dot:

> His Animal Faculties perpetually mounted on his Rational; his Head where his Heels should be, groveling on the Earth. And yet, with all his Faults, he set up to be a universal Reformer and Corrector of Abuses . . . sharing deeply all the while in the very same Pollutions he pretends to sweep away.[151]

Combativeness dogged by pessimism characterized the spirit not only of Swift and Hogarth but also of Callot, Balzac, Daumier, and in Kris and Gombrich's day, David Low. Like their Enlightenment counterparts, these critics recognized that masks—even propagandistic ones—against the intention of their wearers revealed essential truths, an insight Daumier transformed into a tool for documenting social realities and confronting political propaganda. A combativeness that resisted the impulse to fatalism: the *sub rosa* conflict within caricature defined Kris and Gombrich's wartime antifascism.

CHAPTER 8

BETWEEN PAST AND FUTURE 1945–65

Fragmented Possibilities

In prewar Vienna, the study of caricature and borderline art gave Kris an unsteady but still workable identity as an art historian. In postwar New York, his psychoanalytic practice and research now became the foundation of his professional life and provided the opening to a wider public. Having survived the wreck of Austrian art and politics, he fastened more firmly to the rock of psychoanalysis and its Freudian substratum. He co-edited the abridged publication of the Freud–Fliess correspondence, and in the introduction he stressed the physiological and neurological thinking behind Freud's discoveries.[1] He trained psychiatrists at the New York Psychoanalytic Society, became a founding editor of *The Psychoanalytic Study of the Child*, led research at the Yale Child Study Center, and collaborated with Heinz Hartmann and Rudolph M. Loewenstein to write "a system of psychoanalysis"—the long-delayed realization of his goal to advance a psychoanalytic psychology.[2] In all of these efforts, he attempted to reawaken an interest in Freud as scientist.

Immediately after the war, Kris participated in the Society for the Psychological Study of Social Issues, a branch of the American

Psychological Association. Reminiscent of Lynd's *Knowledge for What?*, the society defined its purpose as "the directing of psychological research toward contemporary problems, making available to citizens outside the psychological profession conclusions drawn from the scientific study of human behavior."[3] Kris contributed to its 1945 publication *Human Nature and Enduring Peace*, in which psychologists, sociologists, and foreign policy analysts debated issues of postwar recovery. The society's working groups regarded the spirit of wartime alliances as the foundation of postwar internationalism, as the volume stated: "[T]he only apparent cause of war involving the three advanced systems [the United States, Britain, and the Soviet Union] would be the most idiotic defensive anxiety and a mounting spiral of armaments, mutual suspicion, and fear."[4]

In the book, the social psychologist Gordon W. Allport described the psychological advantages that derived from an international organization of states. The psychologist of art Rudolf Arnheim analyzed German reconstruction and war crimes trials and called on the tribunals to confront fascism as a global phenomenon, not only as an outcome of German nationalism. Participating in discussions on reconstruction in Japan was Owen Lattimore. A Sinologist on the faculty of Johns Hopkins University and a member of the Institute of Pacific Relations, Lattimore five years later became the first target of Senator Joseph McCarthy's attacks on East Asian policymakers.[5]

In a working group on "public opinion and world order," Kris discussed how professionals in the field of mass communication could most effectively promote internationalism. He warned against adopting the methods of mass advertisers and marketeers. Instead, he advised that opinion pollsters join with communication scholars to undertake scientific studies of how different nations had experienced the impact of war. Such research would provide a foundation for greater mutual understanding: "Interdependence becomes more clearly focused, interests more sharply crystallized; and the information on existing opinion is likely to *engender demand for information* as to the reasons underlying it."[6] In this international effort, world organizations had to produce their own structure of global information and communication. Kris found inspiration for his proposals in *Civilization and Its Discontents*, perhaps Freud's most fatalistic writing, where according to Kris, Freud conveyed that "in spite of determining biological factors changes occur over long periods of time which affect even basic human reactions. These changes may then be evaluated as progress."[7]

After the war, Kris did not seek a position in art history or museum work, and although he worked with Hartmann and Loewenstein on the reformulation of Freudian theory, he never returned to his plan for a comprehensive psychology of art. He fluctuated between accepting the permanently divided nature of his scientific and humanist interests and following his former impulse toward integrating them. In October 1945, he wrote to Gombrich that they could resume their prewar collaboration "if and when I should apply to the Rockefeller Foundation for the grant for studies in the social psychology of art."[8] Three months later he explained in a resigned and clinical tone, "I have moved away so far from the humanities per se that they evoke mainly nostalgic memories."[9] His prewar projects sank into the past or vanished into an uncertain future. Where his scholarly agenda was concerned, Kris wrote, "I have ceased to believe in long term planning."[10]

Years of forced exile and war reinforced the sense of disruption he had first experienced in Vienna. Kris never acquired a stable institutional and intellectual foothold but instead built and rebuilt his work on shifting professional and historical foundations. A great part of his achievement consisted in his ceaseless efforts to respond to those shifts, to heal the fractures they caused in his career and projects, and to draw together the persistently changing perspectives that rose before him. Committed to defending and expanding Freud's original insights, he remained open to new integrative visions but continued to suspect self-contained, unified systems. Yet, as the inward counterpart to this experimentalism, he developed an ever deeper sense of uncertainty and loss and an abiding concern with the problem of personal and collective remembrance. Although his work with Hartmann and Loewenstein placed new psychoanalytic emphasis on the ego's cognitive functions, he hoped eventually to focus his chief attention on a science of memory. The opportunity never appeared.[11]

Before the end of 1945, Gombrich resumed his fellowship at the Warburg Institute, which had become a part of the University of London a year earlier but which still could offer him no permanent academic post.[12] He had expected the monitoring service to be incorporated into the new Labour government's intelligence bureaus and thought momentarily about remaining at the listening post. Kris had urged him to support the Labour ministry:

> My own impulse would be to say that any sort of intelligence in the inter-war [sic] period would be both interesting and rewarding, that to serve a government of which one can approve as fully as one can of the present British government is in itself a good thing.[13]

Gombrich, however, had one overriding inclination: to return to the Warburg Institute. Two years later, Ernst Buschbeck, a former Austrian émigré in London and the recently restored director of the *Kunsthistorisches Museum*, attempted to convince him to return to Austria. On a trip to Paris to organize an exhibition of Austrian art, Buschbeck encountered him and, as Gombrich wrote to Kris, he "tried to persuade me to go to Vienna as a. o. Professor."[14] Gombrich turned down the offer.

In Gombrich, the division between his scientific and humanist impulses, between his wartime activism and postwar pessimism became increasingly sharp bifurcations. Contact with Karl Popper after the war brought the split to the surface. In March 1946, Gombrich wrote to Kris that Popper had received an appointment to the London School of Economics and that both volumes of *The Open Society and Its Enemies* now had appeared in Britain: "Of course he distrusts all history, psychology and so on but this rather stimulates than daunts me."[15] Gombrich looked forward to developing a psychology of art grounded not in a philosophy of history but in a science of perception and he outlined for Kris the theory that remained one of his core insights: "My idea is, of course, that perception never comes first but is conceived in terms of conceptual constructed schemata."[16]

Surveying European affairs, a politically resigned Gombrich sided with Winston Churchill, who earlier that month had given his Iron Curtain speech in Fulton, Missouri: "There is only 'the world' left—but Churchill has said all I could have said, and slightly better, I presume. I do not think that atom bombs are good for the progress of Ghirlandajo research but then . . ."[17]

On the eve of the war, a physicist friend had informed Gombrich of Niels Bohr's theoretical speculations about a so-called uranium bomb: the acquaintance and Gombrich "were both united in hoping that such a weapon might only be dropped on some desert island, to show friend and foe alike that all other ideas of weaponry and warfare had had their day."[18] Bohr himself shared that view, as did several Manhattan Project scientists who wrote the Franck Report petitioning to limit the use of the weapon to a test demonstration. But when the nuclear age became a reality, Gombrich—as reflected in his letter to Kris—rejected the possibility of disarmament. He accepted nuclear weaponry as a tool of Cold War deterrence, adopting a position similar to what Jonathan Schell characterized as nuclear Wilsonianism: "To the nuclear realist's hope for security and the nuclear romantic's longing for greatness, we must add the nuclear Wilsonian's dream of peace based on nuclear terror."[19] In fact, in his final thoughts on the nuclear threat, Gombrich continued to believe that

> despite the brutal conflicts and worrying crises that have broken out since 1945 in various parts of the globe, we have been spared a third world war because we all know only too well that it could mean the end of the history of the world. It isn't a great comfort, but it's better than none at all.[20]

At the Warburg Institute, Gombrich rejoined Saxl's prewar project to assemble Warburg's biography and collected writings. But collaboration revived disagreements over how to evaluate Warburg's contributions to art history and how to make his writings accessible to an English-speaking audience. Nor had Saxl's reticence to publish the caricature book been forgotten.[21] Gombrich, however, remained profoundly conscious of both his professional and personal debt to Saxl. He described for Kris his thoughts on returning to the institute:

> I did find, however, that my six years absence had given me some wholesome distance to the things (while not causing me to forget them[)] and I did find, furthermore, that these years of practical work have made me a bit more ruthless and "expeditif". In short I now think that I'll be able to tackle it and to meet the moral obligation, which, after all, I have in this matter—for without your idea of recommending me to Saxl for the Nachlass I would probably have landed in Auschwitz or somewhere.[22]

In a letter to Kris a year earlier, Gombrich had described what most impressed him about Saxl, the scholar who had organized the Goya exhibition in Vienna and who opened the doors of the Warburg Institute as a refuge to exiles: "at bottom he has a strange anarchic form of true humanity and decency which one can't help liking."[23] In March 1948, Gombrich wrote Kris informing him of Saxl's sudden death at the age of fifty-eight. Gombrich and others experienced a sense of disbelief and disorientation at the thought of working without his presence: "There is nothing left, nobody knows what is going to happen and who his successor might be."[24] He once more recalled Saxl's humane spirit: "His lack of pomposity and his real humanity were irresistible."[25] After Saxl's death, the prewar caricature project became Gombrich's most direct scholarly link to the Viennese past.

The Manuscript Revisited

In May 1947, Kris informed Gombrich that the "largest U.S. publishing house seems to be very interested in publishing the large (original) book on caricatures."[26] Kris had kept in contact with John Marshall, and in April 1948, he wrote to Gombrich that Marshall would support a Rockefeller grant for him to come to the United States, during which time they could discuss the caricature manuscript: "I rather feel that we should be able to find some way of presentation which might interest the publisher and ourselves."[27] For Kris, a return to caricature would provide a new opportunity to explore the social psychology of art; for Gombrich, it meant the chance to develop further his psychology of perception and representation.[28]

Gombrich foresaw significant changes to the prewar book, in part because his own attitude to the manuscript had altered:

> I am still convinced that the basic thesis (Ablösung von Magie) [decline of magic] is sound and that there is much else in the book worth saying. I don't think on the other hand that the book is very well organised and despite the fact that it embraces so much I am not sure that it tells the whole story. I should rather like to link it with another aspect which we would have to discuss and which comes into my "language of the image" hobby.[29]

Kris and Gombrich decided to update the caricature book in two directions. First, they planned to expand the use of social psychology, tracing links from caricature to magic, propaganda, and social aggression. Second, they looked to tie caricature to conceptual constructs in image making. These ambitions meant rewriting the manuscript nearly from scratch.

Before leaving London, Gombrich formulated two outlines for the new book. He sent the first outline—for a work titled "Psychology and Origins of Caricature"—to Kris in August 1948.[30] This blueprint reduced the book from five to four chapters. The first chapter would discuss caricature as both an instrument of imaginary aggression and a technique of visual communication. The second would explain the conditions necessary for the emergence and acceptance of a new, simplified visual language, while the third would follow the development of that language from the artist's sketch to Töpffer's reductionist approach. The last chapter would consider the nature and dissolution of image magic. The prewar manuscript's historical treatment of comic art would be much reduced or deleted altogether. Several months later, Gombrich suggested that the sociological component of the blueprint focus on transformations in perception:

> As far as Caricature is concerned I now feel we may have to stress the institutional, social aspect a little more. One can (and does) "learn" to see caricatures. First in small circles (17th century) then in larger ones. I believe altogether that this problem of learning to understand the artist[']s signs and therewith the interaction between artist and coherent public plays a greater part in the history of art than has been conceded to it.[31]

In July 1949, Gombrich produced a second, more detailed five-chapter outline—with estimated word counts—for a book that restored the title "Caricature" and that reintroduced a portion of the earlier historical perspective. The first chapter would explore differences between caricature—an art form with its own history—and comic art, propaganda, and aggressive image making, which "have no 'history' but exist wherever social conditions permit."[32] The second chapter would focus on the new way of seeing that accompanied caricature, and the third on the dissolution of image magic and the emergence of play with form. The fourth chapter would consider "the persistency of 'primitive' traits"[33] in image making, while a concluding chapter would compare caricature to modernist tendencies in art: "Caricature as a model. The primitive survives disguised as 'art' but confined to comic. When all barriers fall (modern art) new problems arise."[34] Caricature now interested Gombrich less as an example of political art than as an experiment in technique.

By September 1949, when Gombrich arrived in the United States, he and Kris possessed four different drafts or outlines of the caricature book: the prewar manuscript; the abbreviated wartime manuscript perhaps intended for the Warburg Institute's journal; the outline incorporating the new emphasis on a psychology of perception; and the outline giving greater prominence to social psychology. During the next four months, the two scholars attempted to salvage a project that now threatened to break apart. They received encouragement from Siegfried Kracauer, who had taken up research into photography and saw in the caricature project a connection to his own study of visual expression. In October, he wrote to Kris:

> I also learned, that you are engaged in research on caricature, which, I guess, will continue your previous studies in the field. The theme is of interest to me. I am now preparing . . . a book on film aesthetics which begins with an analysis of instantaneous photography and for the rest may involve problems overlapping with yours. Should you feel like it, we might, sometime, come together and discuss this matter.[35]

In January 1950, Gombrich described their progress in a report to Saxl's successor at the Warburg Institute, Henri Frankfort:

> Picking up the threads of our researches before the war, we found ourselves in complete agreement as to which parts could be allowed to stand and which needed revision or re-formulation. I made a first draft of the most crucial chapters and we laid down the argument of the remaining ones in some detail. I think that the book is now "on the rails" for we have a clear idea of its scope, size and approach. We want to call it "The Rise of Caricature, An Essay in the Social Psychology of Art".[36]

The ambitiousness of the title, however, betrayed the difficulty of completing the revision. Thirty-five pages in length, the manuscript produced after the war remained a partial product. It included only three brief chapters. The introductory chapter spelled out the extensive aims that Kris and Gombrich still kept in mind for the book:

> To observe the invention of an art form and its development from a studio joke to a social institution, even a social power, should in itself be of considerable interest for it is not often in history that we can speak of real beginnings and watch a growth of this kind.[37]

Caricature portraiture revealed both the psychological components and the social factors that drove artistic experiments:

> We believe that the art of caricature is symptomatic of a degree of freedom on the part of the artist, a freedom both in the social and aesthetic sense, to which the figurative arts attained latest of all media of human expression. It is this thesis about the basically "archaic" character of the figurative arts which is to be tested and made explicit through the material of this book. We hope that it may justify the subtitle of this essay. For though caricature itself remains a genre on the fringe of art—caricatures of permanent value are rather rare—a study of its history and its working may help us to lay bare certain mechanisms of artistic creation which remain submerged in the subtler and richer textures of great art.[38]

A social psychology of caricature would thus reveal the gradual emergence of modern artistic freedom.

The second chapter, following roughly the outline that Gombrich wrote in the previous year, explored comic images from the ancient world to the twentieth century. But it sharply dissociated the evolution of caricature from the rise of political art and excluded the history of the broadsheet altogether. Analysis of political art and propaganda now belonged specifically to social scientists and opinion researchers:

> The output of political pamphlets and illustrated broadsides may serve as an indication of what issues stirred the masses and—more

> interesting still, what political forces were out deliberately to enlist the support of the masses ... It is a history which affords much interest to the historian of public opinion and its manipulation—but its relevance to the history of caricature is only evident at one point—the point when caricature in our sense, portrait caricature is first used systematically as one of the methods of pictorial propaganda—and this point is not reached before the middle of the eighteenth century.[39]

Only the relation of caricature to effigies remained of historical interest: "To the social psychologist they [effigies] serve to show how deeply rooted and universal is the belief in the identity between image and imaged—the root of all image magic."[40] Modern caricature emerged when Swiftian self-observation and intellectual awareness allowed the beholder to enjoy, rather than fear, critical images:

> They [effigies] show us how jealously the individual guards his likeness ... Perhaps we have here one of the reasons why mock portraiture as a harmless joke could only see the light when the fear of the artist's power over the image had receded and when a few enlightened individuals had learn[ed] to laugh about that self love which guards the [one's] own likeness as a part of the self.[41]

Not Daumier's republican art but Swift and Hogarth's moral and psychological studies represented the culmination of caricature.

In the third and last chapter—of which two closely similar versions survive—Kris and Gombrich explored the role of mental projection in portrait art. Like all portrait artists, caricaturists relied on the beholder's share, on viewers projecting their own visions onto the subject of the image. Reductionist techniques encouraged that process: "the sketch has so much greater chance of being accepted as a good likeness than the elaborate portrait."[42] By generating projections, sketch-like portraits endowed their subjects with new life and drew the viewer further into the process of seeing. Caricature, which simplified the face to its "primary relationships,"[43] and remained in that way constantly open to the beholder, gave both artist and audience the continuous freedom to experiment.

The rough chapters that emerged from Gombrich's trip to the United States became the last draft that he and Kris produced for the caricature book. Those brief chapters examined the regressive power of visual images, explored the psychological ground for the rise of a new art, and analyzed projective mechanisms of visual perception. But these divergent approaches soon became irreconcilable. Before the war, the evolution of a republican art served as one of the book's crucial integrative themes. Without it, the artistic, psychological, and political components that the prewar manuscript brought together began in the early 1950s to split apart.[44]

Caricature and Conceptual Vision

In London, Herbert Read provided a final, indirect impetus to completing the caricature project. Having previously acted as a distant mediator between Kris and the London art public, he now served Gombrich as a guide to reaching English-speaking audiences. During the war, when Marshall asked for his advice on whom to contact in the humanities, Gombrich had recommended Read:

> He [Marshall] mentioned that he had seen the head of a historical Institute here who had new ideas which might be worth supporting but in general he expressed some doubt as to new ideas in this country. He wondered whom he should go and see (in this search for ideas), here I was rather high and dry, I suggested Herbert Read, he asked whether he is "in need of support[.]" I said I did not think he was but he was an excellent sound board for new ideas, and a very nice man.[45]

In April 1947, Gombrich wrote to Kris about his idea for "a book, not exactly popular but readable, say, for the public of Herbert Read's Art and Society."[46] Gombrich apparently kept Read and his audience in mind when finishing *The Story of Art*, which appeared in print in January 1950 and which drew attention to the linkage between caricature and Expressionism. Like Kris's Daumier exhibition and Read's *Art and Society*, Gombrich's *Story of Art* emphasized the challenge that caricature and Expressionism posed to the viewer and art critic:

> Caricature had always been "expressionist", for the caricaturist plays with the likeness of his victim, and distorts it to express just what he feels about his fellow man. As long as these distortions of nature sailed under the flag of humour nobody seemed to find them difficult to understand . . . But the idea of a serious caricature, of an art which deliberately changed the appearance of things not to express a sense of superiority, but maybe love, or admiration, or fear, proved indeed a stumbling block as Van Gogh had predicted.[47]

Immediately after completing *The Story of Art*, Gombrich entered more deeply into the problems of pictorial representation, image recognition, and the psychology of perception—problems that Read had connected to caricature in his review of the King Penguin book. In a letter to Kris in April 1950, Gombrich now discussed taking the caricature project even further into those areas:

> What I would like most would be some theory of selective perception which seems to me important for physiognomic perception. Obviously we register and remember in a physiognomy first those features which contradict our expectations . . . I should like to know how far the expected type, the thing that is not registered, can be equated with the conceptual image of a face. A caricature, after all, is more or less a conceptual image of a face, a "skeleton face" or stereotype face on which the physiongomically [sic] relevant deviation has been entered or superimposed whyle [sic] the rest has remained conceptual.[48]

In the following month, upon receiving his appointment to the Slade Professorship in the Fine Arts, Gombrich began to prepare a program of lectures for Oxford. He wrote to Kris in June, "Caricatura makes no progress."[49] In August, the war scare in Korea led Popper to caution Gombrich against making a planned trip to the European Continent because of what Popper perceived as a looming "war danger."[50] Although Gombrich ignored the warning, it revived his sense of fatalism: "What a world, and how unnecessary and futile it all looks, does it not?"[51]

In April 1951, Gombrich complained to Kris that he had been finding it difficult to write, and attributed the problem to his lecture schedule. But a stimulus to move forward had come from Read:

> Luckily my self[-]respect was somewhat restored when I allowed myself to be bullied into contributing an essay for a symposium called "Aspects of Growth and Form" published by a rather cranky but decent philosopher of science for the Institute of Contemporary Art[s] under Herbert Read's Aegis.[52]

Soon after the war Read had led the effort to create the ICA, which had officially opened in June 1947.[53] Gombrich's wartime recommendation to Marshall on Read's behalf had perhaps assisted the art institute's founding: in 1948, Read reported to the ICA's organizing committee that "John D. Rockefeller had given him an unsolicited gift of $2,500 for the Institute."[54]

At the ICA symposium Gombrich presented his seminal essay on the psychology of art and perception, "Meditations on a Hobby Horse." In a letter to Kris, he explained that he intended the title to echo Swift's "meditations on a broomstick."[55] The ICA talk did, in fact, revisit the fundamental question raised by Swift: To what extent could human beings relinquish their idealized visions of themselves? The answer for Gombrich lay in the psychology of conceptual images and the extent to which people could see themselves within the framework of those images: "At the most primitive level, then, the conceptual image might be identified with what we have called the minimum image—that minimum, that is, which will make it fit into a psychological lock."[56]

Just as Kris had argued that image magic did not depend upon exact likeness between image and object, so Gombrich stressed that the conceptual image did not amount to a visual copy. Rather, it offered markers that guided the audience's own recognitions and triggered their projections. Assisted in this way by the artist, the audience completed the construction of the full image. Gombrich explained to Kris the purpose behind the presentation:

> You understand that my aim is to learn a little more about that indispensable notion "the conceptual image" which seems to me somehow quite wrongly conceived. I am more than ever convinced that the problem of the complete or incomplete image in art is one of the key problems.[57]

The appearance at the ICA seminar now generated a new urge to finish the caricature manuscript:

> It may be pure "Ausred" [evasion] but I have the feeling at present that a little more analysis of the Abbild [likeness] problem will also do the caricature a good deal of good. Everything has obviously an aura of equivalent images[,] both positive and negative ones.[58]

Read, who had been the first audience in Britain for the caricature project, now provided the last inspiration to completing it.

The correspondence between Kris and Gombrich makes no mention of their final decision regarding the caricature project. It is probable that the decision emerged during Gombrich's trip to Harvard in July and August 1951, during which time he visited Kris.[59] In October, Kris worked at revising the essay on caricature that he had presented to the Warburg Institute, which he and Gombrich had published in the *British Journal of Medical Psychology* and which Kris now incorporated into

Psychoanalytic Explorations in Art, published in 1952. Gombrich approved its inclusion and searched out illustrations to go with it.[60]

Focusing on the fate of image magic and the influence of reductionism, Kris removed from the newly revised essay one of the few allusions to political art. To be sure, examples of Low's use of reduction in depicting politicians remained—to which were now added examples from Hogarth's depictions of Whig political leaders. And the reference to Philipon and Daumier's pear appeared—but now without mention of its significance in the struggle for republican freedom or the accompanying reference to Low's political animals. Instead, a more dismal judgment of political caricature followed: "As the pear became the mocking symbol in countless caricatures and cartoons, we witness once more the reduction of the portrait caricature to the stereotype for political imagery."[61] Kris and Gombrich no longer drew attention to caricature as a republican art form but instead stressed its nature as a corrupted, propagandistic medium.

Less than two years later, in April 1954, Gombrich received the invitation to deliver the 1956 A. W. Mellon Lectures at the National Gallery of Art in Washington.[62] He included in his talks what he called "the experiment with caricature," linking it in detail to his investigation of conceptual images in art. In 1960, he published the lectures as *Art and Illusion: A Study in the Psychology of Pictorial Representation*. The three-ringed notebook with the two hundred and fifty-four-page prewar caricature manuscript still remained filed away with his private papers.

Just as Kris had done in his paper in prewar Lucerne, Gombrich in his lectures in postwar Washington approached caricature as an artistic innovation with implications for both art history and psychological science. His understanding of the experiment, however, now departed from what he and Kris put forward in the prewar manuscript. Caricature emerged as the product of changes in cognition and perception. The rise of a new way of seeing, not the decline of magic and the diminishing of unconscious fear, explained its advent. Hogarth, not Daumier, appeared as the inspirational model—for both the caricaturist and Gombrich. As Hogarth intuited and Gombrich detailed, caricaturists configured their portraits from the minimum of visual clues necessary for facial recognition. The nearer one approached a conceptual image or schema, the closer one came to unmasking the personality. Here Gombrich preserved the core insight from the prewar caricature book: the conceptual image—the minimal or irreducible schema—hid within, not behind, the subject's facial mask, and the beholder possessed the capacity to switch perception between the schema and mask.

Gombrich again raised the historical question that had guided his work with Kris: Why had the reductionist approach to visual representation emerged only very late in the development of art? He recalled their prewar response:

> But may it not be that its very power held it in check? . . . To the humble craftsman of earlier periods, the experience may not have been free from half-conscious or unconscious fears . . . These speculations were particularly suggested to me by researches into the history of caricature which I was privileged to undertake with my friend Ernst Kris. Our starting point at the time was the question of why portrait caricature, the playful distortion of a victim's face, makes only so late an appearance in Western art . . . We thought at the time that it was the fear of image magic, the reluctance to do as a joke what the unconscious means very much in earnest, which delayed the coming of that visual game.[63]

Gombrich now argued that the late emergence of caricature derived from the nature of conceptual images: "I still believe these [unconscious] motives may have played their part, but the theory might be generalized. The invention of portrait caricature presupposes the theoretical discovery of the difference between likeness and equivalence."[64] The caricaturist produced not portraits from nature but equivalent identities, which "do not depend on the imitation of individual features so much as on configurations of clues."[65] The ability to create and recognize such identities broadened the range of image making. Caricature thus revealed that artistic experimentation moved forward as the constant creation of new perceptual equivalences between images and reality, or in the language of the prewar manuscript, as the ceaseless discovery of new switches between schema and mask.

Hogarth, the master of stage art, had given impetus and direction to such conceptual experiments and reinventions. Envisioning the world as a theatrical tragicomedy, he created from his store of facial schemas the character types and expressive figures that brought his theater to life: "Hogarth accepted the idea of art as a language and seized eagerly on the possibilities it offered for the creation of characters with which to people his imaginary stage."[66]

Daumier's significance consisted in expanding the English schemas. Gombrich now downplayed the importance of Daumier's powers of direct observation and instead emphasized his capacity for mental projection. When beginning an artwork, Daumier preferred to sketch formless "clouds of lines,"[67] which revealed almost on their own the contours of an image. He remained a vital nineteenth-century experimentalist not by joining the language of art to politics but by pioneering the techniques of Expressionism: "For in and with Daumier the tradition of physiognomic experiment began to be emancipated from that of humor."[68] He became a forerunner of the modernist movements that finally "swept away those restraints and taboos that restricted the artist's choice of means and the freedom of experimentation."[69] In Gombrich's *Art and Illusion*, Daumier confirmed the crucial creative significance of mental constructs—not of political visions.

If *Art and Illusion* set out Gombrich's new direction as both a cultural historian and a psychologist of art, it served also as a remembrance of his beginnings. He dedicated it to the three teachers who influenced his early development. Two of them—Julius von Schlosser and Emanuel Loewy—had died in 1938, the year of the *Anschluss*. The third teacher, Ernst Kris—who helped guide Gombrich's career from their original meeting at the *Kunsthistorisches Museum* in Vienna to his presentation of the Mellon Lectures in Washington—had passed away in February 1957.

Political Dissent and Experimental Conditions

When he later recalled the caricature manuscript, Gombrich explained that the *Anschluss* and the Second World War had brought the project to an end. He did not discuss his and Kris's four-year effort to revive the caricature book after the war.[70] Yet, his explanation remains historically accurate. In the first place, as Freeman Dyson has pointed out, research across disciplinary boundaries became more difficult after the war, both between science and the humanities and within the sciences themselves. Dyson cited the decline in physics of the "mutual admiration and easy mixing of theory and experiment, which seemed natural and necessary in the 1930s" and which had characterized the attitudes of Ernest Rutherford and Albert Einstein.[71] A key reason behind this change, he explained, derived from the growing specialization of theory and experimentation in the 1950s. Increasingly advanced, intricate, and expensive methods and technologies worked against communication across fields. Such specialization of knowledge extended into the humanities, leaving the integrative example of one such as Warburg ever more distant, isolated, and even inconsequential.

The post-1945 social sciences offered a similar picture. Immediately after the war, the émigré sociologist Leo Lowenthal, for example, had used integrated content analysis to dissect the speeches and writings of American right-wing agitators.[72] But in the years that followed, the discipline of applied psychology departed from the integration of scientific, humanist, and political questions such as those posed by Lowenthal—or by the caricature project. It is indicative that during the 1950s the field of classical studies produced perhaps the most outstanding exceptions to this rule. Works such as those by M. I. Finley and Bernard Knox combined literary, historical, and social analyses not only to reinterpret the ancient past but also to highlight the relevance of ancient studies to the effort at reconstructing postwar political culture.[73]

Before the war, the caricature project had gained inspiration from new movements in the art world, but by the 1950s, the visual arts had once more changed direction. Expressionism broke its remaining ties to classical representation and embraced more fully the principles of abstraction. Daumier's political art—now viewed in isolation from his technical mastery—seemed to belong to a fading, irrelevant era.[74] Even Read no longer believed that the creator of Ratapoil deserved a necessary or important place in the history of contemporary sculpture. In sharp contrast to the discussion of caricature and Expressionism in *Art and Society*, Read's 1964 book on the history of modern sculpture alluded to "the odd intrusion of Honoré Daumier, who as early as 1830 was producing busts as superficially 'modern' as any works of Rodin."[75] Read continued:

> But Daumier was a caricaturist, and the kind of deformations made by the caricaturist to secure his satirical emphasis have nothing in common with the formal conceptions of a Rodin (as the satires of Goya, for example, have only a superficial resemblance to Picasso's drawings for his *Guernica*) . . . Any resemblance with the stylistic forms of modern art is therefore "purely coincidental."[76]

In an age committed to non-representational forms, Daumier—who remained devoted to the classical framework in spite, or perhaps because, of his commitment to innovation—had lost his status even as an experimentalist.

Finally, after 1945, the intellectual culture of the Cold War replaced that of antifascism. In its willingness to cross intellectual and geographic boundaries and in its early grounding in a broad antifascist culture, Kris and Gombrich's integrative approach reflected a consciousness rooted in the 1930s, a consciousness that in Europe and the United States had helped sustain their interest in Daumier and political art. That motivating spirit faded when the Popular Front culture, which had been one of their sources of inspiration, fell victim to the Cold War.[77]

In the case of Gombrich, a new kind of pessimism took hold. He chose—almost from desperation—to concentrate his scholarship increasingly on matters of purely visual perception and artistic technique. That fatalism influenced both his conception of Warburg and his understanding of caricature. Having committed himself to the Warburg biography at the height of the interwar crisis, Gombrich wrote and published it long after the war. It now reflected his critique of an art history that linked the transformation of images to progressive, spiritual enlightenment. For a similar reason, his views on the history of caricature changed markedly from the prewar to the postwar eras. Explaining his shift in interpretation, he stated:

> [F]or Kris, caricature replaced image-magic . . . Kris, like Freud, and like Aby Warburg, was completely under the spell of an evolutionist interpretation of human history, imagined as a slow advance from primitive irrationality to the triumph of reason . . . But I considered it [caricature] as a technical innovation rather than as a symptom of a change in human consciousness. No one can deny that we have made enormous technical advances, but it is also true that in other ways we are still savages.[78]

Caricature art represented a series of methodological advances, but not cultural or political progress. Felix Gilbert had detected this withdrawal of political interest in Gombrich's exegetical approach to the Warburg biography, in his emphasis on the philosophic and academic rather than the civic and political contexts of Warburg's life and career:

> The bulk of the work [of the biography] consists in presenting and explaining Warburg's notes. Information about the external

> circumstances of Warburg's life within which his ideas developed seems a later addition rather than a fundamental basis of the work.[79]

In matters of politics and ideas, Gombrich identified perhaps most closely with the outstanding exemplar of the German Enlightenment, the writer G. E. Lessing. Warburg and Freud had seen in Lessing the exemplar of religious toleration and intellectual freedom. For Gombrich, however, he foreshadowed the figure of a conflicted, twentieth-century intellectual. In an essay from the same year as the Mellon Lectures, he wrote:

> Lessing, of course, belongs with all his fibres to the great eighteenth century. But just because he was so thoroughly of his time, his dedicated life refutes those insidious voices who like to tell the writer today that the only way out of the Ivory Tower leads through what they call "commitment" to a creed, party, or faction. Lessing was always engaged, but never committed.[80]

Scholarly dedication and personal remembrance attached Gombrich to the Warburg biography and caricature study, but both projects eventually reflected the fatalism that once again overtook him in the postwar years.

In this context, it is interesting to see that Gombrich, two decades after the war, returned to the prewar caricature manuscript. The book had already crossed two historical and political divides: the caesura in Austria and Germany between the republican and Nazi eras and the chasm that opened in Europe and the United States between the antifascist struggle and the Cold War. Now in the mid-1960s, with the emergence of the New Left and the rise of opposition to the Vietnam War, Gombrich looked again at the prewar draft, and began to revise and retype it. He worked once more on a translation of the foreword, marking the date in red pen: "1965."[81] He added references to the most recent editions of Baudelaire's commentaries and Töpffer's theoretical writings. The process of revision, however, went beyond updating prewar translations and citations. Gombrich added a footnote that included a critique of contemporary politics and the media packaging of candidates:

> We have now paradoxically returned, via Madison Avenue, to the equation of man with his "image", a term now widely extended for the opinion or impression a public figure "projects" wittingly or unwittingly to the outside world. In the cynical parlance of commercial and political advertising, if a product or a man fails, he has given out a "false image"; a political attack is conducted by projecting "counter-images".[82]

And as an example of the technique of producing new configurations out of familiar words and imagery, he cited the title of a review of Gerald Scarfe's satiric images—"Scarfaces"—from a June 1966 issue of the *New Statesman*.[83]

Gombrich clearly envisioned—at least for a time—trying to publish the twice-abandoned book project, and the date 1966 emphasizes that he contemplated this possibility not as a brief impulse but at least for a year. During that period, he incorporated into the manuscript a new example of the power of image magic—the power that, according to the 1936 Vienna exhibition, Daumier channeled into modern political criticism.

Gombrich cited at length a passage from Norman Mailer's famous antiwar speech delivered at Berkeley in 1965. The speech concluded with Mailer calling on American war protesters to send pictures of Lyndon Johnson, upside down, throughout the world:

> Silently, without a word, the photograph of you, Lyndon Johnson, will start appearing everywhere, upside down. Your head will speak out—even to the peasant in Asia—it will say that not all Americans are unaware of your monstrous vanity, overwee[n]ing pride, and doubtful motive . . . And those little pictures will tell the world what

> we think of you and your war in Viet Nam. Everywhere, upside down. Everywhere, everywhere.[84]

Gombrich read Mailer's speech in the June 1965 issue of *The Realist*, where antiwar protesters, through the revived medium of the broadsheet, combined new artistic experimentation with radical political criticism. As in the golden age of caricature, cultural politics in the 1960s relied on unmasking—the response to government authorities who, as Gombrich pointed out, hired professional media agents to mold their public images and who deployed the powers of mass communication to spread their political messages. Through an unimagined circumstance, the New Left now gave revived meaning to the prewar caricature manuscript. Gombrich's willingness to update it showed his awareness of its renewed relevance. Significantly, he decided that the Popular Front-era manuscript needed very few changes to make it current for the new decade of dissent.

For one last time political events encouraged Gombrich to publish his and Kris's experiment in scholarship. Before the war, the Popular Front had offered inspiration; after the war, the New Left's challenge to the Cold War provided the stimulus. Again, what is significant is less the specific nature of the changes that went into the manuscript than the fact of revision itself. The changes did not produce a political book, nor did they incorporate new political insights. Mailer's upside-down LBJ entered the manuscript as an example of revitalized image magic and not as a call for a new political language. But a new political movement helped to stir once more the thought of publishing his and Kris's innovative work of scholarship. Just as in the world before 1939, so also in the world after 1945, the rise of a broadly based political culture of the Left proved vital to encouraging a critical, integrative experiment—or in this case, the revival of such an experiment. Gombrich's return to the manuscript recalls that his pioneering insight into the role of conceptual schemas in visual art originally referred to political as well as mental constructs.

Carefully Gombrich incorporated the changes that seemed to him pertinent, even typing one of the revised pages in single rather than double space so as to preserve the prewar text's original pagination. That small decision deserves emphasis: Gombrich remained intent on keeping the book nearly identical to the prewar version, down to the page numbers. *Art and Illusion* had put forward a new analysis of caricature art, but the book that he considered resurrecting in the 1960s revived his and Kris's original argument from the antifascist era. Once more Gombrich saw the manuscript as belonging to the present. Yet, after having taken such pains, he returned the book to its place in his study. After 1966, he made no further effort to publish it. The manuscript remained in its binder, the outcome of a private experiment that now belonged to personal memory.

The motivating spirit of that memory did reappear in one of Gombrich's finest essays: "The Photographer as Artist." There he reflected on the work of Henri Cartier-Bresson, the photojournalist who, like a Renaissance caricaturist, experimented with classical forms and who, like Kris, identified with the Popular Front. Gombrich—one of the first scholars to interpret the French photographer's work as part of art history—emphasized that Cartier-Bresson had created, to use Kris's phrase, a new twentieth-century realism.[85] In that effort he was Daumier's successor. But Daumier, according to Gombrich, "with his unfailing instinct for the ridiculous and pathetic, remained ultimately an inventor of types rather than an observer of life."[86] More significant was the mediating influence of documentary film and especially of Jean Renoir. Kris's description of Balzac and Daumier for the 1936 Vienna exhibition resonated again in Gombrich's description of the great director who had hired Cartier-Bresson as an assistant on *La Règle du jeu*. Renoir, Gombrich wrote,

> brought it home to us that we could be made to share the tragedies, comedies and tragicomedies of life around us in any setting, as the types and roles which people are made to play in society dissolved before our eyes to show the human being behind the mask.[87]

Cartier-Bresson revived the great experiment that Kris and Gombrich had traced from Renaissance Bologna to contemporary Paris. Trained first as a painter, Cartier-Bresson—like the Carracci long before him—left the studio for the streets where he documented the world around him:

> What he has said many times is that he waits for "the right moment" . . . What is the right moment? It is the moment, we must infer, when the language of reality becomes distinct and distinctive, not in the obvious cliché but through the mutual elucidation and articulation of all the sights within the frame. The capacity to integrate them Cartier-Bresson owes no doubt to the discipline of painting.[88]

The right moment—which Cartier-Bresson also described professionally and poignantly as the decisive moment—offered a model of integration. It combined classical, documentary, and critical visions:

> Nearly all his pictures exhibit that visual balance, that secret geometry of a formal composition which counteracts the impression of the merely fortuitous and the contingent . . . He must have been lying in wait at such a spot with the camera ready for the moment when life entered the scene and completed the design at just the right point.[89]

In a second essay on the photographer, Gombrich speculated that a direct link might exist between Cartier-Bresson's photographic art and the experiment with caricature. Just as in effective caricature, so also in successful photographic portraits,

> we are less aware of individual changes than of their resulting "global" impression. The most striking evidence of this global character of physiognomic likeness is offered by the successful caricature in which all the component features of the face are distorted, without

> affecting the resemblance of the whole. I do not know if Cartier-Bresson has ever indulged in this wicked game, but his drawings in pencil, crayon and pen prove him to be an eager explorer of the varied landscape of the face.[90]

Cartier-Bresson's images overcame a caesura in time, not only in art history but also in Gombrich's own life.

The idea of Cartier-Bresson as Daumier's successor recalls that caricature evolved as an experiment not only with portraiture but also with light. Gombrich in fact included in *Art and Illusion* Daumier's "Advice to a Young Artist" as a technical example of how color indicated degrees of illumination (Plate 16). A quiet masterpiece, the painting depicts an older artist examining the work of his younger colleague. With undisturbed concentration, the elder colleague analyzes the student's experiment, while the novice tries to perceive his trial effort from a new angle of vision. At the same moment, from an unseen origin, shadows are dispelled and the space becomes partially lit. "The abrupt change of tone," Gombrich explains, "brings the sunlight into the gloomy nineteenth-century interior."[91] The artist's studio evokes the features of a dim, isolated reading room, a darkened world into which Daumier has conveyed a source of light.

NOTES

Chapter 1: The Unfinished Project

1. Eric R. Kandel, *The Age of Insight: The Quest to Understand the Unconscious in Art, Mind, and Brain, from Vienna 1900 to the Present* (New York: Random House, 2012), especially chaps. 11–12. For an assessment of Gombrich as an art historian whose work pointed beyond art history, see Christopher S. Wood, "E. H. Gombrich: Art and Illusion: A Study in the Psychology of Pictorial Representation, 1960," in *The Books that Shaped Art History: From Gombrich and Greenberg to Alpers and Krauss*, ed. Richard Stone and John-Paul Stonard (London: Thames & Hudson, 2013), 116–27.
2. Robert Waelder, "Psychoanalysis and History: Application of Psychoanalysis to Historiography," in *The Psychoanalytic Interpretation of History*, ed. Benjamin B. Wolman (New York: Harper Torchbooks, Harper and Row, 1973), 3.
3. As George Makari points out, Kris hoped that Anna Freud's interwar studies of the child would create a bridge to academic psychology. Waelder had studied physics in Vienna before turning to psychoanalysis. See Makari, *Revolution in Mind: The Creation of Psychoanalysis* (New York: HarperCollins, 2008), 441–3.
4. In Vienna, Erik Erikson became intrigued by Kris's notion of regression and self-restitution. After the war, he expanded upon it in his own theory of the stages of ego development, each stage marked by a period of crisis and reconsolidation. On Erikson's early interest in Kris's theory of creativity and ego functioning, see Lawrence J. Friedman, *Identity's Architect: A Biography of Erik H. Erikson* (New York: Scribner, 1999), 70 and 94. Like Erikson, Hans Loewald after the war would also emphasize the phases of the ego's achievement of inward reconsolidation. See Hans W. Loewald, "On the Therapeutic Action of Psychoanalysis" (1960), in *Papers on Psychoanalysis* (New Haven: Yale University Press, 1980), 221–56. Ego consolidation would "follow periods of relative ego disorganization and reorganization, characterized by ego regression" (ibid., 224). Drawing out the therapeutic implications of that insight, Loewald argued that "analysis can be characterized, from this standpoint, as a period or periods of induced ego disorganization and reorganization" (ibid.). The therapeutic process represented a "regressive crisis" (ibid.).
5. See the collection of Warburg's writings in Aby Warburg, *The Renewal of Pagan Antiquity: Contributions to the Cultural History of the European Renaissance*, trans. David

Britt, Getty Research Institute Publications Programs: Texts and Documents (Los Angeles: Getty Research Institute for the History of Art and the Humanities, 1999).

6. See Kandel, *Age of Insight*, especially chaps. 11–12. Kandel emphasizes the importance of Alois Riegl, a founder of the Vienna School, in bringing attention to the beholder's share in art.
7. A collection also of Saxl's correspondence with Kris and Gombrich is in the General Correspondence of the Warburg Institute Archive (hereafter cited as GC, WIA). Letters in the General Correspondence between the institute and Kris and between the institute and Gombrich appear in the folders "Ernst Kris," "Kunsthistorisches Museum (Kris)," and "E. H. Gombrich." Before 1940, Kris and Gombrich corresponded with each other in German; from 1940 on, they corresponded only in English. Prior to the Second World War, correspondence between Kris, Gombrich, and the Warburg Institute was carried on in German, but from 1939 only in English. Translations in the book are my own unless indicated otherwise.
8. See Ernst Kris to E. H. Gombrich, 7 June 1949, Box 6, Ernst Kris Papers, Library of Congress, Washington, DC. Hereafter the Ernst Kris Papers will be cited as EK.
9. See Gombrich to Kris, 2 May 1950, Box 6, EK.
10. See Kris to Gombrich, 28 November 1945; Kris to Gombrich, 9 January 1946; and Gombrich to Kris, 20 April 1947, Box 6, EK.
11. E. H. Gombrich to Ernst Kris, 6 August 1952, Box 6, EK.
12. Plutarch, "Alexander," paragraph 1, in *The Age of Alexander*, trans. Ian Scott-Kilvert (Harmondsworth: Penguin Books, 1973), 252.
13. See Roger Nichols, *Mendelssohn Remembered* (London: Faber and Faber, 1997), 138–9. In our day, Kirk Douglas, also a practitioner of caricature, referred to it as "the actor's obsession." See Kirk Douglas, *I Am Spartacus! Making a Film, Breaking the Blacklist* (New York: Open Road, 2012), 128.
14. For a detailed analysis and compelling narrative of caricature art in French urban culture and society, see Judith Wechsler, *A Human Comedy: Physiognomy and Caricature in 19th Century Paris* (Chicago: University of Chicago Press, 1982).
15. For Baudelaire, Balzac, and Champfleury, see Ségolène Le Men, "Daumier and Printmaking," in *Daumier 1808–1879*, exhibition organized by the National Gallery of Canada, Ottawa, the Réunion des Musées Nationaux/Musée d'Orsay, Paris, and the Phillips Collection, Washington (Ottawa: National Gallery of Canada, 1999), 38–40.
16. See, for example, Ralph E. Shikes, *The Indignant Eye: The Artist as Social Critic in Prints and Drawings from the Fifteenth Century to Picasso* (Boston: Beacon Press, 1969); Ralph E. Shikes and Steven Heller, *The Art of Satire: Painters as Caricaturists and Cartoonists from Delacroix to Picasso* (N.p.: Pratt Graphics Center and Horizon Press, 1984); Diana Donald, *The Age of Caricature: Satirical Prints in the Reign of George III* (New Haven: Yale University Press, 1996); David Bindman, *Hogarth and His Times: Serious Comedy* (Berkeley and Los Angeles: University of California Press, 1997); Mark Hallett, *The Spectacle of Difference: Graphic Satire in the Age of Hogarth* (New Haven: Yale University Press, 1999); John Milner, *Art, War and Revolution in France 1870–1871: Myth, Reportage and Reality* (New Haven: Yale University Press, 2000); and David S. Kerr, *Caricature and French Political Culture 1830–1848: Charles Philipon and the Illustrated Press* (Oxford: Oxford University Press, Clarendon Press, 2000). From September 2011 to March 2012, the Metropolitan Museum of Art presented a comprehensive exhibition on the uses of caricature across time and place. See Constance C. McPhee and Nadine M. Orenstein, *Infinite Jest: Caricature and Satire from Leonardo to Levine* (New York: Metropolitan Museum of Art, 2011). For a brief review of selected art historical approaches to caricature, see Sybille Moser-Ernst and Ursula Marinelli, "Geschichte des Karikaturprojektes Kris/Gombrich: Antworten und offene Fragen," in *Jenseits des Illustrativen: Visuelle Medien und Strategien politischer Kommunikation*, ed. Niels Grüne and Claus Oberhauser (Göttingen: V&R Unipress, 2015), 249–52.

17. Thus, for the special issue of the *Art Journal* edited by Judith Wechsler, "The Issue of Caricature," *Art Journal* 43, no. 4 (Winter 1983), which included articles on photography, the world of nineteenth-century newspapers, Cubism, and the art of cartooning, Gombrich contributed his essay "The Wit of Saul Steinberg" (377–80).
18. Felix Gilbert, *A European Past: Memoirs 1905–1945* (New York: W. W. Norton, 1988), 172.
19. Ibid.
20. Felix Gilbert, "Machiavelli in an Unknown Contemporary Dialogue," *Journal of the Warburg Institute* 1, no. 2 (October 1937): 163–6.
21. Machiavelli and Francesco Guicciardini became the subjects of Gilbert's groundbreaking study of Renaissance political and historical thought, *Machiavelli and Guicciardini: Politics and History in Sixteenth-Century Florence* (Princeton, NJ: Princeton University Press, 1965).
22. Gilbert, "Machiavelli," 164.
23. Ibid., 166.
24. Gilbert, *A European Past*, 187. After the war, Gilbert taught for many years at Bryn Mawr College, before becoming a fellow at the Institute for Advanced Study in Princeton.
25. Ernst Kris and Hans Speier, *German Radio Propaganda: Report on Home Broadcasts During the War*, in association with Sidney Axelrad, Hans Herma, Janice Loeb, Heinz Paechter, and Howard B. White (London: Oxford University Press, 1944), 291.
26. On wartime efforts to use psychoanalysis to interpret the psychology of the Nazi leadership and the impact of those efforts on social science, see Daniel Pick, *The Pursuit of the Nazi Mind: Hitler, Hess, and the Analysts* (Oxford: Oxford University Press, 2012).
27. In his study of Freud, Carl E. Schorske described the pattern of political withdrawal and scientific engagement that began to appear among Austrian intellectuals prior to the First World War. See Schorske, *Fin-de-siècle Vienna: Politics and Culture* (New York: Alfred A. Knopf, 1980), 181–207.
28. Russell Jacoby, *The Repression of Psychoanalysis: Otto Fenichel and the Political Freudians* (Chicago: University of Chicago Press, 1986).
29. Gombrich, "Sir Ernst Gombrich," interview by Adi Wimmer, in *Strangers at Home and Abroad: Recollections of Austrian Jews Who Escaped Hitler*, ed. Adi Wimmer, trans. Ewald Osers (Jefferson, NC: McFarland and Company, 2000), 29. An earlier translation of this interview appeared in Peter Weibel and Friedrich Stadler, eds., *The Cultural Exodus from Austria: Vertreibung der Vernunft* (Vienna: Löcker Verlag, 1993), 333–7.

Chapter 2: Toward a Psychology of Art, 1919–32

1. Gombrich to Kris, 22 December 1945, Box 6, EK.
2. Kris to Gombrich, 28 June 1946, Box 6, EK.
3. Gombrich to Kris, 2 May 1950, Box 6, EK.
4. Anton O. Kris, letter to the author, 6 May 2004. I am indebted to Ernst Kris's son Anton O. Kris and his daughter Anna Kris Wolff for family history and biographical information. For Kris's early life, see also Samuel Ritvo and Lucille B. Ritvo, "Ernst Kris, 1900–1957: Twentieth Century *Uomo Universale*," in *Psychoanalytic Pioneers*, ed. Franz Alexander, Samuel Eisenstein, and Martin Grotjahn (New York: Basic Books, 1966) and Elke Mühlleitner, "Ernst Kris (1900–1957)," in *Biographisches Lexikon der Psychoanalyse: Die Mitglieder der Psychologischen Mittwoch-Gesellschaft und der Wiener Psychoanalytischen Vereinigung 1902–1938* (Tübingen: Edition Diskord, 1992).
5. Anton O. Kris and Anna Kris Wolff, conversation with author, 22 January 2004. Anton Kris and Anna Kris Wolff recalled that although their father did not provide them with formal religious training, he familiarized them with the aesthetic and symbolic heritage of the Church on their travels to Italy after the Second World War. For Kris's university

registration form, see *Matrikel* (Summer 1919–Summer 1922), Universitätsarchiv, Universität Wien. The form lists his religion as Roman Catholic and his father's profession as *Rechtsanwalt*.

6. Anton O. Kris and Anna Kris Wolff, conversation with the author, 22 January 2004.
7. See Betty Kurth, *Das Lustschloss Schönbrunn*, Österreichische Kunstbücher, Band 7 (Vienna: Ed. Hölzel [ca. 1920]), 17.
8. Gombrich to Kris, 25 March 1942, Box 6, EK.
9. E. H. Gombrich, "The Study of Art and the Study of Man: Reminiscences of Collaboration with Ernst Kris (1900–1957)" (1967), in *Tributes: Interpreters of Our Cultural Tradition* (Ithaca, NY: Cornell University Press, 1984), 221. On Kris's attendance at university lectures, see also E. H. Gombrich, preface to *Legend, Myth, and Magic in the Image of the Artist: A Historical Experiment*, by Ernst Kris and Otto Kurz (New Haven: Yale University Press, 1979), ix.
10. Max Dvořák, "Pieter Bruegel the Elder," in *The History of Art as the History of Ideas* (1924), trans. John Hardy (London: Routledge & Kegan Paul, 1984), 77.
11. Ibid.
12. Ibid., 78.
13. Ibid., 79.
14. Ibid., 90–1.
15. Ibid., 96.
16. Ibid. For Dvořák's historical perspectives and methods, see also Dvořák, *Idealism and Naturalism in Gothic Art*, trans. Randolph J. Klawiter (Notre Dame, IN: University of Notre Dame Press, 1967).
17. On Dvořák's theory of art history and reaction to the First World War, see Matthew Rampley, "Max Dvořák: Art History and the Crisis of Modernity," *Art History* 26, no. 2 (April 2003): 214–37.
18. Otto Benesch, "Max Dvořák (1874–1921)" (1957), in *Collected Writings*, edited by Eva Benesch, vol. 4 (London: Phaidon Press, 1973), 310–11. On Dvořák and the Vienna School art historians, see also Benesch, "Die Wiener Kunsthistorische Schule" (1920) and "Max Dvořák: Ein Versuch zur Geschichte der historischen Geisteswissenschaften" (1924 [1922]), in *Collected Writings*, vol. 4.
19. For Kris's attendance at Kraus's one-man performances, see Eric R. Kandel, *In Search of Memory: The Emergence of a New Science of Mind* (New York: W. W. Norton, 2006), 363. For Kraus and the Expressionists, see Schorske, *Fin-de-siècle Vienna*, 322–66.
20. Max Dvořák, "On El Greco and Mannerism," in *History of Art as the History of Ideas*, 104. After the war, the art historian Walter Friedlaender expanded Dvořák's conception of Mannerism and its relevance to modern art history. See Friedlaender, *Mannerism and Anti-Mannerism in Italian Painting* (1925, 1930 [1928–29]), introduction by Donald Posner (New York: Schocken Books, 1965) and *David to Delacroix* (1930), trans. Robert Goldwater (Cambridge, MA: Harvard University Press, 1952).
21. See *Matrikel* (Summer 1919–Summer 1922).
22. On Schlosser's Italian background, see E. H. Gombrich, "Julius von Schlosser," *Burlington Magazine* 74, no. 431 (February 1939), 98.
23. Julius von Schlosser, "History of Portraiture in Wax" (1910–11), trans. James Michael Loughridge, in *Ephemeral Bodies: Wax Sculpture and the Human Figure*, ed. Roberta Panzanelli (Los Angeles: Getty Research Institute, 2008), 172.
24. Ibid.
25. See E. H. Gombrich, *Art and Illusion: A Study in the Psychology of Pictorial Representation* (1960), A. W. Mellon Lectures in the Fine Arts, 1956, National Gallery of Art, Washington, DC, Bollingen Series, XXXV, 5 (Princeton, NJ: Princeton University Press, 1972), 23. According to Gombrich, Croce's influence superseded the early interest Schlosser had shown in the psychology of artistic representation. See E. H. Gombrich, "Art History and Psychology in Vienna Fifty Years Ago," *Art Journal* 44, no. 2 (Summer 1984): 162–4.

26. See, for example, Franz Wickhoff, *Roman Art: Some of Its Principles and Their Application to Early Christian Painting*, trans. Eugénie Strong (London: William Heinemann, 1900).
27. For Schlosser's description of Kris, see Gombrich, "The Study of Art and the Study of Man," 222. Kris also worked as Schlosser's research assistant. See Gombrich, preface to *Legend, Myth, and Magic in the Image of the Artist*, x. On Schlosser's influence on Kris's art historical interests, see Thomas Röske, "Traces of Psychology: The Art Historical Writings of Ernst Kris," *American Imago* 58, no. 1 (Spring 2001): 463–77.
28. Anton O. Kris described his father's political stance in comments at the panel devoted to Ernst Kris's career held at the Winter Meeting, American Psychoanalytic Association, 23 January 2003.
29. See Carl E. Schorske, *Thinking with History: Explorations in the Passage to Modernism* (Princeton, NJ: Princeton University Press, 1998), 105–22.
30. On Kris as a curator, see Gombrich, "The Study of Art and the Study of Man," 222. The historian of Renaissance sculpture, Leo Planiscig, had responsibility for organizing the collection's bronze work, which he described in his *Die Bronzeplastiken: Statuetten, Reliefs, Geräte und Plaketten: Katalog*, Publikationen aus den Sammlungen für Plastik und Kunstgewerbe, ed. Julius Schlosser, vol. 4 (Vienna: Kunstverlag Anton Schroll, 1924).
31. For Bredekamp's analysis of the rise of scientific, especially evolutionary, perspectives within the *Kunst- und Wunderkammer* tradition, see Horst Bredekamp, *The Lure of Antiquity and the Cult of the Machine: The Kunstkammer and the Evolution of Nature, Art and Technology*, trans. Allison Brown (Princeton, NJ: Markus Wiener, 1995). For a discussion of the influence of the *Kunstkammer* tradition within twentieth-century Austrian medicine and literature, see Gitta Honegger, *Thomas Bernhard: The Making of an Austrian* (New Haven: Yale University Press, 2001), 84–8.
32. See Julius von Schlosser, *Die Kunst- und Wunderkammern der Spätrenaissance: Ein Beitrag zur Geschichte des Sammelwesens: Ein Handbuch für Sammler und Liebhaber* (1908), 2nd edition (Leipzig: Klinkhardt and Biermann, 1978), 66–7, 79–86, 97, 101, 109, and 176–8.
33. Christopher S. Wood, introduction to *The Vienna School Reader: Politics and Art Historical Method in the 1930s* (New York: Zone Books, 2000), 31.
34. Emanuel Loewy, *The Rendering of Nature in Early Greek Art*, trans. John Fothergill (London: Duckworth, 1907), 13.
35. E. H. Gombrich, "Sir Ernst Gombrich über seinen Lehrer Emanuel Löwy," interview by Harald Wolf, in *Emanuel Löwy: Ein vergessener Pionier*, ed. Friedrich Brein, Kataloge der Archäologischen Sammlung der Universität Wien, Sonderheft I (Vienna: Verlag des Clubs der Universität Wien, 1998), 64.
36. Emanuel Loewy, "Ursprünge der bildenden Kunst," *Almanach der Akademie der Wissenschaften in Wien* 80 (1930): 277.
37. Anton O. Kris, letter to author, 6 May 2004.
38. For information on Marianne Rie's early education and career, see Mühlleitner, "Marianne Kris (1900–1980)," *Biographisches Lexikon der Psychoanalyse* and Elizabeth Ann Danto, *Freud's Free Clinics: Psychoanalysis and Social Justice, 1918–1938* (New York: Columbia University Press, 2005), 99 and 172.
39. Ernst Kris, interview by K. R. Eissler, 15 June 1953, Box 117, Sigmund Freud Papers, Library of Congress (hereafter cited as SF), 2. Author's translation from the German. On the conception of applied psychoanalysis within the early Freudian movement in Vienna, see Louis Rose, *The Freudian Calling: Early Viennese Psychoanalysis and the Pursuit of Cultural Science* (Detroit: Wayne State University Press, 1998).
40. Kris provided dates for the progress of his career in the letter and curriculum vitae that he wrote for the Society for the Protection of Science and Learning after his emigration to Britain. See Ernst Kris to Society for the Protection of Science and Learning, 4 June

1939, Bodleian MS., Society for the Protection of Science and Learning, 187/1–3, folios 175–7 and 189.

41. See Ernst Kris, *Der Stil "rustique": Die Verwendung des Naturabgusses bei Wenzel Jamnitzer und Bernard Palissy*, Sonderausdruck aus Jahrbuch der kunsthistorischen Sammlungen in Wien, Neue Folge, Band I (Vienna: Verlag von Anton Schroll, 1926), 138. Carlo Ginzburg has discussed pictorial representation in light of its origins in depictions of the dead. See Ginzburg, *Wooden Eyes: Nine Reflections on Distance*, trans. Martin Ryle and Kate Soper (New York: Columbia University Press, 2001), 63–78. In his autobiography, Palissy warned against sacrificing true originality to mere imitation in art. See James S. Amelang, *The Flight of Icarus: Artisan Autobiography in Early Modern Europe* (Stanford, CA: Stanford University Press, 1998), 246–7. On Palissy's craft, see Leonard N. Amico, *Bernard Palissy: In Search of Earthly Paradise* (Paris and New York: Flammarion, 1996).
42. See Ernst Kris, "A Psychotic Sculptor of the Eighteenth Century" (1933 [1932]), in *Psychoanalytic Explorations in Art* (Madison, CT: International Universities Press, 1952), 128–50. For alternative interpretations of Messerschmidt, see Rudolf Wittkower and Margot Wittkower, *Born Under Saturn: The Character and Conduct of Artists: A Documented History from Antiquity to the French Revolution* (New York: W. W. Norton, 1969), 124–32 and Ulrich Pfarr, "Ernst Kris on F. X. Messerschmidt—A Valuable Stimulus for New Research?" *American Imago* 58, no. 1 (Spring 2001): 445–61. Kris published his essay on Messerschmidt in *Imago*, where he returned to the subject a few years later. See Kris, "Comments on Spontaneous Artistic Creations by Psychotics" (1936), in *Psychoanalytic Explorations in Art*, 87–127.
43. See Gombrich, "The Study of Art and the Study of Man," 225–6. Kris had enrolled for biology courses in 1931. Marianne Kris recalled that perhaps he also had determined to renounce the study of medicine after being offered the editorship of *Imago*. See Evonne Levy, "Ernst Kris, *The Legend of the Artist* (1934), and *Mein Kampf*," *Oxford Art Journal* 36, no. 2 (2013): 210–11.
44. Ernst Kris, "The Image of the Artist: A Psychological Study of the Role of Tradition in Ancient Biographies," *Psychoanalytic Explorations in Art*, 83. The essay appeared originally under the title "Zur Psychologie älterer Biographik (dargestellt an der des bildenen Künstlers)" in *Imago* 21 (1935). Later in life, Kris expressed deep regret that he never studied medicine. Anton O. Kris and Anna Kris Wolff, conversation with the author, 23 January 2003.
45. Henry James, *Daumier, Caricaturist* (1890; reprint, London: Rodale Press, 1954), 24.
46. Ibid. Three years after publishing it in the January 1890 issue of *Century Magazine*, James republished the essay, with minor editorial changes, as "Honoré Daumier" in his collection *Picture and Text* (New York: Harper and Brothers, 1893). Each version was reprinted separately in the 1950s. See *Daumier Lithographs: The Human Comedy* (Elvehjem Museum of Art, University of Wisconsin-Madison, 1985), 6.
47. On Seipel's ordination and appointment at Salzburg, see Klemens von Klemperer, *Ignaz Seipel: Christian Statesman in a Time of Crisis* (Princeton, NJ: Princeton University Press, 1972), 31 and 43.
48. On the integral role of anti-Semitism within the Christian Social movement, see Bruce F. Pauley, *From Prejudice to Persecution: A History of Austrian Anti-Semitism* (Chapel Hill, NC: University of North Carolina Press, 1992), 150–73.
49. On Christian Social foreign policy in particular and the party's relation to fascism in general, see Martin Kitchen, *The Coming of Austrian Fascism* (London: Croom Helm, 1980), 144–201. For Seipel's reference to Mussolini as a renewer, the negotiation over an Italian, Austrian, and Hungarian alliance, and the diplomatic confrontation in the South Tyrol, see Klemperer, *Ignaz Seipel*, 329–40.
50. On the reduction in the size of the civil service, see Pauley, *From Prejudice to Persecution*, 90–1.
51. On nationalist protests and anti-Semitic violence at universities in the 1920s, see Pauley, *From Prejudice to Persecution*, 89–101 and 121–5.

52. Karl Kraus, *The Last Days of Mankind*, trans. Alexander Gode and Sue Ellen Wright (New York: Frederick Ungar Publishing, 1974), 3.
53. See Pauley, *From Prejudice to Persecution*, 99. On the link between Kraus's play and his documentary journalism, see Paul Reitter, *The Anti-Journalist: Karl Kraus and Jewish Self-Fashioning in Fin-de-siècle Europe* (Chicago: University of Chicago Press, 2008), 118–19.
54. See Eric Hobsbawm, *Interesting Times: A Twentieth-Century Life* (New York: Pantheon Books, 2002), 168. A. J. P. Taylor commented that perhaps the only inhabitants of the Austrian republic who identified themselves as Austrian citizens rather than as German nationals were diehard Habsburg loyalists, Viennese Jews, and Communists. See Taylor, "The Austrian Illusion," in *Europe: Grandeur and Decline* (London: Penguin Books, 1991), 325–7.
55. See Christopher Long, *Josef Frank: Life and Work* (Chicago: University of Chicago Press, 2002), 117. Trude Wähner eventually emigrated to the United States.
56. Anton O. Kris and Anna Kris Wolff, conversation with the author, 22 January 2004.
57. See Gombrich, "The Study of Art and the Study of Man," 222 and Kris to Society for the Protection of Science and Learning, 4 June 1939, Bodleian MS.

Chapter 3: The Vienna–London Connection, 1932–36

1. For an account of the individualist perspective, philosophic optimism, and social background of the membership of the Austrian Masonic lodges, see Malachi Haim Hacohen, *Karl Popper—The Formative Years, 1902–1945: Politics and Philosophy in Interwar Vienna* (Cambridge: Cambridge University Press, 2000), 41–3 and 47.
2. See E. H. Gombrich and Didier Eribon, *Looking for Answers: Conversations on Art and Science* (New York: Harry N. Abrams, 1993), 29–30.
3. On Asquith's upbringing and education, see Roy Jenkins, *Asquith: Portrait of a Man and an Era* (New York: Chilmark Press, 1964), 13–25. George Dangerfield's caustic but classic portrait of Asquith, published in 1935, still deserves attention. See Dangerfield, *The Strange Death of Liberal England* (New York: Capricorn Books, 1961), 17–18. For Violet Bonham Carter, see Jenkins, introduction to *Lantern Slides: The Diaries and Letters of Violet Bonham Carter 1904–1914*, ed. Mark Bonham Carter and Mark Pottle (London: Weidenfeld and Nicolson, 1996).
4. I am grateful to Professor Richard Gombrich and Leonie Gombrich for information regarding E. H. Gombrich's sisters. Leonie Gombrich, letter to the author, 16 January 2008.
5. For Gombrich's education, see Gombrich, "Sir Ernst Gombrich," interview by Wimmer, 25–30, 133–6. On the Theresianum, see Schorske, *Fin-de-siècle Vienna*, 135.
6. Gombrich and Eribon, *Looking for Answers*, 32.
7. E. H. Gombrich, "An Autobiographical Sketch" (1987), in *Topics of Our Time: Twentieth-Century Issues in Learning and in Art* (Berkeley and Los Angeles: University of California Press, 1991), 13. For Gombrich's early attitude toward Expressionism, see his *The Preference for the Primitive: Episodes in the History of Western Taste and Art* (London: Phaidon Press, 2002), 233.
8. E. H. Gombrich, "Focus on the Arts and Humanities," in *Tributes*, 13–14.
9. Gombrich, "An Autobiographical Sketch," 14. Confronted late in life by a strong revival of interest in Riegl's theories, Gombrich reminded younger art historians that he had been wary of the ideological implications of Riegl's aim to understand art through the artist's will. Riegl, he stated, had not inspired him in the pursuit of art history. See Ján Bakos, "The Vienna School's Hundred and Sixty-Eighth Graduate: The Vienna School's Ideas Revised by E. H. Gombrich" and E. H. Gombrich, "Response from E. H. Gombrich," in *Gombrich on Art and Psychology*, ed. Richard Woodfield (Manchester: Manchester University Press, 1996), 234–61. For a discussion of Riegl's conception of art history, see Margaret Olin, *Forms of Representation in Alois Riegl's Theory of Art*

(University Park, PA: Pennsylvania State University Press, 1992) and Richard Woodfield, et al., *Framing Formalism: Riegl's Work* (Amsterdam: Overseas Publishing Association, 2001).

10. Gombrich, "Focus on the Arts and Humanities," 14. Gombrich published his dissertation in two parts. See E. H. Gombrich, "Zum Werke Giulio Romanos: I. Der Palazzo del Tè," *Jahrbuch der kunsthistorischen Sammlungen in Wien*, Neue Folge, Band 8 (1934): 79–104 and "Zum Werke Giulio Romanos: II. Versuch einer Deutung," *Jahrbuch der kunsthistorischen Sammlungen in Wien*, Neue Folge, Band 9 (1935): 121–50.
11. Gombrich and Eribon, *Looking for Answers*, 41.
12. Gombrich to Kris, 17 August 1940, Box 6, EK.
13. Gombrich ultimately published this research as "Eine verkannte karolingische Pyxis im Wiener Kunsthistorischen Museum," *Jahrbuch der kunsthistorischen Sammlungen in Wien*, Neue Folge, Band 7 (1933): 1–14.
14. Gombrich, "The Study of Art and the Study of Man," 224.
15. Gombrich and Eribon, *Looking for Answers,* 45.
16. Gombrich reproduced "Der Zweifel" in a letter to Carl E. Schorske, in which Gombrich confirmed the date of the student play as 1932. E. H. Gombrich to Carl E. Schorske, 18 December 1994, letter in possession of the author. I am grateful to Carl Schorske for having provided me with the letter and poem.
17. Gombrich to Schorske, 18 December 1994. Underlined in the original.
18. Ibid. Underlined in the original.
19. Ibid.
20. For a description of the events of June 1931, see Pauley, *From Prejudice to Persecution*, 125–7.
21. E. H. Gombrich, "The Exploration of Culture Contacts: The Services to Scholarship of Otto Kurz (1908–1975)" (1979), in *Tributes*, 238.
22. See Gombrich, "Sir Ernst Gombrich," interview by Wimmer, 27–8.
23. Ibid., 28.
24. See Pauley, *From Prejudice to Persecution*, 262.
25. Ibid., 28.
26. Ibid., 29.
27. On Mussolini's role in the February events in Austria, see Kitchen, *The Coming of Austrian Fascism*, 151.
28. On the February events, the *Vaterländische Front*, and anti-Semitism see Pauley, *From Prejudice to Persecution*, 268–72 and Kitchen, *The Coming of Austrian Fascism*, 202–64.
29. Gombrich, "Sir Ernst Gombrich," interview by Wimmer, 29.
30. Ibid. On Benesch, see Charles de Tolnay, "In Memoriam Otto Benesch," in *The Art of the Renaissance in Northern Europe: Its Relation to the Contemporary Spiritual and Intellectual Movements*, by Otto Benesch, revised edition (London: Phaidon Press, 1965), vii–ix and "Österreichische Wissenschaftsemigration" in *The Cultural Exodus from Austria*, ed. Weibel and Stadler, 7.
31. Pauley, *From Prejudice to Persecution*, 167 and 172.
32. Ibid., 168 and 202–3.
33. See Franz Borkenau, *Austria and After* (London: Faber and Faber, 1938).
34. Gombrich and Eribon, *Looking for Answers*, 46–7.
35. Gombrich, "The Study of Art and the Study of Man," 227–8.
36. Anton O. Kris, letters to author, 8 April 2006 and 9 April 2006. The identity of the cardinal is still unknown.
37. See Gombrich, "Sir Ernst Gombrich," interview by Wimmer, 29.
38. For the history of the Hamburg school of thought that developed around Warburg, from the creation of his private library to the founding of his academic institution for the humanities and social sciences, see Emily J. Levine, *Dreamland of Humanists: Warburg, Cassirer, Panofsky, and the Hamburg School* (Chicago: University of Chicago

Press, 2013). Levine explores the school within the context of Hamburg's intersecting social, intellectual, and political worlds. Focusing on changes in image making at the time, Philippe-Alain Michaud examines the connection of Warburg's art history to the contemporaneous emergence of the motion picture. See Michaud, *Aby Warburg and the Image in Motion*, trans. Sophie Hawks (New York: Zone Books, 2004).

39. For comparison of the Renaissance in the work of Warburg and Freud, see Louis Rose, *The Survival of Images: Art Historians, Psychoanalysts, and the Ancients* (Detroit: Wayne State University Press, 2001), 96–105.
40. See Gombrich and Eribon, *Looking for Answers*, 39–40.
41. See Arpad Weixlgärtner and Leo Planiscig, eds., *Festschrift für Julius Schlosser zum 60. Geburtstage* (Zürich: Amalthea Verlag, 1927). Kris's essay, titled "Georg Hoefnagel und der wissenschaftliche Naturalismus," took up the theme of naturalism that he had recently explored in the work of Jamnitzer and Palissy.
42. See the Warburg Library's *Kulturwissenschaftliche Bibliographie zum Nachleben der Antike*, vol. 1, *Die Erscheinungen des Jahres 1931*, (Leipzig: B. G. Teubner, 1934; reprint, Nendeln, Liechtenstein: Kraus-Thomson Organization, Kraus Reprint, 1978) and the Warburg Institute's *A Bibliography of the Survival of the Classics*, vol. 2, *The Publications of 1932–1933*, (London: The Warburg Institute, 1938; reprint, Nendeln, Liechtenstein: Kraus-Thomson Organization, Kraus Reprint, 1978).
43. E. H. Gombrich, letter to the author, 1 March 2000.
44. Fritz Saxl to Ernst Kris, 28 October 1932, GC, WIA. At the end of the war, Edgar Wind had studied art history at the University of Berlin, but he also spent a semester at the University of Vienna, attending the classes of both Dvořák and Schlosser. See Hugh Lloyd-Jones, "A Biographical Memoir," in *The Eloquence of Symbols: Studies in Humanist Art*, by Edgar Wind (Oxford: Oxford University Press, Clarendon Press, 1983), xiv.
45. Ernst Kris and Otto Kurz, *Die Legende vom Künstler: Ein geschichtlicher Versuch* (Vienna: Krystall-Verlag, 1934), [5]. The book was published in English as *Legend, Myth, and Magic in the Image of the Artist: A Historical Experiment,* trans. Alastair Lang and Lottie M. Newman (New Haven: Yale University Press, 1979).
46. Kris and Kurz, *Legend, Myth, and Magic in the Image of the Artist* 66–71. Kris had given his book the working title, "*Daidalos, Die Legende vom Künstler (Ein geschichtlicher Versuch)*." (See Kris to Saxl, 23 April 1934, GC, WIA.) During the Renaissance and Baroque periods, as Kris knew, automated sculptures became among the most highly prized possessions of the *Kunstkammer* collectors. On the fascination with automatons, see Bredekamp, *The Lure of Antiquity and the Cult of the Machine*, 46–51.
47. Kris and Kurz referred to Warburg's 1902 essay "Bildniskunst and florentinisches Bürgertum," republished in the 1932 volume of Warburg's papers, *Die Erneuerung der heidnischen Antike: Kulturwissenschaftliche Beiträge zur Geschichte der europäischen Renaissance*, ed. Gertrud Bing (Leipzig: B. G. Teubner). See Kris and Kurz, *Legend, Myth, and Magic in the Image of the Artist*, 73. The recent English translation appears as "The Art of Portraiture and the Florentine Bourgeoisie" in Warburg, *The Renewal of Pagan Antiquity*, 185–221 and 435–50.
48. Kris and Kurz, *Legend, Myth, and Magic in the Image of the Artist*, 76. Steffen Krüger has described how Kris might have seen in Hitler the most recent and most dangerous example of self-identification with the artist as magicworker. See Krüger, "*Die Legende vom Künstler* als Propagandastrategie," in *Im Dienste des Ich: Ernst Kris heute*, ed. Steffen Krüger and Thomas Röske (Vienna: Böhlau, 2013), 99–117, and "*The Legend of the Artist*: Family Romance and Führer Myth," *American Imago* 71, no. 1 (Spring 2014): 29–51. See also Levy, "Ernst Kris," 209–29. For an analysis and critique of this conception of image making and perception, see David Freedberg, *The Power of Images: Studies in the History and Theory of Response* (Chicago: University of Chicago Press, 1989), 201–5. Freedberg

argues that it is not the unconscious process of perception but instead the conscious creations of the artist that encourage the viewer to seek out lifelike illusions.

49. Kris and Kurz, *Legend, Myth, and Magic in the Image of the Artist*, 49. See Erwin Panofsky, *Idea: Ein Beitrag zur Begriffsgeschichte der älteren Kunsttheorie* (Leipzig: Studien der Bibliothek Warburg, 1924); English edition: *Idea: A Concept in Art History*, trans. Joseph J. S. Peake (Columbia, SC: University of South Carolina Press, 1968).
50. Kris to Saxl, 23 April 1934, GC, WIA. Panofsky himself had conceived of *Idea* itself as a companion study to a lecture on "The Idea of the Beautiful in Plato's Dialogues" presented by Ernst Cassirer at the Warburg Library. See Panofsky, *Idea*, ix, and Levine, *Dreamland of Humanists*, 164–5.
51. Kris to Saxl, 23 April 1934, GC, WIA.
52. Ibid.
53. On the Lucerne Congress, see Ernest Jones, *The Life and Work of Sigmund Freud*, vol. 3 (New York: Basic Books, 1957), 191–2 and Ernest Jones to Sigmund Freud, 20 June 1934, *The Complete Correspondence of Sigmund Freud and Ernest Jones 1908–1939*, ed. R. Andrew Paskauskas (Cambridge, MA: Harvard University Press, Belknap Press, 1993), 737–8.
54. See Ernst Kris, "Zur Psychologie der Karikatur," *Imago* 20, no. 4 (1934): 451. (English version: Ernst Kris, "Psychology of Caricature," in *Psychoanalytic Explorations in Art*, 174.) Translations from the German are Kris's translations for the English version. Page numbers from the English version are included in parentheses.
55. Ibid., 451. (Ibid., 174.)
56. Ibid., 452. (Ibid., 174–5.)
57. Ibid. (Ibid., 175.)
58. Ibid. (Ibid.)
59. Ibid., 454. (Ibid., 177.)
60. Ibid., 455. (Ibid.)
61. Caricature represented a convergence, not divergence, of regressive and cognitive mental acts. On convergence and divergence in mental life, see Anton O. Kris, "Unlearning and Learning Psychoanalysis," *American Imago* 70, no. 3 (Fall 2013): 341–55.
62. "Zur Psychologie der Karikatur," 458. ("Psychology of Caricature," 180.)
63. Ibid., 461. (Ibid., 183.)
64. Ibid., 457. (Ibid., 179.)
65. Fritz Saxl to Ernst Kris, 3 July 1934, GC, WIA. On Read's appointment as editor, see James King, *The Last Modern: A Life of Herbert Read* (London: Weidenfeld and Nicolson, 1990), 117–18.
66. Saxl to Kris, 18 December 1934, GC, WIA.
67. Ernst Kris, review of W. R. Juynboll, *Het komische genre in de ital[i]aansche Schilderkunst gedurende de zeventiende en de achtiende eeuw. Bijdrage tot de geschiedenis van de caricatuur*, in *Burlington Magazine* 66, no. 383 (February 1935): 97. On the Carracci, whose work became crucial to Kris and Gombrich's interpretation of caricature, see Donald Posner, *Annibale Carracci: A Study in the Reform of Italian Painting around 1590*, 2 vols. (London: Phaidon Press, 1971); Margaretha Rossholm Lagerlöf, *Ideal Landscape: Annibale Carracci, Nicolas Poussin and Claude Lorrain* (New Haven: Yale University Press, 1990); and Gail Feigenbaum, "Practice in the Carracci Academy," in *The Artist's Workshop*, ed. Peter M. Lukehart, Studies in the History of Art, 38 (Washington, DC: National Gallery of Art, 1993).
68. See Steffen Krüger, *Das Unbehagen in der Karikatur: Kunst, Propaganda und persuasive Kommunikation im Theoriewerk Ernst Kris'* (Munich: Wilhelm Fink, 2011), 157, and Levy, "Ernst Kris," 216.
69. Kris to Saxl, 24 October 1934, GC, WIA.
70. Kris seems to have kept Schlosser's comment even from Gombrich, only informing Saxl so as to convince him of the importance of finding places for Gombrich and Kurz at the Warburg Institute. In later years Gombrich recalled that Schlosser had deplored

anti-Semitism at the university and had condemned acts of intimidation by the *Deutsche Studentenschaft*. He knew that Schlosser had stopped taking on Jewish doctoral students because, Gombrich explained, he did not believe that he could find them employment. Gombrich also stated, however, that he had been told that Schlosser concluded a postcard to a colleague in Florence with the salutation, "*Heil Hitler*." For Gombrich, Schlosser's "internal contradiction" with regard to the *Anschluss* remained a painful enigma. See E. H. Gombrich, "Einige Erinnerungen an Julius von Schlosser als Lehrer," *Kritische Berichte* XVI, no. 4 (1988): 9.

71. Kris to Saxl, 7 December 1934, GC, WIA.
72. Ibid.
73. Ibid.
74. Ibid.
75. Ibid.
76. Ibid.
77. Ibid.
78. Kris to Saxl, 9 January 1935, GC, WIA. Immediately before the war, Kris did begin work on a new psychology of art. See Kris, "On Inspiration: Preliminary Notes on Emotional Conditions in Creative States," *International Journal of Psycho-Analysis* 20, nos. 3–4 (July–October 1939): 377–89.
79. Bettina Warburg was the daughter of Aby Warburg's brother Paul Warburg, and Edward the son of another brother, Felix Warburg. A naturalized American citizen, Bettina Warburg had trained as a psychiatrist in London. She belonged to the American Psychoanalytic Association, through which she organized and financed the emigration of psychiatrists and psychoanalysts from Germany. The Viennese psychoanalyst Hermann Nunberg, who was married to Marianne Kris's sister, worked with Bettina Warburg in New York. Edward Warburg, also a naturalized American, served as a trustee for the Museum of Modern Art and as the chief financial sponsor for the newly founded American Ballet. See Ron Chernow, *The Warburgs: The Twentieth-Century Odyssey of a Remarkable Jewish Family* (New York: Random House, 1993), 312–13, 342–7, and 439. On Nunberg's career, see Mühlleitner, *Biographisches Lexikon der Psychoanalyse*, 236–7. Kris first approached Bettina Warburg and Edward Warburg about Kurz at the psychoanalytic congress in Lucerne and he kept Saxl informed of his efforts in this regard. See Kris to Saxl, 7 December 1934, GC, WIA.
80. Kris to Saxl, 7 December 1934, GC, WIA.
81. Ernst Kris to Edward Warburg, 8 January 1935, carbon copy, GC, WIA. In German in the original.
82. Ibid.
83. Ibid. Underlined in the original.
84. Edward Warburg to Ernst Kris, 4 March 1935, carbon copy, GC, WIA. In English in the original. Edward Warburg responded only after Bettina Warburg intervened directly with her cousin. See Kris to Saxl, 25 April 1935, GC, WIA.
85. Kris to Saxl, 7 December 1934, GC, WIA.
86. Kris to Saxl, 25 April 1935, GC, WIA. At the time, the future of the Warburg Institute generated severe intrafamilial conflict and bitterness. In 1933, the German government allowed the Warburg Library to move to London on condition that the transfer drew no publicity and that the books traveled to England only as a three-year loan. In 1935, from New York, Felix Warburg exerted pressure within the family to bring the institute to the United States after the loan's expiration. The patriarch and director of the family's financial affairs in Germany, Max Warburg, and his son Eric Warburg strenuously opposed the plan. During 1935, Hitler sought cordial military and diplomatic understandings with the British government—the Anglo-German naval agreement was signed in June. At the same time, the *Völkischer Beobachter* accused the Warburg family of seeking to profit financially from the eventual selling and dispersal of the library. The

German Warburgs therefore expected Hitler's government to cancel the loan and retaliate against the family if the books left England and moved to the United States. Ultimately, Eric Warburg convinced his New York cousins to accept a London home for the institute. In 1936, Samuel Courtauld gave it an endowment and the University of London provided it with space. See Chernow, *The Warburgs*, 407–8.
87. Kris to Saxl, 25 April 1935, GC, WIA.
88. Kris to Saxl, 7 December 1934, GC, WIA.
89. See Gertrud Bing to E. H. Gombrich, 8 January 1935, GC, WIA.
90. Bing to Gombrich, 28 September 1935, GC, WIA. See also Gombrich and Eribon, *Looking for Answers*, 47.
91. On Gombrich's fellowship, see Gombrich and Eribon, *Looking for Answers,* 48–50 and Gombrich, "An Autobiographical Sketch," 19–20.
92. Bing to Gombrich, 13 July 1936, GC, WIA. On his travel, see Kris to Saxl, 2 October 1935, GC, WIA.
93. Kris to Saxl, 25 April 1935, GC, WIA.

Chapter 4: Daumier in Vienna, 1936

1. For a biography of Dantan, see Janet Seligman, *Figures of Fun: The Caricature-Statuettes of Jean-Pierre Dantan* (London: Oxford University Press, 1957).
2. Nothing, unfortunately, is at present known of the donor.
3. [Ernst Kris], *Die Karikaturen des Dantan: Paris-London, 1831–1839, Ausstellung im Corps de Logis der neuen Hofburg*, Herbst, 1933, Kunsthistorisches Museum, Sammlungen für Plastik und Kunstgewerbe (Vienna: J. Weiner, 1933), 3–4.
4. The most notorious writer of local *Kulturpolitik*, Karl Heinrich Waggerl, became an early, outspoken supporter of Hitler. On Austrian *Kulturpolitik* and the *Heimat* movement in literature, see Honegger, *Thomas Bernhard*, 45–54. School textbooks, emphasizing that Austria was a historically German nation, expressed the same views. See George Prochnik, *The Impossible Exile: Stefan Zweig at the End of the World* (New York: Other Press, 2014), 150.
5. On the cultural politics of the Salzburg Festival, see Michael P. Steinberg, *The Meaning of the Salzburg Festival: Austria as Theater and Ideology, 1890–1930* (Ithaca, NY: Cornell University Press, 1990), 84–141 and 196–231.
6. Saxl to Kris, 28 October 1932, GC, WIA.
7. On Sedlmayr's support for *Anschluss*, see Wood, introduction to *The Vienna School Reader*, 12–13 and 36.
8. See Hans Sedlmayr, "Bruegel's *Macchia*," in *The Vienna School Reader*, ed. Wood, 323–76.
9. Dvořák, "Pieter Bruegel the Elder," 91.
10. Ernst Kris and Leo Planiscig, *Kleinkunst der italienischen Frührenaissance: III. Ausstellung*, Juni–Juli 1936, Kunsthistorisches Museum, Sammlungen für Plastik und Kunstgewerbe (J. Weiner: Vienna, [1936]), 3.
11. Vincent van Gogh to Theo van Gogh, July 1885, in *The Letters of Vincent Van Gogh,* ed. Ronald de Leeuw, trans. Arnold Pomerans (London: Penguin Books, 1996), 306. Underlined in the original. On Van Gogh's collection of Daumier lithographs, see Vincent van Gogh to Theo van Gogh, 3 September 1888, 9 September 1888, and 24 September 1888, ibid., 395, 398, and 406.
12. *Conversations with Cézanne,* ed. Michael Doran, trans. Julie Lawrence Cochran (Berkeley and Los Angeles: University of California Press, 2001), 175. Unlike Daumier, Gavarni did not tackle politics, while Forain placed his drawings at the service of the French war effort in 1914. See Edward Lucie-Smith, *The Art of Caricature* (London: Orbis Publishing, 1981), 78, 81, and 92.
13. For a study of Daumier's experimentation in various artistic media, see Bruce Laughton, *Honoré Daumier* (New Haven: Yale University Press, 1996).

14. Daumier's illustrations appeared in volume 9 of *La Comédie humaine*, including depictions of Vautrin and old Goriot from *Le Père Goriot*. See Le Men, "Daumier and Printmaking," 40.
15. Honoré de Balzac, *Lost Illusions*, trans. Herbert J. Hunt (London: Penguin Books, 2004), 299.
16. Ibid., 314. On the themes of spirituality and social criticism in Balzac's work, see for example Philippe Bertault, *Balzac and the Human Comedy*, trans. Richard Monges (New York: New York University Press, 1963). For Balzac as a social novelist and social psychologist, the essential reading remains Georg Lukács, *Studies in European Realism* (New York: Grosset and Dunlap, Universal Library, 1964), 21–84. Judith Wechsler analyzes Balzac's theory and methods of observation and their relation to caricature in *A Human Comedy*, pp. 20–39.
17. Stefan Zweig, *The World of Yesterday*, trans. Benjamin W. Huebsch and Helmut Ripperger (Lincoln, NE and London: University of Nebraska Press, Bison Book, 1964), 431–2.
18. Stefan Zweig, *Balzac*, trans. William and Dorothy Rose (New York: Viking Press, 1946), 40. Zweig's abbreviated study of Balzac appeared posthumously. He had begun the book in exile in London, before coming to the United States and finally Brazil. His wife Lotte ensured that the manuscript reached Zweig from Britain, perhaps, as George Prochnik writes, to encourage or revive an identification with the novelist. For a short time in Brazil, Zweig did work enthusiastically on the biography. For a study of Zweig's life and spirit in exile, see Prochnik, *The Impossible Exile*; on Zweig and Balzac specifically, see pp. 258–9 and 335–6.
19. On the creation, diffusion, and prosecution of Louis-Philippe's caricature as a pear, see Wechsler, *A Human Comedy*, 68–75; Le Men, "Daumier and Printmaking," 40; and Kerr, *Caricature and French Political Culture*, 141–5.
20. Le Men, "Daumier and Printmaking," 40.
21. See T. J. Clark, *The Absolute Bourgeois: Artists and Politics in France 1848–1851* (Berkeley and Los Angeles: University of California Press, 1999), 116–17.
22. Judith Wechsler has traced Daumier's personal struggle in his figure of the jester. See Wechsler, *A Human Comedy*, 170–1.
23. For background to Kris's participation at Pontigny, see Gombrich, "The Study of Art and the Study of Man," 230. On Kris's participation at Pontigny and for conference topics, see Enid McLeod, *Living Twice: Memoirs* (London: Hutchinson Benham, 1982), 59–66, 89–90, 93–4, and 111–12. I am grateful to Steffen Krüger for drawing my attention to McLeod's autobiography.
24. Albert Camus, "Roger Martin du Gard," in *Lyrical and Critical Essays*, trans. Ellen Conroy Kennedy (New York: Vintage Books, 1968), 260.
25. Ibid., 270.
26. Ibid., 272.
27. Roger Martin du Gard, *Jean Barois* (1913), trans. Stuart Gilbert (New York: Viking Press, 1949), 22.
28. Ibid., 62. See also 13–19 and 56–9.
29. Ibid., 180–1.
30. Ibid., 182.
31. Jean Améry, *On Aging: Revolt and Resignation* (1968), trans. John D. Barlow (Bloomington, IN: Indiana University Press, 1994), 84.
32. Jean Améry, *On Suicide: A Discourse on Voluntary Death* (1976), trans. John D. Barlow (Bloomington, IN: Indiana University Press, 1999), 11.
33. Camus, "Roger Martin du Gard," 285. In January 1942, Martin du Gard wrote to Stefan Zweig that the next generation would build the world anew and that their own generation must be able to exit it with dignity. See Prochnik, *The Impossible Exile*, 339. For the career and ideas of Martin du Gard, see David L. Schalk, *Roger Martin du Gard: The Novelist and History* (Ithaca, NY: Cornell University Press, 1967).

34. See McLeod, *Living Twice*, 112. Martin du Gard recalled how André Gide distanced himself from the younger generation who were trying to come to terms with this question at the 1937 conference. See Martin du Gard, *Notes on André Gide* (1951), trans. John Russell (New York: Helen Marx Books, 2005), 79–82. During the war, the Pontigny conference was reconvened at Mount Holyoke College in Massachusetts, bringing together American academics and French scholars-in-exile, including Jean Wahl, Rachel Bespaloff, and Claude Lévi-Strauss. On the wartime meetings and their prewar history, see Christopher Benfey and Karen Remmler, eds., *Artists, Intellectuals, and World War II: The Pontigny Encounters at Mount Holyoke College, 1942–1944* (Amherst, MA: University of Massachusetts Press, 2006).
35. Gombrich, "The Study of Art and the Study of Man," 230. Evonne Levy has suggested that a political critique was also implicit in Kris and Gombrich's research into the Naumburg Cathedral sculptures that they undertook at the same time as the caricature project. See Levy, "Ernst Kris und der Nationalsozialismus: Politische Subtexte in einem verschollenen Experiment über Reaktionen auf die Chorfiguren des Naumburger Doms (1933–1935)," in *Im Dienste des Ich: Ernst Kris heute*, ed. Krüger and Röske, 83–97.
36. See *Honoré Daumier: Zeichnungen, Aquarelle, Lithographien, Kleinplastiken*, Ausstellung, 21 November–21 Dezember 1936 (Vienna: Albertina, Kulturbund, 1936), 5. The exhibition bore the imprimatur of an honorary committee that included Schuschnigg. The Austrian chancellor attended the exhibition's opening (see Levy, "Ernst Kris," 212). The French ambassador to Austria, Gabriel Puaux, was also a member of the committee and assisted as an intermediary, helping to obtain loans from public museums in Paris. In 1938, as France sought to reassert its presence in the Middle East, Puaux was appointed high commissioner in Syria. See Philip Shukry Khoury, *Syria and the French Mandate: The Politics of Arab Nationalism, 1920–1945* (Princeton, NJ: Princeton University Press), 574–5. In the 1960s, Puaux published a political memoir of Austria under Dollfuss and Schuschnigg, *Mort et Transfiguration de l'Autriche 1933–1955* (Paris: Librairie Plon, 1966).
37. Gombrich, "Sir Ernst Gombrich," interview by Wimmer, 133.
38. On the assembling of the exhibition, see *Honoré Daumier*, Ausstellung, 21 November–21 Dezember 1936, 5–6. The Albertina co-sponsored the exhibition with the Austrian *Kulturbund*. Like Kris, Benesch remained in Vienna until the *Anschluss* forced him into exile in the United States. During the war, he published a study of book illustrations from Rubens to Daumier that was both a history of art and history of ideas. See Otto Benesch, *Artistic and Intellectual Trends from Rubens to Daumier as Shown in Book Illustration* (Cambridge, MA: Department of Printing and Graphic Arts, Harvard College Library, 1943). After the war, Benesch returned to Vienna and the Albertina. In 1947, he became the collection's director, a position that he held until 1961. See Barbara Dossi, *Albertina: The History of the Collection and Its Masterpieces* (Munich: Prestel, 1999), 158. After his return, Benesch wrote about the Albertina's history in "A Short History of the Albertina Collection" (1948) and "Die Albertina" (1959), both essays republished in *Collected Writings*, vol. 4. After completing his directorship, he wrote *Master Drawings in the Albertina: European Drawings from the 15th to the 18th Century* (1964), trans. Felice Stampfle and Ruth Kramer (Greenwich, CT: New York Graphic Society Publishers, n.d.).
39. The *Konzerthaus* incident is described in Pauley, *From Prejudice to Persecution*, 272.
40. Kris to Saxl, 10 August [1936], GC, WIA.
41. G. E. R. Gedye, *Betrayal in Central Europe: Austria and Czechoslovakia: Fallen Bastions* (New York: Harper & Brothers, 1939), 186.
42. On the Austro-German understandings, see Gedye, *Betrayal in Central Europe*, 180–91. In Holland, in advance of direct orders from Germany, Seyss-Inquart enforced anti-Semitic legislation modeled on German racial laws. See Raul Hilberg, *The Destruction*

of the European Jews (1961) (New York: Harper and Row, Harper Colophon Books, 1979), 365–82. The International Military Tribunal recorded that the deportation of Jews ordered by Seyss-Inquart entered strongly in his conviction and subsequent execution in 1946 (ibid., 690 and 713). As Nuremberg prosecutor Telford Taylor described, Seyss-Inquart epitomized the mentality of the Austrian civil servant who sought to revive Habsburg imperial ambitions in alliance with Hitler's Greater Germany. Only toward the end of the war did his criminal actions raise qualms in him. See Taylor, *The Anatomy of the Nuremberg Trials: A Personal Memoir* (New York: Skyhorse Publishing, 1993), 439–44.

43. Gedye, *Betrayal in Central Europe*, 192–4.
44. According to Kris in his interview with K. R. Eissler, Freud had decided against Fenichel as editor of *Imago* because "he found Fenichel too doctrinaire. Too doctrinaire means that he had a political opinion and this political opinion could influence his editorial activity" (Kris, interview with K. R. Eissler, 15 June 1953, 1, Box 117, SF). Regarding Freud and Reich—"the prelude to the Fenichel story"—Kris described how Freud drew a distinction between doctrinaire and revolutionary thought: "Here [with Reich] it was clearly, absolutely clearly, his [Freud's] rejection of Marxism as too doctrinaire. If it would have been during the time of revolution [in der Revolution], that would have been something different. But a doctrinaire system was unacceptable. And moreover it, the whole of it, seemed to him too unpsychological. The subordination of psychological thinking to materialism seemed to him implausible" (ibid., 23–4). Author's translation from the German interview. Another example of Freud's attitude toward revolutionary, as opposed to doctrinaire, thinking derives also from this time. In 1932, Freud signed a Left-leaning, antiwar petition circulated by the German physician Dr. Wladimir Eliasberg intended for the Geneva antiwar congress in July. This "call to physicians of all countries" warned that the economic crisis would lead to war. It stated further: "It is Soviet Russia that faces the most immediate threat. An attack on this country, which desires peaceful reconstruction, means a new world war." Author's translation from the German. See Wladimir Eliasberg, Box 24, SF.
45. Cited by Jacoby, *The Repression of Psychoanalysis*, 94. For a discussion of Reich, Fenichel, and Kris, see Jacoby, 83–97. On the cooperation and friction between Reich and Fenichel, and on Reich's important role in the Vienna Psychoanalytic Institute's Technical Seminar and Ambulatorium, where Reich was appointed the first tenured doctor in 1925, see Danto, *Freud's Free Clinics*, 100, 125–6, 160, and 269–71. As George Makari points out, Kris and Waelder attended Reich's Technical Seminar. For a cogent account of the professional and intellectual debates within the interwar psychoanalytic community in Vienna, see Makari, *Revolution in Mind*, 388–466. On the theory and practice of psychology in Vienna in the era of municipal reform, see Sheldon Gardner and Gwendolyn Stevens, *Red Vienna and the Golden Age of Psychology, 1918–1938* (New York: Praeger, 1992).
46. Kris to Saxl, 14 September 1936, GC, WIA.
47. Ibid.
48. Ibid. For National Socialism's use of the word, *Sippe* (kin), see Victor Klemperer, *The Language of the Third Reich: LTI-Lingua Tertii Imperii: A Philologist's Notebook*, trans. Martin Brady (Continuum: London, 2002), 80.
49. Kris to Saxl, 14 September 1936, GC, WIA.
50. Ibid. Underlined in the original.
51. Ibid.
52. Ibid. Von Dehmel, perhaps as Kris's colleague or at Kris's request, later assessed Freud's antiquities at an unusually low value, reducing the tax imposed by the authorities on Freud when he left Vienna. See Mark Edmundson, *The Death of Sigmund Freud: The Legacy of His Last Days* (New York: Bloomsbury, 2007), 116.
53. Ibid.

54. Kris to Saxl, 22 October 1936, GC, WIA.
55. Ibid. On the Warburg Institute, the AAC, and negotiations to keep the institute in England, see Elizabeth Sears, "The Warburg Institute, 1933–1944: A Precarious Experiment in International Collaboration," *Art Libraries Journal* 38, no. 4 (2013): 8–11. See also Dorothea McEwen, "A Tale of One Institute and Two Cities: The Warburg Institute," in *German-Speaking Exiles in Great Britain*, ed. Ian Wallace (Amsterdam: Rodopi, 1999).
56. For a list of exhibitions devoted to Daumier's work, see "Exhibitions," in *Daumier 1808–1879*, exhibition organized by the National Gallery of Canada, Ottawa, the Réunion des Musées Nationaux/Musée d'Orsay, Paris, and the Phillips Collection, Washington, 588–93. Michel Melot has explored the exhibitions of Daumier's works in France, and the nuances of the responses to them, against the background of political conflicts in the Third Republic, not only between republicans and conservatives but also between moderate republicans who emphasized Daumier as a painter and left-wing republicans who stressed Daumier the printmaker and caricaturist. See Michel Melot, "Daumier, Art, and Politics," ibid., 60–9. Kris and Gombrich's Vienna exhibition would reflect most closely the left-wing republican perspective.
57. *Ausstellung Honoré Daumier 1808–1879: Gemälde, Aquarelle, Zeichnungen, Plastik*, 21 February–31 March 1926, Galerie Matthiesen, Berlin (Berlin: Otto Elsner, [1926]). Emil Waldmann, who co-organized the Berlin exhibition and wrote the catalog introduction, assisted Kris in assembling the Vienna exhibition.
58. Otto Benesch, "Honoré Daumier: Zur Ausstellung in der Albertina 1937," *Österreichische Rundschau*, 3 Jg., Heft 2 (1937), reprinted in *Collected Writings*, vol. 4, 106.
59. Ibid.
60. See Melot, "Daumier, Art, and Politics," 64.
61. Kris reproduced these and the following illustrations in the exhibition's catalog.
62. Ernst Kris, "Honoré Daumier" (1936) in *Honoré Daumier*, Ausstellung, 21 November–21 Dezember 1936, 7. Imprisoned in 1944 in one of Hitler's asylums, the writer Hans Fallada recalled a Daumier cartoon given him by a friend: "one of those portraits of parliamentarians that he did by the hundred, with their stupid, sly and brutish faces . . . in my own mind I translated [its title] simply as 'Nazi mug.'" See Fallada, *A Stranger in My Own Country: The 1944 Prison Diary*, trans. Allan Blunden (Cambridge: Polity Press, 2015), 69.
63. Balzac, *Lost Illusions*, 387.
64. See ibid., 391.
65. Thus, as Le Men notes, when he depicted the figure in print, it was "drawn by Daumier from every conceivable angle." See Le Men, "Daumier and Printmaking," 38.
66. Clark, *The Absolute Bourgeois*, 116.
67. Ibid., 117. Édouard Papet writes, "With *Ratapoil*, Daumier simultaneously synthesized and subverted the sculptural genres that predominated toward the end of the July Monarchy: the caricature, the bourgeois statuette, and the commemorative public monument," in Papet, "'He Also Does Sculpture,'" in *Daumier 1808–1879*, exhibition organized by the National Gallery of Canada, Ottawa, the Réunion des Musées Nationaux/Musée d'Orsay, Paris, and the Phillips Collection, Washington, 55–6. For a chronology of the appearance and survival of Ratapoil both in print and in stone, see ibid., 276–87.
68. Jacques Ellul, *Propaganda: The Formation of Men's Attitudes*, trans. Konrad Kellen and Jean Lerner (New York: Vintage Books, 1973), 24.
69. Kris, "Honoré Daumier," 7–8. Clark's analysis, like Kris's, asserts the existence of that identification. See Clark, *The Absolute Bourgeois*, 117. For an examination of Daumier's representations of Don Quixote from the beginning to the end of his career—pre-and post-Ratapoil—see *Daumier 1808–1879*, exhibition organized by the National Gallery of Canada, Ottawa, the Réunion des Musées Nationaux/Musée d'Orsay, Paris, and the Phillips Collection, Washington, 516–41.
70. James, *Daumier*, 24.
71. Ibid., 23.

72. Ibid., 24.
73. Ibid., 30. Judith Wechsler cites Baudelaire's statement in "The Issue of Caricature," 317. Agnes Mongan noted "the writer's pleasure, his puzzlement and his desire to explain both" in James's reaction to coming across Daumier's lithographs in a Left Bank bookshop. See Mongan, introduction to *Honoré Daumier 1808–1879: The Armand Hammer Daumier Collection* (Los Angeles: Armand Hammer Foundation, 1982), 10.
74. Victor Hugo, *Selected Poems of Victor Hugo*, trans. E. H. and A. M. Blackmore (Chicago: University of Chicago Press, 2004), 117.
75. Kris, "Honoré Daumier," 8.
76. Ibid., 9.
77. Ibid.
78. Gertrud Bing, "Fritz Saxl (1890–1948): A Memoir," in *Fritz Saxl 1890–1948: A Volume of Memorial Essays from His Friends in England*, ed. D. J. Gordon (London: Thomas Nelson and Sons, 1957), 9.
79. Saxl to Kris, 27 January 1937, GC, WIA.
80. Gombrich, "The Study of Art and the Study of Man," 230. The certificate of Kris's membership in the *Ordre National de la Légion d'Honneur* is in Box OV 1, EK. No further information is available on the process behind Kris's membership (Jean Beysett, Grande Chancellerie de la Légion d'Honneur, letter to author, 27 October 2004).
81. Leonie Gombrich, conversation with the author, 4 January 2008. On the day of Gombrich's marriage Kris wrote Saxl with the news. See Kris to Saxl, 16 October 1936, GC, WIA. Richard Gombrich became Boden Professor of Sanskrit at Oxford and a leading figure in the field of Buddhist Studies.
82. Gombrich, "Sir Ernst Gombrich," interview by Wimmer, 135.
83. Fritz Saxl, "Why Art History?" (1948), in *Lectures*, vol. 1 (London: The Warburg Institute, University of London, 1957), 355. For a discussion of Saxl's interpretation of *Guernica*, see Rose, *Survival of Images*, 151–2.
84. Ernst Kris, "The Imagery of War," *Dayton Art Institute Bulletin* XV, no. 1 (October 1942): [1–2].
85. Ibid., [5]. For a recent study of the depiction of war in European art, see James Clifton and Leslie M. Scattone, *The Plains of Mars: European War Prints, 1500–1825* (New Haven and London: Yale University Press, 2009).
86. Recently, Carlo Ginzburg has emphasized the significant role of Picasso's own experiment with classicism in the creative and political genesis of *Guernica*. See Ginzburg, "The Sword and the Lightbulb: A Reading of *Guernica*," in *Disturbing Remains: Memory, History, and Crisis in the Twentieth Century*, ed. Michael S. Roth and Charles G. Salas (Los Angeles: Getty Research Institute, 2001), esp. 125–56.

Chapter 5: The Caricature Book, 1936–38

1. Gombrich, "The Study of Art and the Study of Man," 228–9.
2. See Kris to Saxl, 4 February 1937 and Saxl to Kris, 8 February 1937, GC, WIA; Gombrich and Eribon, *Looking for Answers*, 51; and Gombrich, "Sir Ernst Gombrich," interview by Wimmer, 133.
3. Saxl to Kris, 5 March 1937, GC, WIA.
4. Kris to Saxl, 13 October 1937, GC, WIA.
5. *Die Karikatur* (unpublished German ms) and *Caricature* (unpublished English ms), property of the Archive of E. H. Gombrich Estate, at the Warburg Institute Archive, London. © Literary Estate of E. H. Gombrich (hereafter cited as Gombrich Archive, WIA). The question of course arises as to which manuscript should be considered the final prewar version. Both versions have equal status. The London translation of the Viennese manuscript was the version intended for publication and the analysis here follows that translation. It utilizes the Vienna manuscript to fill in certain gaps, but it

does not offer new English translations, with the exception of the foreword, which Gombrich translated only partially into English. I have preserved the unedited punctuation and grammar of Gombrich's English version, and have included original German phrases with the English where such clarification seemed useful. It is not yet possible to determine exactly when Gombrich completed the English translation. The Gombrich Archive possesses partial drafts of lectures on caricature that Gombrich adapted from the caricature book years after he and Kris ended the book project: a four-page draft, "The Caricature Style"; a partial draft of lectures, pages numbered 3–104; and a thirteen-page manuscript of a radio talk in German, "Das Wesen der Karikatur." Gombrich thus incorporated various ideas from the book manuscript into his writings throughout his career.

6. Foreword to *Caricature* ms, page inserted in *Die Karikatur*. Underlined in the original.
7. Ibid.
8. Ibid.
9. Ibid. Author's translation.
10. Ibid. Author's translation.
11. Gombrich described Kris's intention in his letter to the author, 1 March 2000. See also Gombrich and Eribon, *Looking for Answers,* 51.
12. Ernst Kris and E. H. Gombrich, *Caricature* ms, 2. Underlined in the original.
13. Ibid., 12.
14. Ibid., 14–15.
15. Ibid., 25.
16. Ibid., 26.
17. Ibid., 30.
18. Ibid., 33.
19. Ibid., 35.
20. Ibid., 36. Underlined in the original.
21. Ibid., 42–3.
22. Ibid., 53. Here Gombrich translated *Kippcharakter* as "character switch" rather than "switch character" as he did throughout the remainder of the manuscript.
23. Freud perhaps anticipated this interpretive approach in *Civilization and Its Discontents*, where he explained the limits of the analogy between archeology and psychoanalysis. There he wrote that in the mind, unlike the archeological site, various layers co-resided or overlapped: "[A]ll the earlier phases of development continue to exist alongside the latest one . . . And the observer would perhaps only have to change the direction of his glance or his position in order to call up the one view or the other." See *The Standard Edition of the Complete Psychological Works of Sigmund Freud*, ed. James Strachey (London: Hogarth Press and the Institute of Psycho-Analysis, 1953–1974), vol. 21, p. 70.
24. Kris and Gombrich, *Caricature* ms, 54–5.
25. Ibid., 105.
26. Ibid., 106.
27. Ibid., 106 n. 1.
28. Ibid.
29. Ibid.
30. Ibid., 86.
31. Ibid., 87.
32. Ibid., 88.
33. Ibid.
34. Ibid., 90.
35. Ibid.
36. Ibid., 111–12.

37. Ibid., 112.
38. Ibid., 116.
39. Ibid., 117.
40. Ibid., 118.
41. Ibid., 119.
42. Ibid.
43. Ibid., 125.
44. Ibid., 119.
45. Ibid., 143.
46. Ibid., 155.
47. Ibid., 156.
48. Ibid.
49. Ibid.
50. Ibid., 161.
51. Ibid.
52. Ibid., 163.
53. Ibid., 166.
54. Ibid., 167.
55. Ibid. Melot has pointed out that in the early 1830s Daumier lithographs shared in the Romantic rebellion and received support from French Romantics, including Hugo; under the Second Empire, however, classicists approvingly linked his caricatures to a lost humanism. See Melot, "Daumier, Art, and Politics," 65–6. Between the two world wars, an edition of Daumier's antiwar lithographs was published in Germany. See *Daumier on War*, introduction by Hans Rothe (1926; reprint, New York: Da Capo Press, 1977).
56. Kris and Gombrich, *Caricature* ms, 168.
57. Ibid.
58. Ibid., 172–3.
59. Ibid., 173.
60. Ibid.
61. Ibid., 175
62. Ibid., 174.
63. Ibid., 175.
64. Ibid., 176.
65. Ibid. Underlined in the original.
66. Ibid., 178.
67. Ibid., 180.
68. Ibid., 181.
69. Ibid., 182.
70. Ibid., 183.
71. Ibid., 183.
72. Ibid., 184.
73. Ibid.
74. Ibid., 184.
75. Ibid., 185.
76. Ibid., 185n.
77. Ibid., 185–6.
78. Ibid., 186n. Pierre Cabanne similarly likened Daumier to Balzac in their shared interest in nocturnal luminance—for what it revealed in the shadow world around them and for its magnetic effect on viewers. See Pierre Cabanne, *Daumier*, trans. Lisa Davidson (Paris: Vilo Publishing, Les éditions de l'Amateur, 1999), 7.
79. Kris and Gombrich, *Caricature* ms, 189.
80. Ibid., 191.

81. Ibid., 191n.
82. Ibid., 193. Italics added.
83. Ibid.
84. Ibid., 200.
85. Ibid., 201.
86. Ibid.
87. Ibid.
88. Ibid., 202. Underlined in the original.
89. Ibid., 203.
90. Ibid., 204.
91. Ibid., 204–5. Underlined in the original.
92. Ibid., 209.
93. Ibid., 209–10.
94. Ibid., 213.
95. Ibid.
96. Ibid., 213–14. In the London manuscript, Gombrich omitted the sentence referring to the Dadaists, Klee, and Ernst (*Die Karikatur* ms, 213). The translation of this sentence is my own.
97. Ibid., 214. Underlined in the original.
98. Years later, Edgar Wind criticized both caricature drawing and Expressionist art, arguing that "Expressionist painting as a whole, even with such remarkable talents as Beckmann and Kirchner, became caught in that most cantankerous of genres, the serious cartoon; but that was not just a German obsession." See Wind, *Art and Anarchy* (New York: Alfred A. Knopf, 1964), 133. According to Wind, caricature had cut itself off from its political and social moorings: "The fact that the best cartoonists of our age have abandoned their medium for the grand manner, or confine themselves to weird social burlesque in the style of Thurber, may possibly account for the scarcity of talent in current political caricature. Or has modern conformism become so strong that caricature, deprived of its topical role, can display itself only as a 'fine art'?" (ibid., 133–4.)
99. Kris and Gombrich, *Caricature* ms, 217.
100. Ibid., 218.
101. Ibid., 219.
102. Ibid., 219–20.
103. Ibid., 221–2.
104. Ibid., 222. Underlined in the original.
105. Ibid., 223.
106. Ibid., 228–9.
107. Ibid., 230.
108. Ibid., 234n.
109. Ibid., 243–4.
110. Ibid., 244.
111. Ibid., 254.
112. Primo Levi, *The Periodic Table* (1975), trans. Raymond Rosenthal (New York: Alfred A. Knopf, Everyman's Library, 1996), 37.

Chapter 6: From Vienna to London and New York, 1938–41

1. On the *British Journal of Medical Psychology* and the British Psychoanalytic Society, see Adam Phillips, *Winnicott* (London: Penguin Books, 2007), 39–41. For Freud, Rickman, Rivers, and Jones, see Jones to Freud, 25 January 1920, 364; Freud to Jones, 8 February 1920, 368; Jones to Freud, 1 October 1920, 391; Freud to Jones, 12 October 1920, 393; and Jones to Freud, 15 June 1921, 430, *Complete Correspondence of Sigmund Freud and Ernest Jones 1908–1939*. In the 1920s, Rickman helped organize the London Clinic for

Psychoanalysis and joined its staff. See Danto, *Freud's Free Clinics*, 151 and 168. For biographical information and a collection of Rickman's writings, including reports for the War Office in the Second World War, see John Rickman, *Selected Contributions to Psycho-Analysis* (London: Karnac, 2003) and John Rickman, *No Ordinary Psychoanalyst: The Exceptional Contributions of John Rickman*, ed. Pearl King (London: Karnac, 2003).

2. Ernst Kris and E. H. Gombrich, "The Principles of Caricature," *British Journal of Medical Psychology* 17 (1938): 319.
3. Ibid.
4. Ibid., 322. Italics in the original.
5. Ibid., 321 n.1.
6. Ibid., 324.
7. Ibid., 331. Italics in the original.
8. Ibid., 337.
9. Ibid.
10. Ibid., 340.
11. Ibid., 337.
12. Ibid., 341.
13. Ibid., 319 n.1.
14. Ernst Kris and Leo Planiscig, *Gefälschte Kunstwerke: V. Ausstellung*, September–Oktober 1937, Kunsthistorisches Museum, Sammlungen für Plastik und Kunstgewerbe (J. Weiner: Vienna, [1937]), 3. Months earlier Kris and Planiscig had presented an exhibition of trial pieces sculpted by late Renaissance artists, including Giambologna and Bernini, which emphasized that the experimental process—not the final product—represented what was authentic in art. See Ernst Kris and Leo Planiscig, *Bozzetti und Modelletti der Spätrenaissance und des Barock: IV. Ausstellung*, Dezember 1936–Jänner 1937, Kunsthistorisches Museum, Sammlungen für Plastik und Kunstgewerbe (J. Weiner: Wien, [1936–7]). *Bozzetto* referred to the sketch and *modelletto* to the final design.
15. Kris and Planiscig, *Gefälschte Kunstwerke*, 3.
16. Ibid., 4.
17. Ibid., 3.
18. That same treacherous nakedness reappeared after the Second World War when politicians, lawyers, clerics, and academics all claimed that Austria had in actuality been the first republican victim of Hitler. On the persistence of the myth of Austria as Hitler's first victim, see Hella Pick, *Guilty Victim: Austria from the Holocaust to Haider* (London: I. B. Tauris, 2000).
19. On Innitzer's support for the *Anschluss*, his efforts to protect Church interests, and his attempts to accommodate Hitler, see Pauley, *From Prejudice to Persecution*, 298–9 and Evan Burr Bukey, *Hitler's Austria: Popular Sentiment in the Nazi Era, 1938–1945* (Chapel Hill, NC: University of North Carolina Press, 2000), 35–6 and 96–106.
20. See *The Vienna School Reader*, ed. Wood, 12–13.
21. Leonie Gombrich, conversation with the author, 4 January 2008.
22. Anton O. Kris, letter to the author, 30 December 2007 and Anton O. Kris and Anna Kris Wolff, conversation with the author, 17 January 2008. In recounting to his son the story of his final days in Vienna, Kris never specified which branch of the police called him in for questioning. For recollections of the *Anschluss* see, for example, Kandel, *In Search of Memory*; George Clare, *Last Waltz in Vienna: The Rise and Destruction of a Family* (New York: Holt, Rinehart and Winston, 1982); and Egon Schwarz, *Refuge: Chronicle of a Flight from Hitler*, trans. Philip Boehm, Hildegarde and Hunter Hannum, and Caroline Wellbery (Riverside, CA: Ariadne Press, 2002). George Steiner recalls that period through the life of his Viennese father. See Steiner, *Errata: An Examined Life* (New Haven: Yale University Press, 1998).
23. Consul to Warburg Institute, Imperial Institute Buildings, South Kensington, 6 May 1938, GC, WIA. The month of Kris's emigration is incorrectly recorded as June in

Herbert Haupt's *Jahre der Gefährdung: Das Kunsthistorische Museum 1938–1945* (Vienna: Kunsthistorisches Museum, 1995), 10. On the forced emigration from Austria, see Edward Timms and Ritchie Robertson, eds., *The Austrian Exodus: The Creative Achievements of Refugees from National Socialism*, Austrian Studies VI (Edinburgh: Edinburgh University Press, 1995).

24. P. A. Lemoisne, "Preface," *Exhibition of a Century of French Caricature 1750–1850 with some English Caricatures of the Napoleonic Period*, 10 March–6 April 1939 (The Anglo-French Art and Travel Society, 1939), 8.
25. Ibid., 10.
26. Ibid.
27. Gombrich and Eribon, *Looking for Answers,* 51. The reader was Edgar Wind, from whom Saxl had drawn information about psychoanalysis as early as 1932. Saxl, however, might also have been concerned with the possible impact on the status of a foreign institute in Britain. Years later, Gombrich referred to "a certain reluctance to publish a book which took many of its examples from topical cartoons such as those by David Low who was then at the height of his powers." (Quoted in Levy, "Ernst Kris," 214 n. 28.)
28. Ibid.
29. On the King Penguin series, see Jeremy Lewis, *Penguin Special: The Life and Times of Allen Lane* (London: Penguin Books, 2005), 143–5.
30. Ernst Kris and E. H. Gombrich, *Caricature* (Harmondsworth: Penguin Books, 1940), 5.
31. Ibid., 14.
32. Ibid., 15.
33. Ibid., 17.
34. Ibid., 22.
35. Ibid., 24.
36. Clive Bell, review of *Portraits of Christ,* by Ernst Kitzinger and Elizabeth Senior and *Caricature*, by Ernst Kris and E. H. Gombrich, in *New Statesman and Nation* (22 February 1941): 196. Bell shared Read's principled pacifism. His discomfort with new mass media and technological culture reflected both his commitment to the intellectual world of Bloomsbury and his attachment to the countryside and his country estate. In 1937, Bell's son Julian was killed defending the Spanish republic at the battle of Brunete. See Peter Stansky and William Abrahams, *Journey to the Frontier: Two Roads to the Spanish Civil War* (Chicago: University of Chicago Press, 1966), 38 and 394–6.
37. Bell, review of *Portraits of Christ* and *Caricature*, 196.
38. On Piper as a wartime artist, see Henry Pelling, *Britain and the Second World War* (Glasgow: William Collins and Sons, 1970), 322–3 and Frances Spalding, *British Art since 1900* (London: Thames & Hudson, 1986), 128–39. After the war, CEMA became reincarnated as the Arts Council.
39. John Piper, "One Shilling, Coloured," *The Spectator* (14 March 1941): 290.
40. Review of *Caricature* by Ernst Kris and E. H. Gombrich, in *Times Literary Supplement* (8 March 1941): n.p.
41. Herbert Read, *Art and Society* (New York: Macmillan, 1937), 251–2.
42. On the New Burlington exhibition, see King, *The Last Modern*, 170–1. Just two years earlier, Read had published his *Art Now: An Introduction to the Theory of Modern Painting and Sculpture* (New York: Harcourt, Brace and Company, 1936). On artistic rebellion and the suppression of art in interwar Germany, see John Willett, *Art and Politics in the Weimar Period: The New Sobriety, 1917–1933* (New York: Da Capo Press, 1996).
43. Herbert Read, foreword to *Kokoschka: Life and Work,* by Edith Hoffmann (London: Faber and Faber, 1947), 8.
44. Ibid.

45. On Goya's influence on British satirical art, see Reva Wolf, *Goya and the Satirical Print in England and on the Continent, 1730–1850* (Boston: David R. Godine and Boston College Museum of Art, 1991). On Read's role in the display of *Guernica*, see King, *The Last Modern*, 171–2.
46. Herbert Read, *Contemporary British Art* (Harmondsworth: Penguin Books, 1951), 23.
47. Ibid.
48. Ibid., 27.
49. See Asa Briggs, *The BBC: The First Fifty Years* (Oxford: Oxford University Press, 1985), 114–15.
50. Herbert Read, "Multum in Parvo," review of *Portraits of Christ*, by Ernst Kitzinger and Elizabeth Senior, and *Caricature*, by Ernst Kris and E. H. Gombrich, *The Listener* (27 February 1941): 305.
51. Ibid., 305–6.
52. Ibid., 305.
53. On recruitment and staffing, see Olive Renier and Vladimir Rubinstein, *Assigned to Listen: The Evesham Experience 1939–43* (London: BBC External Services, 1986), 15–16; Asa Briggs, *The History of Broadcasting in the United Kingdom*, vol. 3, *The War of Words*, revised edition (Oxford: Oxford University Press, 1995), 170–3; and Briggs, *The BBC: The First Fifty Years*, 175 and 188–9. On BBC governance, see Asa Briggs, *Governing the BBC* (London: British Broadcasting Corporation, 1979).
54. Jessica Mitford, *Hons and Rebels* (New York: New York Review Books, 2004), 179–80.
55. "(Walter) ERNST KRIS," Bodleian MS., Society for the Protection of Science and Learning, 189/1–2, folio 177. For the date of the curriculum vitae, see folio 189.
56. See Kris, Curriculum Vitae, Rockefeller Foundation, Record Group 1.1, Series 200, Sub-series R, Box 260, Folder 3098.
57. See Pelling, *Britain and the Second World War*, 315–16, and Daniel Snowman, *The Hitler Emigres: The Cultural Impact on Britain of Refugees from Nazism* (London: Pimlico, 2003), 105–6.
58. See Pelling, *Britain and the Second World War*, 86.
59. See Christopher Andrew, *Her Majesty's Secret Service: The Making of the British Intelligence Community* (New York: Penguin Books, 1987), 479.
60. See Pelling, *Britain and the Second World War*, 87.
61. Andrew, *Her Majesty's Secret Service*, 480.
62. Ernst Kris to Esther Simpson, 10 July 1940, Bodleian MS., Society for the Protection of Science and Learning, 189/1–2, folio 199.
63. Kris to Simpson, 20 August 1940, folio 205v.
64. Ernst Kris to Mark Abrams, 5 September 1940, Box 2, EK. Abrams, a monitor whom Kris had trained in England, headed the BBC Research Department in fall 1940. See Ernst Kris to S. Lawford Childs, 10 October 1940, Box 2, Folder 15, EK.
65. Kris to Abrams, 5 September 1940, Box 2, EK.
66. Ibid.
67. Ibid.
68. Ernst Kris to W. N. Newton, 6 September 1940, Box 2, Folder 15, EK.
69. Ernst Kris to John Salt, 15 November 1940, Box 2, Folder 17, EK. Salt was a BBC program director whose responsibilities eventually included monitoring, counter-propaganda, and overseas intelligence.
70. Ernst Kris to Mark Abrams, 22 December 1940, Box 2, EK.
71. On the University in Exile, the role of the Rockefeller Foundation, and the friction between the school and the foundation, see Peter M. Rutkoff and William B. Scott, *New School: A History of the New School for Social Research* (New York: Free Press, 1986), 84–106.
72. See Sears, "The Warburg Institute, 1933–1944," 9.

73. See Hans Speier, "Introduction: Autobiographical Notes," in *The Truth in Hell and Other Essays on Politics and Culture, 1935–1987* (Oxford: Oxford University Press, 1989), 14–15.
74. Ibid., 15.
75. Kris to Salt, 15 November 1940, Box 2, Folder 17, EK.
76. On Marshall's role at the Rockefeller Foundation, in particular his efforts to build contacts in Europe in the 1930s, see William J. Buxton, "John Marshall and the Humanities in Europe: Shifting Patterns of Rockefeller Foundation Support," *Minerva* 41, no. 2 (2003): 133–53. For the appraisal committee's report, see p. 141.
77. On Marshall's contributions to the study of politics and mass communication, see Brett Gary, *The Nervous Liberals: Propaganda Anxieties from World War I to the Cold War* (New York: Columbia University Press, 1999), 85–93.
78. See Paul F. Lazarsfeld, "An Episode in the History of Social Research: A Memoir," in *The Intellectual Migration: Europe and America, 1930–1960*, ed. Donald Fleming and Bernard Bailyn (Cambridge, MA: Harvard University Press, Belknap Press, 1969), 275–6. On Marshall's support for Eisler, see Buxton, "Marshall," 134 n.8 and 152.
79. Quoted in Rutkoff and Scott, *New School*, 89. On the split within the Rockefeller Foundation over providing support for Jewish scholars, see ibid., 95–6.
80. On the contrasting efforts of the Rockefeller and Ford Foundations, see Buxton, "Marshall," pp. 148–9. On Marshall and antifascism, see Gary, *Nervous Liberals*, 107–8.
81. Ernst Kris, Curriculum Vitae, Rockefeller Foundation, Record Group 1.1, Series 200, Sub-series R, Box 260, Folder 3098, Rockefeller Archive Center.
82. Ibid.
83. John Marshall, Interviews, 12 December 1940, Rockefeller Foundation, Record Group 1.1, Series 200, Sub-series R, Box 260, Folder 3098. Hereafter cited as Interviews.
84. Marshall, Interviews. The Institute for Propaganda Analysis, which provided teachers with guidance on how to instruct students and the public in recognizing propaganda, professed political indifference to the source of propaganda. See Ralph W. Tyler, "Implications of Communications Research for the Public Schools" (1942 [1941]), in *Print, Radio, and Film in a Democracy*, ed. Douglas Waples (Chicago: University of Chicago Press, 1942), 155 and Gary, *Nervous Liberals*, 78.
85. Quoted in Ernst Kris, "The 'Danger' of Propaganda," *American Imago* 2, no. 1 (1941), 8 n. 7.
86. See Gary, *Nervous Liberals*, 67–8.
87. Marshall, Interviews. Lasswell strongly recommended Kris to Marshall, although he described Kris as "someone whose speculation must be kept in touch with the evidence" (Marshall, Interviews). For Lasswell's recommendation, see Harold Lasswell to John Marshall, 15 December 1940, Rockefeller Foundation, Record Group 1.1, Series 200, Sub-series R, Box 260, Folder 3098. Gary discusses Kris and Lasswell's views of the wartime role of social science. See Gary, *Nervous Liberals*, 118–21.
88. Marshall, Interviews. Kris gave a similar, albeit abbreviated, account of the interview: "I gave them my conditions: That I was not 'neutral,' that I would not associate with anybody who had ever been neutral or anti-British at any time of his life, etc. . . . I had a three-hour conference with their coordinator for radio and propaganda research, Lasswell, who flatly accepted all I wanted . . ." (Kris to Salt, 15 December 1940, Box 2, Folder 17, EK).
89. Kris and Speier, *German Radio Propaganda*, 35.
90. Ibid., 36.
91. Resolution, 21 March 1941, Rockefeller Foundation, Record Group 1.1, Series 200, Sub-series R, Box 260, Folder 3098.
92. Kris to Salt, 1 February 1941, Box 2, Folder 18, EK.
93. Kris and Speier, *German Radio Propaganda*, v.
94. See Speier, "Autobiographical Notes," 6–14, and Rutkoff and Scott, *New School*, 107–13.

95. Hans Speier, "The Truth in Hell: Maurice Joly and *The Protocols of the Wise Men of Zion*," in *The Truth in Hell*, 283. The anti-Semitic authors who invented *The Protocols of the Elders of Zion* plagiarized from Joly's dialogue, transforming Joly's descriptions of Bonapartist political strategies into the protocols of a supposed Jewish world conspiracy. Speier wrote his essay to guard Joly from undeserved taint and preserve his status as an important political theorist. For a commentary on the history of Joly's essay and its contemporary relevance, see Carlo Ginzburg, "Representing the Enemy: On the French Prehistory of the *Protocols*," in *Threads and Traces: True, False, Fictive*, trans. Anne C. Tedeschi and John Tedeschi (Berkeley and Los Angeles: University of California Press, 2012).
96. Speier, "The Truth in Hell," 281.
97. Ibid., 282.
98. Ibid.
99. Speier, "Autobiographical Notes," 23. For a discussion of Speier's participation in the Totalitarian Communication Project and his move from the New School to Washington, see Daniel Morris Bessner, "The Night Watchman: Hans Speier and the Making of the American National Security State" (Ph.D. diss., Duke University, 2013), 129–42.
100. News of the Hitler–Stalin Pact hit Lynd particularly hard. See Gary, *Nervous Liberals*, 93–4.
101. See Ernst Kris and Howard White, "The German Radio Home News in Wartime," in *Radio Research 1942–1943*, ed. Paul Lazarsfeld and Frank Stanton (New York: Duell, Sloan and Pearce, Essential Books, 1944; reprint: New York: Arno Press, 1979), 181–208. On radio research at Columbia, see Lazarsfeld, "Episode in the History of Social Research," 304–5, 310–13, and 326–31.
102. Robert S. Lynd and Helen Merrell Lynd, *Middletown: A Study in Modern American Culture* (New York: Harcourt Brace Jovanovich, 1929, 1957). In 1935 the Lynds returned to Muncie to study the effects of the Depression. See Robert S. Lynd and Helen Merrell Lynd, *Middletown in Transition: A Study in Cultural Conflicts* (New York: Harcourt Brace Jovanovich, 1937, 1965). For a recent extension of the Middletown study, see Dan Rottenberg, ed., *Middletown Jews: The Tenuous Survival of an American Jewish Community* (Bloomington, IN: Indiana University Press, 1997).
103. On Kracauer and Adorno, see Martin Jay, *The Dialectical Imagination: A History of the Frankfurt School and the Institute of Social Research, 1923–1950* (Boston: Little, Brown, 1973), 21–2 and 66.
104. This account is based on material from David Culbert, "The Rockefeller Foundation, the Museum of Modern Art Film Library, and Siegfried Kracauer, 1941," *Historical Journal of Film, Radio and Television* 13, no. 4 (1993): 495–511.
105. In her work Barry explored how motion pictures transformed visual art. In a letter to Kris, she explained that movie fragments and not primitive residues provided the material of supposedly unconscious, surrealist symbolism, writing that "my own preoccupation with the surrealists is to establish (as I believe) that much of their visual imagery comes from forgotten but very concrete memories of early French films seen in their early years i.e. 1901–1912" (Iris Barry to Ernst Kris, 9 May 1945, Box 2, EK). Like Kris and Gombrich, she concluded that primitivism was in crucial part not a primordial revival but a contemporary creation.
106. Iris Barry to John Marshall, 14 May 1941, in Culbert, "Rockefeller Foundation," 499. In the wartime social sciences, Adorno also emphasized the necessity of "content analysis." See T. W. Adorno, "Scientific Experiences of a European Scholar in America," trans. Donald Fleming, in *The Intellectual Migration: Europe and America, 1930–1960*, ed. Fleming and Bailyn, 344.
107. John Marshall to Henry Allen Moe, John Simon Guggenheim Memorial Foundation, quoted in Culbert, "Rockefeller Foundation," 505. Carlo Ginzburg, in "Details, Early

Plans, Microanalysis: Thoughts on a Book by Siegfried Kracauer" (*Threads and Traces*, 186), has pointed out that Kracauer's interpretation of film also showed the influence of Panofsky.

108. Siegfried Kracauer, *From Caligari to Hitler: A Psychological History of the German Film* (Princeton, NJ: Princeton University Press, 1947), 71.
109. Siegfried Kracauer, "Film 1928," in *The Mass Ornament: Weimar Essays*, trans. Thomas Y. Levin (Cambridge, MA: Harvard University Press, 1995), 320.
110. Siegfried Kracauer, "Propaganda and the Nazi War Film" (1942), supplement to *From Caligari to Hitler*, 299.
111. Ibid., 303. On the propaganda studies of Kris, Kracauer, and Adorno, see Louis Rose, "Interpreting Propaganda: Successors to Warburg and Freud in Wartime," *American Imago* 60, no. 1 (Spring 2003): 122–30, and "Daumier in Vienna: Ernst Kris, E. H. Gombrich, and the Politics of Caricature," *Visual Resources: An International Journal of Documentation* 23, nos. 1–2 (March–June 2007): 39–64.
112. Schapiro had first urged Kracauer to seek Barry's support in the United States. On Schapiro's support for and disagreements with Kracauer, see Mark M. Anderson, "Siegfried Kracauer and Meyer Schapiro: A Friendship," *New German Critique*, no. 54 (Fall 1991): 19–29.
113. Meyer Schapiro, "The New Viennese School" (1936), in *The Vienna School Reader*, ed. Wood, 459.
114. Ibid., 482.
115. Kris to Salt, 1 February 1941, Box 2, Folder 18, EK.
116. See Gary, *Nervous Liberals*, 121–2. Kris, with other psychoanalysts, did provide advice to Walter Langer as he constructed his wartime case study of Hitler for the OSS. See Pick, *Pursuit of the Nazi Mind*, 133–4. Pick's book includes a history of the OSS's interest in psychological analysis (108–22) as well as an examination of the content and fate of Langer's report (128–52). Like Kris, Erik Erikson also devoted attention to propaganda analysis. See Erikson, "Hitler's Imagery and German Youth," *Psychiatry* 5, no. 4 (November 1942): 475–93, and "Comments on Anti-Nazi Propaganda" (1945), in *A Way of Looking at Things: Selected Papers from 1930 to 1980*, ed. Stephen Schlein (New York: W. W. Norton, 1987).
117. Kris provided essential support to exiled family members. During the First World War, his older brother Paul, who had helped prepare Kris's path toward Catholicism, had been a prisoner of war in Russia; after the war, he practiced law in Paris. In 1938, in an Austrian journal for refugees in France, he published legal advice to Austrian exiles, recommending that they seek protection in France by defining themselves as ex-Austrians. The designation carried a political message but no legal weight. Paul emigrated to Brazil via Portugal. Ernst Kris sent funds to him and his wife, and also helped his two nieces in Britain (Anton O. Kris and Anna Kris Wolff, conversation with the author, 17 January 2008). On Paul Kris in Paris, see Franz Goldner, *Austrian Emigration 1938–1945* (New York: Frederick Ungar, 1979), 2. Kris shared with Saxl the responsibility for supporting Betty Kurth, who now lived in London. See Kris to Bing, 6 November 1942, GC, WIA.
118. Kris to Salt, 7 January 1941, Box 2, Folder 18, EK.
119. Kris to Bing, 6 November 1942, GC, WIA.
120. Discussing his father's emigration, Anton O. Kris concluded, "I don't think he ever recovered from leaving England." Quoted in Emily A. Kuriloff, *Contemporary Psychoanalysis and the Legacy of the Third Reich: History, Memory, Tradition* (New York: Routledge, 2014), 39. Kuriloff explores diverse experiences of exile among psychoanalysts from the perspective of an interpersonal psychoanalyst.
121. Kris and Speier, *German Radio Propaganda*, 36.
122. Prior to *German Radio Propaganda*, Kris had completed several studies on mass communication, propaganda, and political terror, including "German Censorship

Instructions for the Czech Press," *Social Research* 8, no. 2 (May 1941): 238–46; "Morale in Germany," *American Journal of Sociology* 47, no. 3 (November 1941): 352–61; "Mass Communication under Totalitarian Governments" (1942 [1941]), in *Print, Radio, and Film in a Democracy*, ed. Waples; "German Propaganda Instructions of 1933," *Social Research* 9, no. 1 (February 1942): 46–81; "The Covenant of the Gangsters," *Journal of Criminal Psychopathology* 4, no. 3 (January 1943): 445–58; and "Danger and Morale," *American Journal of Orthopsychiatry* 14, no. 1 (January 1944): 147–55.

123. "Expert Analyzes Nazi Propaganda," *New York Times*, 8 December 1940. The article described Kris as a "Viennese psychologist" who had been on "the teaching staff of the Psychoanalysis Institute in Vienna" and "the war head of the monitoring service of the British Broadcasting Company." The illustration that accompanied the article would have confirmed Kris's concerns about the difficulty of countering Nazi propaganda in the United States: a photograph showed an elderly gentleman in bowler and overcoat, in undisturbed peace, feeding the swans in London's Battersea Park.
124. Ernst Kris, "The Place of the Audience in German Propaganda," ms, n.d., 14–15, Box 17, Folder 2, EK. Here Kris makes his own application of ideas developed by Freud in *Group Psychology and the Analysis of the Ego*. Kris explored Le Bon's theories and the Freudian response further in an unpublished essay that he co-authored with a member of the Rockefeller research team, Hans Herma. See Ernst Kris and Hans Herma, "Hitler's Views on Propaganda and Le Bon's Psychology of the Crowd: A Study in the Sociology of Knowledge," ms, n.d., Box 17, Folder 2, EK.
125. Ernst Kris, "Some Problems of War Propaganda: A Note on Propaganda New and Old," *Psychoanalytic Quarterly* 12 (1943): 387–8. For a study of Kris as propaganda analyst, see Krüger's *Das Unbehagen in der Karikatur*.
126. Ibid., 399.

Chapter 7: War Work, 1941–45

1. Gombrich to Kris, 2 November 1944, Box 6, EK.
2. Gombrich to Kris, 3 January 1945, Box 6, EK.
3. E. H. Gombrich, "Myth and Reality in German Wartime Broadcasts" (1969), in *Ideals and Idols: Essays on Values in History and in Art* (London: Phaidon Press, 1979), 104–5.
4. Ibid., 105.
5. Elias Canetti, *Party in the Blitz: The English Years* (New York: New Directions Books, 2005), 9.
6. Fritz Saxl and Rudolf Wittkower, *British Art and the Mediterranean* (1948; reprint with a preface by Rudolf Wittkower, London: Oxford University Press, 1969). Katia Mazzucco discusses the 1941 Warburg Institute exhibition from which the book derived, including a review by Herbert Read, in "1941 *English Art and the Mediterranean*: A Photographic Exhibition by the Warburg Institute in London," *Journal of Art Historiography* 5 (December 2011): 1–28. For a brief biography of Saxl, see Bing, "Fritz Saxl (1890–1948): A Memoir," in *Fritz Saxl 1890–1948*, ed. Gordon. On the CEMA photo exhibitions, see Gombrich to Kris, 16 August 1943, Box 6, EK.
7. For political themes in Saxl's lectures, see Rose, *Survival of Images*, 133–53.
8. Bing to Gombrich, 13 September 1939, GC, WIA.
9. On the wartime difficulties confronting the Warburg Institute, see Sears, "The Warburg Institute," 12–14.
10. E. H. Gombrich to Esther Simpson, 12 April 1939, Bodleian MS., Society for the Protection of Science and Learning, 187/1–3, folio 249.
11. Bing to Gombrich, 13 September 1939, GC, WIA.
12. Gombrich to Bing, 14 September 1939, GC, WIA.

13. See Pelling, *Britain and the Second World War*, 47–8.
14. Gombrich to Bing, 8 October 1939, GC, WIA. Underlined in the original.
15. Gombrich to Bing, 8 October 1939, GC, WIA.
16. See Ernst Kris and E. H. Gombrich, *Caricature: An Essay on Its History and Meaning*, ms, n.d., Box 17, EK. Kris saved the text of the essay, while Gombrich kept the appendix on art and physiognomy, the subject that he intended eventually to submit to Wittkower.
17. Kris and Gombrich, "Caricature: An Essay on Its History and Meaning," Hist. Probl. 12, Box 17, EK. It is possible that Gombrich was referring to this manuscript when he recalled the difficulty of publishing a work that included Low's caricatures. For Low's creation, see *The Complete Colonel Blimp*, ed. Mark Bryant (London: Bellew Publishing, 1991).
18. E. H. Gombrich, "Art and Propaganda," *The Listener* (7 December 1939): 1119.
19. Ibid., 1120.
20. Ibid., 1120.
21. Bing to Gombrich, 12 October 1939, GC, WIA.
22. See Gombrich and Eribon, *Looking for Answers*, 58 and Gombrich, "Myth and Reality in German Wartime Broadcasts," 93.
23. Richard Marriott, quoted in Renier and Rubinstein, *Assigned to Listen*, 16.
24. Gombrich to Bing, 21 February 1940, GC, WIA.
25. Ibid. Three years before the war, the archeologist Sir Leonard Woolley, who had undertaken excavations at Ur for the British Museum, published his book *Abraham: Recent Discoveries and Hebrew Origins* (London: Faber and Faber, 1936).
26. Gombrich to Bing, 21 February 1940, GC, WIA.
27. Gombrich to Bing, 11 May 1940, GC, WIA. Underlined in the original.
28. See Gombrich to Kris, 2 January 194[1] (the year was mistakenly typed as "1940") and n.d. [ca. February 1942], Box 6, EK.
29. See Gombrich to Kris, 7 October 1940, Box 6, EK. Amadea Gombrich did not remain in Edinburgh, but eventually moved to London to find work. In 1942, she married Sir John Forsdyke, director of the British Museum, at Westminster Abbey. See Gombrich to Kris, 25 March 1942, Box 6, EK.
30. Gombrich to Bing, 6 June 1940, GC, WIA. Underlined in the original.
31. Gombrich to Bing, 7 July 1940, GC, WIA. By the end of the month, Gombrich had learned the address—"A.I.C. Huyton near Liverpool, Camp 3, House 166"—and relayed it to Esther Simpson of the AAC. See Gombrich to Simpson, 30 July 1940, Bodleian MS, Society for the Protection of Science and Learning, 187/1–3, folio 258. Gombrich told Kris of his father's and Kurz's internment in a letter the following month. See Gombrich to Kris, 17 August 1940, Box 6, EK.
32. E. H. Gombrich to Rudolf Wittkower, 25 July 1940, GC, WIA.
33. Gombrich to Kris, 7 October 1940, Box 6, EK. For first-person accounts of the internment camps, see Snowman, *The Hitler Emigres*, 107–15.
34. Ibid.
35. For Lady Violet Bonham Carter's intervention, see Gombrich to Kris, 23 July 1941, Box 6, EK. For efforts by the Gombrichs to find a home and secure work, see Gombrich to Kris, 25 March 1942 and 25 November 1942, Box 6, EK.
36. See Gombrich to Kris, 25 November 1942 and 16 November 1943, Box 6, EK.
37. See Gombrich to Kris, 23 July 1941, Box 6, EK. See also Gombrich and Eribon, *Looking for Answers,* 62, and Sears, "The Warburg Institute, 1933–1944," 13.
38. [Saxl] to Gombrich, 7 August 1941, GC, WIA. Underlined in the original.
39. See Gombrich to Kris, 21 August 1941; n. d. [ca. February 1942]; and 25 March 1942, Box 6, EK.
40. T. Rowlandson and A. C. Pugin, *The Microcosm of London* (London: King Penguin Books, 1943; revised edition, 1947), 5.
41. Ibid., 7.

42. Ibid.
43. Ibid., 6.
44. Gombrich to Saxl, 20 August 1940, GC, WIA. See E. H. Gombrich, "The Artist and the Art of War," *The Listener* (29 August 1940): 311–12.
45. E. H. Gombrich, preface to *Assigned to Listen*, by Renier and Rubinstein, 7.
46. Gombrich to Kris, 21 August 1941, Box 6, EK.
47. Gombrich to Kris, n. d. [ca. February 1942], Box 6, EK.
48. Ibid.
49. See Briggs, *The BBC: The First Fifty Years*, 207–8.
50. Gombrich to Kris, n. d. [ca. February 1942], Box 6, EK.
51. Ibid. On Oliver Whitley's background, work, and resignation, see Asa Briggs, *The History of Broadcasting in the United Kingdom*, vol. 2, *The Golden Age of Wireless*, revised edition (Oxford: Oxford University Press, 1995), 399, and vol. 3, *War of Words*, 171 and 330–1.
52. Gombrich to Bing, 23 June 1941, GC, WIA. Ellipses in the original.
53. On Eden and appeasement, see R. A. C. Parker, *Chamberlain and Appeasement: British Policy and the Coming of the Second World War* (New York: St. Martin's Press, 1993), 45–57 and 93–123; William R. Rock, *British Appeasement in the 1930s* (New York: Norton, 1977), 4–5 and 75–82; and A. J. P. Taylor, *English History 1914–1945* (New York: Oxford University Press, 1970), 379–80 and 421–3.
54. On the Economic Warfare division, its Special Operations Executive, and Dalton's tenure, see Andrew, *Her Majesty's Secret Service*, 475–7. One of the most detailed case studies and one of the most moving accounts of democratic antifascism is E. P. Thompson's history of the service of his brother, Frank Thompson, in E. P. Thompson, *Beyond the Frontier: The Politics of a Failed Mission: Bulgaria 1944* (Stanford, CA: Stanford University Press, 1997).
55. On domestic reform and the war effort, see Pelling, *Britain and the Second World War*, 130–1, 168, and 181–5.
56. Ibid., 133, 158–9, and 185–6.
57. For example, he wrote to Salt in January 1941: "The wave of anti-British feeling, which is still alive and kept alive by Moscow and Berlin, is a danger which we have no reason to minimize" (Kris to Salt, 7 January 1941, Box 2, Folder 18, EK).
58. See Kris and Speier, *German Radio Propaganda,* 214, 223–4, 284–5, 436–7, and 481–2.
59. Ibid., 285.
60. See Gombrich to Kris, 14 February 1941, Box 6, EK.
61. Gombrich to Saxl, 27 March 1941, GC, WIA. For background on the life, works, and political thought of Gerald of Wales, see Robert Bartlett, *Gerald of Wales, 1146–1223* (Oxford: Oxford University Press, Clarendon Press, 1982).
62. For a recent discussion of the dual state interpretation of fascism, see Robert O. Paxton, *The Anatomy of Fascism* (New York: Alfred A. Knopf, 2004), 121–2.
63. Gombrich to Kris, 23 July 1941, Box 6, EK.
64. Gombrich to Kris, 14 February 1941, Box 6, EK.
65. Gombrich to Kris, 3 April 1941, Box 6, EK. In interviews with the psychiatrist Leon Goldensohn at the Nuremberg trials, Fritzsche again depicted Germans as fighting the two world wars only as wars of national defense. He asserted that the Second World War became a war of atrocities and a war to exterminate the Jews because the Nazis had defensively adopted the methods of Russian and German Communists and because French resistance fighters and Russian partisans began attacks on Germans. According to him, before the rise of the resistance and partisan movements in France, the Germans administered a "peaceful occupation" and in Russia "people were almost happy." See Leon Goldensohn, *The Nuremberg Interviews: An American Psychiatrist's Conversations with the Defendants and Witnesses*, ed. Robert Gellately (New York: Vintage Books, 2005), 65–7. Fritzsche also criticized as counter-productive the crude propaganda of

Julius Streicher (ibid., 71–3) and the anti-Church ideology of Alfred Rosenberg (ibid., 74–5). But as Telford Taylor pointed out, in broadcasts after the invasion of Russia, Fritzsche's characterization of Nazi Germany as victim included describing Germany as subject to "a new wave of international Jewish-democratic-bolshevistic agitation." See Taylor, *Anatomy of the Nuremberg Trials*, 463. Fritzsche was acquitted at Nuremberg, but immediately upon release he was brought before the city's Denazification Court (*Spruchkammer*), convicted, and sentenced to nine years of hard labor. He was pardoned in 1950 and died in 1953 (ibid., 612). On the organization of propaganda in Germany from 1933 to 1945, see David Welch, *The Third Reich: Politics and Propaganda* (London: Routledge, 1993).

66. Gombrich to Kris, 23 July 1941, Box 6, EK. Underlined in the original. Gombrich revived the analysis of propaganda contained in his letters from 1941 in his Creighton Lecture delivered nearly thirty years later. See Gombrich, "Myth and Reality in German Wartime Broadcasts."
67. Kris to Gombrich, 2 January 1942 [misdated 1941], Gombrich Archive, WIA.
68. Ibid.
69. Gombrich to Kris, 29 January 1942, Box 6, EK. Underlined in the original.
70. Ibid.
71. Ibid.
72. Ibid.
73. Ibid. Even Charles de Gaulle, with his Catholic monarchist lineage and anti-Marxist animus, when urged by his interior minister to arrest Jean-Paul Sartre during the May 1968 student revolt, replied, "You cannot imprison Voltaire."
74. Ibid. Years after the war Gombrich returned to this question of how to create viable revolutionary propaganda—one that "implies some kind of correspondence between inwardness and outward sign"—as a part of his exploration of schematized or ritualized expression. See Gombrich, "Ritualized Gesture and Expression in Art" (1966), in *The Image and the Eye: Further Studies in the Psychology of Pictorial Representation* (London: Phaidon Press, 1982), 74.
75. On efforts to formulate an antifascist philosophy during the war, see James D. Wilkinson, *The Intellectual Resistance in Europe* (Cambridge, MA: Harvard University Press, 1981).
76. Gombrich to Kris, 25 March 1942, Box 6, EK.
77. Ibid. Underlined in the original.
78. Ibid. During the war, in "The Subject of Poussin's *Orion*" for the *Burlington Magazine* 84, no. 491 (February 1944), Gombrich pointed out how Poussin contained the problem of violence within his vision of nature: "he too conceived the ancient tale of violence and magic as a veiled and esoteric 'hieroglyph' of nature's changing course" (41). Reprinted in Gombrich, *Symbolic Images*, 3rd edition (London: Phaidon Press, 1985), 122.
79. A further demonstration of the interweaving of Gombrich's political and scholarly concerns was a four-page, typescript essay he sent to Kris entitled "Some Axioms, Musing and Hints on Hearing." Dated 15 June 1945, the essay analyzed how auditory perception and mental projection interacted in the work of translating radio broadcasts. He wrote the analysis for fellow monitors. Gombrich to Kris, 15 June 1945 and 23 September 1945, Box 6, EK. In Aby Warburg's case, Charlotte Schoell-Glass has convincingly interpreted his art history as an indirect mode of political engagement, specifically the means through which Warburg confronted the growth of political anti-Semitism in Germany. See Charlotte Schoell-Glass, *Aby Warburg and Anti-Semitism: Political Perspectives on Images and Culture*, trans. Samuel Pakucs Willcocks (Detroit: Wayne State University Press, 2008).
80. On Vansittart's participation in the Hoare–Laval negotiations and his contribution to the Munich discussions, see Norman Rose, *Vansittart: Study of a Diplomat* (London:

William Heinemann, 1978), 175–80 and 221–30. For a concise character sketch of Vansittart at the time of Munich, see Taylor, *English History 1914–1945*, 405. On Vansittart's ties to and role within the intelligence community, see Andrew, *Her Majesty's Secret Service*, 342–3, 350, 383–5, 414–17, 424, and 429. On the communications between Vansittart, Halifax, Italian representatives, and the War Cabinet in the crucial days before the fall of France, see Ian Kershaw, *Fateful Choices: Ten Decisions that Changed the World, 1940–1941* (New York: Penguin Press, 2007), 31–47.

81. For the succession of printings, see Robert Vansittart, *Black Record: Germans Past and Present* (London: Hamish Hamilton, 1941), [iv].
82. Vansittart, *Black Record*, 18. Italics in the original.
83. Ibid., 19.
84. Ibid., 8.
85. Ibid., 14.
86. Ibid., 10.
87. See ibid., 20 and 24.
88. See ibid., 13 and 55.
89. On the reactions to Vansittart's BBC talks and on his wartime relations to the Foreign Office and to Dalton, see Norman Rose, *Vansittart*, 237–49 and Pelling, *Britain and the Second World War*, 260–1.
90. Vansittart, *Black Record*, 52.
91. Ibid., 54.
92. Ibid.
93. Ibid.
94. Using Tacitus to debate political theories and justify nationalist ideologies had a long European history from the Renaissance to Nazi Germany. Christopher B. Krebs traces that history in *A Most Dangerous Book: Tacitus' Germania from the Roman Empire to the Third Reich* (New York: W. W. Norton, 2011). The exiled Italian scholar and future Warburg fellow Arnaldo Momigliano counted the *Germania* as one of "the one hundred most dangerous books ever written" (quoted in Krebs, 22). The centuries of debate over how to interpret Tacitus had particular relevance to Momigliano. A classicist from a religiously orthodox and socially assimilated Jewish family, Momigliano—like thousands of Italian academics—swore a loyalty oath to Mussolini. He joined the Fascist party and in 1938 sought exemption from the anti-Semitic Racial Laws as a party member. Mussolini's government ignored the request and deprived him of his university professorship. Momigliano found eventual refuge in England. During the war, the Nazis murdered his parents, who had also joined the Fascist party but who eventually found temporary safety in France. See William V. Harris, "The Silences of Momigliano," *Times Literary Supplement* (12 April 1996) and Michael P. Steinberg, "Arnaldo Momigliano and the Facts," in *Judaism Musical and Unmusical* (Chicago: University of Chicago Press, 2007), 141–65. At the time of the Vansittart controversy, Momigliano was at work on his manuscript on Tacitus' ideas of power and freedom; after the war he published his essay on Tacitus and the response to Roman tyranny. See Arnaldo Momigliano, "The First Political Commentary on Tacitus" (1947), *Essays in Ancient and Modern Historiography* (Middletown, CT: Wesleyan University Press, 1982), 205–29. See also Riccardo Di Donato, "Arnaldo Momigliano from Antiquarianism to Cultural History," in *Momigliano and Antiquarianism: Foundations of the Modern Cultural Sciences*, ed. Peter N. Miller (Toronto: University of Toronto Press, 2007), 70–2.
95. See Heinrich Fraenkel, *Vansittart's Gift to Goebbels: A German Exile's Answer to Black Record* (London: Fabian Society, [n.d.]), 9.
96. Victor Gollancz, *Shall Our Children Live or Die? A Reply to Lord Vansittart on the German Problem* (London: Victor Gollancz, 1942), 5. According to Gollancz, as many as a half-million copies of *Black Record* might have been purchased, from which he concluded that as many as three million read Vansittart's book (ibid.).

97. George Orwell, "London Letter to *Partisan Review*," 15 April 1941, in *The Collected Essays, Journalism and Letters of George Orwell*, vol. 2, *My Country Right or Left 1940–1943*, ed. Sonia Orwell and Ian Angus (New York: Harcourt Brace Jovanovich, 1968), 114.
98. Ibid.
99. George Orwell, "London Letter to *Partisan Review*," 1 January 1942, ibid., 175.
100. Ibid.
101. Ibid., 176. The Austrian socialist leadership in exile called for a workers' antifascist uprising throughout Greater Germany, whereas Austrian conservatives revived the notion of Austrian patriotism and a return to the *status quo ante*. On the politics of the Austrian émigré community in England, see Goldner, *Austrian Emigration 1938 to 1945*, 14–17 and 120–8.
102. See Rose, *Vansittart*, 262–4.
103. Gombrich to Kris, 2 January 194[1], Box 6, EK.
104. Ibid.
105. Ibid. Himmler, pan-German educators, and Nazi propagandists in fact claimed that Tacitus provided an original account of dormant racial characteristics that National Socialism would revive and reanimate in the present. See Krebs, *A Most Dangerous Book*, 214–44.
106. Gombrich to Kris, 29 January 1942, Box 6, EK. Underlined in the original.
107. With Franz Neumann and Herbert Marcuse, Felix Gilbert worked in the OSS on political analyses that could assist with counter-propaganda. For example, with Marcuse, Gilbert co-authored a report on the political influence of the traditional Prussian aristocracy and officer corps in Nazi Germany, concluding that British and American propagandists had overemphasized their role and thereby diverted attention from the far more significant influence of industrialists, modern militarists, and middle-class nationalists and intellectuals—in other words, German fascism and not Prussian imperial ambition was now the enemy, and British and American counter-propaganda had to reflect that fact. See "The Significance of Prussian Militarism for Nazi Imperialism: Potential Tensions in United Nations Psychological Warfare (October 20, 1943)" in Franz Neumann, Herbert Marcuse, and Otto Kirchheimer, *Secret Reports on Nazi Germany: The Frankfurt School Contribution to the War Effort* (Princeton, NJ: Princeton University Press, 2013), 61–73. In summer 1944, Gilbert returned to England to work in the London OSS office (ibid., 61).
108. E. H. Gombrich, "Kokoschka in his Time" (1986), in *Topics of Our Time*, 147.
109. Gombrich to Kris, 25 March 1942, Box 6, EK. Underlined in the original.
110. Ernst Kris, "The Covenant of the Gangsters," 446. As Kris knew from his monitoring activity, Goebbels used *Black Record* to try to plant the fear of harsh retaliation. See Pelling, *Britain and the Second World War*, 261.
111. Kris, "The Covenant of the Gangsters," 457.
112. Ibid., 456.
113. Ibid., 457.
114. Ibid.
115. Robert S. Lynd, *Knowledge for What? The Place of Social Science in American Culture* (Princeton, NJ: Princeton University Press, 1939, 1948).
116. Gombrich to Kris, 16 August 1943, Box 6, EK.
117. Ibid.
118. Kris to Gombrich, 18 September [1943], Gombrich Archive, WIA.
119. Ibid.
120. Ibid.
121. Ibid.
122. Ibid. Underlined in the original.
123. Gombrich to Kris, 16 November 1943, Box 6, EK.

124. David Hume, "Of National Characters," in *Selected Essays*, ed. Stephen Copley and Andrew Edgar (Oxford: Oxford University Press, World's Classics, 2008), 113. In that essay Hume wrote that "a nation is nothing but a collection of individuals" (ibid., 114) subject to the varying associative influences of government, economy, foreign relations, and political revolution. Because, according to Hume, "the human mind is of a very imitative nature" (ibid., 115), individuals were further influenced in their thoughts and feelings by group behavior and especially by figures of authority.
125. Ibid. Underlined in the original.
126. Ibid.
127. Kris and Speier, *German Radio Propaganda*, 79.
128. Gombrich to Kris, 2 April 1943, Box 6, EK.
129. Ibid. Underlined in the original. In Germany, Cardinal Michael Faulhaber's Advent sermons in 1933 told German Catholics that the Christian religion, not pre-Christian culture, united the German people and that Christianity possessed historical and theological ties to Judaism. Still, he never protested publicly against Nazi anti-Semitism, he accepted the idea of a German racial community, and he re-emphasized the message that Christianity had supplanted Judaism. Bishop Clemens August von Galen openly opposed the Nazi euthanasia program. See Saul Friedländer, *Nazi Germany and the Jews*, vol. 1, *The Years of Persecution, 1933–1939* (New York: HarperCollins Publishers, HarperPerennial, 1997), 47–8 and 183–4; Michael Phayer, *The Catholic Church and the Holocaust, 1930–1965* (Bloomington, IN: Indiana University Press, 2000) 15, 45, 75, and 81; and Krebs, *A Most Dangerous Book*, 214–17.
130. For a description of the *Kulturkampf* in Austria see Radomír Luža, *Austro-German Relations in the Anschluss Era* (Princeton, NJ: Princeton University Press, 1975), 182–91.
131. Gombrich to Kris, 2 April 1943, Box 6, EK. Underlined in the original.
132. Ibid. Underlined in the original.
133. Ibid.
134. Gombrich to Kris, 16 August 1943, Box 6, EK.
135. Ibid.
136. Edmund Burke, *A Philosophical Enquiry into the Origin of Our Ideas of the Sublime and Beautiful* (1759), ed. Adam Phillips (Oxford: Oxford University Press, World's Classics, 1990), 152. Emphasis in the original.
137. Ibid., 153. For a wartime analysis of the emotive origins and implications of Nazi language, see Klemperer, *Language of the Third Reich*, 236–45.
138. Gombrich to Kris, 16 November 1943, Box 6, EK.
139. Gombrich to Kris, 12 April 1944, Box 6, EK.
140. E. H. Gombrich, "Kokoschka in his Time," 147. For discussion of Leftist resistance after 1934 to fascism in Austria—including Socialist, Communist, and labor resistance—see Martin Kitchen, "The Austrian Left and the Popular Front," in *The Popular Front in Europe*, ed. Helen Graham and Paul Preston (London: Macmillan Press, 1987), 35–57 and Herbert Steiner, "The Role of the Resistance in Austria, with Special Reference to the Labor Movement," in *Resistance Against the Third Reich, 1933–1990*, ed. Michael Geyer and John W. Boyer (Chicago: University of Chicago Press, 1994), 167–72.
141. See Kris, "Some Problems of War Propaganda." The values expressed in this article were also reflected in lectures that he delivered at the New School. See Rutkoff and Scott, *New School*, 139.
142. Gombrich to Kris, 16 November 1943, Box 6, EK.
143. Ibid.
144. See Gombrich to Kris, 12 April 1944, Box 6, EK.
145. Gombrich to Kris, 3 January 1945, Box 6, EK.

146. Ibid.
147. Ibid.
148. Gombrich to Kris, 23 September 1945, Box 6, EK.
149. Gombrich to Kris, 23 March 1946, Box 6, EK.
150. Jonathan Swift, "A Meditation upon a Broom-Stick" (1703), in *The Basic Writings of Jonathan Swift*, intro. by Claude Rawson (New York: The Modern Library, 2002), 663.
151. Ibid.

Chapter 8: Between Past and Future, 1945–65

1. Ernst Kris, introduction (1954) to Sigmund Freud, *The Origins of Psychoanalysis: Letters to Wilhelm Fliess, Drafts and Notes: 1887–1902*, ed. Marie Bonaparte, Anna Freud, and Ernst Kris (New York: Basic Books, 1977), 3–47.
2. Kris to Gombrich, 3 October 1945, Box 6, EK. See Heinz Hartmann, Ernst Kris, and Rudolph M. Loewenstein, *Papers on Psychoanalytic Psychology* (Madison, CT: International Universities Press, 1964). Nellie Thompson describes this phase of Kris's professional career in her "Ernst Kris in America," *American Imago* 71, no. 4 (December 2014): 353–74. Eli Zaretsky makes the point that even as the effort to systemize Freud's psychology led Kris and his colleagues to emphasize a positivistic language that described psychic conflict in quantifiable terms, at the same time they recommended replacing the term "ego" with "self" in the discussion of narcissism so as to emphasis the person's relation to the world, anticipating intersubjective psychoanalysis. See Zaretsky, *Secrets of the Soul: A Social and Cultural History of Psychoanalysis* (New York: Alfred A. Knopf, 2004), 294 and 311–12.
3. *Human Nature and Enduring Peace*, ed. Gardner Murphy (Boston: Houghton Mifflin Company, 1945), vii.
4. Ibid., 237–8.
5. On McCarthy's vendetta against Lattimore and its effect on Lattimore's life and career, see Ellen Schrecker, *Many Are the Crimes: McCarthyism in America* (Boston: Little, Brown, 1998), 244–54.
6. *Human Nature and Enduring Peace*, ed. Murphy, 406. Emphasis in the original.
7. Ibid., 407. In the following year, Kris returned to the question of postwar social relations in "Notes on the Psychology of Prejudice," *English Journal* 35, no. 6 (June 1946): 304–8.
8. Kris to Gombrich, 3 October 1945, Box 6, EK.
9. Kris to Gombrich, 9 January 194[6] (the letter is misdated "1945"), Box 6, EK.
10. Ibid.
11. On the role of Kris in creating a psychoanalytic theory of cognition, see Kandel, *In Search of Memory*, 54–5 and 367–8, and Kandel, *The Age of Insight*, chaps. 11–12. Anton O. Kris noted Kris's unrealized aim to pursue research into memory (Anton O. Kris, conversation with the author, 17 January 2008).
12. In December 1945, Saxl submitted a request to the Ministry of Labour for Gombrich's reinstatement, writing, "Dr. Gombrich was granted permission to work at this Institute in April, 1936. He joined the BBC on 11th December, 1939, was approved for Auxiliary War Service employment on 20th February, 1940 and again on 21st March, 1943, and will terminate his employment at the BBC on the 14th of this month." Saxl to Manager, Employment Exchange, Ministry of Labour and National Service, 4 December 1945, GC, WIA.
13. Kris to Gombrich, 3 October 1945, Box 6, EK. The possibility of integrating the listening post with official intelligence operations at the Foreign Office or Ministry of Information had been discussed when the monitoring service was created, but the plans had been placed on hold. See Briggs, *History of Broadcasting in the United Kingdom*, vol. 3, *War of Words*, 171.

14. Gombrich to Kris, 20 December 1947, Box 6, EK. On Buschbeck's return to Austria, see Gombrich to Kris, 23 March 1946, Box 6, EK.
15. Gombrich to Kris, 23 March 1946, Box 6, EK. The two volumes of Karl Popper's *The Open Society and Its Enemies* (vol.1, *The Spell of Plato*, and vol. 2, *The High Tide of Prophecy: Hegel, Marx, and the Aftermath*) had appeared the previous year (George Routledge and Sons, 1945).
16. Gombrich to Kris, 23 March 1946, Box 6, EK.
17. Ibid.
18. E. H. Gombrich, *A Little History of the World*, trans. Caroline Mustill (New Haven: Yale University Press, 2005), 281.
19. Jonathan Schell, *The Seventh Decade: The New Shape of the Nuclear Danger* (New York: Henry Holt and Company, Metropolitan Books, 2007), 69.
20. Gombrich, *Little History of the World*, 282.
21. See Gombrich to Kris, 20 April 1947 and 27 February 1948, Box 6, EK.
22. Gombrich to Kris, 23 March 1946, Box 6, EK. Gombrich later wrote a memoir of Saxl for a collection of Saxl's writings. See his introduction to *A Heritage of Images*, by Fritz Saxl (Harmondsworth: Penguin Books, Peregrine Books, 1970). For a discussion of Gombrich's return to the Warburg biography specifically, see Matthew Finch, "Ernst Gombrich and the Memory of Aby Warburg: Emotion, Identity and Scholarship" (Ph.D. diss., Queen Mary, University of London, February 2007). Carlo Ginzburg explores the dual historical tradition of Warburg and Gombrich within the Warburg Institute in "From Aby Warburg to E. H. Gombrich: A Problem of Method," in *Clues, Myths, and the Historical Method*, trans. John and Anne C. Tedeschi (Baltimore: Johns Hopkins University Press, 1989).
23. Gombrich to Kris, 20 April 1947, Box 6, EK.
24. Gombrich to Kris, 24 March 1948, Box 6, EK.
25. Ibid.
26. Kris to Gombrich, 13 May 1947, Box 6, EK.
27. Kris to Gombrich, 6 April 1948, Box 6, EK.
28. Before the end of the war, Kris had begun to return to his prewar plan for a psychology of art and creativity. See Kris, "Approaches to Art" (1944), in *Psychoanalysis Today*, ed. Sandor Lorand (New York: International University Press, 1944) and "Art and Regression," *Transactions of the New York Academy of Sciences* 6, no. 7 (May 1944): 236–50.
29. Gombrich to Kris, 24 April 1948, Box 6, EK.
30. The outline is dated 5 August 1948 and accompanied the letter from Gombrich to Kris, 7 August 1948, Box 6, EK.
31. Gombrich to Kris, 9 January 1949, Box 6, EK.
32. Gombrich to Kris, outline for "Caricature," 16 July 1949, [1], Box 6, EK.
33. Ibid.
34. Ibid., [2].
35. Siegfried Kracauer to Ernst Kris, 17 October 1949, in *Siegfried Kracauer-Erwin Panofsky Briefwechsel 1941–1966*, ed. Volker Breidecker (Berlin: Akademie Verlag, 1996), 97.
36. E. H. Gombrich to Henri Frankfort, 15 January 1950, [1], Box 6, EK. It was Frankfort who in 1948 finally converted Gombrich's fellowship into a permanent position at the institute.
37. Ernst Kris and E. H. Gombrich, "The Rise of Caricature: An Essay in the Social Psychology of Art," ms, I.2, Gombrich Archive, WIA.
38. Ibid., I./3.
39. Ibid., II./7–8.
40. Ibid., II.10.
41. Ibid., II.11.

42. Ibid., /III/2.
43. Ibid., /III/8.
44. Kris's negative reaction to Erik Erikson's attempt to integrate the study of history, art, and ego psychology in his *Childhood and Society* might reflect in part Kris's own pessimism toward such efforts at this time. See Friedman, *Identity's Architect*, 239 and 294.
45. Gombrich to Kris, 2 November 1944, Box 6, EK. Gombrich's judgment could also have been influenced by Read's willingness at Routledge to consider publishing the first volume of Popper's *The Open Society and Its Enemies*. See Gombrich and Eribon, *Looking for Answers*, 122.
46. Gombrich to Kris, 20 April 1947, Box 6, EK. Two years earlier, Read's *Art and Society* (London: Faber and Faber, 1945) had appeared in a second edition.
47. E. H. Gombrich, *The Story of Art*, 4th edition (London: Phaidon Press, 1951), 423.
48. Gombrich to Kris, 22 April 1950, Box 6, EK.
49. Gombrich to Kris, 7 June 1950, Box 6, EK.
50. Gombrich to Kris, 9 August 1950, Box 6, EK.
51. Ibid.
52. Gombrich to Kris, 23 April 1951, Box 6, EK. Lancelot Law Whyte was the philosopher of science who edited the symposium.
53. See King, *The Last Modern*, 235–7.
54. Ibid., 241.
55. Gombrich to Kris, 23 April 1951, Box 6, EK.
56. E. H. Gombrich, "Meditations on a Hobby Horse or the Roots of Artistic Form" (1951), in *Meditations on a Hobby Horse and Other Essays on the Theory of Art*, 4th edition (London: Phaidon Press, 1985), 8.
57. Gombrich to Kris, 23 April 1951, Box 6, EK.
58. Ibid.
59. See Gombrich to Kris, 23 April 1951 and 15 August 1951, Box 6, EK.
60. See Gombrich to Kris, 12 October 1951 and 23 October 1951, Box 6, EK.
61. Kris and Gombrich, "Principles of Caricature," in *Psychoanalytic Explorations in Art*, 196.
62. Gombrich to Kris, 4 April 1954, Box 6, EK.
63. Gombrich, *Art and Illusion*, 342–3.
64. Ibid., 343.
65. Ibid., 345.
66. Ibid., 350.
67. Ibid., 353.
68. Ibid., 355.
69. Ibid., 357–8. For a discussion of Gombrich's concept of progress in art in *Art and Illusion* and reactions to that concept within art history, see Wood, "E. H. Gombrich: Art and Illusion," 122–7.
70. See Gombrich, "The Study of Art and the Study of Man," 230; Gombrich, "An Autobiographical Sketch," 19; and Gombrich, "Magic, Myth and Metaphor: Reflections on Pictorial Satire," in *The Uses of Images: Studies in the Social Function of Art and Visual Communication* (London: Phaidon Press, 1999), 190–1. In the last of these essays, Gombrich stated that when he and Kris saw each other ten years after the completion of the 1937 manuscript they "had both gained some distance from their pet ideas" (ibid., 191). He did not refer to their attempts to rewrite the manuscript for possible publication at that time. In 1983, the director and writer Jonathan Miller conducted an interview with Gombrich for the BBC, now published in Miller, *On Further Reflection: 60 Years of Writing* (New York: Overlook Press, 2014). There Gombrich spoke of Kris's invitation "to join him in an investigation of the history of caricature" and recalled its importance to his later work: "caricature, of course, raises many psychological problems, including problems of perception. So I was introduced very early in my life to the

general problems of images rather than of great works of art; after all, nobody would claim that every successful caricature is a great work of art" (ibid., 105–6). He noted further that he continued this line of research after arriving in 1936 at the Warburg Institute, "which concerned itself no less with the symbolic meaning of humble images than with that of great works of art" (ibid., 106).

71. Freeman Dyson, *The Scientist as Rebel* (New York: New York Review Books, 2006), 252.
72. Leo Lowenthal and Norbert Guterman, *Prophets of Deceit: A Study of the Techniques of the American Agitator* (New York: Harper & Brothers, 1949). The preface included an acknowledgment to Kris.
73. See, for example, M. I. Finley, *The World of Odysseus* (New York: Viking Press, 1954) and Bernard Knox, *Oedipus at Thebes: Sophocles' Tragic Hero and His Time* (New Haven: Yale University Press, 1957). Alice L. Conklin's *In the Museum of Man: Race, Anthropology, and Empire in France, 1850–1950* (Ithaca: Cornell University Press, 2013) described how antifascist political culture helped move the discipline of anthropology toward both a more humanistic perspective and a more social scientifically based field methodology. The change included reorganizing the *Musée de l'Homme* in Paris to serve a wider public. In the United States, although divisions persisted between the humanities, sciences, and arts, interdisciplinary work between the social and mental sciences themselves continued to receive substantial university and foundation support, with cognitive psychology as both a leading field and a center of conflict for such work. See Jamie Cohen-Cole, *The Open Mind: Cold War Politics and the Sciences of Human Nature* (Chicago: University of Chicago Press, 2014), esp. 76–103.
74. Willibald Sauerländer, reviewing the Daumier exhibition organized by the Staatliche Graphische Sammlung in Munich, wrote that even today "the popularity of his works often goes no further than finding them entertaining and misses their explosive political significance and the physiognomic perceptiveness. Daumier's prints reflect a critical public culture that has largely been forgotten." See Sauerländer, "The Genius of the Other Daumier," trans. David Dollenmayer, *New York Review of Books* 60, no. 3 (21 February 2013): 17. From October 2013 to January 2014, the Royal Academy in London, however, organized a new exhibition of Daumier's artwork. See the catalog and essays, *Daumier: Visions of Paris* (London: Royal Academy Publications, 2013).
75. Herbert Read, *Modern Sculpture: A Concise History* (London: Thames and Hudson, 1964), 12.
76. Ibid. On the vitality and struggles of postwar British realism, see James Hyman, *The Battle for Realism: Figurative Art in Britain During the Cold War 1945–1960* (New Haven and London: Yale University Press, 2001). Hyman emphasizes that, as the realist movement confronted "the post-surrealist concerns" of figures such as Read and the growing Abstract Expressionist movement of the 1950s, British realist art also experienced an internal conflict between modernist realism and social realism (ibid., 3).
77. The director Milos Forman revived that political interest in his film, *Goya's Ghosts* (Sony Pictures, 2006). Forman traces Goya's visions to the public and political realities of Bourbon and Napoleonic Spain: the torture, tribunals, and invasion that occurred in the name of God and liberation and that haunted Goya in his last years.
78. Gombrich and Eribon, *Looking for Answers*, 52–3. See also Gombrich, "Magic, Myth and Metaphor," 191.
79. Felix Gilbert, "From Art History to the History of Civilization: Aby Warburg" (1972), review of *Aby Warburg: An Intellectual Biography*, by E. H. Gombrich, in *History: Choice and Commitment* (Cambridge, MA: Harvard University Press, Belknap Press, 1977), 424. Catherine Soussloff pointed to a similar de-emphasizing of political context in Gombrich's interpretation of Oskar Kokoschka and Karl Kraus. See Catherine M. Soussloff, "Portraiture and Assimilation in Vienna: The Case of Hans Tietze and Erica Tietze-Conrat," in *Diasporas and Exiles: Varieties of Jewish Identity*, ed. Howard Wettstein (Berkeley and Los Angeles: University of California Press, 2002), 149 n.45.

80. E. H. Gombrich, "The Diversity of the Arts: The Place of the *Laocoon* in the Life and Work of G. E. Lessing (1729–1781)" (1956), in *Tributes*, 49.
81. Kris and Gombrich, foreword to *Caricature* ms, Gombrich Archive, WIA.
82. Kris and Gombrich, *Caricature* ms, 119.
83. Ibid., 239n.
84. Ibid., 220.
85. On Gombrich's significance for the recognition of Cartier-Bresson, see Pierre Assouline, *Henri Cartier-Bresson: A Biography*, trans. David Wilson (London: Thames and Hudson, 2005), 228–32. Assouline points out that Gombrich included Cartier-Bresson in the updated editions of *The Story of Art* as early as 1972.
86. E. H. Gombrich, "The Photographer as Artist: Henri Cartier-Bresson" (1978), in *Topics of Our Time*, 200. Daumier's interests in fact included photography, and like Cartier-Bresson, although he accepted captions as a journalistic necessity, he preferred to have the image speak for itself. See Le Men, "Daumier and Printmaking," 38 and 42.
87. Gombrich, "The Photographer as Artist," 200.
88. Ibid., 201–2.
89. Ibid., 202.
90. E. H. Gombrich, "The Mysterious Achievement of Likeness" (1997), in *Tête à Tête: Portraits by Henri Cartier-Bresson*, by Henri Cartier-Bresson (Boston: Little, Brown, Bulfinch Press Book, 1998), [ii].
91. Gombrich, *Art and Illusion*, 55–6.

BIBLIOGRAPHY

I. Archives

Bodleian MS. Society for the Protection of Science and Learning. Oxford University.

Ernst Kris Papers (EK). Manuscript Division, Library of Congress, Washington, DC.

Estate of E. H. Gombrich (Gombrich Archive). Unpublished manuscripts, property of the Archive of E. H. Gombrich Estate, at the Warburg Institute Archive, London. ©Literary Estate of E. H. Gombrich.

Rockefeller Foundation. Rockefeller Archive Center. Sleepy Hollow, NY.

Sigmund Freud Papers (SF). Manuscript Division, Library of Congress, Washington, DC.

Warburg Institute Archive (WIA). General Correspondence (GC). University of London.

II. Ernst Kris and E. H. Gombrich on Caricature

Gombrich, E. H. "The Style of Caricature." Ms, 4 pp. © Literary Estate of E. H. Gombrich.

——. Partial drafts of lectures on caricature. Ms, pp. 3–104. © Literary Estate of E. H. Gombrich.

——. "Das Wesen der Karikatur." Ms, pp. 1–13. © Literary Estate of E. H. Gombrich.

Honoré Daumier: Zeichnungen, Aquarelle, Lithographien, Kleinplastiken. Ausstellung, 21 November–21 Dezember 1936. Vienna: Albertina, Kulturbund, 1936.

Kris, Ernst. *Die Karikaturen des Dantan: Paris-London, 1831–1839.* Ausstellung im Corps de Logis der neuen Hofburg, Herbst, 1933. Kunsthistorisches Museum, Sammlungen für Plastik und Kunstgewerbe. Vienna: J. Wiener, 1933.

——. "Zur Psychologie der Karikatur," *Imago* 20, no. 4 (1934): 450–66.

——. "The Psychology of Caricature," *International Journal of Psychoanalysis* 17, no. 3 (1936): 285–303.

——. Review of W. R. Juynboll, *Het komische genre in de ital[i]aansche Schilderkunst gedurende de zeventiende en de achtiende eeuw. Bijdrage tot de geschiedenis van de caricatuur.* In *Burlington Magazine* 66, no. 383 (February 1935): 97.

——. "Honoré Daumier" (1936). In *Honoré Daumier: Zeichnungen, Aquarelle, Lithographien, Kleinplastiken.* Ausstellung, 21 November–21 Dezember 1936. Vienna: Albertina, Kulturbund, 1936.

———. "The Psychology of Caricature." In *Psychoanalytic Explorations in Art*. Madison, CT: International Universities Press, 1952.

Kris, Ernst, and E. H. Gombrich. "The Principles of Caricature." *British Journal of Medical Psychology* 17 (1938): 319–42. Delivered as a lecture at the Warburg Institute, London on 25 May 1937. Expanded version published as "The Principles of Caricature," in *Psychoanalytic Explorations in Art*. Madison, CT: International Universities Press, 1952.

———. *Die Karikatur*. Ms, 254 pp. © Literary Estate of E. H. Gombrich.

———. *Caricature*. Ms, 254 pp. © Literary Estate of E. H. Gombrich.

———. *Caricature*. King Penguin Books. Harmondsworth: Penguin Books, 1940.

———. *Caricature: An Essay on Its History and Meaning*. Ms, 129 pp. Ernst Kris Papers.

———. "Appendix: Caricature and Physiognomics." Ms, 13 pp. © Literary Estate of E. H. Gombrich.

———. "The Rise of Caricature: An Essay in the Social Psychology of Art." Ms, 35 pp. © Literary Estate of E. H. Gombrich.

III. Works Cited

Adorno, T. W. "Scientific Experiences of a European Scholar in America." Translated by Donald Fleming. In *The Intellectual Migration: Europe and America, 1930–1960*, edited by Donald Fleming and Bernard Bailyn. Cambridge, MA: Harvard University Press, Belknap Press, 1969.

Amelang, James S. *The Flight of Icarus: Artisan Autobiography in Early Modern Europe*. Stanford, CA: Stanford University Press, 1998.

Améry, Jean. *On Aging: Revolt and Resignation* (1968). Translated by John D. Barlow. Bloomington, IN: Indiana University Press, 1994.

———. *On Suicide: A Discourse on Voluntary Death* (1976). Translated by John D. Barlow. Bloomington, IN: Indiana University Press, 1999.

Amico, Leonard N. *Bernard Palissy: In Search of Earthly Paradise*. Paris and New York: Flammarion, 1996.

Anderson, Mark M. "Siegfried Kracauer and Meyer Schapiro: A Friendship." *New German Critique*, no. 54 (Fall 1991): 19–29.

Andrew, Christopher. *Her Majesty's Secret Service: The Making of the British Intelligence Community*. New York: Penguin Books, 1987.

Arnheim, Rudolf. "A New Laocoön: Artistic Composites and the Talking Film" (1938). In *Film as Art*. Berkeley and Los Angeles: University of California Press, 1957.

Assouline, Pierre. *Henri Cartier-Bresson: A Biography*. Translated by David Wilson. London: Thames and Hudson, 2005.

Ausstellung Honoré Daumier 1808–1879: Gemälde, Aquarelle, Zeichnungen, Plastik. 21 February–31 March 1926. Galerie Matthiesen, Berlin. Berlin: Otto Elsner, 1926.

Bakos, Ján. "The Vienna School's Hundred and Sixty-Eighth Graduate: The Vienna School's Ideas Revised by E. H. Gombrich." In *Gombrich on Art and Psychology*, edited by Richard Woodfield. Manchester: Manchester University Press, 1996.

Balzac, Honoré de. *Lost Illusions*. Translated by Herbert J. Hunt. London: Penguin Books, 2004.

Bartlett, Robert. *Gerald of Wales, 1146–1223*. Oxford: Oxford University Press, Clarendon Press, 1982.

Bell, Clive. "King Penguins." Review of *Portraits of Christ*, by Ernst Kitzinger and Elizabeth Senior, and *Caricature*, by Ernst Kris and E. H. Gombrich. *New Statesman and Nation* (22 February 1941): 196.

Benesch, Otto. "Die Wiener Kunsthistorische Schule" (1920). In *Collected Writings*, edited by Eva Benesch. Vol. 4. London: Phaidon Press, 1973.

——. "Max Dvořák: Ein Versuch zur Geschichte der historischen Geisteswissenschaften" (1924 [1922]). In *Collected Writings*, edited by Eva Benesch. Vol. 4. London: Phaidon Press, 1973.

——. "Honoré Daumier: Zur Ausstellung in der Albertina 1937" (1937). In *Collected Writings*, edited by Eva Benesch. Vol. 4. London: Phaidon Press, 1973.

——. *Artistic and Intellectual Trends from Rubens to Daumier as Shown in Book Illustration.* Cambridge, MA: Department of Printing and Graphic Arts, Harvard College Library, 1943.

——. *The Art of the Renaissance in Northern Europe: Its Relation to the Contemporary Spiritual and Intellectual Movements* (1945). Revised edition. London: Phaidon Press, 1965.

——. "A Short History of the Albertina Collection" (1948). In *Collected Writings*, edited by Eva Benesch. Vol. 4. London: Phaidon Press, 1973.

——. "Max Dvořák (1874–1921)" (1957). In *Collected Writings*, edited by Eva Benesch. Vol. 4. London: Phaidon Press, 1973.

——. "Die Albertina" (1959). In *Collected Writings*, edited by Eva Benesch. Vol. 4. London: Phaidon Press, 1973.

——. *Master Drawings in the Albertina: European Drawings from the 15th to the 18th Century* (1964). Translated by Felice Stampfle and Ruth Kramer. Greenwich, CT: New York Graphic Society Publishers, n.d.

Benfey, Christopher, and Karen Remmler, eds. *Artists, Intellectuals, and World War II: The Pontigny Encounters at Mount Holyoke College, 1942–1944.* Amherst, MA: University of Massachusetts Press, 2006.

Bertault, Philippe. *Balzac and the Human Comedy*. Translated by Richard Monges. New York: New York University Press, 1963.

Bessner, Daniel Morris. "The Night Watchman: Hans Speier and the Making of the American National Security State." Ph.D. diss., Duke University, 2013.

Bindman, David. *Hogarth and His Times: Serious Comedy*. Berkeley and Los Angeles: University of California Press, 1997.

Bing, Gertrud. "Fritz Saxl (1890–1948): A Memoir." In *Fritz Saxl 1890–1948: A Volume of Memorial Essays from His Friends in England*, edited by D. J. Gordon. London: Thomas Nelson and Sons, 1957.

Borkenau, Franz. *Austria and After*. London: Faber and Faber, 1938.

Bredekamp, Horst. *The Lure of Antiquity and the Cult of the Machine: The Kunstkammer and the Evolution of Nature, Art and Technology.* Translated by Allison Brown. Princeton, NJ: Markus Wiener, 1995.

Briggs, Asa. *Governing the BBC.* London: British Broadcasting Corporation, 1979.

——. *The BBC: The First Fifty Years.* Oxford: Oxford University Press, 1985.

——. *The History of Broadcasting in the United Kingdom.* Vol. 2, *The Golden Age of Wireless.* Revised edition. Oxford: Oxford University Press, 1995.

——. *The History of Broadcasting in the United Kingdom.* Vol. 3, *The War of Words.* Revised edition. Oxford: Oxford University Press, 1995.

Bukey, Evan Burr. *Hitler's Austria: Popular Sentiment in the Nazi Era, 1938–1945.* Chapel Hill, NC: University of North Carolina Press, 2000.

Burke, Edmund. *A Philosophical Enquiry into the Origin of Our Ideas of the Sublime and the Beautiful* (1759). Edited by Adam Phillips. Oxford: Oxford University Press, World's Classics, 1990.

Buxton, William J. "John Marshall and the Humanities in Europe: Shifting Patterns of Rockefeller Foundation Support." *Minerva* 41, no. 2 (2003): 133–53.

Cabanne, Pierre. *Honoré Daumier: Painter of the Human Comedy.* Translated by Lisa Davidson. Paris: Vilo Publishing, Les éditions de l'Amateur, 1999.

Camus, Albert. *Lyrical and Critical Essays.* Translated by Ellen Conroy Kennedy. New York: Vintage Books, 1968.

Canetti, Elias. *Party in the Blitz: The English Years.* New York: New Directions Books, 2005.

Chernow, Ron. *The Warburgs: The Twentieth-Century Odyssey of a Remarkable Jewish Family*. New York: Random House, 1993.
Clare, George. *Last Waltz in Vienna: The Rise and Destruction of a Family 1842–1942*. New York: Holt, Rinehart and Winston, 1982.
Clark, T. J. *The Absolute Bourgeois: Artists and Politics in France 1848–1851*. Berkeley and Los Angeles: University of California Press, 1999.
Clifton, James, and Leslie M. Scattone. *The Plains of Mars: European War Prints, 1500–1825*. New Haven and London: Yale University Press, 2009.
Cohen-Cole, Jamie. *The Open Mind: Cold War Politics and the Sciences of Human Nature*. Chicago: University of Chicago Press, 2014.
The Complete Colonel Blimp. Edited by Mark Bryant. London: Bellew Publishing, 1991.
The Complete Correspondence of Sigmund Freud and Ernest Jones 1908–1939. Edited by R. Andrew Paskauskas. Cambridge, MA: Harvard University Press, Belknap Press, 1993.
Conklin, Alice L. *In the Museum of Man: Race, Anthropology, and Empire in France, 1850–1950*. Ithaca: Cornell University Press, 2013.
Conversations with Cézanne. Edited by Michael Doran. Translated by Julie Lawrence Cochran. Berkeley and Los Angeles: University of California Press, 2001.
Culbert, David. "The Rockefeller Foundation, the Museum of Modern Art Film Library, and Siegfried Kracauer, 1941." *Historical Journal of Film, Radio and Television* 13, no. 4 (1993): 495–511.
Dangerfield, George. *The Strange Death of Liberal England*. New York: Capricorn Books, 1961.
Danto, Elizabeth Ann. *Freud's Free Clinics: Psychoanalysis and Social Justice, 1918–1938*. New York: Columbia University Press, 2005.
Daumier 1808–1879. Exhibition organized by the National Gallery of Canada, Ottawa, the Réunion des Musées Nationaux/Musée d'Orsay, Paris, and the Phillips Collection, Washington. Ottawa: National Gallery of Canada, 1999.
Daumier Lithographs: The Human Comedy. Elvehjem Museum of Art, University of Wisconsin-Madison, 1985.
Daumier on War. Introduction by Hans Rothe. 1926. Reprint. New York: Da Capo Press, 1977.
Daumier: Visions of Paris. London: Royal Academy Publications, 2013.
Di Donato, Riccardo. "Arnaldo Momigliano from Antiquarianism to Cultural History." In *Momigliano and Antiquarianism: Foundations of the Modern Cultural Sciences*, edited by Peter N. Miller. Toronto: University of Toronto Press, 2007.
Donald, Diana. *The Age of Caricature: Satirical Prints in the Reign of George III*. New Haven: Yale University Press, Paul Mellon Centre for Studies in British Art, 1996.
Dossi, Barbara. *Albertina: The History of the Collection and Its Masterpieces*. Munich: Prestel, 1999.
Douglas, Kirk. *I Am Spartacus! Making a Film, Breaking the Blacklist*. New York: Open Road, 2012.
Dvořák, Max. *The History of Art as the History of Ideas* (1924). Translated by John Hardy. London: Routledge and Kegan Paul, 1984.
——. *Idealism and Naturalism in Gothic Art*. Translated by Randolph J. Klawiter. Notre Dame, IN: University of Notre Dame Press, 1967.
Dyson, Freeman. *The Scientist as Rebel*. New York: New York Review Books, 2006.
Edmundson, Mark. *The Death of Sigmund Freud: The Legacy of His Last Days*. New York: Bloomsbury, 2007.
Ellul, Jacques. *Propaganda: The Formation of Men's Attitudes*. Translated by Konrad Kellen and Jean Lerner. New York: Vintage Books, 1973.
Erikson, Erik H. "Hitler's Imagery and German Youth." *Psychiatry* 5, no. 4 (November 1942): 475–93.

——. "Comments on Anti-Nazi Propaganda" (1945). In *A Way of Looking at Things: Selected Papers from 1930 to 1980*, edited by Stephen Schlein. New York: W. W. Norton, 1987.

"Expert Analyzes Nazi Propaganda." *New York Times*, 8 December 1940.

Fallada, Hans. *A Stranger in My Own Country: The 1944 Prison Diary*. Translated by Allan Blunden. Cambridge: Polity Press, 2015.

Feigenbaum, Gail. "Practice in the Carracci Academy." In *The Artist's Workshop*, edited by Peter M. Lukehart. Studies in the History of Art, 38. Washington, DC: National Gallery of Art, 1993.

Finch, Matthew. "Ernst Gombrich and the Memory of Aby Warburg: Emotion, Identity and Scholarship." Ph.D. diss., Queen Mary, University of London, February 2007.

Finley, M. I. *The World of Odysseus*. New York: Viking Press, 1954.

Forman, Milos, dir. *Goya's Ghosts*. Sony Pictures, 2006.

Fraenkel, Heinrich. *Vansittart's Gift to Goebbels: A German Exile's Answer to Black Record*. London: Fabian Society, n.d.

Freedberg, David. *The Power of Images: Studies in the History and Theory of Response*. Chicago: University of Chicago Press, 1989.

Freud, Sigmund. *Jokes and Their Relation to the Unconscious* (1905). In Vol. 8, *The Standard Edition of the Complete Psychological Works of Sigmund Freud*, edited by James Strachey. London: Hogarth Press and the Institute of Psycho-Analysis, 1953–1974.

——. *Group Psychology and the Analysis of the Ego* (1921). In Vol. 18, *The Standard Edition of the Complete Psychological Works of Sigmund Freud*, edited by James Strachey. London: Hogarth Press and the Institute of Psycho-Analysis, 1953–1974.

——. *Civilization and Its Discontents* (1930 [1929]). In Vol. 21, *The Standard Edition of the Complete Psychological Works of Sigmund Freud*, edited by James Strachey. London: Hogarth Press and the Institute of Psycho-Analysis, 1953–1974.

——. *Moses and Monotheism: Three Essays* (1939 [1934–1938]). In Vol. 23, *The Standard Edition of the Complete Psychological Works of Sigmund Freud*, edited by James Strachey. London: Hogarth Press and the Institute of Psycho-Analysis, 1953–1974.

Friedländer, Saul. *Nazi Germany and the Jews*. Vol. 1, *The Years of Persecution, 1933–1939*. New York: HarperCollins Publishers, HarperPerennial, 1997.

Friedlaender, Walter. *Mannerism and Anti-Mannerism in Italian Painting* (1925, 1930 [1928–29]). Introduction by Donald Posner. New York: Schocken Books, 1965.

——. *David to Delacroix* (1930). Translated by Robert Goldwater. Cambridge, MA: Harvard University Press, 1952.

Friedman, Lawrence J. *Identity's Architect: A Biography of Erik H. Erikson*. New York: Scribner, 1999.

Gardner, Sheldon, and Gwendolyn Stevens. *Red Vienna and the Golden Age of Psychology, 1918–1938*. New York: Praeger, 1992.

Gary, Brett. *The Nervous Liberals: Propaganda Anxieties from World War I to the Cold War*. New York: Columbia University Press, 1999.

Gedye, G. E. R. *Betrayal in Central Europe: Austria and Czechoslovakia: Fallen Bastions*. New York: Harper and Brothers, 1939.

Gilbert, Felix. "Machiavelli in an Unknown Contemporary Dialogue." *Journal of the Warburg Institute* 1, no. 2 (October 1937): 163–6.

——. *Machiavelli and Guicciardini: Politics and History in Sixteenth-Century Florence*. Princeton, NJ: Princeton University Press, 1965.

——. "From Art History to the History of Civilization: Aby Warburg" (1972). Review of *Aby Warburg: An Intellectual Biography*, by E. H. Gombrich. In *History: Choice and Commitment*. Cambridge, MA: Harvard University Press, Belknap Press, 1977.

——. *A European Past: Memoirs 1905–1945*. New York: W. W. Norton, 1988.

Gilbert, Felix, and Herbert Marcuse. "The Significance of Prussian Militarism for Nazi Imperialism: Potential Tensions in United Nations Psychological Warfare (October 20, 1943)." In Franz Neumann, Herbert Marcuse, and Otto Kirchheimer, *Secret Reports on*

Nazi Germany: The Frankfurt School Contribution to the War Effort. Princeton, NJ: Princeton University Press, 2013.

Ginzburg, Carlo. *Clues, Myths, and the Historical Method.* Translated by John and Anne C. Tedeschi. Baltimore: Johns Hopkins University Press, 1989.

——. "The Sword and the Lightbulb: A Reading of *Guernica*." In *Disturbing Remains: Memory, History, and Crisis in the Twentieth Century*, edited by Michael S. Roth and Charles G. Salas. Los Angeles: Getty Research Institute, 2001.

——. *Wooden Eyes: Nine Reflections on Distance.* Translated by Martin Ryle and Kate Soper. New York: Columbia University Press, 2001.

——. *Threads and Traces: True, False, Fictive.* Translated by Anne C. Tedeschi and John Tedeschi. Berkeley and Los Angeles: University of California Press, 2012.

Goldensohn, Leon. *The Nuremberg Interviews: An American Psychiatrist's Conversations with the Defendants and Witnesses*, edited by Robert Gellately. New York: Vintage Books, 2004.

Goldner, Franz. *Austrian Emigration 1938 to 1945.* New York: Frederick Ungar, 1979.

Gollancz, Victor. *Shall Our Children Live or Die? A Reply to Lord Vansittart on the German Problem.* London: Victor Gollancz, 1942.

Gombrich, E. H. "Eine verkannte karolingische Pyxis im Wiener Kunsthistorischen Museum." *Jahrbuch der kunsthistorischen Sammlungen in Wien*, Neue Folge, Band 7 (1933): 1–14.

——. "Zum Werke Giulio Romanos: I. Der Palazzo del Tè." *Jahrbuch der kunsthistorischen Sammlungen in Wien*, Neue Folge, Band 8 (1934): 79–104.

——. "Zum Werke Giulio Romanos: II. Versuch einer Deutung." *Jahrbuch der kunsthistorischen Sammlungen in Wien*, Neue Folge, Band 9 (1935): 121–50.

——, "Julius von Schlosser." *Burlington Magazine* 74, no. 431 (February 1939): 98–9.

——. "Art and Propaganda." *The Listener* (7 December 1939): 1118–20.

——. "The Artist and the Art of War." *The Listener* (29 August 1940): 311–12.

——. "The Subject of Poussin's *Orion*." *Burlington Magazine* 84, no. 491 (February 1944): 37–41. Reprinted in *Symbolic Images.* 3rd edition. London: Phaidon Press, 1985.

——. *The Story of Art.* 4th edition London: Phaidon Press, 1951.

——. "Meditations on a Hobby Horse or the Roots of Artistic Form" (1951). In *Meditations on a Hobby Horse and Other Essays on the Theory of Art.* 4th edition. London: Phaidon Press, 1985.

——. "The Diversity of the Arts: The Place of the *Laocoon* in the Life and Work of G. E. Lessing (1729–1781)" (1956). In *Tributes: Interpreters of Our Cultural Tradition.* Ithaca, NY: Cornell University Press, 1984.

——. *Art and Illusion: A Study in the Psychology of Pictorial Representation* (1960). A. W. Mellon Lectures in the Fine Arts, 1956. National Gallery of Art, Washington, DC. Bollingen Series, XXXV, 5. Princeton, NJ: Princeton University Press, 1972.

——. "Ritualized Gesture and Expression in Art" (1966). In *The Image and the Eye: Further Studies in the Psychology of Pictorial Representation.* London: Phaidon Press, 1982.

——. "The Study of Art and the Study of Man: Reminiscences of Collaboration with Ernst Kris (1900–1957)" (1967). In *Tributes: Interpreters of Our Cultural Tradition.* Ithaca, NY: Cornell University Press, 1984.

——. "Myth and Reality in German Wartime Broadcasts" (1969). In *Ideals and Idols: Essays on Values in History and in Art.* London: Phaidon Press, 1979.

——. Introduction to *A Heritage of Images*, by Fritz Saxl. Harmondsworth: Penguin Books, Peregrine Books, 1970.

——. "The Photographer as Artist: Henri Cartier-Bresson" (1978). In *Topics of Our Time: Twentieth-Century Issues in Learning and in Art.* Berkeley and Los Angeles: University of California Press, 1991.

——. "The Exploration of Culture Contacts: The Services to Scholarship of Otto Kurz (1908–1975)" (1979). In *Tributes: Interpreters of Our Cultural Tradition.* Ithaca, NY: Cornell University Press, 1984.

——. Preface to *Legend, Myth, and Magic in the Image of the Artist: A Historical Experiment*, by Ernst Kris and Otto Kurz. New Haven: Yale University Press, 1979.

——. "The Wit of Saul Steinberg." *Art Journal* 43, no. 4 (Winter 1983): 377–80.

——. "Art History and Psychology in Vienna Fifty Years Ago." *Art Journal* 44, no. 2 (Summer 1984): 162–4.

——. *Aby Warburg: An Intellectual Biography.* 2nd edition. Chicago: University of Chicago Press, 1986.

——. Preface to *Assigned to Listen: The Evesham Experience 1939–43*, by Olive Renier and Vladimir Rubinstein. London: BBC External Services, 1986.

——. "Einige Erinnerungen an Julius von Schlosser als Lehrer." *Kritische Berichte* XVI, no. 4 (1988): 5–9.

——. "Kokoschka in his Time" (1986). In *Topics of Our Time: Twentieth-Century Issues in Learning and in Art.* Berkeley and Los Angeles: University of California Press, 1991.

——. "An Autobiographical Sketch" (1987). In *Topics of Our Time: Twentieth-Century Issues in Learning and in Art.* Berkeley and Los Angeles: University of California Press, 1991.

——. "Magic, Myth and Metaphor: Reflections on Pictorial Satire" (1990). In *The Uses of Images: Studies in the Social Function of Art and Visual Communication.* London: Phaidon Press, 1999.

——. "Response from E. H. Gombrich." In *Gombrich on Art and Psychology*, edited by Richard Woodfield. Manchester: Manchester University Press, 1996.

——. "The Mysterious Achievement of Likeness" (1997). In *Tête à Tête: Portraits by Henri Cartier-Bresson*, by Henri Cartier-Bresson. Boston: Little, Brown, Bulfinch Press Book, 1998.

——. "Sir Ernst Gombrich über seinen Lehrer Emanuel Löwy" (1997). Interview by Harald Wölf. In *Emanuel Löwy: Ein vergessener Pionier*, edited by Friedrich Brein. Kataloge der Archäologischen Sammlung der Universität Wien. Sonderheft I. Vienna: Verlag des Clubs der Universität Wien, 1998.

——. "Sir Ernst Gombrich." Interview by Adi Wimmer. In *Strangers at Home and Abroad: Recollections of Austrian Jews Who Escaped Hitler*, edited by Adi Wimmer, translated by Ewald Osers. Jefferson, NC: McFarland and Company, 2000.

——. *A Little History of the World.* Translated by Caroline Mustill. New Haven: Yale University Press, 2005.

Gombrich, E. H., and Didier Eribon. *Looking for Answers: Conversations on Art and Science* (1991). New York: Harry N. Abrams, 1993.

Hacohen, Malachi Haim. *Karl Popper—The Formative Years, 1902–1945: Politics and Philosophy in Interwar Vienna.* Cambridge: Cambridge University Press, 2000.

Hallett, Mark. *The Spectacle of Difference: Graphic Satire in the Age of Hogarth.* New Haven: Yale University Press, 1999.

Harris, William V. "The Silences of Momigliano." *Times Literary Supplement*, 12 April 1996.

Haupt, Herbert. *Jahre der Gefährdung: Das Kunsthistorische Museum 1938–1945.* Vienna: Kunsthistorisches Museum, 1995.

Hilberg, Raul. *The Destruction of the European Jews* (1961). New York: Harper and Row, Harper Colophon Books, 1979.

Hobsbawm, Eric. *Interesting Times: A Twentieth-Century Life.* New York: Pantheon Books, 2002.

Honegger, Gitta. *Thomas Bernhard: The Making of an Austrian.* New Haven: Yale University Press, 2001.

Hugo, Victor. *Selected Poems of Victor Hugo.* Translated by E. H. and A. M. Blackmore. Chicago: University of Chicago Press, 2004.

Human Nature and Enduring Peace. Edited by Gardner Murphy. Boston: Houghton Mifflin Company, 1945.

Hume, David. "Of National Characters." In *Selected Essays*, edited by Stephen Copley and Andrew Edgar. Oxford: Oxford University Press, World's Classics, 2008.

Hyman, James. *The Battle for Realism: Figurative Art in Britain During the Cold War 1945–1960.* New Haven and London: Yale University Press, 2001.
Jacoby, Russell. *The Repression of Psychoanalysis: Otto Fenichel and the Political Freudians.* Chicago: University of Chicago Press, 1986.
James, Henry. *Daumier, Caricaturist* (1890). Reprint, London: Rodale Press, 1954.
——. "Honoré Daumier." In *Picture and Text.* Harper and Brothers, 1893.
Jay, Martin. *The Dialectical Imagination: A History of the Frankfurt School and the Institute of Social Research, 1923–1950.* Boston: Little, Brown, 1973.
Jenkins, Roy. *Asquith: Portrait of a Man and an Era.* New York: Chilmark Press, 1964.
——. Introduction to *Lantern Slides: The Diaries and Letters of Violet Bonham Carter 1904–1914,* edited by Mark Bonham Carter and Mark Pottle. London: Weidenfeld and Nicolson, 1996.
Jones, Ernest. *The Life and Work of Sigmund Freud.* Vol. 3. New York: Basic Books, 1957.
Kandel, Eric R. *In Search of Memory: The Emergence of a New Science of Mind.* New York: W. W. Norton, 2006.
——. *The Age of Insight: The Quest to Understand the Unconscious in Art, Mind, and Brain, from Vienna 1900 to the Present.* New York: Random House, 2012.
Kerr, David S. *Caricature and French Political Culture 1830–1848: Charles Philipon and the Illustrated Press.* Oxford: Oxford University Press, Clarendon Press, 2000.
Kershaw, Ian. *Fateful Choices: Ten Decisions that Changed the World, 1940–1941.* New York: Penguin Press, 2007.
Khoury, Philip Shukry. *Syria and the French Mandate: The Politics of Arab Nationalism, 1920–1945.* Princeton, NJ: Princeton University Press, 1987.
King, James. *The Last Modern: A Life of Herbert Read.* London: Weidenfeld and Nicolson, 1990.
Kitchen, Martin. *The Coming of Austrian Fascism.* London: Croom Helm, 1980.
——. "The Austrian Left and the Popular Front." In *The Popular Front in Europe,* edited by Helen Graham and Paul Preston. London: Macmillan Press, 1987.
Kitzinger, Ernst, and Elizabeth Senior. *Portraits of Christ.* King Penguin Books. Harmondsworth: Penguin Books, 1940.
Klemperer, Klemens von. *Ignaz Seipel: Christian Statesman in a Time of Crisis.* Princeton, NJ: Princeton University Press, 1972.
Klemperer, Victor. *The Language of the Third Reich: LTI-Lingua Tertii Imperii: A Philologist's Notebook* (1947). Translated by Martin Brady. Continuum: London, 2002.
Knox, Bernard. *Oedipus at Thebes: Sophocles' Tragic Hero and His Time.* New Haven: Yale University Press, 1957.
Kracauer, Siegfried. "Film 1928" (1928). In *The Mass Ornament: Weimar Essays.* Translated by Thomas Y. Levin. Cambridge, MA: Harvard University Press, 1995.
——. "Propaganda and the Nazi War Film" (1942). In *From Caligari to Hitler: A Psychological History of the German Film.* Princeton, NJ: Princeton University Press, 1947.
——. *From Caligari to Hitler: A Psychological History of the German Film.* Princeton, NJ: Princeton University Press, 1947.
Kraus, Karl. *The Last Days of Mankind.* Translated by Alexander Gode and Sue Ellen Wright. New York: Frederick Ungar Publishing, 1974.
Krebs, Christopher B. *A Most Dangerous Book: Tacitus' Germania from the Roman Empire to the Third Reich.* New York: W. W. Norton, 2011.
Kris, Anton O. "Unlearning and Learning Psychoanalysis." *American Imago* 70, no. 3 (Fall 2013): 341–55.
Kris, Ernst. *Der Stil "rustique": Die Verwendung des Naturabgusses bei Wenzel Jamnitzer und Bernard Palissy.* Sonderausdruck aus Jahrbuch der kunsthistorischen Sammlungen in Wien. Neue Folge. Band I. Vienna: Verlag von Anton Schroll, 1926.

——. "Georg Hoefnagel und der wissenschaftliche Naturalismus." In *Festschrift für Julius Schlosser zum 60. Geburtstage*, edited by Arpad Weixlgärtner und Leo Planiscig. Zürich: Amalthea Verlag, 1927.

——. "A Psychotic Sculptor of the Eighteenth Century" (1933 [1932]). In *Psychoanalytic Explorations in Art.* Madison, CT: International Universities Press, 1952.

——. "The Image of the Artist: A Psychological Study of the Role of Tradition in Ancient Biographies" (1935). In *Psychoanalytic Explorations in Art.* Madison, CT: International Universities Press, 1952.

——. "Comments on Spontaneous Artistic Creations by Psychotics" (1936). In *Psychoanalytic Explorations in Art.* Madison, CT: International Universities Press, 1952.

——. "On Inspiration: Preliminary Notes on Emotional Conditions in Creative States." *International Journal of Psycho-Analysis* 20, nos. 3–4 (July–October 1939): 377–89.

——. "The Place of the Audience in German Propaganda [n.d.]," ms. Ernst Kris Papers. Manuscripts Division. Library of Congress.

——. "The 'Danger' of Propaganda." *American Imago* 2, no. 1 (1941): 3–42.

——. "German Censorship Instructions for the Czech Press." *Social Research* 8, no. 2 (May 1941): 238–46.

——. "Morale in Germany." *American Journal of Sociology* 47, no. 3 (November 1941): 352–61.

——. "Mass Communication under Totalitarian Governments" (1942 [1941]). In *Print, Radio, and Film in a Democracy*, edited by Douglas Waples. Chicago: University of Chicago Press, 1942.

——. "German Propaganda Instructions of 1933." *Social Research* 9, no. 1 (February 1942): 46–81.

——. "The Imagery of War." *Dayton Art Institute Bulletin* 15, no. 1 (October 1942): [1–5].

——. "The Covenant of the Gangsters." *Journal of Criminal Psychopathology* 4, no. 3 (January 1943): 445–58.

——. "Some Problems of War Propaganda: A Note on Propaganda New and Old." *Psychoanalytic Quarterly* 12 (1943): 381–99.

——. "Danger and Morale." *American Journal of Orthopsychiatry* 14, no. 1 (January 1944): 147–55.

——. "Approaches to Art" (1944). In *Psychoanalysis Today*, edited by Sandor Lorand. New York: International University Press, 1944.

——. "Art and Regression." *Transactions of the New York Academy of Sciences* 6, no. 7 (May 1944): 236–50.

——. "Public Opinion and World Order: A Group of Questions Answered by Jerome Bruner, Gerhart Saenger, Harold Lasswell, Ernst Kris, H. H. Remmers." In *Human Nature and Enduring Peace*, edited by Gardner Murphy. Third Yearbook of the Society for the Psychological Study of Social Issues. Boston: Houghton Mifflin, 1945.

——. "Notes on the Psychology of Prejudice." *English Journal* 35, no. 6 (June 1946): 304–8.

——. *Psychoanalytic Explorations in Art.* Madison, CT: International Universities Press, 1952.

——. Introduction (1954) to Sigmund Freud, *The Origins of Psychoanalysis: Letters to Wilhelm Fliess, Drafts and Notes: 1887–1902*, edited by Marie Bonaparte, Anna Freud, and Ernst Kris. New York: Basic Books, 1977.

Kris, Ernst, Heinz Hartmann, and Rudolph M. Loewenstein. *Papers on Psychoanalytic Psychology*. Madison, CT: International Universities Press, 1964.

Kris, Ernst, and Hans Herma, "Hitler's Views on Propaganda and Le Bon's Psychology of the Crowd: A Study in the Sociology of Knowledge," ms. Ernst Kris Papers. Manuscripts Division. Library of Congress.

Kris, Ernst, and Otto Kurz. *Die Legende vom Künstler: Ein geschichtlicher Versuch.* Vienna: Krystall-Verlag, 1934.

——. *Legend, Myth, and Magic in the Image of the Artist: A Historical Experiment*. Revised by Otto Kurz. Translated by Alastair Lang and Lottie M. Newman. New Haven: Yale University Press, 1979.

Kris, Ernst, and Leo Planiscig. *Kleinkunst der italienischen Frührenaissance*. III. Ausstellung, Juni–Juli 1936. Kunsthistorisches Museum, Sammlungen für Plastik und Kunstgewerbe. Vienna: J. Wiener, 1936.

——. *Bozzetti und Modelletti der Spätrenaissance und des Barock*. IV. Ausstellung, Dezember 1936–Jänner 1937. Kunsthistorisches Museum, Sammlungen für Plastik und Kunstgewerbe. Vienna: J. Wiener, 1936–37.

——. *Gefälschte Kunstwerke: Katalog*. V. Ausstellung, September–Oktober 1937. Kunsthistorisches Museum, Sammlungen für Plastik und Kunstgewerbe. Vienna: J. Wiener, 1937.

Kris, Ernst, and Hans Speier. *German Radio Propaganda: Report on Home Broadcasts During the War*. In association with Sidney Axelrad, Hans Herma, Janice Loeb, Heinz Paechter, and Howard B. White. London: Oxford University Press, 1944.

Kris, Ernst, and Howard White. "The German Radio Home News in Wartime." In *Radio Research 1942–1943*, edited by Paul F. Lazarsfeld and Frank N. Stanton. New York: Duell, Sloan and Pearce, Essential Books, 1944. Reprint, New York: Arno Press, 1979.

Krüger, Steffen. *Das Unbehagen in der Karikatur: Kunst, Propaganda und persuasive Kommunikation im Theoriewerk Ernst Kris'*. Munich: Wilhelm Fink, 2011.

——. "*Die Legende vom Künstler* als Propagandastrategie." In *Im Dienste des Ich: Ernst Kris heute*, edited by Steffen Krüger and Thomas Röske, 99–117. Vienna: Böhlau, 2013.

——. "*The Legend of the Artist*: Family Romance and Führer Myth." *American Imago* 71, no. 1 (Spring 2014): 29–51.

Kuriloff, Emily A. *Contemporary Psychoanalysis and the Legacy of the Third Reich: History, Memory, Tradition*. New York: Routledge, 2014.

Kurth, Betty. *Das Lustschloss Schönbrunn*. Österreichische Kunstbücher, Band 7. Vienna: Ed. Hölzel [ca. 1920].

Lagerlöf, Margaretha Rossholm. *Ideal Landscape: Annibale Carracci, Nicolas Poussin and Claude Lorrain*. New Haven: Yale University Press, 1990.

Laughton, Bruce. *Honoré Daumier*. New Haven: Yale University Press, 1996.

Lazarsfeld, Paul. F. "An Episode in the History of Social Research: A Memoir." In *The Intellectual Migration: Europe and America, 1930–1960,* edited by Donald Fleming and Bernard Bailyn. Cambridge, MA: Harvard University Press, Belknap Press, 1969.

Le Men, Ségolène. "Daumier and Printmaking." In *Daumier 1808–1879*. Exhibition organized by the National Gallery of Canada, Ottawa, the Réunion des Musées Nationaux/Musée d'Orsay, Paris, and the Phillips Collection, Washington. Ottawa: National Gallery of Canada, 1999.

Lemoisne, P. A. "Preface." *Exhibition of a Century of French Caricature 1750–1850 with some English Caricatures of the Napoleonic Period*. 10 March–6 April 1939. The Anglo-French Art and Travel Society, 1939.

The Letters of Vincent Van Gogh. Edited by Ronald de Leeuw. Translated by Arnold Pomerans. London: Penguin Books, 1996.

Levi, Primo. *The Periodic Table* (1975). Translated by Raymond Rosenthal. New York: Alfred A. Knopf, Everyman's Library, 1996.

Levine, Emily J. *Dreamland of Humanists: Warburg, Cassirer, Panofsky, and the Hamburg School*. Chicago: University of Chicago Press, 2013.

Levy, Evonne. "Ernst Kris und der Nationalsozialismus: Politische Subtexte in einem verschollenen Experiment über Reaktionen auf die Chorfiguren des Naumburger Doms (1933–1935)." In *Im Dienste des Ich: Ernst Kris heute*, edited by Steffen Krüger and Thomas Röske, 83–97. Vienna: Böhlau, 2013.

——. "Ernst Kris, *The Legend of the Artist* (1934), and *Mein Kampf*." *Oxford Art Journal* 36, no. 2 (2013): 209–29.

Lewis, Jeremy. *Penguin Special: The Life and Times of Allen Lane*. London: Penguin Books, 2005.

Lloyd-Jones, Hugh. "A Biographical Memoir." In *The Eloquence of Symbols: Studies in Humanist Art*, by Edgar Wind. Oxford: Oxford University Press, 1983.

Loewald, Hans W. "On the Therapeutic Action of Psychoanalysis" (1960). In *Papers on Psychoanalysis*. New Haven: Yale University Press, 1980.

Loewy, Emanuel. *The Rendering of Nature in Early Greek Art* (1900). Translated by John Fothergill. London: Duckworth and Co., 1907.

——. "Ursprünge der bildenden Kunst." *Almanach der Akademie der Wissenschaften in Wien* 80 (1930): 275–95.

Lowenthal, Leo and Norbert Guterman. *Prophets of Deceit: A Study of the Techniques of the American Agitator*. New York: Harper & Brothers, 1949. (Republished in Leo Lowenthal. *False Prophets: Studies on Authoritarianism*. New Brunswick, NJ: Transaction Books, 1987.)

Lucie-Smith, Edward. *The Art of Caricature*. London: Orbis Publishing, 1981.

Lukács, Georg. *Studies in European Realism*. New York: Grosset and Dunlap, Universal Library, 1964.

Luža, Radomír. *Austro-German Relations in the Anschluss Era*. Princeton, NJ: Princeton University Press, 1975.

Lynd, Robert S. *Knowledge for What? The Place of Social Science in American Culture*. Princeton, NJ: Princeton University Press, 1939, 1948.

Lynd, Robert S., and Helen Merrell Lynd. *Middletown: A Study in Modern American Culture*. New York: Harcourt Brace Jovanovich, 1929, 1957.

——. *Middletown in Transition: A Study in Cultural Conflicts*. New York: Harcourt Brace Jovanovich, 1937, 1965.

McEwen, Dorothea. "A Tale of One Institute and Two Cities: The Warburg Institute." In *German-Speaking Exiles in Great Britain*, edited by Ian Wallace. Amsterdam: Rodopi, 1999.

McLeod, Enid. *Living Twice: Memoirs*. London: Hutchinson Benham, 1982.

McPhee, Constance C., and Nadine M. Orenstein. *Infinite Jest: Caricature and Satire from Leonardo to Levine*. New York: The Metropolitan Museum of Art, 2011.

Makari, George. *Revolution in Mind: The Creation of Psychoanalysis*. New York: HarperCollins, 2008.

Martin du Gard, Roger. *Jean Barois*. Translated by Stuart Gilbert. New York: Viking Press, 1949.

——. *Notes on André Gide*. Translated by John Russell. New York: Helen Marx Books, 2005.

Matrikel (Summer 1919–Summer 1922), Universitätsarchiv, Universität Wien.

Mazzucco, Katia. "1941 *English Art and the Mediterranean*: A Photographic Exhibition by the Warburg Institute in London." *Journal of Art Historiography* 5 (December 2011): 1–28.

Melot, Michel. "Daumier, Art, and Politics." In *Daumier 1808–1879*. Exhibition organized by the National Gallery of Canada, Ottawa, the Réunion des Musées Nationaux/Musée d'Orsay, Paris, and the Phillips Collection, Washington. Ottawa: National Gallery of Canada, 1999.

Michaud, Philippe-Alain. *Aby Warburg and the Image in Motion*. Translated by Sophie Hawks. New York: Zone Books, 2004.

Miller, Jonathan. *On Further Reflection: 60 Years of Writing*. New York: Overlook Press, 2014.

Milner, John. *Art, War and Revolution in France 1970–1871: Myth, Reportage and Reality*. New Haven: Yale University Press, 2000.

Mitford, Jessica. *Hons and Rebels*. New York: New York Review Books, 2004.

Momigliano, Arnaldo. "The First Political Commentary on Tacitus" (1947). In *Essays in Ancient and Modern Historiography*. Middletown, CT: Wesleyan University Press, 1982.

Mongan, Agnes. Introduction to *Honoré Daumier 1808–1879: The Armand Hammer Daumier Collection*. Los Angeles: Armand Hammer Foundation, 1982.

Moser-Ernst, Sybille, and Ursula Marinelli. "Geschichte des Karikaturprojektes Kris/ Gombrich: Antworten und offene Fragen." In *Jenseits des Illustrativen: Visuelle Medien und Strategien politischer Kommunikation*, edited by Niels Grüne and Claus Oberhauser. Göttingen: V&R Unipress, 2015.

Mühlleitner, Elke. *Biographisches Lexikon der Psychoanalyse: Die Mitglieder der Psychologischen Mittwoch-Gesellschaft und der Wiener Psychoanalytischen Vereinigung 1902–1938*. Tübingen: Edition Diskord, 1992.

Nichols, Roger. *Mendelssohn Remembered*. London: Faber and Faber, 1997.

Olin, Margaret. *Forms of Representation in Alois Riegl's Theory of Art*. University Park, PA: Pennsylvania State University Press, 1992.

Orwell, George. *The Collected Essays, Journalism and Letters of George* Orwell. Vol. 2, *My Country Right or Left 1940–1943*. Edited by Sonia Orwell and Ian Angus. New York: Harcourt Brace Jovanovich, 1968.

Panofsky, Erwin. *Idea: Ein Beitrag zur Begriffsgeschichte der älteren Kunsttheorie*. Leipzig: Studien der Bibliothek Warburg, 1924. English edition: *Idea: A Concept in Art Theory*. Translated by Joseph J. S. Peake. Columbia, SC: University of South Carolina Press, 1968.

Papet, Édouard. "'He Also Does Sculpture.'" In *Daumier 1808–1879*. Exhibition organized by the National Gallery of Canada, Ottawa, the Réunion des Musées Nationaux/Musée d'Orsay, Paris, and the Phillips Collection, Washington. Ottawa: National Gallery of Canada, 1999.

Parker, R. A. C. *Chamberlain and Appeasement: British Policy and the Coming of the Second World War*. New York: St. Martin's Press, 1993.

Pauley, Bruce F. *From Prejudice to Persecution: A History of Austrian Anti-Semitism*. Chapel Hill, NC: University of North Carolina Press, 1992.

Paxton, Robert O. *The Anatomy of Fascism*. New York: Alfred A. Knopf, 2004.

Pelling, Henry. *Britain and the Second World War*. Glasgow: William Collins and Sons, 1970.

Pfarr, Ulrich. "Ernst Kris on F. X. Messerschmidt—A Valuable Stimulus for New Research?" *American Imago* 58, no. 1 (Spring 2001): 445–61.

Phayer, Michael. *The Catholic Church and the Holocaust, 1930–1965*. Bloomington, IN: Indiana University Press, 2000.

Phillips, Adam. *Winnicott*. London: Penguin Books, 2007.

Pick, Daniel. *The Pursuit of the Nazi Mind: Hitler, Hess, and the Analysts*. Oxford: Oxford University Press, 2012.

Pick, Hella. *Guilty Victim: Austria from the Holocaust to Haider*. London: I. B. Tauris, 2000.

Piper, John. "One Shilling, Coloured." Review of *Portraits of Christ*, by Ernst Kitzinger and Elizabeth Senior, and *Caricature*, by Ernst Kris and E. H. Gombrich. *The Spectator* (14 March 1941): 290.

Planiscig, Leo. *Die Bronzeplastiken: Statuetten, Reliefs, Geräte und Plaketten: Katalog*. Publikationen aus den Sammlungen für Plastik und Kunstgewerbe, edited by Julius Schlosser. Vol. 4. Vienna: Kunstverlag Anton Schroll, 1924.

Popper, Karl R. *The Open Society and Its Enemies*. Vol. 1, *The Spell of Plato*. London: George Routledge and Sons, 1945.

Popper, Karl R. *The Open Society and Its Enemies*. Vol. 2, *The High Tide of Prophecy: Hegel, Marx, and the Aftermath*. London: George Routledge and Sons, 1945.

Posner, Donald. *Annibale Carracci: A Study in the Reform of Italian Painting around 1590*. 2 vols. London: Phaidon Press, 1971.

Prochnik, George. *The Impossible Exile: Stefan Zweig at the End of the World*. New York: Other Press, 2014.

Puaux, Gabriel. *Mort et Transfiguration de l'Autriche 1933–1955*. Paris: Librairie Plon, 1966.

Rampley, Matthew. "Max Dvořák: Art History and the Crisis of Modernity." *Art History* 26, no. 2 (April 2003): 214–37.

Read, Herbert. *Art Now: An Introduction to the Theory of Modern Painting and Sculpture*. New York: Harcourt, Brace and Company, 1936.

——. *Art and Society*. New York: Macmillan, 1937.

——. "Multum in Parvo." Review of *Portraits of Christ*, by Ernst Kitzinger and Elizabeth Senior, and *Caricature*, by Ernst Kris and E. H. Gombrich. *The Listener* (27 February 1941): 305–6.

——. *Art and Society*. 2nd edition. London: Faber and Faber, 1945.

——. Foreword to *Kokoschka: Life and Work*, by Edith Hoffmann. London: Faber and Faber, 1947.

——. *Contemporary British Art*. Harmondsworth: Penguin Books, 1951.

——. *Modern Sculpture: A Concise History*. London: Thames and Hudson, 1964.

Reitter, Paul. *The Anti-Journalist: Karl Kraus and Jewish Self-Fashioning in Fin-de-siècle Europe*. Chicago: University of Chicago Press, 2008.

Renier, Olive, and Vladimir Rubinstein. *Assigned to Listen: The Evesham Experience, 1939–1943*. London: BBC External Services, 1986.

Review of *Caricature* by Ernst Kris and E. H. Gombrich. In *Times Literary Supplement*, 8 March 1941.

Rickman, John. *No Ordinary Psychoanalyst: The Exceptional Contributions of John Rickman*. Edited by Pearl King. London: Karnac, 2003.

——. *Selected Contributions to Psycho-Analysis*. London: Karnac, 2003.

Ritvo, Samuel, and Lucille B. Ritvo. "Ernst Kris, 1900–1957: Twentieth Century *Uomo Universale*," in *Psychoanalytic Pioneers*, edited by Franz Alexander, Samuel Eisenstein, and Martin Grotjahn. New York: Basic Books, 1966.

Rock, William R. *British Appeasement in the 1930s*. New York: Norton, 1977.

Rose, Louis. *The Freudian Calling: Early Viennese Psychoanalysis and the Pursuit of Cultural Science*. Detroit: Wayne State University Press, 1998.

——. *The Survival of Images: Art Historians, Psychoanalysts, and the Ancients*. Detroit: Wayne State University Press, 2001.

——. "Interpreting Propaganda: Successors to Warburg and Freud in Wartime." *American Imago* 60, no. 1 (Spring 2003): 122–30.

——. "Daumier in Vienna: Ernst Kris, E. H. Gombrich, and the Politics of Caricature." *Visual Resources: An International Journal of Documentation* 23, nos. 1–2 (March–June 2007): 39–64.

Rose, Norman. *Vansittart: Study of a Diplomat*. London: William Heinemann, 1978.

Röske, Thomas. "Traces of Psychology: The Art Historical Writings of Ernst Kris." *American Imago* 58, no. 1 (Spring 2001): 463–77.

Rottenberg, Dan, ed. *Middletown Jews: The Tenuous Survival of an American Jewish Community*. Bloomington, IN: Indiana University Press, 1997.

Rowlandson, T., and A. C. Pugin. *The Microcosm of London*. London: King Penguin Books, 1943; revised edition, 1947.

Rutkoff, Peter M., and William B. Scott. *New School: A History of the New School for Social Research*. New York: Free Press, 1986.

Sauerländer, Willibald. "The Genius of the Other Daumier." Translated by David Dollenmayer. *The New York Review of Books* 60, no. 3 (21 February 2013): 17–18.

Saxl, Fritz. "Why Art History?" (1948). In *Lectures*. Vol. 1. London: The Warburg Institute, University of London, 1957.

Saxl, Fritz, and Rudolf Wittkower. *British Art and the Mediterranean*, 1948. Reprint, with a preface by Rudolf Wittkower, London: Oxford University Press, 1969.

Schalk, David L. *Roger Martin du Gard: The Novelist and History*. Ithaca, NY: Cornell University Press, 1967.

Schapiro, Meyer. "The New Viennese School" (1936). In *The Vienna School Reader: Politics and Art Historical Method in the 1930s*, edited by Christopher S. Wood. New York: Zone Books, 2000.

Schell, Jonathan. *The Seventh Decade: The New Shape of the Nuclear Danger*. New York: Henry Holt and Company, Metropolitan Books, 2007.

Schlosser, Julius von. "History of Portraiture in Wax" (1910–11). Translated by James Michael Loughridge. In *Ephemeral Bodies: Wax Sculpture and the Human Figure*, edited by Roberta Panzanelli. Los Angeles: Getty Research Institute, 2008.

——. *Die Kunst- und Wunderkammern der Spätrenaissance: Ein Beitrag zur Geschichte des Sammelwesens: Ein Handbuch für Sammler und Liebhaber* (1908). 2nd edition. Leipzig: Klinkhardt and Biermann, 1978.

Schoell-Glass, Charlotte. *Aby Warburg and Anti-Semitism: Political Perspectives on Images and Culture*. Translated by Samuel Pakucs Willcocks. Detroit: Wayne State University Press, 2008.

Schorske, Carl E. *Fin-de-siècle Vienna: Politics and Culture.* New York: Alfred A. Knopf, 1980.

——. *Thinking with History: Explorations in the Passage to Modernism.* Princeton, NJ: Princeton University Press, 1998.

Schrecker, Ellen. *Many Are the Crimes: McCarthyism in America*. Boston: Little, Brown, 1998.

Schwarz, Egon. *Refuge: Chronicle of a Flight from Hitler*. Translated by Philip Boehm, Hildegarde and Hunter Hannum, and Caroline Wellbery. Riverside, CA: Ariadne Press, 2002.

Sears, Elizabeth. "The Warburg Institute, 1933–1944: A Precarious Experiment in International Collaboration." *Art Libraries Journal* 38, no. 4 (2013): 7–15.

Sedlmayr, Hans. "Bruegel's *Macchia*" (1934). In *The Vienna School Reader: Politics and Art Historical Method in the 1930s*, edited by Christopher S. Wood. New York: Zone Books, 2000.

Seligman, Janet. *Figures of Fun: The Caricature-Statuettes of Jean-Pierre Dantan.* London: Oxford University Press, 1957.

Shikes, Ralph E. *The Indignant Eye: The Artist as Social Critic in Prints and Drawings from the Fifteenth Century to Picasso*. Boston: Beacon Press, 1969.

Shikes, Ralph E., and Steven Heller. *The Art of Satire: Painters as Caricaturists and Cartoonists from Delacroix to Picasso.* N.p.: Pratt Graphics Center and Horizon Press, 1984.

Siegfried Kracauer-Erwin Panofsky Briefwechsel 1941–1966. Edited by Volker Breidecker. Berlin: Akademie Verlag, 1996.

Snowman, Daniel. *The Hitler Emigres: The Cultural Impact on Britain of Refugees from Nazism.* London: Pimlico, 2003.

Soussloff, Catherine M. "Portraiture and Assimilation in Vienna: The Case of Hans Tietze and Erica Tietze-Conrat." In *Diasporas and Exiles: Varieties of Jewish Identity*, edited by Howard Wettstein. Berkeley and Los Angeles: University of California Press, 2002.

Spalding, Frances. *British Art since 1900.* London: Thames & Hudson, 1986.

Speier, Hans. *The Truth in Hell and Other Essays on Politics and Culture, 1935–1987*. New York: Oxford University Press, 1989.

Stansky, Peter, and William Abrahams. *Journey to the Frontier: Two Roads to the Spanish Civil War.* Chicago: University of Chicago Press, 1966.

Steinberg, Michael P. *The Meaning of the Salzburg Festival: Austria as Theater and Ideology, 1890–1930.* Ithaca, NY: Cornell University Press, 1990.

——. "Arnaldo Momigliano and the Facts." In *Judaism Musical and Unmusical.* Chicago: University of Chicago Press, 2007.

Steiner, George. *Errata: An Examined Life*. New Haven: Yale University Press, 1998.

Steiner, Herbert. "The Role of the Resistance in Austria, with Special Reference to the Labor Movement." In *Resistance Against the Third Reich, 1933–1990*, edited by Michael Geyer and John W. Boyer. Chicago: University of Chicago Press, 1994.

Swift, Jonathan. "A Meditation upon a Broom-stick" (1703). In *The Basic Writings of Jonathan Swift*. Introduction by Claude Rawson. New York: The Modern Library, 2002.

Taylor, A. J. P. *English History 1914–1945*. New York: Oxford University Press, 1970.

——, "The Austrian Illusion." In *Europe: Grandeur and Decline*. London: Penguin Books, 1991.

Taylor, Telford. *The Anatomy of the Nuremberg Trials: A Personal Memoir*. New York: Skyhorse Publishing, 1993.

Thompson, E. P. *Beyond the Frontier: The Politics of a Failed Mission: Bulgaria 1944*. Stanford, CA: Stanford University Press, 1997.

Thompson, Nellie. "Ernst Kris in America." *American Imago* 71, no. 4 (December 2014): 353–74.

Timms, Edward, and Ritchie Robertson, eds. *The Austrian Exodus: The Creative Achievements of Refugees from National Socialism*. Austrian Studies VI. Edinburgh: Edinburgh University Press, 1995.

Tolnay, Charles de. "In Memoriam Otto Benesch." In *The Art of the Renaissance in Northern Europe: Its Relation to the Contemporary Spiritual and Intellectual Movements*, by Otto Benesch. Revised edition. London: Phaidon Press, 1965.

Tyler, Ralph W. "Implications of Communications Research for the Public Schools" (1942 [1941]). In *Print, Radio, and Film in a Democracy*, edited by Douglas Waples. Chicago: University of Chicago Press, 1942.

Vansittart, Robert. *Black Record: Germans Past and Present*. London: Hamish Hamilton, 1941.

Waelder, Robert. "Psychoanalysis and History: Application of Psychoanalysis to Historiography." In *The Psychoanalytic Interpretation of History*, edited by Benjamin B. Wolman. New York: Harper Torchbooks, Harper and Row, 1973.

Warburg, Aby. *Die Erneuerung der heidnischen Antike: Kulturwissenschaftliche Beiträge zur Geschichte der europäischen Renaissance*. Edited by Gertrud Bing. Leipzig: B. G. Teubner, 1932.

——. *The Renewal of Pagan Antiquity: Contributions to the Cultural History of the European Renaissance*. Translated by David Britt. Getty Research Institute Publications Programs: Texts and Documents. Los Angeles: Getty Research Institute for the History of Art and the Humanities, 1999.

[Warburg Institute.] *A Bibliography of the Survival of the Classics*. Vol. 2, *The Publications of 1932–1933*. London: The Warburg Institute, 1938. Reprint, Nendeln, Liechtenstein: Kraus-Thomson Organization, Kraus Reprint, 1978.

[Warburg Library.] *Kulturwissenschaftliche Bibliographie zum Nachleben der Antike*. Vol. 1, *Die Erscheinungen des Jahres 1931*. Leipzig: B. G. Teubner, 1934. Reprint, Nendeln, Liechtenstein: Kraus-Thomson Organization, Kraus Reprint, 1978.

Wechsler, Judith. *A Human Comedy: Physiognomy and Caricature in 19th Century Paris*. Chicago: University of Chicago Press, 1982.

——. "The Issue of Caricature." *Art Journal* 43, no. 4 (Winter 1983): 317–18.

Weibel, Peter, and Friedrich Stadler, eds. *The Cultural Exodus from Austria: Vertreibung der Vernunft*. Vienna: Löcker Verlag, 1993.

Weixlgärtner, Arpad, and Leo Planiscig, eds. *Festschrift für Julius Schlosser zum 60. Geburtstage*. Zürich: Amalthea Verlag, 1927.

Welch, David. *The Third Reich: Politics and Propaganda*. London: Routledge, 1993.

Wickhoff, Franz. *Roman Art: Some of Its Principles and Their Application to Early Christian Painting*. Translated by Eugénie Strong. London: William Heinemann, 1900.

Wilkinson, James D. *The Intellectual Resistance in Europe*. Cambridge, MA: Harvard University Press, 1981.
Willett, John. *Art and Politics in the Weimar Period: The New Sobriety, 1917–1933*. New York: Da Capo Press, 1996.
Wind, Edgar. *Art and Anarchy*. New York: Alfred A. Knopf, 1964.
Wittkower, Rudolf, and Margot Wittkower. *Born Under Saturn: The Character and Conduct of Artists: A Documented History from Antiquity to the French Revolution*. New York: W. W. Norton, 1969.
Wolf, Reva. *Goya and the Satirical Print in England and on the Continent, 1730–1850*. Boston: David R. Godine and Boston College Museum of Art, 1991.
Wood, Christopher S. "E. H. Gombrich: Art and Illusion: A Study in the Psychology of Pictorial Representation, 1960." In *The Books that Shaped Art History: From Gombrich and Greenberg to Alpers and Krauss*, edited by Richard Stone and John-Paul Stonard. London: Thames & Hudson, 2013.
——. Introduction to *The Vienna School Reader: Politics and Art Historical Method in the 1930s*. New York: Zone Books, 2000.
Woodfield, Richard, ed. *Gombrich on Art and Psychology*. Manchester: Manchester University Press, 1996.
Woodfield, Richard, et al. *Framing Formalism: Riegl's Work*. Amsterdam: Overseas Publishers Association, 2001.
Woolley, Leonard. *Abraham: Recent Discoveries and Hebrew Origins*. London: Faber and Faber, 1936.
Zaretsky, Eli. *Secrets of the Soul: A Social and Cultural History of Psychoanalysis*. New York: Alfred A. Knopf, 2004.
Zweig, Stefan. *Balzac*. Translated by William and Dorothy Rose. New York: Viking Press, 1946.
——. *The World of Yesterday*. Translated by Benjamin W. Huebsch and Helmut Ripperger. Lincoln and London: University of Nebraska Press, Bison Book, 1964.

INDEX

INDEX